Nicholas

'Malcolm Guite ha[s]
in its perspective a
investigation [that] [...] [...]
[...] Grovier, *Times Literary Supplement*

'There is much to praise in *Mariner* – not least that it is a 470-page book unapologetically devoted to interpreting, and celebrating, a single poem. That Guite neither sexes up his manuscript nor curbs his religious enthusiasm gives his interpretation an impressive dose of integrity.'

Frances Wilson, *New Statesman*

'Forcefully and convincingly argued.'

The Telegraph

'The story of Coleridge's life does undoubtedly echo that of his poem. This is a book that provides rewarding rereadings of both.'

Nick Rennison, *The Sunday Times*

'Malcolm Guite's new biography is ingeniously structured around the Mariner . . . Guite has an unerring eye for the memorable anecdote . . . He writes with passion about Coleridge's distinctive Christian theology. Coleridge was surely one of the inspirations for Sherlock Holmes. His life would make a great movie. I wonder who should be cast as Silas Tomkyn Comberbache?'

The Times

'Guite is a serious and substantive critic, and there is more about Coleridge's greatest poem here than in any work published in the last quarter-century. I imagine that this book may become a classic of Christian spirituality, a text for retreats, and, if it does, it will help resurrect Coleridge's own reputation in that regard.'

The Tablet

'This book – which is full of judiciously chosen quotations from Coleridge's mesmerising letters and notebooks – is a splendid celebration of the grizzled figure who "stoppeth one of three" and the tragic artist who created him.'

The Times

'In this remarkable book, using a very close reading of *The Rime of the Ancient Mariner* as an armature, Guite attempts to make good this lacuna and to use Coleridge's evolving religion – to build up a view of the poet's visionary life . . . excellent and richly compelling reading.'

The Irish Catholic

'This is a superior life of Coleridge . . . Guite has complete mastery of the primary and secondary literature [and] master-fully interweaves sections from the *Mariner* with episodes from Coleridge's unfolding life to both enhance our appreciation of Coleridge's poetic powers and to bring us up to speed on all that is known of his later life.'

The Heythrop Journal

'Malcolm Guite has established himself as one of the leading Christian poets of our time. This positions him to offer a distinctive reading of a poetic giant of the past, S. T. Coleridge. As expected, *Mariner* is exceptionally rich, penetrating and absorbing.'

Jeremy Begbie, Duke University

'An illuminating close reading of the poem, relating it at every point to the subsequent course of Coleridge's life, he shows us why it remains so important for our culture.'

The Church Times

'A profound exploration of the human condition . . . Guite also draws out the continuing relevance of Coleridge's life and writing to our own time.'

Transpositions

'Alongside impressive close readings of the text . . . a fully rounded Coleridge emerges from these pages.'

Catholic Herald

'*Mariner* is not only beautifully (and evocatively) written, it is also deeply compassionate.'

Methodist Recorder

'It's rare for me to say this about a book, but *Mariner* is astonishing . . . I came away with an awareness that most of Coleridge's modern biographers have downplayed the man's faith, and you can't understand his great poem without understanding the faith it springs from.'

Tweetspeak

'The "biker priest" who revived a Christian reading of *The Rime of the Ancient Mariner* . . . found himself "blown away" by Coleridge's account of God and creative genius.'

The Times

'Insightful and sympathetic commentary.'

Catholic Herald

'Malcolm Guite makes a case for the importance of faith to Coleridge, and his significance as a spiritual writer . . . The poem, according to Guite, has much to say about our own times.'

Crosslight Magazine

For my mother Shiona

First published in Great Britain in 2017 by Hodder & Stoughton
An Hachette UK company

This paperback edition first published in 2018

2

Copyright © Malcolm Guite, 2017

The right of Malcolm Guite to be identified as the Author of the Work has been
asserted by him in accordance with the Copyright, Designs and Patents Act 1988.

A CIP catalogue record for this title is available from the British Library

ISBN 978 1 473 61107 8
eBook ISBN 978 1 473 61106 1

Typeset by Hewer Text UK Ltd, Edinburgh
Printed and bound in the UK by Clays Ltd, St Ives plc

Hodder & Stoughton policy is to use papers that are natural, renewable
and recyclable products and made from wood grown in sustainable
forests. The logging and manufacturing processes are expected to
conform to the environmental regulations of the country of origin.

Hodder & Stoughton Ltd
Carmelite House
50 Victoria Embankment
London EC4Y 0DZ

www.hodder.co.uk

Nicholas Temple

MARINER

A Voyage with
Samuel Taylor Coleridge

Malcolm Guite

HODDER

Contents

The Ancient Mariner keeps watch at Watchet Harbour: like his mariner,
Coleridge endured the agony of loneliness and despair but also like him he
survived the ordeal, was rewarded with a visionary experience of transfigured
beauty in the world

Introduction

This book is written to take you on a journey: a journey into the hidden life of a great poet, and a journey into your own hidden life; a journey up towards mountaintop moments of vision and a journey down, fathoms deep beneath the travelling keel of your consciousness. This is a journey made possible for us, perhaps even made necessary, because it was made first by Samuel Taylor Coleridge. In *The Rime of the Ancient Mariner*, a poem whose depths and heights, whose darkness and light, were prophetic both of Coleridge's own life and of ours, he has given us, if we can learn to read it, a chart that maps both our souls and our world.

This one poem, originally begun as a quickly sketched popular gothic ballad, a disposable poem, to be sold to a magazine to fund a walking tour, was to become in the hands and imagination of Coleridge no throwaway but a unique and always generative visionary work. First published in 1798, worked on and reworked until its publication in its full form with the gloss in 1817 and further slight changes even to the last edition in Coleridge's life-time in 1834, *The Rime of the Ancient Mariner* has never ceased to compel, baffle, intrigue and ultimately delight its readers from the end of the eighteenth to the beginning of the twenty-first century. It has been the subject of major critical essays and reviews and indeed of entire books. It has been seen as the central myth of the new Romantic Movement, the first truly symbolist poem, a poem of pure imagination, a moral tale, an immoral tale, a farrago of superstitions, a profound Christian allegory, a drug-fuelled nightmare, a poem of psychological disintegration, a vision of final integration, and in more recent times, a prophetic ecological warning. It would seem that each generation, as it looks into the mysterious and reflective depths of this poem, finds something telling, particular and intimate speaking to their soul.

The poem itself, like *The Odyssey* before it, has the classic shape of a journey out and back again. An unnamed ship, the purpose of whose journey we are never told, leaves the familiar and sails south, across 'the line' into the southern hemisphere, and comes at last to great ice floes in the Antarctic. The sailors are lost in fog and surrounded by ice but are befriended by an albatross. This mysterious bird, which has been hailed by the men 'as a Christian soul' and has shared the ship's hospitality, guides the ship through the ice, round Cape Horn and into the unknown Pacific.

But this narrative is suddenly interrupted as a wedding guest, to whom the tale is being told, notices a terrible change in the mariner's expression:

The ancient Mariner inhospitably killeth the pious bird of good omen.

"God save thee, ancient Mariner!
From the fiends, that plague thee thus!—
Why look'st thou so?"—With my cross-bow
I shot the Albatross.

(Lines 79–82 with gloss)

The rest of the poem goes on to explore the profound spiritual and material consequences of this seemingly random deed, which as the poem proceeds, takes on the resonance and spiritual significance of the primal fall of humankind, and the fall of each of us. The crew make themselves complicit in the deed by taking a purely instrumental view of the bird, first saying it was a bird of good omen and blaming the mariner and then changing their mind and saying it was right to kill the bird as it had brought the fog and mist.

But the albatross has its own proper life and meaning, and eventually they learn, but only through the medium of a dream, that they have disturbed a delicate balance and grieved the Polar Spirit, the deeply hidden, but living essence of that hemisphere who 'loved the bird, that loved the man that shot him with his bow'.

The poem goes on to tell of the death of the other sailors and of the survival of the mariner, in an agony of helpless guilt and isolation in which he curses himself and every other living thing and wishes only to die. And then we have an extraordinary scene of transformation in which the mariner is suddenly able to see the world anew, on its own terms, and without sole reference to himself, and in which he finally blesses the 'happy living things' against whose whole web of life he has offended. The rest of the poem tells of his growing spiritual awareness; his penance and expiation of the curse; his visitation by angels and his final return, purged and transformed, to the place where he began; of his meeting with a hermit; of the sacrament of confession, the recovery of faith and a new mission to tell his own transformative tale to those who need to hear it.

Astonishingly, every one of these narrative elements can be paralleled in Coleridge's life as he came to live it *after* the composition of this poem. I shall bring out these parallels as we look at each section of the poem in detail in the second part of this book. But, briefly, one might observe that, like his mariner, Coleridge sailed away from home and all that was familiar, both outwardly in his life-changing voyages to Germany and Malta, and inwardly in his journey deep into the nightmare world of opium addiction and high into the rarefied regions of metaphysical speculation. Like his mariner, Coleridge endured the agony of loneliness, despair and suicidal thoughts, but also like him he survived the ordeal, was rewarded with a visionary experience of transfigured beauty in the world and returned from his voyage into extremity with a new sense of purpose. Just as the mariner met the pilot and the hermit at the moment his ship was sinking, and was rescued by them, so Coleridge was rescued from the shipwreck of addiction and despair by Dr Gillman, with whom he lived for the last years of his life. In that final phase he became, like his mariner, a life-transforming teacher, sharing a spiritual vision which linked love and prayer with a new humility towards God and nature. Not surprisingly, Coleridge later came to identify himself with the mariner, yet when he wrote the poem he had never even been to sea and none of these adventures had yet befallen him.

So, how did he come to write it? What sources were woven into the poem? What intuitions, dreams and apprehensions were bodied forth in its strange and vivid imagery? These are some of the questions we will seek to answer in this book. Coleridge's poem sends us out on a journey around the world, down towards the South Pole, up again through equatorial heat and drought, and finally home transformed. In the opening verses the mariner glances briefly back at what he is leaving behind: 'the kirk, the hill, the light-house top' – then turns forwards and braces himself for adventure. So we will do the same as we step on board with Coleridge, and begin our journey with and through the poem.

In the first part of this book, we will look back with him, glancing over his shoulder, at the rich series of events and influences that led him to the moment, at the age of twenty-five, when he could begin the poem. I have called this first part of the book 'Prelude: The Growth of a Poet's Mind', deliberately borrowing the title that was later given to Wordsworth's great poem. It was not, of course, Wordsworth's original title, for *The Prelude* was only published posthumously and Wordsworth always referred to it as his 'poem to Coleridge'. Coleridge never wrote his own 'Prelude' precisely because he was pouring so much of his time, his poetic and intellectual energy, into enabling Wordsworth to write his. As Richard Holmes consistently shows in his two-volume biography, and Coleridge later came to realise, it was Coleridge's insistent and almost obsessive deference to Wordsworth that undermined his own sense of himself as a poet and took away the confidence he needed to write his own poetry. Nevertheless, I hope in this Prelude to show what Wordsworth called 'the spots of time', the insights, points of development and growth, which brought Coleridge to the point where he could produce his early masterpiece in *The Ancient Mariner*. Then, in Part II, we will look forward, through the lens of the poem itself, at Coleridge's life and take the adventure that comes. From here on the shape and structure of this book and of our journey will follow the beautiful seven-part structure that Coleridge gave his poem.

But first, let us briefly consider four key features of the poem that made it so significant for Coleridge and can make it significant for us, too.

Prophetic Framing

Though *The Ancient Mariner* was begun in 1797 when Coleridge was only twenty-five, it was an astonishingly prescient poem. As Coleridge himself came to realise much later, the shape of this story was to be the shape of his own life. With an uncanny clarity, image after image, and event after event in the poem became emblems of what Coleridge was later to suffer and discover. In the rich and honest notebooks Coleridge kept throughout his life he came in the end to recognise and refer to himself as 'the mariner'.

This prescient nature of the poem, the sense that new depths open out when we read it with both the early and the later Coleridge in mind, is further intensified by two of the poem's 'framing' devices. The first is the fact, embedded in the narrative of the poem itself, that an old man tells the story to a younger

5 *Wrote poem @ 25*

man, and that the encounter between them is predestined, and is for the younger man's benefit. The poem opens with a wedding guest, eager to get to the festivities, being singled out and stopped by the mariner and compelled to hear the story whether he wills or no: 'held' by the mariner's 'glittering eye'. By the end of the story the younger man has been so affected by the tale that he turns from the wedding and changes the course of his life:

He went like one that hath been stunned,
And is of sense forlorn:
A sadder and a wiser man,
He rose the morrow morn.

(Lines 622–5, last lines of the poem)

In retrospect, it is possible to imagine the wedding guest as the youthful Coleridge and the mariner as the older and wiser Coleridge returning to teach and guide his younger self.

The other 'framing device' unique to this poem is the famous 'gloss' which was added by Coleridge, nearly twenty years later, to the version published in 1817. Here indeed Coleridge created a beautiful counterpoint to his youthful voice and a more profound interpretation of the poem than he himself could have written when he composed it. This gloss, in which the young man's original text is opened out by the older poet's subsequent experience of life, forms the key to my own interpretation and my decision to use the poem itself as a key to Coleridge's life story.

The Sacred Power of Self-Intuition

One may well ask how it was that Coleridge came to write such a prescient poem, to invoke imaginatively as it were a narrative shape which he himself was yet to fill. Coleridge himself suggests an illuminating answer. In 1817 he published his two most important books: *Sibylline Leaves*, the collection of his poetry that contains *The Ancient Mariner*, in its full form and published for the first time under Coleridge's name, and *Biographia Literaria* or *Biographical Sketches of My Literary Life and Opinions*. This latter book was intended as a companion volume to the poems and contains many powerful insights into the workings of the poetic imagination. We shall be looking at these insights in greater detail later in this book. But to answer our immediate question about how a poem might be so full of intuitive foresight, here is a passage from the *Biographia* which gives us an image with which to think about the imagination's power of shaping prescience, or, as Coleridge calls it in this passage, 'sacred power of self-intuition':

> They and only they can acquire the philosophic imagination, the sacred power of self-intuition, who within themselves can inter-pret and understand the symbol, that the wings of the air-sylph are forming within the skin of the caterpillar; those only, who feel in their own spirits the same instinct, which impels the chrys-alis of the horned fly to leave room in its involucrum for anten-nae yet to come. They know and feel, that the potential works in them, even as the actual works on them.[1]

Here Coleridge advances the beautiful suggestive idea that the poetic imagination can hold open for us a shape or a space we have yet to grow into. The great works of art and literature are, as it were, making room for our future insights, giving us the shapes, the stories, the images into which the undeveloped antennae of our inner life can grow.

If this is true of the narrative shape and the imagery of *The Ancient Mariner*, it follows that the poem is more than just an individual's story. It is also a profound exploration of the human condition, of our fallenness and, as Coleridge says in the gloss, our 'loneliness and fixedness'. Yet the poem also offers hope, release and recovery. Indeed, it goes further than giving parables, images and emblems of our spiritual and psychological depths, for it also turned out to be prescient and prophetic of the whole ecological movement with its rooting of human evil in an act of needless violence against another species. In this poem, recovery consists in learning to love our fellow creatures, a motif that anticipates many modern concerns. So in the following pages I will try to draw out the way the poem also tells that tale, and how it voices the concerns of generations born long after Coleridge's death, including our own.

Spiritual Force

There have of course been many books on Coleridge generally, and on *The Rime of the Ancient Mariner* in particular, but, in the present book, I will be seeking to redress a strange imbalance in some of them – even some of the very best of them: the failure to engage seriously with the rich spirituality that pervades his work, and particularly with the depth and reach of Coleridge's Christian faith.

The Road to Xanadu,[2] John Livingston Lowes' great study of the sources of *Kubla Khan* and *The Rime of the Ancient Mariner*, is an exhaustive exploration of all that went in to the making of the poems, but doesn't really apply that learning either to Coleridge's subsequent life or indeed our own life and times, as I intend to do. Molly Lefebure's ground-breaking book *Samuel Taylor Coleridge: A Bondage of Opium*[3] not only brought a greater understanding of the debilitating addiction with which Coleridge had to struggle for most of his adult life, but relates it well to some of the imagery in *The Ancient Mariner*. Indeed, it is she who points out in passing that the older Coleridge, in his notebooks, identified himself with his own mariner and used the imagery of his poem to describe the agony of his nightmares and withdrawal symptoms, but she does not pursue or develop the link more systematically across his life. However, her expertise about addiction is telling and I will be drawing on her insights to talk about how strikingly relevant Coleridge's poem, and indeed his life story, is to a culture like our own, so dominated by various forms of addictive and obsessive behaviour.

Finally, there is Richard Holmes's magisterial two-volume biography of Coleridge,[4] essential reading for anyone who wants to study him in depth. Holmes is highly readable and has brilliant insights, especially into the younger Coleridge. But though his second volume, *Coleridge: Darker Reflections*, dealing with the older Coleridge, is extensive and detailed, it seems to me that Holmes's account does not give Coleridge's Christian faith the really central place it should have, nor does it have the theological focus and reach necessary to bring out the depth and originality of Coleridge's contribution to Christian thinking. Of course, as a biographer, he notes that Coleridge returned to faith and wrote some profound and influential theology, but Holmes is not really engaged with, or sympathetic to, that faith, and his selections from the notebooks and letters underplay it. In particular, he takes only occasional notice of Coleridge's rich and compelling prayer life, for which there is abundant evidence as many of his prayers are written out in his notebooks.

In fact, the return to prayer accompanies the key turning point in *The Ancient Mariner*, the moment in which he is freed from the albatross. For the mariner moves from an agonising inability to pray –

I look'd to Heaven, and tried to pray;
But or ever a prayer had gusht,
A wicked whisper came, and made
My heart as dry as dust.

(Lines 244–7)

– to a renewed gift of prayer, released by a return to imaginatively transfigured vision, which changes everything:

The spell begins to break.
> The self-same moment I could pray;
> And from my neck so free
> The Albatross fell off, and sank
> Like lead into the sea.
>
> *(Lines 288–91 with gloss)*

As we will see in the following pages, prayer, both achieved and despaired of, both abandoned and recovered, weaves constantly in and out of Coleridge's letters, notebooks, conversation and actual practice. For Coleridge, as for the mariner, prayer and vision went hand in hand, and the recovery of prayer in his life was not a matter of conventional piety but of spiritual survival. His experience of what he called 'the Night-mare Life-in-Death' made prayer, itself, a matter of life and death.

Prophetic Moment: A Poem on the Threshold

Though Coleridge gave *The Ancient Mariner* a medieval setting and the verse was meant to imitate early ballads, it was written in the midst of that massive shift in the way we see things and configure the world, which issued from the Enlightenment. The poem is fully alive to that shift and crisis and is indeed a parable about its failings and problems and a prophecy about their resolution. Thomas Pfau, the cultural historian, has shown, in his excellent recent book *Minding the Modern*,[5] how *The Ancient Mariner* engages with the problems of alienation and anomie, with the crisis over the very nature of personhood which modernity has brought us. He goes so far as to say that *The Ancient Mariner* is 'A parable about the philosophical predicament of modernity' (p. 454) and in the final section of his book, 'Retrieving the Human',

Coleridge emerges as something of a hero and a prophet for our times: an opinion with which I entirely concur.

One aspect of the Enlightenment which had huge implications for modernism was the divorce between reason and imagination and the consequent reduction of knowledge itself to a so-called 'objective' realm of quantifiable fact from which all value or meaning had been drained, which in turn led to a reductive, mechanistic and purely material account of the cosmos.

Coleridge was living and working in the midst of this process. He saw from within, as it developed, the deadening effect of a falsely rationalistic and materialist philosophy. As a leading figure in the 'Romantic Movement' he was already part of the reaction against a purely mechanical and materialist view of the world, but unlike some of the other Romantic poets he was concerned with more than creating beautiful fantasies as an alternative to grim reality. He wanted to challenge the philosophers on their own ground and show that the insights of imagination are insights into reality itself. In particular he wanted to deliver his age from what he called 'the tyranny of the eye', to alert us to the formative reality of invisible qualities and values to counterbalance our obsession with 'visible' facts, with the quantifiable, with dead things that can only be weighed and measured.

When at last Coleridge published *The Rime of the Ancient Mariner* under his own name and with his own interpretative gloss in 1817 he prefaced the whole poem with an epigraph: a quotation in Latin from a work by Thomas Burnet: *Arcaeologiae Philosophicae*, a seventeenth-century work which combined mysticism and science, of which Coleridge possessed a 1692 edition. The very fact that he chose to preface his poem with a passage from such a work signalled that he no longer regarded *The Mariner* as a piece of gothic frippery but saw it as a serious contribution to our spiritual understanding. The content of the quotation that Coleridge selected makes his intentions for the whole poem even clearer:

> I readily believe that there are more invisible beings in the universe than visible. But who will declare to us the nature of all these, the rank, relationships, distinguishing characteristics and qualities of each? What is it they do? Where is it they dwell? Always the human intellect circles around the knowledge of these mysteries, never touching the centre. Meanwhile it is, I deny not, oft-times well pleasing to behold sketched upon the mind, as upon a tablet, a picture of the greater and better world; so shall not the spirit, wonted to the petty concerns of daily life, narrow itself over much, nor sink utterly into trivialities. But meanwhile we must diligently seek after truth, and maintain a temperate judgement, if we would distinguish certainty from uncertainty, day from night.[6]

Two key elements from this epigraph are especially relevant to this poem: 'I readily believe that there are more invisible beings in the universe than visible'; and second, from the central part of the passage, an encouragement for us 'to behold sketched upon the mind, as upon a tablet, a picture of the greater and better world; so shall not the spirit, wonted to the petty concerns of daily life, narrow itself over much nor sink utterly into trivialities'. These elements alert us to two key features in the poem, opening our minds to a deeper reading. We are asked to remember the reality of the invisible as well as the visible, to remember that there is always more both to our cosmos and to our own minds than we can at any given moment comprehend. Indeed, a large part of the power and purpose of Coleridge's poetry is to make the invisible realities visible to us, to clothe them for a moment in visible symbols, which can move and change us. The second element also touches on one of the central themes of *The Rime of the Ancient Mariner* and, more widely, one of Coleridge's most important assertions as a poet: the danger that the petty concerns of daily life, the apparent ordinariness of a world taken for granted, should narrow the mind and sink it into triviality. Burnet's way of curing this is to suggest that the mind should behold a greater and a better world. Certainly Coleridge's method in this poem is to take us out of the realm of the familiar, transferring us both literally and metaphorically to an entirely different hemisphere and opening the mind to heights and depths, sublimities and horrors, which are the visible representation of the mind's own invisible potentialities.

Throughout our reading of this poem we must have this sense of expansion: of height, of depth, of unrealised potential, of being more and more in touch with invisible realities glimmering through the visible.

Although Coleridge is best known for a handful of brilliant poems written in the course of a few miraculous years when he was a young man at the end of the eighteenth century, it is less well known that he spent the rest of his life, the first thirty-four years of the nineteenth century, reflecting on the meaning of that intense experience: of having been the mind through which great works of imagination had been revealed. In this reflection Coleridge found himself compelled to reject the mechanistic, clockwork cosmos of Newton, to reject the distant and detached clock-maker that passed for God with many of his contemporaries. Instead he rediscovered for himself the mysterious and suddenly present God who spoke to Moses from the burning bush, and called himself 'I AM', the mysterious and all-sustaining Word made flesh at Bethlehem, and the life-giving Holy Spirit through whom the imaginations of poets are kindled. After all his peregrinations, Coleridge, like his mariner, found haven and firm footing at last in the land of the Trinity.

As we come to the end of the Enlightenment project, the shortcomings of which Coleridge so strongly attacked while he was in the midst of it, and as we find the purely material and mechanical models of reality less and less adequate to our experience, we may find in Coleridge's writings essential guides for the seas we have to navigate in the 'post-modern' era.

Prelude

The Growth of a Poet's Mind

The lighthouse top at Watchet Harbour: the beacon of vision, the light of reason, and a lifelong delight in philosophy

CHAPTER ONE

The Kirk, the Hill, the Lighthouse Top

The ship was cheered, the harbour cleared,
Merrily did we drop
Below the kirk, below the hill,
Below the light house top.

(Lines 21–4)

Coleridge describes his mariner setting out on the voyage and glancing back as, one by one, the kirk, the hill, the lighthouse top – the familiar landmarks of home – drop out of sight below the horizon, and he turns forwards to face the unknown. As we look at Coleridge's life before he wrote *The Ancient Mariner*, these three familiar landmarks may, helpfully, stand as emblems for important aspects of that life. 'The kirk' may stand not only for the church itself, but also for the formative influence of its vicar, Coleridge's father, and for Coleridge's own first reading of the Bible and the Prayer Book, reading which never deserted him, and in the end deeply renewed him. 'The hill' may stand for his rich early experiences of nature, not only in climbing the hills of his Devon childhood, but more importantly following the streams he loved uphill towards their source. Finally, 'the light-house top' may stand for the light of reason, the beginnings of his education, and his early and lifelong delight in philosophy.

The Kirk

Coleridge was born in the small Devonshire town of Ottery St Mary on 21 October 1772, the youngest of the Reverend John

Coleridge's ten children. If we were trying to reconstruct the infancy and early childhood of anybody in Coleridge's father's generation or earlier, we would find it very difficult to do so, for the polished, decorous, guarded and Augustan culture of the early and mid-eighteenth century in which John Coleridge flourished placed little importance on childhood, and indeed dressed children as little adults and waited impatiently for them to grow up and be useful. It was Coleridge's and Wordsworth's generation, and indeed primarily these two very poets, who shifted the entire culture around them, and opened up that keen interest in the intense experience of childhood and that remarkable reverence for the insights of the child which still form part of our outlook now.

We have a rich source for understanding Coleridge's childhood experience in the poet's own writings. In his notebooks and letters and in his poetry itself he reached back to understand the forces that had shaped him for good and ill, and wrote about them with extraordinary intensity. Indeed, he would later define a poet as a person who retained a child's capacity for intense vision and wonder: 'In the Poet was comprehended the man who carries the feelings of Childhood onto the powers of Manhood, who with a soul unsubdued, unshackled by custom, can contemplate all things with the freshness, with the wonder of a child . . .'[1]

One of Coleridge's earliest memories, a memory of listening to the church bells of Ottery St Mary's, is preserved for us in a passage from *Frost at Midnight*, an important poem to which we will be returning later in more detail:

> . . . oft
> With unclosed lids, already had I dreamt
> Of my sweet birth-place, and the old church-tower,
> Whose bells, the poor man's only music, rang
> From morn to evening, all the hot Fair-day,
> So sweetly, that they stirred and haunted me

With a wild pleasure, falling on mine ear
Most like articulate sounds of things to come![2]

This would have been a vivid experience for the young child. In those days on feasts and 'Fair-days' the chimes of St Mary's were sometimes rung for as long as twelve hours at a stretch, resonating from the two huge bell-towers which were part of the church's substantial fourteenth-century foundation. Young Coleridge, released from other tasks on the hot Fair-day, and roaming upstream beside his beloved River Otter, would have heard the bells right up the valley.

There is a great deal to be learnt about Coleridge's feelings and formation even in this brief passage: not simply that he was child of the vicarage, and that in a profound way, his mature theology would eventually return to the place where he began, the life of the Church of England, integrating sacred and secular in the rhythms and patterns of community life; but we glimpse also his instinctive empathy for 'the poor man' and his understanding that the poor and the marginalised need their music too. Indeed, his whole poetic, and to some degree political effort would be to take 'high culture' out of the drawing rooms of the well-off and give it back to the people, so that they might hear their own voice 'with a clean new music in it', in Seamus Heaney's phrase. Finally, Coleridge seems to locate in this very early experience of hearing the bells an intensely personal apprehension which would mark the deepest character of his later writing: a sense of a 'wild haunting', a presentiment of things to come, a feeling that even apparently 'senseless and inarticulate' things are, could we but hear them, trembling on the brink of speech. The poet presents us with the image of the child haunted with wild pleasure by something which, though not articulate yet, would become articulate just as a listening child himself would one day speak to spellbound listeners.

Another great source of information on Coleridge's early childhood comes in a series of autobiographical letters to his friend Tom Poole. These letters give us a picture of a wayward, precocious, sensitive and intense child, utterly open to the heights and depths of what life had to bring him.

The Ancient Mariner contains a line in which we are told the wedding guest listened like 'a three years' child' but by the age of three Coleridge had become not only a listener but also a reader and a declaimer!

In the second of his autobiographical letters to Poole,[3] when he was twenty-four and had just become Poole's neighbour in Nether Stowey, Coleridge tells his friend that at the close of 1775 (when he was then aged three) 'I could read a chapter in the Bible'! In the next letter, describing the years 1775–8, when he was between three and six, Coleridge opens cheerily, 'These three years I continued at the reading school', and even tells us a little of what he was reading for fun:

We know of his childhood of letters

My Father's Sister kept an *every-thing* Shop at Crediton – and there I read thro' all the gilt-cover little books that could be had at that time, & likewise all the uncovered tales of Tom Hickathrift, Jack the Giant-killer, &c & &c &c &c – / – – and I used to lie by the wall, and *mope* – and my spirits used to come upon me suddenly, & in a flood – & then I was accustomed to run up and down the church-yard, and act over all I had been reading on the docks, the nettles, and the rank-grass. – At six years old I remember to have read Belisarius, Robinson Crusoe, & Philip Quarle [Quarll] – and then I found the Arabian Nights' entertainments – one tale of which (the tale of a man who was compelled to seek for a pure virgin) made so deep an impression on me (I had read it in the evening while my mother was mending stockings) that I was haunted by spectres, whenever I was in the dark – and I distinctly remember the anxious & fearful eagerness, with which

I used to watch the window, in which the books lay – & whenever the Sun lay upon them, I would seize it, carry it by the wall, & bask, & read –.[4]

The first thing to note about this passage is the *active* imagination with which Coleridge responded to his reading: 'I was accustomed to run up and down the church-yard, and act over all I had been reading on the docks, the nettles, and the rank-grass.' It is an extraordinary vision, this wonder-child acting out the great mythopoeic fairy-tales – *Jack the Giant Killer* and the tales of *Arabian Nights* – but enacting them on the sacred ground of the church. In a sense, that image beautifully embodies what would be his life's mission: bringing together the active, shaping spirit of the imagination, on the one hand, and the traditions and mysteries of Christianity, on the other. Indeed, in another of his autobiographical letters to Poole he himself makes the link between his reading of fairy-tales and the opening of his mind to new ways of finding truth in faith and philosophy, and in this letter he anticipates a great deal of modern thinking about the right place of imagination and fairy-tale in the raising of children, when he makes a defence of stories of giants, magicians and genii:

For from my early reading of Faery Tales, & Genii &c &c – my mind had been habituated *to the Vast* -& I never regarded my senses in any way as the criteria of my belief. I regulated all my creeds by my conceptions not by my *sight* – even at that age. Should children be permitted to read Romances, & Relations of Giants & Magicians, & Genii? – I know all that has been said against it; but I have formed my faith in the affirmative. – I know no other way of giving the mind a love of 'the Great', & 'the Whole'. – Those who have been led to the same truths step by step thro' the constant testimony of their senses, seem to me to want a sense which I possess – They contemplate nothing but *parts* – and all *parts* <u>are necessarily little</u> – and the Universe to them is but a mass of *little things.* – It is true, that the mind *may* become credulous & prone to superstition by the former method – but are not the Experimentalists credulous even to madness in believing any absurdity, rather than believe the grandest truths, if they have not the testimony of their own senses in their favor? – I have known some who have been *rationally* educated, as it is styled. They were marked by a microscopic acuteness; but when they looked at great things, all became a blank & they saw nothing – and denied (very illogically) that any thing could be seen; <u>and uniformly put the negation of a power for the possession of a power</u> – & called the want of imagination Judgment . . .[5]

Coleridge wrote this letter at the age of twenty-four and it was already clear to him that the awakened imagination of the child can and should become a gift and power available to the adult. This passage also introduces one of the great themes of Coleridge's life and work: his heroic resistance to the reductivism which had begun in his era, and has nearly choked and destroyed ours. <u>By reductivism I mean the entire cast of mind that always presumes that everything apparently great or mysterious can be reduced to its smallest parts and 'explained', that is to say 'explained away'.</u> We see it in the aggressive 'New Atheism' of our own time; we see it in the kind of reductivism that relies on phrases <u>like 'just'</u> or <u>'only' or 'merely'</u>, the kind of thinking that wants to see the whole of human culture as merely the unwinding of a selfish gene. Coleridge not only saw this danger but also saw its essential absurdity, its philosophical shallowness, <u>its blind obsession with parts and refusal to contemplate the whole.</u> As we will see, these issues are raised with great force through the imaginative frame and narrative of *The Ancient Mariner*, and addressed by Coleridge throughout his life, especially in his final brilliant synthesis of

Coleridge recognizing
power of child's
mind thru his own experience

imagination, faith and philosophy in the *Biographia Literaria*. But this is to anticipate.

Coleridge's active or even overactive imaginative life, fuelled by *The Arabian Nights*, could have its shadow side, for if *The Arabian Nights* was the source of his first supernatural imaginative rapture, it was also the source of dreadful nightmares which pursued him all his life. So he wrote to Poole, in a passage we have already cited: 'I was haunted by spectres'. This phrase will be resonant for readers of *The Ancient Mariner* with its spectral ship and its 'Night-mare Life-in-Death' (line 193). It is also interesting to note the sheer power of the presence of the physical book itself for the young Coleridge, his obsessive watching of it, and his deep need for the light of the sun to cleanse and safeguard these imaginative voyages. There is another sense, too, in which the arena of imagination is both framed and guarded by the larger and equally supernatural framing of 'the Kirk'. Later in the same letter he says to Poole:

> – I suppose, you know the old prayer –
> Matthew! Mark! Luke! & John!
> God bless the bed which I lie on.
> Four Angels round me spread,
> Two at my foot & two at my bed [head] –

> This prayer I said nightly – & most firmly believed the truth of it.
> – Frequently have I, half-awake & half-asleep, my body diseased & fevered by my imagination, seen armies of ugly Things bursting in upon me, & these four angels keeping them off.[6]

Once more we see, even so early in his childhood, key elements that he would weave into *The Ancient Mariner*: the invading nightmares, the desperate need for and power of prayer, the intervention of angels.

Childhood weaves into poem

But there was more to Coleridge's childhood, of course, than simply the intense listening and precocious reading of a gifted and imaginative child. Coleridge was the youngest of ten, a gift to his father's mature years and the apple of his mother's eye, for his father was fifty-three and his mother forty-five when he was born. This sense of being the last, the special, perhaps the unexpected child, had a double-edge; as Coleridge memorably and paradoxically put it: 'my father was very fond of me, and I was my mother's darling — in consequence, I was very miserable'.[7]

From the outset, both sibling love and sibling rivalry were a deep part of Coleridge's formation. He felt very close to his older sister Anne, whom he called *Nancy*, feelings perhaps intensified in recollection of her untimely death at twenty-one. The nearest to Coleridge in age was Francis, called 'Frank'. If Coleridge was doted on by his mother, then perhaps, almost by way of compensation, his nurse, Molly, who had most of the practical rearing of the children, doted instead on Frank; and, according to Coleridge, gave Coleridge himself nothing but hard words and blows. Out of these tensions arose perhaps the single most significant episode in Coleridge's childhood; certainly it was an episode to which he returned again and again in memory and in notebooks, and the atmosphere and imagery of which entered deeply into his poetry, and returned to him sometimes in both dream and nightmare. What started as a squabble between brothers over food suddenly escalated into rage, into running away, and indeed into a near-death experience. Let us hear Coleridge tell the story of what happened in his own words:

I had asked my mother one evening to cut my cheese *entire*, so that I might toast it: this was no easy matter, it being a *crumbly* cheese – My mother however did it – / I went into the garden for some thing or other, and in the mean time my Brother Frank *minced* my cheese, 'to disappoint the favorite'. I returned, saw the exploit, and in an agony of passion flew at Frank – he

pretended to have been seriously hurt by my blow, flung himself
on the ground, and there lay with outstretched limbs – I hung
over him moaning & in a great fright – he leaped up, & with a
horse-laugh gave me a severe blow in the face – I seized a knife,
and was running at him, when my Mother came in & took me by
the arm – / I expected a flogging – & struggling from her I ran
away, to a hill at the bottom of which the Otter flows about one
mile from Ottery. – There I stayed; my rage died away; but my
obstinacy vanquished my fears – & taking out a little shilling
book which had, at the end, morning & evening prayers, I very
devoutly repeated them – thinking *at the same time* with inward
& gloomy satisfaction, how miserable my Mother must be! – I
distinctly remember my feelings when I saw a Mr Vaughan pass
over the Bridge, at about a furlong's distance – and how I watched
the Calves in the fields beyond the river. It grew dark – & I fell
asleep – it was towards the latter end of October – & it proved a
dreadful stormy night – / I felt the cold in my sleep, and dreamt
that I was pulling the blanket over me, & actually pulled over me
a dry thorn bush, which lay on the hill – in my sleep I had rolled
from the top of the hill to within three yards of the River, which
flowed by the unfenced edge of the bottom. – I awoke several
times, and finding myself wet & stiff, and cold, closed my eyes
again that I might forget it. – In the mean time my Mother waited
about half an hour, expecting my return, when the *Sulks* had
evaporated – I not returning, she sent into the Church-yard, &
round the town – not found! – Several men & all the boys were
sent to ramble about & seek me – in vain! My Mother was almost
distracted – and at ten o'clock at night I was *cry'd* by the crier in
Ottery, and in two villages near it – with a reward offered for me.
– No one went to bed – indeed, I believe, half the town were up
all one night! To return to myself – About five in the morning or
a little after, I was broad awake; and attempted to get up & walk
– but I could not move – I saw the Shepherds & Workmen at a

distance – & cryed but so faintly, that it was impossible to hear me 80 yards off – and there I might have lain & died – for I was now almost given over, the ponds & even the river near which I was lying, having been dragged. – But by good luck Sir Stafford Northcote, who had been out all night, resolved to make one other trial, and came so near that he heard my crying – He carried me in his arms, for near a quarter of a mile; when we met my father & Sir Stafford's Servants. – . . . I was put to bed – & recovered in a day or so – but I was certainly injured – For I was weakly, & subject to the ague for many years after – .[8]

Holmes and a number of Coleridge's other biographers observe in this episode the first expression of a pattern which they see repeated again and again in Coleridge's life: the sudden *agony of passion* in the midst of an apparently calm scenario, the rapid alternation between feeling hurt himself and feeling total empathy for the one who has hurt him and against whom he has lashed out, and then the *bolt*, the flight, and even in the midst of the flight, a deep sensitivity to and awareness of all his surroundings, and then the pride that will not let him return immediately, and yet the secret longing to be found, and finally the dangerous extremities, the taking of things so far that when at last he wants to cry out and return he is incapable of it. It is certainly true that all these elements, and often in that order, do recur at various times of crisis in Coleridge's life. But I would not want to suggest that this episode was formative in the sense of being determinative. So much of Coleridge's later thought explores the mystery of our freedom. Whatever pressures may be pushing us one way, we can sometimes suddenly move to the other, for both good and ill. There is a further curious detail in this story as Coleridge tells it, and that is that this highly alarmed and emotional seven-year-old nevertheless had a little book of prayers in his pocket, and knew how to read and use them ('I very devoutly repeated them').

There could never have been a time, from his childhood onwards, in which he didn't have 'a little shilling book', or even a weighty folio, somewhere about his person. Also typical of the essence of Coleridge, and anticipating things to come, is the extraordinary honesty and psychological acuteness with which he describes his divided mind – divided not simply between obstinacy and fear, but also between real devotion and an equally real desire to upset his mother: 'I very devoutly repeated them – thinking *at the same time* with inward & gloomy satisfaction, how miserable my Mother must be!' It is this quality of observing all that goes on in our minds at the same time, the worthy as well as the unworthy, which makes him such an honest, helpful and compelling figure for his readers. But it is also worth reflecting that for the infant who heard the church bells, for the three-year-old who could read a chapter of the Bible out loud, for the five-year-old who enacted his fairy-tales in the churchyard, and for the seven-year-old who could devoutly read Evensong in the midst of running away, the whole frame of Anglican Christianity – whatever his subsequent departures and returns – was part of his world, and formed a permanent and generative element in the language with which he spoke and thought. If the mariner was to see the kirk itself drop away below the horizon as he set off on his voyage, he would still find that the deep structure of Christian thought, its heights and depths, its loss and redemption, would always be with him.

Before the kirk drops for the time being below our horizon, let us consider the part played by its central figure, Coleridge's father, Ottery's vicar and schoolmaster. In *Biographia Literaria*, Coleridge gives us an affectionate but partly comic picture of his father as an innocent abroad, a genial but perhaps slightly hapless would-be scholar who had written a great new theory of Latin grammar completely ignored by all, and who bemused his congregation in this small market town by quoting the Bible to them in

Hebrew on the grounds that it was the language of the Holy Spirit. In fact, recent scholarship has taken Coleridge's father rather more seriously, and delineated what an astonishing achievement it was that brought him from humble and unlearned origins to be the possessor of a Cambridge degree, author of several books, and the key leader, communicator and educator of his own community. In 2014 the great Coleridgean scholar J.C.C. Mays produced a monumental work *Coleridge's Father: Absent Man, Guardian Spirit*,[9] which may change our views of him forever. Whatever humorous deprecations there may be in *Biographia Literaria*, Coleridge certainly drew deeply throughout his life on the precious times he had alone with his father: walks and conversations, which glowed all the more intensely in the poet's mind against the dark background of his father's untimely death when Coleridge was nine. One example of such a walk and talk with his father illustrates this most clearly. In the very same letter that describes his disastrous flight from home, he says this about his father:

My Father (who had so little of parental ambition in him, that he had destined his children to be Blacksmiths &c, & had accomplished his intention but for my Mother's pride & spirit of aggrandizing her family) – my father had however resolved that I should be a Parson. I read every book that came in my way without distinction – and my father was fond of me, & used to take me on his knee, and hold long conversations with me. I remember, that at eight years old I walked with him one winter evening from a farmer's house, a mile from Ottery – & he told me the names of the stars – and how Jupiter was a thousand times larger than our world – and that the other twinkling stars were Suns that had worlds rolling round them – & when I came home, he shewed me how they rolled round – / . I heard him with a profound delight & admiration; but without the least

Looks back on relationter better

28

mixture of wonder or incredulity. For from my early reading of
Faery Tales, & Genii &c &c – my mind had been habituated *to
the Vast* –[10]

The first thing to note about this remarkable passage is that it is
not just the heavens that are vast and marvellously furnished, it is
also the mind of the vicar of Ottery St Mary's! The Christianity
into which Coleridge was born, to which he would eventually
return, and which he himself would profoundly renew and
re-envisage, was not some narrow bigotry or closed-down, text-
bound literalism. Coleridge's local vicar was not a flat-earther.
John Coleridge was familiar with the great developments in
astronomy that had taken place during his lifetime. He did not see
the working of reason or the enlargement of the mind through
the discoveries of science as in any sense a threat to his faith.
When he came home and showed his son, perhaps with marbles
on a board, how these other worlds rolled around, he was not
only showing him a piece of astronomy, he was also showing him
that curiosity about the world, and an imaginative grasp of
science, were not necessarily inimical to faith.

The Hill

On that strange night-flight up the hill Coleridge had been running
away from his mother, but there was another sense in which he
was returning to his mother, a sense in which he was profoundly,
as Wordsworth called him, a 'child of nature'. The nurturing of
mind and imagination he received upon the hill above the kirk in
Ottery, and his long rambling following the River Otter upwards
till it was a stream in the hills and brought him to magical caves,
was as profound and spiritually nourishing as anything he received
directly from his parents. The hill here stands as an emblem of
nature, but for Coleridge himself the truest emblem was not so

much the hill itself as the streams which rose within, and flowed from it.

In *The Prelude*, Wordsworth gives us a glimpse of Coleridge, the exiled schoolboy in London, closing his eyes and returning by *internal light*, in an intense act of imagination, to the hill and streams of his childhood:

> I speak to thee, my Friend! to thee,
> Who, yet a liveried schoolboy, in the depths
> Of the huge city, on the leaded roof
> Of that wide edifice, thy school and home,
> Wert used to lie and gaze upon the clouds
> Moving in heaven; or, of that pleasure tired,
> To shut thine eyes, and by internal light
> See trees, and meadows, and thy native stream,
> Far distant, thus beheld from year to year
> Of a long exile.[11]

This passage is made all the more poignant by the fact that it was addressed to Coleridge in the midst of a longer and deeper exile than that of the schoolboy, addressed to him when he was indeed the mariner *alone on a wide, wide sea*, self-exiled across the Mediterranean in Malta. Even as he faced his demons there, Wordsworth was remembering Coleridge remembering the River Otter. But let us hear directly from Coleridge himself about that *dear native stream* in which he nearly drowned, but which was also happily to prove a source and sustenance for so much of his life.

The image of an inexhaustible river, a fountain of life and light, a force to be reckoned with, runs through all Coleridge's writing and emerges afresh at key points in his life. He was fascinated by the river as something seen, but whose source is unseen. This fascination goes right back to his childhood, to the days when with his friends he tried to find the source of the River Otter, a river which was the subject of his first accomplished poem, 'To the River Otter', written when he was still an undergraduate, where already the sense of surface and depth, movement and transparency, had entered his imagination:

> What happy and what mournful hours, since last
> I skimmed the smooth thin stone along thy breast,
> Numbering its light leaps! Yet so deep imprest
> Sink the sweet scenes of childhood that mine eyes
> I never shut amid the sunny ray, but straight
> With all their tints thy waters rise,
> Thy crossing plank, thy marge with willows grey,
> And bedded sand that veined with various dyes
> Gleamed through thy bright transparence! . . .[12]

As Coleridge matured both as a man and a writer, he left the cloying sweetness of that early style behind; but the river, which was its subject, continued to flow through his mind and inform his thought. Indeed, one of the first poems he planned with Wordsworth, in the same year that he wrote *The Ancient Mariner*, was to have been an epic following a stream from its first source to the time it meets the sea. And it was also in that year that Coleridge wrote *Kubla Khan*, the great river poem which we shall look at in much more detail later. All we need note here is that even as he celebrates the River Otter and its source in his childhood he already implies that the waters of a corresponding imaginative river, or perhaps river of imagination, rise within him.

This visionary remembrance of the river of his childhood, written long after, is made particularly poignant and intense by the sudden and complete catastrophe, from the child's point of view, which brought his childhood to an end. When Coleridge was nine, his father went off to Plymouth to see Frank, Coleridge's only slightly older brother, settled and apprenticed as a midshipman. He returned home in apparent good health and high spirits, but that very night he died suddenly, probably of a heart attack.

John Coleridge's death changed everything. The vicarage went with his job. Coleridge's mother found herself at once bereaved, homeless, deprived of income, and having to provide as best she could for such a large family. This may account in some degree for what follows, and for the tragic break in real trust and affection between Coleridge and his mother. Friends of the family, rallying round, and trying to find places and support for the numerous children with whom Anne Coleridge could not cope on her own, told her they could get young Sam presented at Christ's Hospital, a charity school in London, whose board, lodging and education was sometimes provided free to the sons of the clergy, particularly those in material distress. We can see why she took up the offer, but we can equally see how traumatic it was for Coleridge to lose a beloved father, to be wrenched away from his home and family and sent off to the sparse diet, grim regime, savage beatings and above all exile and loneliness which was the experience of most boys in a London charity school. What is more, he was sent away even before it was strictly necessary, even before the school-place was available, and packed off to an uncle in London three months before school started. For now he bade farewell to *the hill* above Ottery St Mary's and all it stood for, but *the lighthouse top*, the rich life of the mind, was just ahead of him.

The Lighthouse Top

If *the kirk* and *the hill* that drop away from the mariner may stand for the formative influences of church and nature, then in this part of Coleridge's life we will see *the lighthouse top*, the light shed not by nature but by human endeavour; the light of learning, of philosophy, of history and poetry, begins to shine more brightly.

However dark some of his school experiences may have been, it was at Christ's Hospital that Coleridge was given an incomparable grounding, not only in Latin and Greek but in the whole tradition of literature from which he would draw so fully and to which he would contribute so richly. But, as we have noted, he was shipped off to an uncle before he ever got to school, and in that strange pre-school interlude, there are also many foreshadowings of his later life.

Uncle John Bowden was a 'character' – indeed almost a Dickensian character before Dickens' time. He kept a tobacconist's near the Stock Exchange, and worked for an underwriter part-time, but seems to have spent a great deal of time escaping from both these occupations, and from his own family, into the many taverns and coffeehouses of London, taking the astonished and astonishing young Coleridge with him. Here's how Coleridge tells the story in his fifth and last autobiographical letter to Poole, starting with a description of his uncle:

> – He was generous as the air & a man of very considerable talents – but he was a Sot [drunkard]. – He received me with great affection, and I stayed ten weeks at his house . . . My Uncle was very proud of me, & used to carry me from Coffee-house to Coffee-house, and Tavern to Tavern, where I drank, & talked & disputed, as if I had been a man – / . Nothing was more common than for a large party to exclaim in my hearing, that I *was a prodigy*, &c &c &c – so that, while I remained at my Uncle's, I was most completely spoilt & pampered, both mind & body.[13]

Here we have a first instance of '*Coleridge the Talker*',[14] brilliant, loquacious, the centre of attention, expanding his wings and the minds of his audience amid the smoke, the drink, and the gregarious clatter and chatter of a London pub. We can also imagine how he flung himself into that world with its thrills of intoxicating drinks, its flattering pleasures of being an honorary 'grown-up', and its almost constant attention, as both an escape from and a compensation for the traumatic loss of his father with which he had not yet really come to terms.

The contrast between pub sessions with his disreputable uncle and the Spartan rigours and disciplines of Christ's Hospital must have been almost unbearable, as Coleridge moved from being spoiled and indulged in pubs to the strict regime, poor food and frequent beatings of his school life.

But if the physical life at school was dark and shadowed, the great lighthouse of intellectual and imaginative life burnt all the more brightly, and Coleridge first showed here those extraordinary powers of resilience and recovery that were to serve him well through the coming traumas of his life. For what the school did provide him with was access to books, and the learning and skill with which to enjoy them: 'My whole Being was, with eyes closed to every object of present sense, to crumple myself up in a sunny Corner, and read, read, read.'[15]

Indeed, Coleridge's access to books was greatly enlarged by an extraordinary incident, which again tells us a huge amount about the man he was to become. This was a story that he told to James Gillman. One day, when Coleridge was 'skipping school' to walk the streets of London, or 'skulking', as it was then called, he was so actively reliving and imagining his reading, in this case, the tale of Leander swimming the Hellespont, that he 'thrust his hands before him as if in the act of swimming' and accidentally struck the pocket of a passing stranger. In what could have been an early episode of *Oliver*, the man seized him and lifted him up and accused him of picking his pocket. Things might have gone very badly for Coleridge at this point, but the affronted man was astonished when the young urchin he had seized enthusiastically explained that he wasn't picking a pocket, but rather swimming the Hellespont, pretending he was Leander swimming towards his beloved Hero. The gentleman was 'so struck and delighted by the novelty of the thing'[16] that, far from dragging the young lad off to the authorities, he gave him instead a subscription for three years to the King Street Lending Library! We can still marvel at this wonderful piece of spontaneous and particular beneficence by an unnamed stranger, which has borne such great fruit. And Coleridge made the most of it. His reading was voracious, and at this stage completely undiscriminating; he simply read and absorbed everything: 'I read through the catalogue, folios and all, whether I understood them, or did not understand them, running all risks in skulking out to get the two volumes which I was entitled to have daily.'[17]

However comprehensive and indiscriminate the reading which so deeply stocked his mind with the ideas and images of his later poetry, certain key themes did begin to emerge as Coleridge entered his teenage years. One of these was a real interest in philosophy, particularly the writings of Plato and the Neo-Platonists, many of whose insights, as we shall see, deeply and subtly inform *The Rime of the Ancient Mariner*. Part of our evidence for this arises from the testimony of a great friend he made at Christ's and kept throughout his life – for Coleridge's eloquence and his gift for friendship never deserted him, and sustained him through his worst days – the wonderful Charles Lamb.

Here is Lamb's justly famous encomium of Coleridge as he was when they met as schoolboys in Christ's Hospital:

> Come back into memory, like as thou wert in the dayspring of thy fancies, with hope like a fiery column before thee – the dark pillar not yet turned – Samuel Taylor Coleridge – Logician, Metaphysician, Bard – How have I seen the casual passer through the cloisters stand still, intranced with admiration (while he weighed the disproportion between the speech and the garb of

the young Mirandula), to hear thee unfold, in thy deep and sweet intonations, the mysteries of Jamblichus, or Plotinus (for even in those years thou waxedst not pale at such philosophic draughts), or reciting Homer in his Greek, or Pindar – while the walls of the old Grey Friars re-echoed to the accents of the inspired charity-boy![18]

Holmes suggests that Lamb does not take Coleridge entirely seriously in this passage: 'Neoplatonic mystics and Gnostics have the air of being plucked out of a conjuror's hat, and there is a certain undercurrent of affectionate mockery.'[19] I would disagree with that assessment. Far from being plucked out of a conjuror's hat, Coleridge's early and deep reading, not only of Plato, but also particularly of these more mystic Neo-Platonists, laid an important foundation for his transfigured and transfiguring view of the world, on which he drew for the rest of his life. We will look at the relevance of these writers in greater detail later, especially when we come to consider the ultimate meanings of the sun and the moon in *The Rime of the Ancient Mariner*, but it is worth even at this point just briefly outlining some of their main ideas. Essential to Coleridge's understanding of Plato is the idea that everything in the world of appearances or 'phenomena' reflects and corresponds with a greater and truer reality of which it is in some sense an 'image, echo or shadow'. Whereas Plato sought to remove us from the world of the senses, which show us only shadows, and to transcend the passing phenomena, Plotinus, Iamblichus and the other Neo-Platonists believed that the images and phenomena of this world could themselves be portals and windows to the radiance beyond them. The scholarly work that has demonstrated how deeply Coleridge drew on this mystical Neo-Platonic tradition is John Beer's two seminal books, *Coleridge the Visionary* and *Coleridge's Poetic Intelligence*. Beer sums up his conclusions in *Coleridge the Visionary*:

> If there is one common thread in Coleridge's spiritual quest, it is his conviction that by meditating on the material universe, men will come to understand the realm of the spiritual, and, correspondingly, the scientist who bears in mind metaphysical truths will find in them the solution to his problems and the true interpretation of physical phenomena.[20]

The 'inspired charity boy' may not have seen the full implications of these texts as he cited them in Greek for his friends, but Coleridge's capacious memory retained everything, and the mature poet drew on them to great and wonderful effect.

If one panel of the 'light-house top' shone out with the writings of ancient philosophers, another shone with a new, glorious and entirely unexpected light, suddenly unveiled by dramatic events in France. Coleridge was just seventeen when the French Revolution began and the Bastille fell in 1789. He was caught up in all the excitement, fervour and marvel of this epoch-making event, as were almost all the others of his generation. As Wordsworth said, 'Bliss was it in that dawn to be alive / But to be young was very heaven!'[21] 'Dawn' is the key word here, bringing with it the sense of new beginnings and new hopes. We are not yet dealing with the dreadful dénouement of these events when that dawn would lead to the terror unleashed on Paris in the noonday of the French Revolution. But in this dawn, as France shook off the shackles of the *ancien régime*, everything seemed possible. The perfection of human society seemed to be within everyone's grasp, and indeed, for all his immersion in the books of the past, Coleridge was then and remained throughout his life keenly aware of the political and social issues of his day, fiercely ardent for justice, so it is not surprising to know that the fall of the Bastille was the occasion of his first thoroughgoing ode. As poetry, it is still immature, marred by the late eighteenth-century poetic mannerisms and personifications which Coleridge and

Wordsworth would later sweep away. The poem ends with a great peroration, pleading for Britain to cast off her chains just as France has done:

Shall France alone a Despot spurn?
Shall she alone, O Freedom, boast thy care?
Lo, round thy standard Belgia's heroes burn,
Tho' Power's blood-stain'd streamers fire the air,
And wider yet thy influence spread,
Nor e'er recline thy weary head,
Till every land from pole to pole
Shall boast one independent soul!
And still, as erst, let favour'd Britain be
First ever of the first, and freest of the free![22]

The tone of that final, ringing couplet seems more appropriate to 'Land of Hope and Glory' than to a universalist revolutionary hymn. At this point Coleridge, still a schoolboy and bound by all the rules of Christ's Hospital, was scarcely among the 'freest of the free'. However, help was at hand, and it arose, as always for Coleridge, through his gift for friendship.

Among the friends Coleridge made in Christ's Hospital was a young man called Tom Evans who lived near the school and invited him to escape it on weekends and share the life of his warm and hospitable family. Evans had also lost his father, but the household of his generous mother and, happily for Coleridge, his three teenage sisters, became a real haven. Together with two other friends, Bob Allen and Val Le Grice, he would go out walking with the three Evans sisters, Anne, Eliza and Mary. He was still recollecting these happy last days at Christ's Hospital as late as 1822 when he wrote to his friend Thomas Allsop of 'a sudden reawakening of schoolboy feelings and notions':

And Oh! From 16 to 19 what hours of Paradise had Allen and I
in escorting the Miss Evanses home on a Saturday, who were then
at a Millaner's [*sic*], whom we used to think, and who I believe
really was, such a nice Lady—and we used to carry thither of a
summer morning the pillage of the Flower Gardens within six
miles of Town with Sonnet of Love-rhyme wrapped round the
Nose-gay.

To be feminine, kind, and *genteelly* (i.e. what I should now
call, neatly) drest—these were the only accomplishments to
which my Head, Heart, or Imagination had any polarity—and
what I was then, I still am.[23]

Indeed, in this quasi-paradisal Indian summer of his late teens
and last schooldays, Coleridge seems to have persuaded himself
that he was in love with Mary Evans, with consequences we shall
see in the next chapter. Unfortunately it was also in this last year
at Christ's, probably as a result of swimming rivers with these
friends in the chilly autumn, that Coleridge had his most severe
bout thus far of the rheumatic fever that would return intermit-
tently and cause so many complications, not least of which was
the long-term consequence of the medical treatment he received
at school and subsequently used himself – heavy doses of laudanum, a commonly prescribed opiate.

*Coleridge's early life described
in the opening lines & stanza's.*

[handwritten annotation]

Coleridge's rooms at Jesus College Cambridge: 'I became a proverb to the University for Idleness – the time, which I should have bestowed on the academic studies, I employed in dreaming out wild schemes of impossible extrication'

CHAPTER TWO

Jesus and the Dragoons

From the point of view of Coleridge's family, and particularly that of his eldest brother, the now 'Reverend' George Coleridge, who had assumed the role of *pater familias*, the whole purpose of Coleridge's education at Christ's was that he should proceed to one of the two Universities where he would either become a fellow and have an academic life or, like most of his university contemporaries, and like George before him, leave university for life as a vicar in the Church of England. So, in the autumn of 1791, Coleridge duly proceeded to Jesus College Cambridge, with which Christ's Hospital had strong links, on a scholarship for which his Christ's schoolmaster Boyer had personally recommended him. The story of Coleridge's Cambridge days, a story he both veiled and retold, often to comic effect, in his later life, was a strange mixture of genius and naivety, passionate engagement and escapist delirium, alternating bouts of intense hard work and almost manic dissipation.

He arrived during the university vacation when there was almost nothing going on at Jesus College, so he spent his first few weeks at Cambridge staying with a friend and mentor from Christ's, Thomas Middleton, a capable and brilliant scholar at Pembroke College, who was later to become the Bishop of Calcutta. Coleridge took directions from Middleton, in the absence of the Director of Studies at Jesus, to begin his reading and study in both mathematics and classics, which would be essential for passing his first Cambridge exams. Middleton leaves us with a picture of long evenings in his rooms at

41

Coleridge arrives @ Jesus College

Pembroke, both of them reading Greek classical texts, Pindar and Euripides, the silence broken only by the pot shots they took with pistols at the large rats which infested Middleton's room. So Coleridge began with a great gust of hard work and good-will, as he wrote to George, who had very much become a substitute father:

> After tea . . . I read classics . . . If I were to read on as I do now — there is not the least doubt, that I should be a Classical Medallist, and a very high Wrangler — but *Freshmen* always *begin* very *furiously*. I am reading Pindar, and composing Greek verse, like a mad dog. I am very fond of Greek verse.[1]

This fondness of Greek verse was to lead both to his first proper academic success, winning a prize after his first year for a Greek ode, and also as a first statement of what was to be a lifelong and passionate struggle for rights and human justice, for it was a Greek ode on the slave trade. However, once term started, and he was back in his own College and away from the virtuous example of Middleton at Pembroke, things changed. As he said in the same letter to George, 'There is no such thing as discipline at our College. There was once they say, but so long ago that no one remembers it.'[2]

We have to remember that the Cambridge of Coleridge's day, as well as attracting some of the most brilliant students of their generation, was also the mere pen and playground for the sons of the English 'squirearchy' and aristocracy. Many of them were used to loose living, had a high-handed disregard for those around them, and were simply biding time with no intention of taking a degree, until they could get back to their fathers' estates. Drunkenness, violence and 'whoredom' was sometimes the rule rather than the exception. But Coleridge did gradually gather around him at Jesus a group of friends who, while certainly on

occasion wild and drunken, were also deep readers and passion-
ately engaged in the political and moral issues of their day. Val Le
Grice, one of his friends from Christ's, summed up the atmosphere of evenings in Coleridge's rooms very vividly:

> what evenings I have spent in those rooms! . . . when Aeschylus,
> and Plato, and Thucydides were pushed aside, with a pile of
> lexicons etc, to discuss the pamphlets of the day. Ever and anon,
> a pamphlet issued from the pen of Burke. There was no need of
> having the book before us. Coleridge had read it in the morn-
> ing, and in the evening he would repeat whole pages
> verbatim.[3]

We can learn a great deal from this little glimpse, about Coleridge
and Cambridge, in the juxtaposition between Greek classics on
the one hand, and 'the pamphlets of the day' on the other. For
Val Le Grice it may well have been a case of pushing the one
aside to make room for the other, and like many mediocre
students before and after him, he may have kept his academic
learning in a sealed compartment which neither admitted light
from his contemporary life nor shed any upon it, but not so
Coleridge. As he was to demonstrate brilliantly in his Greek ode
on the slave trade, for Coleridge the luminous and mystical
insights of Plato on the one hand, and the sharp analysis of real-
politik in Thucydides on the other, were always relevant to the
way we live now. Throughout his life, Coleridge would react to
the great works of the past not as dead monuments of scholarship but (as he would say of the Bible) as 'the living educts of the
Imagination',[4] constantly bringing new insights to bear on
contemporary life.

Second, we have a glimpse here of Coleridge's extraordinary
memory. He could read the latest of Burke's brilliant pamphlets
(these pamphlets were almost certainly those about the debate

of the slave trade abolition movement being put forth by Wilberforce in Parliament) in the morning, and recite pages verbatim in the evening. When we come later to consider the almost magical way in which passages and images from the furthest reach of his voluminous reading could be transformed into moving symbols and images in *The Rime of the Ancient Mariner*, we must think of him not as running back and forth to libraries and indexes, somehow to manufacture an obscure and scholarly poem, but, on the contrary, as drawing happily and freely on the vast resources of 'my memory, tenacious and systematizing'.[5]

The Ode on the Slave Trade

The university offered a prize for an ode in imitation of Sappho, clearly intended to encourage thorough Greek scholarship, though there was already a strong tradition that these classical competition poems not only could, but should be written about contemporary subjects. This was partly, of course, to ensure that the competitors did not simply manufacture a cento of classical quotations but were obliged to compose afresh. But it also had a perhaps unintended consequence of bringing contemporary social and political concerns, as it were in a Trojan horse, right into the heart of the classical curriculum. Indeed, one such competition, only seven years earlier, had massive consequences not only for British politics and law, but for the whole world. In 1785, Thomas Clarkson, then an undergraduate at St John's College Cambridge, put in for a prize for the best Latin essay, and chose the subject '*Anne liceat invitos in servitutem dare?*' – 'Is it lawful to make slaves of others against their will?' Clarkson decided to discuss slavery not just in the ancient world, but in modern times too. While seeking out the first-hand testimony of sugar merchants in London and ship owners in Bristol, Clarkson became aware of the full horrors of the slave trade and his own country's massive involvement in it. He became an impassioned campaigner upon leaving Cambridge, and soon recruited another former student at St John's, William Wilberforce, to be the spokesperson for the anti-slave movement in Parliament, while he himself continued to be its main researcher and organiser outside Parliament. Clarkson and Coleridge were later to become firm friends, and when Clarkson, much later in life, exhausted by his continuous campaigning and bitterly disappointed by the failure of the anti-slavery motion in Parliament, fell into depression and despondency, and began to doubt his faith and succumb to his opium addiction, he turned to Coleridge for advice and support. Part II of this book will look more closely at Coleridge's moving response to Clarkson's request, a response that would encourage and energise both men in their struggles against both the evil of institutional slavery and the hidden slavery of their private addictions.

At this stage, Coleridge was probably unaware that he was following in Clarkson's footsteps as he began work on his Greek ode, but he certainly was aware of the campaign itself, and of Wilberforce's constantly frustrated attempts to change the law in Parliament. Even as Coleridge began to compose in Greek, he was keeping up with the pamphlets of the day. Although slavery had been technically abolished in England in 1772 (the year of Coleridge's birth), the vast hideous and lucrative international trade in enslaved human beings continued to flourish, largely in British hands and to Britain's economic advantage. The philosopher David Hartley, after whom Coleridge called his first son, tried as early as 1776 to introduce an abolition movement in Parliament, with no success. The really serious campaign began with the formation of a committee by Clarkson and Wilberforce in 1787, and their first motion in Parliament in May 1789. This was defeated on the grounds that there was, allegedly, insufficient evidence that slaves were being mistreated, which led Clarkson to a prolonged period of further research and preparation. The second bill, including his carefully documented evidence of the sheer inhumanity and suffering visited on the slaves, was presented to Parliament in April 1791. Again, it was rejected. Wilberforce introduced the bill a third time in the spring of 1792, right in the midst of the period in which Coleridge was preparing his poem. This may have influenced the Latin title he gave his Greek ode, *Sors misera servorum in insulis indiae occidentalis* – 'The unhappy fate of the slaves in the West Indian islands'. In spite of support from Burke, Fox, Pitt and Sheridan, in a debate which Burke described as containing 'the greatest eloquence ever displayed in the House'[6] – in spite of all that, the anti-slavery bill was again defeated. Le Grice's account of those evenings in which Coleridge recited Burke refer in fact to 1792, while Coleridge was composing the ode, so it is clear that he was still following the debates in Parliament. Although Coleridge was thinking about the topic as early as 1791, and intending to write for the competition, the competition was officially announced in January 1792. Coleridge composed the poem that spring, was awarded the prize, and recited his poem on commencement day, 3 July 1792.

Coleridge never translated the poem into English himself but J.C.C. Mays provides a helpful prose translation in his edition of the *Poetical Works*. The ode opens with a studiedly classical dramatic speech addressed to Death personified. Coleridge tells Death that if he visits the slaves in their agony, so dark is their fate that Death, himself, will be their harbinger of freedom and be doing them good: death will be their only release. Indeed, Death himself becomes a kind of rescuer:

Thou art terrible indeed, yet thou dwellest with Liberty, stern Lord!

When on thy dark pinions, looking down on the swelling of the sea, they return with aether-roaming feet to their native country.

Then in the sixth to ninth strophes of the poem, Coleridge talks movingly about how he feels the pain of the slaves as though he had experienced it within himself:

Woe is me how often has a mist come over my tearful eyes, as often as my heart too has groaned! For with the suffering enslaved race, I sorrow deeply in sympathy as they groan in unutterable sorrow, as they circle in the eddies of their hateful labours, children of Necessity.

He is unsparing of the details:

Alas, the unsleeping Whip urges them on toil-wearied before Dawn has wakened the Sun.

Then, in far more radical phrases than the syndics of Cambridge University may have expected, he turns to address directly those who were presently profiting from the slave trade:

O ye who revel in the ills of Slavery, O feeders on the groans of the wretched, insolent sons of Excess, shedders of own brothers' blood, does not the inescapable Eye see these things? Does not Nemesis threaten fire-breathing reprisal? Do you hear? Or do you not hear? How winds shake the ground at its roots, and the recesses of earth groan beneath, and the depths roar terribly, pledging those below to wrath against the killers!

And finally, in case it was not already clear to his readers that he was speaking about the very things being debated that spring in

the British Parliament, he introduces Wilberforce himself into the
poem:

> Lo! I see a Herald of Pity, his head as it were shaded with boughs
> of love! Lo! I hear the golden gladness of thy words, Wilberforce![7]

It is clear that at this stage he thought Wilberforce, who so clearly
had right on his side, would succeed, and in a burst of optimism
buoyed up perhaps by the same hopes that had been released in
him by the French Revolution, he writes,

> Suffering will expire, overcome by the stranger-helping lightning-
> flash of Justice.
>   No longer will the charmless Charm of Gold oppress the
> African shores.[8]

Alas, it would not be until 1807 that the slave trade was finally
abolished by Parliament, after twenty years of tireless campaigning by Clarkson and Wilberforce.

Radicalism and Religion

There is a sharp contrast between the way in which the university permitted, and even applauded, claims for liberty and
human rights which addressed the situation in distant islands
(and did so in an ancient language) and the way it prosecuted
one of its own members for expressing these same liberal views
in English. Once more, Coleridge was caught up in the events,
and once more he was defending liberty. The case concerned
William Frend, the Fellow of Jesus, Coleridge's own College,
who had published a pamphlet called *Peace and Union*, doubtless one of the 'pamphlets of the day' that was being read in
Coleridge's rooms. *Peace and Union* criticised Britain's

declaration of war against France, and attacked the Prime Minister William Pitt for oppressive war taxation. But it also set forth both Deist and Republican ideas. As a consequence, Frend was tried in the Senate House throughout May 1793 on the double charges of sedition and defamation of the Church of England. It was the Rationalist Deism which became the focus of the trial, since Fellows of all Colleges in Oxford and Cambridge were supposed to sign up to the 39 Articles of the Church of England. Coleridge followed the trial each day in the public gallery and joined in the student heckling of the prosecutors. Indeed, there is a story that on one day the heckling was so bad that the Senior Proctor was sent to arrest one man who had particularly distinguished himself. That man was Coleridge, but when the Proctor moved through the crowd, he ended up seizing an undergraduate with a deformed arm who could not possibly have been responsible for the slow hand-clap that had caused offence, and so could not be expelled or punished.

There are differing explanations of how the switch took place and Coleridge got off the hook; whether by a ruse, by good luck, or by a deliberate and charitable error in Coleridge's favour. This latter interpretation was the way Coleridge explained it years later to his friend, the newspaper editor Daniel Stuart.[9] Coleridge had had a narrow escape. If he had been taken before the Proctor he would almost certainly have been expelled. What lay behind the University's expulsion of Frend, who was indeed convicted and deprived of his fellowship and living, was a fear of 'Jacobinism': a fear fostered and exploited by Pitt's repressive government that there might be growing up in England a fifth column of radical extremists who would help France, with whom England was at war, perhaps even preparing the ground for a French invasion. These fears were largely unfounded. English radicals were certainly inspired by the ideals of the French Revolution, but also, as we shall see, were horrified by the violent

Terror in which it resulted, and ultimately deeply disillusioned when Revolutionary France turned out to be an imperial aggressor, particularly in her attack on neutral Switzerland. But these political developments were still to come. At this point, for Coleridge, and for many of his contemporaries, the Jacobin and Republican cause seemed so much more on the right side, and with the people, than the British Government and its Established Church. Indeed, as Coleridge continued, after his anti-slavery ode, to seek out and become involved with those actively campaigning against the slave trade, he became aware that most of them were other dissenters in religion. Clarkson was a Quaker; Wilberforce, while remaining an Anglican, was a fairly radical evangelical, not the usual Establishment type, part of the so-called Clapham Sect. But many of those who seemed to be doing most in practical ways to work for a fairer, or more liberal England, were in fact Unitarians. So it is not surprising that though he was the son of a Church of England vicar, and revered the memory of his father, Coleridge's religious views were moving in a Unitarian direction.

Unitarians of the time did not necessarily reject the idea that God could be considered as a Trinity as well as a Unity or indeed deny the divinity of Christ, as most Unitarians would now; they simply deemed that it was not *necessary* to believe these things in order to be saved. As we will see from Coleridge's own testimony later, even at his most apparently Unitarian phase, he always had a strong focus on Christ as a centre in his spiritual life.

We might say that, looking back on this volatile period of his youth from the standpoint of a profoundly held and deeply integrated Christian faith, and indeed Anglican adherence in his later life, Coleridge might have been tempted to underplay the extent of either his radicalism or his doubts, but I don't think he is guilty of this. And fortunately we also have the contemporary evidence of letters written at the time, which give us a powerful and clear account of what Coleridge was going through. After the crisis of his indebtedness, his 'bolt to London' and enlistment in the Dragoons, an extraordinary adventure which we are about to relate, Coleridge wrote a series of letters to his brother George, freely confessing and analysing where he had gone wrong morally and intellectually, and speaking very frankly of both his doubts and insights. So, in March of 1794, looking back on this period in the previous year, and perhaps on some of the radical thinking that had led up to it, he writes with extraordinary self-awareness about his present confused state of faith:

> I long ago theoretically and in a less degree experimentally knew the necessity of Faith in order to regulate Virtues — nor did I ever seriously disbelieve the existence of a future State — In short, my religious Creed bore and perhaps bears a correspondence with my mind and heart — I had too much Vanity to be altogether a Christian — too much tenderness of Nature to be utterly an Infidel, fond of the dazzle of Wit, fond of subtlety of Argument, I could not read without some degree of pleasure the levities of Voltaire, or the reasonings of Helvetius — but tremblingly alive to the feelings of humanity, and su[s]ceptible of the charms of Truth my Heart forced me to admire the beauty of Holiness in the Gospel, forced me to *love* the Jesus, whom my Reason (or perhaps my *reasonings*) would not permit me to *worship* — My Faith therefore was made up of the Evangelists and the Deistic Philosophy — a kind of *religious Twilight* — I said — *perhaps bears* – Yes! my Brother — for who can say — *Now* I'll be a Christian — Faith is neither altogether voluntary or involuntary — We cannot believe what we choose – but we certainly can cultivate such habits of thinking and acting, as will give force and effective Energy to the arguments on either side— .[10]

51

In the midst of all these alternations of excitement, doubt and some rabble-rousing rhetoric, Coleridge had also been trying again to obtain the scholarships that might have led to an academic career, in this case the Craven Scholarship. He became one of the four finalists in an intense and all-consuming competition, a rigorous series of examinations, but in the end, in this second year at Cambridge, he failed to win either the Craven or any of the other awards, such as the Browne medal. After the immense effort of the Craven, he seems to have had a physical and emotional collapse, and was confined to his room with abscesses, especially an abscessed tooth, which in the end had to be removed. Opium was administered to make the pain bearable and it was recommended he continue to use it during the convalescence. Opium, of course, was completely legal, widely available and used for a variety of complaints. We will look at it later when we consider the beginning and subsequent aspects of Coleridge's addiction. But for now and in what follows we get a sense of his earliest experiences using it for psychological or physical relief, or release. He is just beginning to draw back the dreadful crossbow which will in the end shoot a fatal bolt into his own consciousness, the vast winged spirit of his creative imagination. But he doesn't know that yet. As he writes casually to Mary Evans, with whom he was still exchanging flirtatious endearments:

> Are you asleep, my dear Mary? — I have administered rather a strong Dose of Opium — : however, if in the course of your Nap you should chance to dream, that — I am with the ardour | of fraternal friendship |Your affectionate S. T. Coleridge — you will never have dreamt a truer dream in all *your born days*.[11]

Once he'd recovered from these abscesses and gathered his strength again for university life, he began to take a more realistic view of his circumstances. He felt now that there was no chance he would obtain a fellowship in the College, which would have set him up for life. The obvious alternative, which most students would take, unless they were going back to inherited land, would be a conventional career in the Church. This is certainly what his brothers and family hoped he would choose. But this was just the period when he was having doubts on both moral and theological grounds about the claims of the Established Church, as the letter to his brother makes clear. He still had a faith of sorts and he admired 'the beauty and holiness of the Gospel' but could not, with integrity, sign up to the full claims of the 39 Articles of Religion which he would have been obliged to do if he was ordained in the Church of England. But equally, he had failed to win the College fellowship which would have been a viable alternative to ordination. With no chance of pursuing either of these careers, Coleridge had little incentive to pursue his studies, and spent less of his time and energy on his formal coursework and more on his profound and concentrated efforts in the fields of poetry, philosophical inquiry and political idealism. However, these intense periods of study and reflection alternated (perhaps for sheer relief from the tensions they generated) with increasingly wild and expensive bouts of dissipation and partying.[12] But the indulgences and expenditure were always followed, for Coleridge, by equally strong bouts of remorse and even of nearly suicidal depression. A further event that occurred to destabilise him towards the end of this second year at Cambridge was the news of his brother Frank's death in India. Deemed to be the most brilliant, handsome and adventurous of the Coleridge brothers, Frank, having become an army officer in India, had shot himself during a bout of delirium and fever. Perhaps the memory of his brother, and a strange, even guilt-driven desire to take his place, may have influenced what happened next.

A Very Indocile Equestrian

This summer of 1793 makes a strange prelude, a little space of charming and perhaps nostalgic calm before the storm and drama that were to unfold that autumn. That summer, Coleridge, knowing he was in debt and that he would have to disclose the extent of that debt to his family, decided to return home to Ottery to spend time with them and perhaps recoup and renew the springs of his inspiration on the banks of the Otter. He had an awkward meeting with George as 'head of the family'. George doubtless gave Coleridge a piece of his mind and plenty of good advice, but also, happily, enough money, as he thought, to pay his Cambridge debts. Interestingly, it emerges from his correspondence with George at this point that Coleridge, having grasped that he wouldn't secure a fellowship, was clearly beginning to see himself as a professional writer, and told George all about his plans to publish new translations into English verse of the great classical writers:

> I am now employing myself omni Marte in translating the best Lyric Poems from the Greek, and the modern Latin Writers – which I mean, in about half-a-year's time, to publish by Subscription. By means of Caldwell, Tuckett, & Middleton I can ensure more than two hundred Subscribers; so that this and frugality will enable me to pay my debts, which have corroded my Spirits greatly for some time Past.[13]

By contrast to these solemn protestations of respectable industry and frugal living, and perhaps as compensation for them, Coleridge also seems to have indulged in playful fantasy on the banks of his beloved river. On one occasion he took a party of ladies with him up to the 'Pixie's Parlour', a cave further upstream on the Otter where Coleridge and his brothers had carved their initials, and which was associated in the local Devon folklore with fairies and pixies. In the same spirit in which, as a child, he had enacted the fairy-tales he had been reading, so here at this cave, with its magical associations, he declared and crowned one of the ladies 'The Faery Queen'. The poem 'Songs of the Pixies', which commemorates this event, is still mannered and sentimental, not yet in the mature style that was to come; but it nevertheless begins an imaginative exploration of the combination of the river, the cave and magic which would lead to the masterpiece *Kubla Khan*. It was also this summer that he composed his first really great poem, the sonnet 'To the River Otter', quoted earlier.

One would have thought that with the backing of his brothers, money to clear his debts to his tutor, and a renewal at the springs of his childhood inspiration, Coleridge would have returned to Cambridge rested, and in a more stable frame of mind, ready perhaps to mature and settle down to the tasks in hand. It was not to be. It is difficult to establish from the letters the exact sequence of events, but it seems that instead of returning directly to Cambridge at the end of this vacation, Coleridge went first to London, perhaps secretly to see Mary Evans but also to roister and carouse with his friends from Christ's, Charles Lamb and company. It may be at this point that he both rekindled his love for Mary and despaired of it. It seems she had another suitor who could give her financial stability, which Coleridge knew that he could not offer, and he felt it would, therefore, be wrong to speak of his love. It may be that the excesses and expenditures that seem to have taken place at this time were partly a reaction and response to that dilemma. Whatever the case, we learn from a later letter that by the time Coleridge did get back to Cambridge he had wasted most of the money that his brothers had gathered together for him. This is how he describes to George his

55

departure from the 'fair Road' that his brothers had prepared for him:

> When the state of my affairs became known to you and by your exertions and my Brothers' generous Confidence a fair Road seemed open to extrication—Almighty God! what a sequel! I loitered away more money on the road, and in town than it was possible for me to justify to my Conscience—and when I returned to Cambridge a multitude of petty embarrassments buzzed round me, like a nest of Hornets—Embarrassments, which in my wild carelessness I had forgotten, and many of which I had contracted almost without knowing it—So small a sum remained, that I could not mock my Tutor with it.[14]

Coleridge back in Cambridge, penniless and still in debt, anxious about Mary, too embarrassed to tell his brothers what he'd done (at this stage), seems to have panicked, rushed back to London, rushed back again to Cambridge, contemplated suicide, rushed back to London, bought an Irish lottery ticket, didn't win (though he got a good poem out of it), rushed back again to Cambridge, and then finally, on 24 November, left again for London in desperation. Again, the same letter, written just before his rescue in February, gives us a sense of the pace of events, and of Coleridge's life being completely out of control:

> My agitations were delirium—I formed a Party, dashed to London at eleven o'clock at night, and for three days lived in all the tempest of Pleasure—resolved on my return—but I will not shock your religious feelings. I again returned to Cambridge— staid a week—such a week! Where Vice has not annihilated sensibility, there is little need of a Hell! On Sunday night I packed up a few things, went off in the mail, staid about a week in a strange way, still looking forward with a kind of recklessness to

the dernier resort of misery—an accident of a very singular kind
prevented me, and led me to adopt my present situation—where
what I have suffered—but enough, may he, who in mercy dispen-
seth Anguish be gracious to me![15]

'The *dernier resort* of misery' is here a euphemism for suicide, but
the 'accident of a very singular kind' was, of all things, a meeting
with an army recruiting officer. Coleridge accepted the six-guinea
bounty that was paid upon recruiting and enlisted as a volunteer
private in the 15th Light Dragoons. The only goods he had in the
world were a small bundle of books, and the clothes and greatcoat he was standing in. Perhaps because his greatcoat was clearly
marked with the initials 'S.T.C.', Coleridge chose to assume the
whimsical pseudonym 'Silas Tomkins Comberbache', and gave
that name to the recruiting officer. If one catches the sense in
Comberbache of a load merely encumbering the back of a poor
horse, the name proved very apt; for Coleridge became, in his own
phrase, 'a very indocile equestrian'.[16] What followed was tragi-
comedy of the highest order. Coleridge proved incapable not only
of riding a horse, but even of grooming it, or maintaining his own
arms and accoutrements in the clean and efficient manner that
was required.

  And yet somehow, Coleridge's capacity to talk his way out of
a crisis and to win friends allowed him to get by. His fellow
soldiers began to look after his horse and equipment for him, as
he in turn wrote their love letters for them – a very reasonable
exchange. But there seem also to have been some sensible and
sympathetic officers who found a way of extricating young
Comberbache from the perils and difficulties of actually riding
and found another task for him, to which he turned out to be
very well suited. He was seconded from Reading, where his regiment had gone, to Henley-on-Thames, as 'unfit to ride'. He was
given orders instead to nurse a fellow dragoon who was seriously

ill with what turned out to be smallpox. The two men were isolated in a single room, the 'pesthouse' in the grounds of Henley workhouse, and here Coleridge nursed his comrade for a fortnight through fever and delirium in what must have been putrid and appalling conditions: a bucket of disinfectant and a plate of slops for the men to eat were deposited grimly at the door of the pesthouse each day, and Coleridge was just left to get on with it. Clearly both men could have died, but both survived. Though Coleridge was later to talk in comic terms of his equestrian adventures, he never referred to this grim fortnight, but it may be from this Henley pesthouse that he draws some of the darker imagery of *The Ancient Mariner*:

He despiseth
the creatures of
the calm,

The many men, so beautiful!
And they all dead did lie:
And a thousand thousand slimy things
Lived on; and so did I.

(Lines 236–9 with gloss)

But the curse
liveth for him in
the eye of the
dead men.

The cold sweat melted from their limbs,
Nor rot nor reek did they:
The look with which they looked on me
Had never passed away.

(Lines 253–6 with gloss)

Certainly, after the highly privileged 'bubble' of Cambridge University life, this prolonged spell as an ordinary private soldier among recruits, many of them poor and desperate, enlarged Coleridge's capacities for empathy and compassion, and taught him a great deal about human life that he might not have learned in any other way.

 In the meantime, as we can imagine, his family and friends were panicking and fearful that perhaps he had indeed committed suicide, and were making searches everywhere. Coleridge himself was later to tell a number of entertaining anecdotes about how his true identity and whereabouts came to be known. One story has him stepping out from a sentry box and correcting a passing officer, who happened to ascribe to Euripides a quotation that was really from Sophocles. The officer at once recognised a gentleman in distress. In another story, an officer inspecting the stables finds a cry for help in Latin graffiti on the wall.[17] The officers of the regiment may well indeed have been wondering just who Private Comberbache really was. But it seems that the real truth came through Coleridge's former Christ's Hospital and London friends who eventually got in touch with George Coleridge and told him where his brother was and who managed to get a letter forwarded to Coleridge via a fellow Jesus College undergraduate called Tucker. The letter from George reached Coleridge on 6 February, and for two days he was too distraught and embarrassed to open it. But eventually he opened it and wrote a frank and extraordinary reply. The two most striking things about this brief letter are that Coleridge seemed as bewildered by his own behaviour as his family was, and that somehow in the midst of this drama he was still seeking to interpret events within a spiritual and even explicitly theological frame. Indeed, the struggle in the letter is to keep all the powerful elements, both emotional and spiritual, at work in him, somehow still connected. He moves in the letter from speaking of his soul, to his mind and to his heart.

> My more than brother! What shall I say . . . O my wayward soul! I have been a fool even to madness. What shall I dare to promise? My mind is illegible to myself—I am lost in the labyrinth, the trackless wilderness of my own bosom. Truly may I say—I am wearied of being saved. My frame is chill and torpid— The Ebb and Flow of my hopes & fears has stagnated into

recklessness—one wish only can I read distinctly in my heart—
that it were possible for me to be forgotten as tho' I had never
been![18]

Holmes dismisses this letter as 'hysterical'[19] and while of course
there is an element of hysteria, there are also some profound
statements worth reflecting on, the chief of which is Coleridge's
remarkable comment about the problem for him of self-
knowledge: 'My mind is illegible to myself—I am lost in the
labyrinth, the trackless wilderness of my own bosom.' Legibility,
clarity of meaning, the desire to make every shape and sound
intelligible, was to be at the heart of Coleridge's whole life and
work; so one can imagine the disorientation and anomie of this
experience of illegibility, even to himself. But one should also
pause to consider that image of being lost in the labyrinth and
in the trackless wilderness, and ask what it must have been like,
even in these last throes of adolescence, to possess such a mind
as Coleridge's. For most people, managing the balance between
head and heart, between intellect and intuition, is sometimes
difficult. But to do so possessing the mind of Coleridge must
have been almost impossible. When we consider that he once
said at the age of twenty-four that he had read everything, and
that he retained everything that he read; that in every book he
read, he read the books to which that book referred (as John
Livingston Lowes has so ably demonstrated); that for every
argument on one side of a debate he habitually elaborated and
often wrote down the counter-argument; that he was accustomed to see and to explore both sides of every question – the
sheer intricacy, multiplicity, breadth and depth of thought that
was available to Coleridge, the almost ceaseless activity of what
he later called 'the circling energies' of his reason, must have
been sometimes exhilarating, but sometimes unbearable. The
labyrinth of his mind was so vast and intricate that to be lost

for a while in it himself must have been a dreadful and frightening experience. Coleridge goes on with great psychological acuity to note the alternations of ecstatic height and depressive depth which characterised his nature, and interestingly, to figure these in terms of the movement of the sea: 'The Ebb and Flow of my hopes & fears'. But characteristically, he sees the recklessness that has brought him to this pass not as the product of one extreme or the other, but actually as a kind of stagnation and a lurid calm between them. In an extraordinary and paradoxical phrase he speaks of 'The Ebb and Flow' having 'stagnated into recklessness'. All this, as we shall see, informs the meaning of both the tidal movements and the stagnation of the sea in *The Rime of the Ancient Mariner* (see pages 207–208) The image of stagnation was only too close at hand as Coleridge wrote this letter, for he and his companion were not yet out of the pesthouse and it was there he was writing. And here we have the one glimpse of what he was facing physically in that little room: 'Intolerable images of horror! They haunt my sleep, they enfever my dreams! O that the shadow of Death were on my eyelids, that I were like the loathsome form by which I now sit!'[20] Clearly at this point he thought his companion was dead, and wishes to be dead himself: 'O that without guilt I might ask of my Maker Annihilation!'[21]

And yet even in this profound despair he is praying, he is thinking of God as his Maker. Indeed, the juxtaposition and capitalisation of 'Maker' and 'Annihilation' tell us a great deal about the almost intolerable polarities between which Coleridge was living. But the letter concludes with an appeal for prayer: 'My brother, my brother! pray for me, comfort me, my brother! I am very wretched, and, though my complaint be bitter, my stroke is heavier than my groaning.'[22]

Coleridge's brothers George and James did indeed bring comfort to their lost brother, and set about the exacting task of rescuing him from his predicament, for this was easier said than done. At one point they thought it would be a matter of raising money to buy Coleridge out of the army, but the army insisted that they must first find a replacement recruit. Eventually, thanks to the intervention of a kind officer and the many importunities of Coleridge's family, a compromise was found and they decided to let Coleridge go on medical grounds. Private S.T. Comberbache was discharged as 'insane', 10 April 1794.[23]

Coleridge was not insane, but we must enquire what his state of mind was and what the effect of the whole crisis of these last few months was on his self-awareness. One consequence of the Reverend George Coleridge's kindness and patience in these days with his wild younger brother was that Coleridge confided in him in a series of frank, reflective and self-revelatory letters. In February of 1794 he wrote to George in terms which at once express and critique the conventional piety of the 'repenting prodigal'.

> Sweet in the sight of God and celestial Spirits are the tears of Penitence—the pearls of heaven—the Wine of Angels! Such has been the language of Divines—but Divines have exaggerated.— Repentance may bestow that tranquillity, which will enable man to pursue a course of undeviating harmlessness, but it cannot restore to the mind that inward sense of Dignity, which is the Parent of every kindling Energy! I am not what I was:— *Disgust*—I *feel*, as if I had jaundiced all my Faculties.[24]

This strange passage combines real repentance with mockery of the pious language of repentance. You can see Coleridge wants both to express and to reject the deliberately cloying phrases 'the pearls of heaven' and 'the wine of angels' and to seek behind these conventional and saccharine phrases the real psychological truth about repentance, which is that it is difficult and bitter; but that does not make his repentance any the less genuine, rather the more so; and while he is mocking conventional piety, he is certainly not mocking God. The end of this passage is particularly interesting, first because it tells us that Coleridge's concern is not at any point for his outward image or respectability, but entirely for the integrity of his inward state. He laments the loss; seeks but cannot find the restoration of 'that inward sense of Dignity'. Dignity here, I think, really means a sense of self-worth or integrity, and its loss represents a loss of confidence in his ability to manage his own powers. But this letter is not so much about mere loss of dignity as about a paralysing sense of self-disgust. The feeling of disgust and self-loathing was one with which Coleridge would have to wrestle during key periods throughout his life. And even as he tells us here that disgust extinguishes the 'kindling energies', he was nevertheless able to give permanent and powerful expression to that disgust not only for himself but also for posterity in the telling lines in *The Ancient Mariner*: 'And a thousand thousand slimy things / Lived on; and so did I.'[25]

Interestingly, he goes on to say that the inward sense of dignity is 'the Parent of every kindling energy'. In that phrase 'every kindling energy' we see the first sparks of Coleridge in his mature brilliance, in his account of the mind as a meeting of reciprocal and circling energies, his sense of the intellect as itself an active and kindling light, not merely a blank and passive receptor to the outside senses. Perhaps the greatest characteristic of his mature poetry, particularly *The Rime of the Ancient Mariner* itself, is its 'kindling energy' – *kindling* in the sense that it not only expresses the lights and energies that were already in Coleridge's imagination, but also kindles to new flame and form the imaginations of each new generation of readers.

Later in this same letter Coleridge brings against himself another charge with which his later critics were only too ready to lambast him: that of idleness. When we look at the huge achievement represented by his collected works, and even when we consider the sheer amount of work, especially in intensive and systematic reading, that Coleridge had already put in, we may well feel that idleness was one of the last things with which he should have charged himself. But it is interesting to see what he himself meant by that term. Here is what he says:

> I became a proverb to the University for Idleness- the time, which I should have bestowed on the academic studies, I employed in dreaming out wild schemes of impossible extrication. It had been better for me, if my Imagination had been less vivid—I could not with such facility have shoved aside Reflection! How many and how many hours have I stolen from the bitterness of Truth in these soul-enervating Reveries—in building magnificent edifices of Happiness on some fleeting shadow of Reality![26]

So this so-called 'idleness' was not blank enervation, and Coleridge was certainly no couch potato. Note how *active* this idleness is: dreaming wild schemes, pursuing a vivid imagination and building magnificent edifices. Although these, as Coleridge called them, 'soul-enervating Reveries' were unproductive at the time in academic terms, they were also an exercise of just those faculties of his shaping spirit of imagination, from which the immortal poems of his *annus mirabilis* would arise. It is also interesting to note that he is indulging these long reveries well before the time of his serious indulgence in, or addiction to, opium. Opium may have exaggerated these and made them genuinely more enervating, but at this stage they were a playful and fruitful preparation of the rich soil of Coleridge's imagination. Indeed, in the combination here of the fleeting shadow and the magnificent edifice built through the imagination we have already a faint foreshadowing of *Kubla Khan*.

THE

WATCHMAN.

No. I.

TUESDAY, MARCH 1, 1796.

Published by the Author, S. T. COLERIDGE,
Bristol:
And fold by the Bookfellers and Newfcarriers in Town and Country.

THAT ALL MAY KNOW THE TRUTH;

AND THAT THE TRUTH MAY MAKE US FREE!

AMONG the calamities which eventually have produced the moft important bleffings, we may particularize
the capture of Conftantinople by the Turks in 1453.
The number of learned Greeks, whom this event drove
into the Weft, in conjunction with the recent difcovery
of printing, kindled the love of knowledge in Europe,
and fupplied opportunities for the attainment of it.
Princes emulated each other in the patronage of men of
ability, and endeavoured to excite a fpirit of literature
among their fubjects, by every encouragement which
their rude policy fuggefted, or the genius of the age would
permit. The firft fcanty twilight of knowledge was fuf-
ficient to fhew what horrors had refulted from ignorance;
and no experience had yet taught them that general illumi-
nation is incompatible with undelegated power. This
incipient diffufion of truth was aided by the Lutheran
fchifm, which roufed the Clergy of Europe from their
long doze of fenfuality, and by the keen goading of religious controverfy forced each party into literary exertion. And after the Reformation it was fortunate for the
interefts of Britain, that the Puritans, her firft partizans
for civil and religious freedom, were greatly inferior to
their antagonifts in acquired knowledge. The govern-
B   ment

'THAT ALL MAY KNOW THE TRUTH; AND THAT THE TRUTH MAY MAKE US FREE':
the 'seditious' opening salvo of *The Watchman*

CHAPTER THREE

To Nether Stowey via Utopia

By the time of Coleridge's discharge he had entirely missed the Lent term and the Cambridge Easter term was well underway. He returned on 11 April 1794 to face formal discipline, which included being confined to College grounds and being given some very dull translations to do as an academic exercise. It also involved an extra year before he could take his degree, which would not be possible till the remote distance of Christmas 1795. Coleridge began again at Cambridge meekly enough, but it was clear that through the crisis and adventures of the last few months he had in some sense outgrown the undergraduate role to which he was asked to return; and that, even were he to stay the course for the next two years, the only prospect his Cambridge degree would hold out to him would be a career as a respectable clergyman, something to which Coleridge believed himself to be unsuited (though years later he would write an impassioned plea to the young literati of England, begging them to become Anglican clergymen![1]). The brief month of term remaining was not enough to re-inure him to the cloistered walls, and when the holidays began and he set off from Cambridge in mid-June, not for home, but on a walking tour of England and Wales with a fellow undergraduate, there was a sense of the bird flying free from the cage and new adventures beginning. He would not return to Cambridge, and would never complete his degree.

As he strides out from Cambridge that June day, at a great pace that would take him to Oxford in just two days, on the first of the many walking tours which became so significant for his life and poetry, we have a sense of the real Coleridge coming into focus, of his becoming before our very eyes the man who has equally enthralled, intrigued and infuriated his many biographers. At the start of this tour he bought the first of his famous notebooks with a portable ink-horn and so began the lifetime habit of brilliant and acute observation, both of nature and of himself, and ultimately of the connection between the two, which was to form the centre of his mature work. He and his companion Joseph Hucks had intended to stop over only for a few days in Oxford to catch up with some of Coleridge's old school friends who had gone to 'the other University' before proceeding on to Wales. But they ended up staying a full three weeks in Oxford, as the first of Coleridge's many 'kindling energies' kindled a friendship and indeed started a more than philosophical fire with the unlikely figure of Robert Southey.

Southey, a twenty-year-old poet from Bristol with a head full of radical and republican ideas, but from a staunchly conservative family, had been introduced to Coleridge by his Christ's Hospital friend, Bob Allen. The two poets immediately struck sparks. Like Coleridge, Southey had lost a parent, and like Coleridge his respectable family had destined him for the quiet but secure life of an Anglican clergyman, for which Oxford was the proper preparation. As soon as they met, both men recognised their mutual need to rebel, to escape the dull and crushing expectations of their families, on whom they still depended for support, and somehow build something new for themselves. They immediately set about building 'a magnificent edifice of happiness' on a fleeting shadow of reality, and that edifice was the great 'Pantisocratic scheme' for a new life on new principles in the New World.

The word 'Pantisocracy' was invented by Coleridge, as combining the Greek 'pan' for 'all' and 'isocratia' for 'government'. So this was to be not an *aristocracy*, but a *pantisocracy*: all members of a community were to govern their society equally. One might object that the word democracy would have done equally well, but Coleridge in inventing this word had something more in mind. Contemporary democracies, in so far as they existed at all, delegated power from the people to elected representatives, so in some sense the 'demos' – the people – were still not directly in power. In the small community that Coleridge and Southey were imagining it would be possible for everybody to debate and take part directly in all decisions.

Its philosophical foundations drew on a combination of the writings of Rousseau and William Godwin. From Rousseau they took the idea of the 'noble savage' and the 'return to nature': the idea that it was only the degrading human customs and institutions of the *ancien régime* that gave rise to inequalities, and that, left to themselves in a natural environment, humans would naturally form a perfect society. From Godwin's *Inquiry Concerning Political Justice* they took the idea of anarchy as a form of perfection and liberation; that the imposition of law by others, even as it attempts to reform, is precisely what deforms the soul; that a mutually renewed and constantly self-chosen covenant between individuals in a society without any form of government was not only possible but desirable. Both of these extraordinarily optimistic philosophies had been given a new lease of life by the French Revolution, and a whole generation began to dare to believe that the dreams of these philosophers really would come true.

There was also a practical example, as they saw it, of a new beginning in America to inspire them, in Joseph Priestley and the American emigration movement. For in April of that year, the month in which Coleridge returned to Cambridge, Priestley had set off to found an ideal Unitarian community in America. Although in his much later account of these things in the *Biographia Literaria*, Coleridge was to play down these hopes, there is plenty of evidence from his letters and notebooks of how

Takes up
political
reform

seriously he took this at the time. In one of the notebooks of 1805 during a time of crisis in Malta, he looked back at that time, and wrote, 'Then came that stormy time when America really inspired Hope, & I became an exalted Being.'[2] Holmes quotes this fragmentary note, though he omits the very interesting phrase that precedes it in the note, describing the time between the release from the Dragoons and the beginning of Pantisocracy: 'I have lain for hours together awake at night, groaning & *praying*'.

The French Revolution had instilled in Southey and Coleridge, and many of their generation, high hopes for a permanent radical improvement of living conditions for all humanity achieved at a national level by change of regime and constitution. Those hopes were dashed by the Terror and France's rapid transition from fragile democracy to political tyranny. The two men saw Pantisocracy as an alternative, small-scale way of achieving the change they wanted. Despairing of top-down, national, political revolution, they hoped that the emergence of radical small communities living at a local level by the principles of 'Liberty, Equality and Fraternity' would effect a gradual change in society from the bottom up.

Southey and Coleridge certainly took their new scheme seriously enough to begin almost immediately recruiting others. And suddenly, to the amazement and consternation of the hapless Hucks, the Welsh walking tour became a Pantisocratic recruiting drive. Coleridge and Southey's radical idealism and dreams of American equality didn't always go down well in Wales. For example, they were almost thrown out of a pub in Bala when Coleridge proposed a toast to General Washington. The extended tour eventually brought him back to Bristol, Southey's hometown, and the two men took rooms together in College Street as a headquarters from which they hoped to put their new scheme into effect. They lit upon the idea of founding their community with an initial colony of twelve men and twelve women, sharing all

Becoming regiment

things equally, and set about recruiting in Bristol since Wales had been so unsuccessful.

Their first recruit was Robert Lovell. Son of Bristol Quaker parents, Lovell was already open to some of the pair's radical ideas when he studied with Southey at Balliol College, Oxford. Like Southey, he reckoned himself a poet. Lovell did not stay in the scheme long but his involvement had momentous consequences for both Coleridge and Southey, because it was through Lovell that they met their future wives.

Lovell was courting, and was soon engaged to a girl called Mary Fricker. The Fricker family consisted of a widowed mother who kept a dress shop, one ne'er-do-well son, George, and five beautiful daughters, four of marriageable age, clearly a magnet for three aspiring radical poets. When Robert Lovell married Mary Fricker, and Robert Southey became engaged to Edith Fricker, while new Pantisocratic recruit George Burnett took an interest in Martha Fricker, Coleridge was inevitably expected to show an interest in the remaining girl, Sara,[3] and he duly did. He and Southey conducted their courtship and entered into their marriages on a tide of enthusiasm for the new Pantisocratic scheme, which may have blinded their judgement. Coleridge certainly thought so later when in a letter to Southey he said that under Southey's influence he had 'mistaken the ebullience of *schematism* for affection, which a moment's reflection might have told me, is not a plant of so mushroom a growth . . . but my whole Life has been a series of Blunders! God have mercy upon me—for I am a most miserable Dog'—[4]

We will shortly relate how the bubble of 'ebullient schematism' burst and with what consequences, but it is worth reflecting with Coleridge himself at this point not so much on the youthful naivety of the Pantisocratic scheme, as on the deeper motivations and nobler moments of vision which were bound up with it, for those deeper motivations remained throughout Coleridge's life,

Panistacracy

and the nobler vision eventually clarified into great poetry and visionary prose. Looking back on these heady months fifteen years later in 1809 in his journal *The Friend*, Coleridge reflected on the way he and his generation had had their imaginations in different ways 'kindled' by the 'general conflagration' of the French Revolution.

> My feelings, however, and imagination did not remain unkindled in this general conflagration; and I confess I should be more inclined to be ashamed than proud of myself, if they had! I was a sharer in the general vortex, though my little World described the path of its Revolution in an orbit of its own. What I dared not expect from constitutions of Government and whole Nations, I hoped from Religion and a small Company of chosen Individuals—

Coleridge goes on in this piece to use one of his many wonderful metaphors of flight to account both for the lift-off and the come-down of the Pantisocratic scheme, perhaps gently but only implicitly suggesting the extent to which the scheme itself was full of hot air:

> When we had gradually alighted on the firm ground of common sense, from the gradually exhausted Balloon of youthful Enthusiasm, though the air-built Castles, which we had been pursuing, had vanished with all their pageantry of shifting forms and glowing colours, we were yet free from the stains and impurities which might have remained upon us, had we been travelling with the crowd of less imaginative malcontents, through the dark lanes and foul bye roads of ordinary Fanaticism.[5]

I think the key and strangely neglected sentence in this later account by Coleridge of the Pantisocratic dream is 'What I dared not expect from constitutions of Government and whole Nations,

I hoped from Religion and a small Company'. In the end it was these two elements – the profound religious impulse, the deepening spiritual life on the one hand, and the intensity and closeness of relationships in a 'small Company' where imagination could be kindled and vision shared on the other – that were to remain the constants in Coleridge's many wanderings.

Even though this passage from *The Friend* was written many years later when Coleridge had returned to a more Christian faith, it remains true that this early radicalism was, for Coleridge, strongly inspired by his reading of the gospel. For example, in a letter to his brother George about how best to establish true liberty and equality, Coleridge defends himself from accusations of abandoning faith, pointing out that his dislike of the present forms of Anglican Christianity does not mean he's not passionate about Christ:

> You ask me what the friend of universal equality *should* do. I answer—'Talk not politics—*Preach the Gospel!*'
>
> Yea, my brother! I have at all times in all places exerted my power in defence of the Holy One of Nazareth against the learning of the historian, the libertinism of the wit, and (his worst enemy) the mystery of the bigot.[6]

In the end it was a combination of things which deflated the Pantisocratic balloon: primarily it was deep disagreement between Southey and Coleridge about how to put their principles into practice, and then massive pressure from both their families, but particularly Southey's, which finally undid things. The first shock from Coleridge's point of view came from the discovery that in spite of long nights talking about liberty, equality and fraternity, about having all things in common, owning no private property, and equal opportunity for all, Southey was still naively assuming that they would take servants with them who would live in separate quarters, and that the women in their company would not be part of the full Pantisocratic democracy and debates. Coleridge was appalled, and it began to dawn on him that Southey, born and bred a gentleman, had really no conception of what democracy or equality actually were. This proved rapidly to be the case. The original plan had been that all twelve Pantisocratic couples would each put £125 into a common purse, to purchase their land and tools, which would all then be jointly owned; Southey, however, wished to reserve some of his own money and to keep a separate private annuity. By this time the writing was more than on the wall. When they found they could neither recruit all twelve couples nor afford the journey to America and the land there, Southey proposed that they start with a joint venture farming in Wales, but he was already making other plans. He had been promised a further allowance from his family if he bailed out of the scheme, which is exactly what he did in November of 1795. Coleridge felt deeply betrayed, not least because he himself, with some painful conflicts of feeling, had turned down similar offers from his own family; what is more, he had, at least from his perspective, painfully wrenched his heart away from Mary Evans to fit in with the general Fricker scheme of things. He wrote Southey a long, agonised letter, going through the whole story from start to finish:

> Your conversation, when George Burnett repeated it to me . . . It scorched my throat. Your private resources were to remain your individual property, and every thing to be separated on five or six acres. In short we were to commence Partners in a petty Farming Trade. This was the Mouse of which the Mountain Pantisocracy was at last safely delivered! I received the account with Indignations & Loathings of unutterable Contempt'[7]

Southey had not burnt his boats, and could always turn to his family for financial support, but Coleridge still saw the deepest part of the vision, in its sense both of religion and of new beginnings in a small company, and was determined to live by its principles. And for Coleridge this included marrying Sara and setting up a new household.

Two letters, both to Southey, are particularly relevant if we are to understand both the tensions and the potentials between which this marriage took place. Coleridge as we know had originally been in love with Mary Evans but never clear about the degree to which his love was returned, or whether marriage was possible, and all this time, Southey, although he knew about Mary, was nevertheless urging Coleridge on to propose to Sara because it fitted in so well with the great scheme. Even as late as the end of 1794, Coleridge was writing to Southey about the agony of wrenching himself from Mary, whether or not he had any real chance with her. Of Mary, he says,

> To *love her*, Habit has made unalterable: I had placed her in the sanctuary of my Heart, nor can she be torn from thence but with the Strings that grapple it to life. This Passion, however, divested as it now is of all Shadow of Hope, seems to lose it's disquieting Power. Far distant, and never more to behold or hear of her, I shall sojourn in the Vale of Men, sad and in loneliness, yet not unhappy . . . Had I been united to her, the Excess of my Affection would have effeminated my Intellect. I should have fed on her looks as she entered into the room, I should have gazed on her footsteps when she went out from me.[8]

Then, turning his attentions from Mary, whom he is losing, towards Sara, he writes,

> To lose her!—I can rise above that selfish pang. But to marry another—O Southey! bear with my weakness. Love makes all things pure and heavenly like itself,—but to marry a woman whom I do *not* love, to degrade her whom I call my Wife by making her

the Instrument of low Desire—and on the removal of a desultory Appetite to be perhaps not displeased with her Absence!— Enough!—These refinements are the wildering Fires, that lead me into vice. Mark you, Southey! *I will do my duty.*[9]

Such was the state of affairs at the end of December 1794, though it is fair to say that by the time of Coleridge's marriage to Sara in October of 1795, things had changed a little. Once he had made up his mind to climb entirely on board the Pantisocratic balloon, Coleridge did in fact find himself genuinely affectionate towards, and indeed enamoured of, Sara; and when, just a month after his marriage, he wrote the bitter letter to Southey from which we quoted, he summed up things between himself and Sara like this:

> you remember what a Fetter I burst [his love for Mary], and that it snapt as if it had been a sinew of my heart. However I returned to Bristol, and my addresses to Sara, which I at first paid from Principle, not Feeling, from Feeling & from Principle I renewed; and I met a reward more than proportionate to the greatness of the Effort. I love and I am beloved, and I am happy.[10]

Indeed, there is real evidence that Coleridge and Sara were very happy together in the first few years of their marriage, and that Coleridge's application of 'principle and virtue', as he saw it, did blossom into real love and affection. This seems clear from one of the first great poems of his more mature style, which was first drafted around this time, *The Eolian Harp*. There are many versions of this poem from as early as August 1795, the month before his marriage, and he was still clearly working on it and making corrections up to February 1796.[11]

The poem starts with the two of them sitting softly embracing in front of their cottage door, for on marriage they moved into a little cottage in Clevedon, not far from Bristol.

Sara + Coleridge 76

My pensive Sara! thy soft cheek reclined
Thus on mine arm, most soothing sweet it is
To sit beside our cot, our cot o'ergrown
With white-flowered Jasmin, and the broad-leaved Myrtle,
(Meet emblems they of Innocence and Love!)
And watch the clouds, that late were rich with light,
Slow saddening round, and mark the star of eve
Serenely brilliant (such should wisdom be)
Shine opposite! How exquisite the scents
Snatched from yon bean-field! and the world so hushed!
The stilly murmur of the distant Sea
Tells us of Silence.[12]

Then comes the frank eroticism in which the sounds, the songs
and moans of the Eolian Harp as the wind blows through it are
compared with the coy maid half yielding to her lover:

. . . And that simplest Lute,
Placed length-ways in the clasping casement, hark!
How by the desultory breeze caressed,
Like some coy maid half yielding to her lover,
It pours such sweet upbraiding, as must needs
Tempt to repeat the wrong! And now, its strings
Boldlier swept, the long sequacious notes
Over delicious surges sink and rise,
Such a soft floating witchery of sound
As twilight Elfins make, when they at eve
Voyage on gentle gales from Fairy-Land . . .[13]

Already we have in this sequence a series of essential and characteristic Coleridgean notes: the patient attention to nature as a
source of wisdom, the rich and sensuous celebration of love, and
the sense of the magical and transformative in the 'witchery of

sound', twilight Elfins, the voyage on gales from Fairy-Land. The rest of the poem completes a quintessentially Coleridgean itinerary: the celebration of variety in the midst of 'the one Life within us and abroad', the synesthetic moulding and combining power of imagination allowing us to hear 'a light in sound, a sound-like power in light', the sudden leaps of thought and philosophical speculation:

> And what if all of animated nature
> Be but organic Harps diversely framed,
> That tremble into thought, as o'er them sweeps
> Plastic and vast, one intellectual breeze,
> At once the Soul of each, and God of all?[14]

Running through it all is the deep religious sense, the spiritual awareness, which even in this early poem, finally turns back to Christ. And the one who brings him back is Sara; she is the beloved woman who,

> . . . biddest me walk humbly with my God.
> Meek daughter in the family of Christ! . . .
> For never guiltless may I speak of him,
> The Incomprehensible! save when with awe
> I praise him, and with Faith that inly feels;
> Who with his saving mercies healèd me,
> A sinful and most miserable Man,
> Wildered and dark, and gave me to possess
> Peace, and this Cot, and thee, heart-honoured Maid![15]

The peace in that particular 'Cot' was not destined to last long. Coleridge found his business more and more transpiring in Bristol itself; it was there he lectured, and there he produced the copies of his new journal, *The Watchman*.

It was also in Bristol that he found the friend and publisher Joseph Cottle, who would eventually publish not only the first volume of Coleridge's own poetry but also *The Lyrical Ballads*, the book Wordsworth and Coleridge wrote together and published anonymously, and which is now seen as the real beginning and founding of the Romantic Movement in English poetry. It was in Bristol too that the real struggle, politically and spiritually, against the iniquities of the slave trade was taking place, for Bristol was the centre of that trade. By the end of that summer Coleridge knew he would have to move back to Bristol and leave their idyllic honeymoon cottage. Reflecting on that departure in a poem, he also recognised the dissonance between the Romantic writer's retreat away from the press and throng of life, on the one hand, and the need for the revolutionary poet to engage and suffer alongside the people for whom he was writing, on the other. So in *Reflections on Having Left a Place of Retirement*, he writes:

Ah! quiet Dell! dear Cot, and Mount sublime!
I was constrain'd to quit you. Was it right,
While my unnumber'd Brethren toil'd and bled,
That I should dream away the entrusted Hours
On rose-leaf Beds, pampering the coward Heart
With feelings all too delicate for use?[16]

The poem also gives us a useful summary of what Coleridge was hoping to achieve in Bristol through his public lectures and journalism:

I therefore go, and join head, heart, and hand,
Active and firm, to fight the bloodless fight
Of Science, Freedom, and the Truth in CHRIST.[17]

79

'Science, Freedom & The Truth in Christ' was in fact the motto for Coleridge's new journal, *The Watchman*, an heroic but ultimately unsuccessful venture, in which he first showed the astonishing bursts of energy and hard work of which his supposedly indolent nature was always capable. The journal may well have done a great deal of good in raising consciousness, in urging boycotts of those imports such as sugar and rum, tainted and stained with the blood of slaves. It was also very important that in *The Watchman* Coleridge showed time and again that slavery was entirely contrary to the spirit and teachings of Jesus in the Gospels. This needed to be said very clearly because at this time almost all the bishops of the Established Church were voting against Wilberforce's attempts to abolish slavery. However, *The Watchman* was a financial disaster for Coleridge, leaving him in debt, and cumbered with many unsold copies. Some of these were eventually used as no more than fire-lighters in the Nether Stowey fireplace, not quite the national conflagration he had hoped to begin! Perhaps its greatest long-term influence was to recall to a complacent English Establishment the really radical nature of the claims and teachings of Christ.

When Coleridge put out a prospectus for *The Watchman* in February 1796, with the motto 'That all may know the Truth, and that the Truth may make us free!!' he was advised to remove the motto as it might be seen as seditious, and he had to point out to the lawyer who gave this advice that it was in fact a direct quotation from John's Gospel.[18] A good flavour of this journal, and of Coleridge's Bristol lecture from which it drew, is the 'Essay on the Slave Trade', delivered by Coleridge on 16 June 1795 in the Assembly coffeehouse on the quay at Bristol. It was one thing for an undergraduate to write a Greek ode against the slave trade in the distant common rooms of Cambridge, quite another to deliver a lecture in English against slavery in a coffeehouse upon the very quay against which the slaving ships drew up.

The whole essay moves between acute economic and philosophical analysis on the one hand and powerful appeal to the Gospels on the other. Coleridge quite correctly saw that the root cause of the slave trade was profitable trade in the commodities the slaves produced, demand for the consumption of which was artificially and constantly stimulated. So he opens with startling clarity, pointing the finger not at some distant set of slave traders or sea captains whom it would be easy for the comfortable of Bristol to excoriate, but at his own audience, at himself, indeed at all of us.

> Whence arise our Miseries? Whence arise our Vices? From *imaginary* Wants. No man is wicked without temptation, no man is wretched without a cause. But if each among us confined his wishes to the actual necessaries and real comforts of Life, we should preclude all the causes of Complaint and all the motives to Iniquity . . .
>
> And indeed the evils arising from the formation of *imaginary* Wants, have in no instance been so dreadfully exemplified, as in this inhuman Traffic. We receive from the West-India Islands Sugars, Rum, Cotton, Logwood, Cocoa, Coffee, Pimento, Ginger, Indigo, Mahogany, and Conserves. Not one of these articles are necessary; indeed with the exception of Cotton and Mahogany we cannot truly call them even useful: and not one of them is at present attainable by the poor and labouring part of Society. In return we export vast quantities of necessary Tools, Raiment, and defensive Weapons, with great stores of Provision. So that in this Trade as in most others the Poor are employed with unceasing toil first to raise, and then to send away the Comforts, which they themselves absolutely want, in order to procure idle superfluities for their Masters. If this Trade had never existed, no one human being would have been less comfortably cloathed, housed, or nourished.[19]

81

stimulated wants
for unnecessary
goods

Most of this lucid analysis would still hold true today for the many evils inflicted not only on other human beings but on the environment from the rise of global consumerism, whose imaginary wants are stimulated artificially by an insidiously manipulative advertising industry. It is also telling how Coleridge here links the fate of the slaves in their absolute poverty with that of the English poor in their relative poverty, and that the first time he uses the word 'masters', it is not in relation to the slaves and the slave masters, but to the 'captains of industry' who are exploiting the English poor in the new manufacturing industries.

Meanwhile though, in addition to the labour of producing copy and seeing to printing, Coleridge constantly had to travel on speaking tours to drum up support and subscribers. Looking back on this period years later, he gives an entertaining and essentially comic account of his efforts; but at the time, they were serious and desperate. In a hectic five weeks at the beginning of 1796 he visited Worcester, Birmingham, Derby and Sheffield, speaking in public halls and preaching in Unitarian chapels, often to as many as a thousand people at a time. But it was all in vain, and *The Watchman* never produced the living for himself, Sara and his soon-to-be burgeoning family, for Sara was pregnant. Coleridge summed up the situation in a letter to Joseph Cottle:

My dear Sir

It is my business & duty to thank God for all his dispensations, and to believe them the best possible — but, indeed, I think I should have been more thankful, if he had made me a journeyman Shoemaker, instead of an 'Author by Trade'! — I have left my friends, I have left plenty — I have left that ease which would have secured a literary immortality, and have enabled me to give the public works conceived in moments of inspiration, and polished with leisurely solicitude . . . — So I am forced to write for bread — write the high flights of poetic enthusiasm, when every minute

I am hearing a groan of pain from my Wife — groans, and complaints, & sickness! — The present hour I am in a quickset hedge of embarrassments, and whichever way I turn a thorn runs into me —. The Future is cloud & thick darkness — Poverty perhaps, and the thin faces of them that want bread, looking up to me! — Nor is this all — my happiest moments for composition are broken in upon by the reflection of — I *must* make haste — I am too late! — I am already months behind! I have received my *pay* before hand! — O, way-ward & desultory Spirit of Genius! ill canst thou brook a task-master! The tenderest touch from the hand of *Obligation* wounds thee like a scourge of Scorpions! —

I have been composing in the fields this morning, and came home to write down the first rude Sheet of my Preface . . . I have not seen it; but I guess it's [*sic*] contents. I am writing as fast as I can – depend on it, you shall not be out of pocket for me! I feel what I owe you – & independently of this I love you as a friend – Indeed so much that I regret that *you* have been my Copy-holder – / If I have written petulantly forgive me – God knows, I am sore all over – God bless you & believe me, that setting grati-tude aside I love and esteem you & have your interest at heart full as much as my own –

S. T. Coleridge[20]

First, we should note that like almost all of Coleridge's letters, the contents, however mundane, are framed by the divine. He begins and ends with reference to God, which is by no means usual for the time and Coleridge's circle, as one can see from the letters of Lamb and Hazlitt. Second, we can see that even as Coleridge is lamenting his real difficulties, the sheer power, verve and indeed humour of his literary genius is still shining through, as in the pithy and effective image of the 'quickset hedge of embarrass-ments'. Third, it's worth noting that however hard-pressed and beset by the failure, at least financially, are his current endeavours,

83

Coleridge is sublimely confident of his own gifts. He knows that however 'wayward and desultory', he is still possessed of the 'Spirit of Genius'. Of course the whole purpose of the letter is to send an excuse for not having 'done his homework', but Cottle could be in little doubt that the man making the excuse was exceptional, one of the great men of the age. Finally, there is the wonderful throwaway line, 'I have been composing in the fields this morning', which opens up all the depth of Coleridge's engagement with nature; and indeed also lays bare an essential part of his technique as a poet: he did indeed compose outdoors and while he was walking, one reason why his poetry often includes natural imagery; indeed, perhaps it was his morning walk that gave him the image of the hedge for this letter.

This letter is the first in a long series of vivid and entertaining excuses for late work and missed deadlines, letters which Coleridge sent at regular intervals to his exasperated publishers for the rest of his life. However, thanks to Cottle's admirable patience and the energy and industry of both publisher and poet, 'The Preface' to which this letter refers was written and typeset and appeared at the beginning of *Poems on Various Subjects* by S. T. Coleridge, late of Jesus College, Cambridge. This was Coleridge's first volume of poetry and it was published in April of 1796, a year of significant transition for Coleridge. Even as his Pantisocratic bubble burst, even as *The Watchman* expired in a welter of debt and unpaid bills, something new was being born: Coleridge the poet was coming forward to take centre stage. That same year he would leave Bristol and begin his life afresh in Nether Stowey with new friends and new vision, making for himself in some sense a 'Susquehanna of the heart'.

Before we journey with him to Nether Stowey, to the visionary landscape and the intense *annus mirabilis* in which Coleridge will compose *The Mariner* and *Kubla Khan*, we must record one more extraordinary moment from these heady Bristol days. Sometime in the autumn of 1795, just around the time of his marriage, a remarkable meeting took place in a most unlikely setting. Coleridge, by then very well known as a political and religious radical, a daring poet who was published in the more liberal newspapers, and known locally as a campaigner against the slave trade on which Bristol's wealth was based, was invited to 7 Great George Street, the townhouse of John Pinney, a rich West Indies sugar merchant. Considering that Coleridge had regularly campaigned for a boycott of the slave and sugar trades, this was pretty remarkable. In fact, Pinney was increasingly uncomfortable with the trade and with the sources of his wealth in the slave plantation of which he eventually divested himself. Ironically, when Pinney did 'disinvest" and sell his West Indian plantations it was far worse for those slaves, for Pinney had treated them less cruelly than many, and the estates were bought by a man notorious for his cruelty.[21]

It may be that inviting the likes of Coleridge into his elegant drawing room was the beginning of a change in Pinney, but there was another reason for inviting Coleridge. Also present was another guest, a poet who wished to meet Coleridge – a quiet, brooding Northerner called Wordsworth. On that autumn evening in Bristol neither poet knew how momentous this meeting would be, but Wordsworth immediately recognised something great in Coleridge and wrote of their brief encounter. 'Coleridge was at Bristol part of the time I was there, I saw but little of him. I wished indeed to have seen more – his talent appears to be very great.'[22]

By the time *Poems on Various Subjects* finally appeared in April of 1796, Coleridge was almost too exhausted to savour the moment and the achievement. It was well and widely reviewed, although Coleridge's style was developing so rapidly that within a year he was to be embarrassed by the sub-Miltonic diction of many of these poems, particularly 'Religious Musings', the poem

Wordsworth & Coleridge meet

on which he had originally thought its reputation would rest. In fact, the best things in it were the harbingers of his more relaxed and refined style; poems like *The Eolian Harp*. In May of that year, Coleridge did the sensible thing and went away with the now-pregnant Sara for a fortnight's holiday. The place he chose was Nether Stowey, the beautiful Somerset village nestled at the foot of the Quantock Hills, where, two years earlier, in 1794, he had met the philanthropic tanner Tom Poole, whose radical polit-ical leanings and sense of practical charity had already led him to find ways to ameliorate the lives of those around him in Nether Stowey. On 13 May 1796 Coleridge printed the last issue of *The Watchman*, signing off with the motto drawn from scripture: 'Oh watchman thou hast watched in vain'. That episode was over and Coleridge and Sara went down to stay with Tom Poole and recover.

The time with Poole at Nether Stowey, much of it spent in his beautiful garden and orchard under the blossoms drinking cider, making and reciting poems, and setting the world to rights, gave Coleridge a chance to take stock and reflect. He was no longer an irresponsible college student off on one jaunt or adventure after another, confident that his family would always bail him out. He would soon be a father, with mouths to feed and a family to care for, and yet, more than ever, he felt the profound and powerful calling of his muse, knowing full well that he could scarcely rely on poetry for a living. He considered the possibility of starting a school or taking in lodgers or boarders as a tutor. He also consid-ered taking a post as a Unitarian minister, since he had been so welcomed by the Unitarian community when he joined them in campaigning against the slave trade. Even this early, though, his theology was moving back more fully in a Trinitarian direction. Deep in his heart, he knew that neither of these alternatives was his true calling, but that he must necessarily provide for his family. He set this dilemma out fully to Poole. Poole – a self-educated man who had benefited enormously from sitting at Coleridge's feet and imbibing all he had to offer, and who made his own book-room available not only to Coleridge but also to many others in his village – came up with a creative and generous third alternative. He and a group of seven or eight friends each pledged themselves to contribute five guineas annually 'as a trifling mark of their esteem, gratitude and admiration'.[23] This would give Coleridge an annual income of about £40 to supplement whatever else he could make by his writing and perhaps also by an adventure in home gardening and self-sufficiency. For the other part of Poole's plan was that Coleridge should move to Nether Stowey and to a cottage adjacent to Tom's garden that had land enough for the Coleridges to grow some of their own food, keep hens and geese and perhaps a pig. Coleridge was deeply moved by the offer, as he wrote to Poole.

> If it were in my power to give you any thing which I have not already given, I should be oppressed by the letter now before me – but no! I feel myself rich in being poor; and because I have nothing to bestow, I know how much I have bestowed . . . God be ever praised for all things. –[24]

There were still many things to be done. In September, while they were back at Bristol, Sara was delivered of her first child, a boy they named Hartley, after the philosopher. And she needed time to settle and recover before a move. There were debts to be paid, obligations to be met, before the Coleridges could leave Bristol, but eventually, just after Christmas in 1796, on a freezing night, they arrived in Nether Stowey, where Coleridge was to begin an intense period of creative endeavour, literary and personal growth in which he would write the poems that would make his name, chief of which would be *The Rime of the Ancient Mariner*.

Harts returning to trinity

87

The overarching and interlacing trees on the path between Coleridge's cottage and Wordsworth's lodge witnessed the rooting and branching of their fruitful friendship

CHAPTER FOUR

A Network of Friendships

With Coleridge's arrival in Nether Stowey, all the elements that allowed the writing of *The Rime of the Ancient Mariner* gradually fell into place. The year from the spring of 1797 through to the spring of 1798 was the *annus mirabilis* that brought to birth not only Coleridge's greatest poetry, but also the beginning of Wordsworth's greatest writing, and the composition and the publication of their epoch-making joint work *The Lyrical Ballads*. For all these reasons, this year can be seen as the birth of the Romantic Movement in English literature.

Of course, our chief concern will be with *The Rime of the Ancient Mariner* itself, but before we look at the poem in detail in Part II of this book, we shall look at the factors that attended and enabled its birth. This includes the network of friendships that inspired and sustained the writing, the deep reading and confident poetic preparation in which Coleridge was engaging, and the renewal of the springs of his own imagination which was provided by his many walks following springs and rivers, both alone and with William and Dorothy Wordsworth, through the landscape around the Quantocks. Coleridge's sense of renewal is expressed in the three great visionary poems which, as it were, framed and nurtured the composition of *The Mariner: This Lime-Tree Bower My Prison* written in July 1797, *Kubla Khan* in October 1797 and *Frost at Midnight*, written in the February of 1798.[1]

William, Dorothy and More

1797 was the year in which the brief meeting between Wordsworth and Coleridge in Bristol was to blossom into friendship and a literary collaboration in which each poet discovered and drew out the best in the other; in which each recognised, and in one sense gave to the other, the gift of their true self and vocation. There would come a time when this friendship was shadowed, a time when either might paralyse rather than perfect the other's gifts, and that shadowing and darkening of what had once been life-giving is itself one of the great themes of *The Ancient Mariner*. But for now in this miraculous year, the friendship was for both poets, like the living albatross, a gift of wings and flight, lifting them to heights of which neither without the other would have been capable.

When Coleridge moved to Nether Stowey, Wordsworth and his sister Dorothy were living at Racedown near Pilsdon in Dorset in a house provided for them by John Pinney, the conscience-stricken Bristol sugar merchant who had first introduced Coleridge to Wordsworth. The two poets had, in the meantime, been corresponding, and in April of 1797 Wordsworth made a detour to Nether Stowey on a journey from Racedown to Bristol in order to visit Coleridge. Tom Poole played host to the two poets, who by now were familiar with each other's works. At this point they were both attempting to write verse tragedies, not the form for which either would become famous, and they began to read to each other from work in progress. The great conversation had begun.

Wordsworth's brief visit was followed by an invitation to Coleridge to come to Racedown for a longer stay, and in June of that year he walked the forty miles to see them, arriving on the evening of 5 June with the completed first draft of his tragedy *Osorio* sticking out of his pocket. He was standing leaning on a field gate when Dorothy, sitting in the garden of Racedown Lodge, caught sight of him. At that moment, rather than keeping to the road, Coleridge leapt over the gate 'and bounded down a pathless field'[2] to meet them. That impetuosity and energy, the willingness to push past boundaries for the sake of friendship and poetry, were to be keynotes throughout their friendship and lives together.

If the Wordsworths captivated Coleridge at this point, then he was probably unaware of how deeply he was doing the same for them. It is worth hearing from Dorothy Wordsworth, rather than her more taciturn brother William, about the impact Coleridge made:

> You had a great loss in not seeing Coleridge. He is a wonderful man. His conversation teems with soul, mind and spirit. Then he is so benevolent, so good tempered and cheerful, and, like William, interests himself so much about every little trifle.
>
> At first I thought him very plain, that is, for about three minutes; he is pale and thin, has a wide mouth, thick lips, and not very good teeth, longish loose-growing half-curling rough black hair. But if you hear him speak for five minutes you think no more of them.
>
> His eye is large and full, not dark but grey; such an eye as would receive from a heavy soul the dullest expression; but it speaks every emotion of his animated mind; it has more of the 'poet's eye in a fine frenzy rolling' than ever I witnessed. He has fine dark eye-brows and an overhanging forehead.[3]

In this intense and vivid passage, it is worth noting the brief phrase 'his conversation teems with soul, mind and spirit'. Considering that Dorothy had only just met Coleridge this is an extraordinary and prescient list. His conversation itself is emphasised in Richard Armour and Raymond Howes' great book

Coleridge the Talker, which brings together all the contemporary responses to and accounts of Coleridge's conversation we have. The book makes clear that Coleridge's conversation was brilliant not just in the conventional sense of being studded with witticisms or *bon mots*, but in a much fuller and larger sense of being illuminating and formative in the same way that his great poetry is. Indeed, Armour and Howes contend that his genius found even greater expression in spontaneous and improvised talk than it did in formal writing. Whether or not this is the case, it is certainly true that the Conversation Poems, a genre he had invented and begun to compose this year, in which the reader seems to hear the poet in intimate conversation with them, are among the best things that he ever wrote. Dorothy's choice of the word 'teems' also goes to the heart of Coleridge's genius, which is the sheer, generative gift, the life-giving profusion of his imagination. Though we can never hear his conversation, readers of his notebooks and letters can get a glimpse of this teeming mind, from which a super-abundance and overflow of ideas and images seem constantly to be streaming.

The second prescient and telling thing in Dorothy's account is her playful allusion to Shakespeare's description of the ideal or archetypal poet in *A Midsummer Night's Dream*.

> The poet's eye in a fine frenzy rolling,
> Doth glance from heaven to earth, from earth to heaven;
> And as imagination bodies forth
> The forms of things unknown, the poet's pen
> Turns them to shapes, and gives to airy nothing
> A local habitation and a name.[4]

Dorothy was the first of many to notice the power and light in Coleridge's eyes and link it with the mariner, whose 'glittering eye' had power to hold and compel the listener.[5]

But, in fact, the whole of Shakespeare's account of 'the poet' is helpful for understanding Coleridge. Coleridge's great gift as a poet was imagination itself; his great gift as a prose writer was in leading his reader into a deeper understanding of the imagination. In the end Coleridge traced the living stream of the imagination back up to what he believed to be its origin in the creative act of God's imagination, whereby the world came into being. As Coleridge would later put it: 'The primary IMAGINATION I hold to be the living Power and prime Agent of all human perception, and as a repetition in the finite mind of the eternal act of creation in the infinite I AM.'[6]

Coleridge himself, reflecting on Shakespeare, would find in the working of the playwright's imagination helpful analogies for what he believed to be the shaping work of nature, and finally behind that the work of God's 'shaping spirit'. All this was still to come, but somehow, Dorothy foreshadowed it in these few words.

Coleridge was certainly aware of Dorothy's extraordinary gift of discernment and intuition, and in some ways his friendship with her is as important and generative of his poetry as was his friendship with Wordsworth himself. This is how he described Dorothy to Joseph Cottle, who would publish *Lyrical Ballads* later that year.

> She is a woman indeed!—in mind. I mean. & heart—for her person is such that if you expected to see a pretty woman, you would think her ordinary—if you expected to find an ordinary woman, you would think her pretty!—But her manners are simple, ardent, impressive . . .

> In every motion her most innocent soul
> Outbeams so brightly, that who saw would say,
> Guilt was a thing impossible in her.—

Her information various – her eyes watchful in minutest observation of nature – and her taste a perfect electrometer – it bends, protrudes, and draws in, at subtle beauties & most recondite faults.[7]

Like Dorothy's description of Coleridge, his description of Dorothy takes us through the outer towards the inner, towards the mind and heart. It is also interesting to note his appreciation of Dorothy's eye for detail: 'her eye watchful for the minutest observation of nature'. We now know from the publication of her journals and letters that Wordsworth owed an enormous amount to Dorothy, whose observation and indeed actual writing is used in Wordsworth's poetry in the minutest detail. However, it was Coleridge's account of Wordsworth in another letter to Cottle which was again, presciently, to express both the intimacy and the ambivalence of their relationship.

Wordsworth admires my Tragedy—which gives me great hopes. Wordsworth has written a Tragedy himself. I speak with heartfelt sincerity & (I think) unblended judgement, when I tell you, that I feel myself a *little man by his* side; & yet do not think myself the less man, that I formerly thought myself.—His Drama is absolutely wonderful. You know I do not commonly speak in such abrupt & unmingled phrases—& therefore will the more readily believe me.[8]

The two contrasting phrases in this account, on the one hand 'gives me great hopes' and on the other 'I feel myself a little man by his side', represent the two poles between which Coleridge's friendship with Wordsworth moved. On the one hand, there can be no doubt that Wordsworth's initial recognition and encouragement of Coleridge's genius confirmed his vocation as a poet and developed his craft and technique. All that he admired in the clarity and simplicity of style that Wordsworth had already achieved helped to purge Coleridge of the clogging sub-Miltonic poeticisms that encumber so much of his early verse. So, without Wordsworth he would not have risen to the great heights of this *annus mirabilis*. On the other hand, as the relationship developed, and particularly after Coleridge moved from his own native West Country to be with Wordsworth in his native North Country, the balance of the relationship changed and it is arguable that Wordsworth's refusal to include *Christabel* in the second edition of the *Lyrical Ballads* and the displacement of *The Ancient Mariner* to the end of that edition had a crushing effect on Coleridge and took away from him some of the very confidence in his poetry that Wordsworth had helped to instil. All of this was to come, though it is strangely foreshadowed in *The Ancient Mariner*.

Describing this year, so momentous for these two poets, and for English poetry, scholars have not unnaturally focused on the friendship of the two men, but in fact the wider webs of friendship that sustained them both are equally important, reaching well beyond Dorothy as the third in their self-named 'trinity'.[9] As we have seen, without Tom Poole's generosity to Coleridge and confidence in him, his continued hospitality and friendship, and his warmth and openness to the other friends as they came to Nether Stowey, drawn by the excitement of what had begun to happen there, the miraculous events of this year would not have taken place. Among those friends – who met more often than not in Tom Poole's orchard, parlour and book-room, rather than in Coleridge's tiny, smoky and overcrowded cottage – were, in addition to the Wordsworths, Charles Lamb (Coleridge's oldest friend going back to schooldays), John Thelwall (the radical republican whom Coleridge loved and was trying to convert from his atheism – but not his radicalism – and whose stay was to cause so much offence and concern in the district), and often younger men: ardent disciples, like the young William Hazlitt, whose later accounts of this vital summer were to be so influential.

Included in this list of essential and close-hearted conversation partners and friends in the first months of 1797 should, of course, be Sara Coleridge. We know from Coleridge's letters to her and hers to him, and from poems like *The Eolian Harp*, that Sara, who was bright and well educated, took a real part in Coleridge's inner and spiritual life (as well as his outer and domestic life). It is only as the year progresses, as the relationship with the Wordsworths becomes more intense, as the key conversations start to take place on the roads and trackways of this beautiful countryside rather than around the domestic hearth, that we begin to sense the first encroaching shadows of distance and isolation that would eventually grow between Coleridge and Sara. We also know, from a jotting in the notebooks from around 1796–7, that Coleridge was aware of this tension and trying to heal it: 'Mem – not to adulterize my time by absenting myself from my wife –'[10]

Of course, Sara was caught up in the care and work brought on by the birth of their son Hartley, but it is equally true that, unlike most men of the period, Coleridge also took part in the rearing, nursing and care of Hartley.

We are *very* happy – & my little David Hartley grows a sweet boy – & has high health – he laughs at us till he makes us weep for very fondness. – You would smile to see my eye rolling up to the ceiling in a Lyric fury, and on my knee a *Diaper* pinned, to warm.[11]

We get a sense of the energy, joy and laughter of those first few months at Stowey, in the way Coleridge ends this letter to Thelwall:

I send and receive to and from Bristol every week – & will transcribe that part of your last letter & send it to Reed.

I raise potatoes & all manner of vegetables; have an Orchard; & shall raise Corn with the Spade enough for my family. – We have two pigs, & Ducks & Geese. A Cow would not answer the keep: for we have whatever milk we want from T. Poole.

– God bless you & your affectionate ST Coleridge
Sara's love to you . . .[12]

The natural movement from I am happy to 'we are very happy' and even the little post-script 'Sara's love to you', all make it clear that Sara is still at this stage (early in February) very much included in everything.

For all his gregarious nature Coleridge was, as we have seen, also subject to deep bouts of melancholia or depression. His friendships helped him to deal with that, but it never went away. There is a fascinating letter from early April 1797 written to Joseph Cottle, his publisher, clearly after and under the stimulus of Wordsworth's first visit to Nether Stowey, that tells us a great deal both about the seriousness with which Coleridge took his vocation as a poet and the difficulties with which he had to contend. He begins the letter apologising for being dull and despondent in his last meeting with Cottle and explains why in the following terms:

But when last in Bristol the day I meant to have devoted to you was such a day of sadness, that I could *do nothing*. – On the Saturday, the Sunday, and the ten days after my arrival at Stowey I felt a depression too dreadful to be described

So much I felt my genial spirits droop!
My hopes all flat, nature within me seem'd
In all her functions weary of herself.[13]

Two things are worth noting here. First, the depression itself. Like many great minds, Coleridge had to cope with severe mood swings and with a capacity for sorrow that was at least as deep as his capacity for joy. The very openness and sensitivity that were his essential gifts as a poet left him vulnerable to depression. But Coleridge's way of expressing the depression is equally significant; he naturally borrows the language of Milton in *Samson Agonistes* to express his own pain; indeed, he does not so much borrow it, as make it his own. It is clear that for Coleridge, Milton is not simply an august figure from the past but also a contemporary and intimate companion. Coleridge goes on immediately after this passage in the letter to mention Wordsworth's visit:

> Wordsworth's conversation, &c roused me somewhat; but even now I am not the man I have been – and I think never shall. A sort of calm hopelessness diffuses itself over my heart. – Indeed every mode of life which has promised me bread and cheese, has been, one after another torn away from me – but God remains.[14]

Again, it is characteristic that he can be roused by conversation and yet sink so swiftly back into depression. What Coleridge calls 'a sort of calm hopelessness' in this letter is eventually bodied forth in his poetry as the 'doldrums' in which the mariner's ship is trapped. His direct assertion that 'God remains' is typical, even as he surveys both mental and financial distress. That God should remain was a central concern of Coleridge's at this time and for the rest of his life. This confirmed theological concern is clear in a couple of sentences later where he says: 'I employ myself now on a book of Morals in answer to Godwin, and on my Tragedy.' The tragedy that we have already mentioned is *Osorio*. Intended for Drury Lane it was rejected the first time around but years later, revised and retitled *Remorse*, it was an unexpected West End hit and came to Coleridge's rescue, bailing him out financially and emotionally in 1813 at a time when he was near his lowest ebb. The play is an exploration of the mystery of human evil, the problem of pain, in the midst of a world of beauty.

The 'Book of Morals in Answer to Godwin' was never written as a book, though in the end it was realised as an actual conversation with Godwin himself. William Godwin was a radical sceptic, indeed, technically an anarchist, whose book *An Enquiry Concerning Political Justice* had done so much to inspire Coleridge's Pantisocratic ideal and would go on to inspire the radicalism of Percy Bysshe Shelley. Godwin was married to Mary Wollstonecraft, author of *A Vindication of the Rights of Woman* and the mother of Mary Shelley. Coleridge entirely understood and empathised with the Godwins' radical call for social justice, though Godwin was entirely sceptical in religious matters. Coleridge hoped he could persuade Godwin that believing in the God to whom the life and teachings of Jesus Christ pointed would be the most radical option and the best foundation for social justice. Indeed, many years later, when Godwin had moved from atheism to theism, he wrote 'my theism, if such I may be permitted to call it, consists in a reverent and soothing contemplation of all that is beautiful, grand, or mysterious in the system of the universe . . . into this train of thinking I was first led by the conversations of S T Coleridge'.[15] So, even in these twin projects – the unwritten Godwin book and *Osorio* – we see theology and poetry going hand in hand and complementing each other.

In some ways the best account of this network of friendships, both wide and close, a network in which each friend discerns and brings out the best in the other, is given not by a scholar or biographer writing directly about this period, but by another great writer who had experience of the kindling and deepening that such friendships and collaborations can bring. C.S. Lewis's essay on friendship in his seminal book *The Four Loves* has often been mined by scholars as giving a first-hand insight into the way the Oxford Inklings worked as a group of writers, resonating with one another, providing helpful mutual criticism by ultimately sharing a vision in a close group without thought of further fame or consequence, but a vision which nevertheless changes the world around them and flows from them into a wider literature.[16]

It could be argued that friendships are of practical value to the Community. Every civilised religion began in a small group of friends. Mathematics effectively began when a few Greek friends got together to talk about numbers and lines and angles. What is now the Royal Society was originally a few gentlemen meeting in their spare time to discuss things which they (and not many others) had a fancy for. What we now call the 'Romantic Movement' was once Mr Wordsworth and Mr Coleridge talking incessantly (at least Mr Coleridge was) about a secret vision of their own.[17]

Reading for an Epic

If Coleridge was stimulated and encouraged in his vocation by the company of living poets like Wordsworth and literary friends like Lamb, he was also stimulated and engaged in a 'communion with the dead' through his constant reading and re-reading of the great poets and philosophers of the past, as well as the wide reach of his reading in contemporary science and travel writing. Reading for Coleridge was never a passive thing – his mind was not, in his own phrase, 'a lazy on-looker'[18] – but he was fully engaged and involved, always annotating the books in the margins of the pages themselves as well as making citations, jottings and analysis in his own notebooks. Because of these habits we have an exceptionally good idea of all he read and of his responses to his reading. John Livingston Lowes' magisterial work *The Road to Xanadu* follows Coleridge through each volume he reads and shows how each book he read led him to read others mentioned in notes or bibliographies, and how his mind made the most extraordinary connections between the wide variety of books that he would be reading simultaneously. The publication in six large volumes of Coleridge's marginalia makes it clear that he had what can only be described as a long and sustained conversation with many of these books throughout his life. But during the course of this year, as his vocation as a poet clarified and deepened, so did his sense of depth and purpose in reading. The final section of the letter to Cottle quoted above takes us most deeply and clearly into Coleridge's frame of mind at this period and for many years to come and shows both the range of his reading and the end to which he believed it should be directed. After observing that the company of Wordsworth has made him realise that there was something too facile, too shallow and glib in Southey's rapidly composed poetry, Coleridge goes on to suggest how he thought he himself ought to prepare for writing an epic, and it is clear from this and from other notebooks and letters that he had begun to harbour epic ambitions. Just as Milton's words had come to him in expressing his feelings at the start of this letter, so Milton is now his exemplar:

> Observe the march of Milton – his severe application, his laborious polish, his deep metaphysical researches, his prayers to God before he began his great poem, all that could lift and swell his intellect, became his daily food. I should not think of devoting less than 20 years to an Epic Poem. Ten to collect materials

and warm my mind with universal science. I would be a tolerable Mathematician, I would thoroughly know Mechanics,
Hydrostatics, Optics, and Astronomy, Botany, Metallurgy,
Fossilism, Chemistry, Geology, Anatomy, Medicine – then *the
mind of man* – then the *minds of men* – in all Travels, Voyages
and Histories. So I would spend ten years – the next five to the
composition of the poem – and the five last to the correction
of it.

So I would write haply not unhearing of that divine and
rightly whispering Voice, which speaks to mighty minds of
predestinated Garlands, starry and unwithering. God love you,

S. T. Coleridge.[19]

Now there may be something a little tongue in cheek in the extrav-
agance of these proposals, but there is also an underlying seriousness and, indeed, an agenda that Coleridge endeavoured to follow.
It is certainly true, for Coleridge, as it was for Milton, that 'all
that could lift and swell his intellect became his daily food'. And
it is also true that Coleridge's efforts in poetry were also accompanied by deep metaphysical researches and 'prayers to God'
before he began.

Moving on from his backward glance at Milton, Coleridge's
reading list for writing an epic poem itself makes fascinating
reading. We have grown used to the deep and debilitating split in
our culture between the arts and sciences, used to thinking of the
arts as warm and genial and the sciences as cold and factual, but
Coleridge insists, he must '*warm*' his 'mind with universal
science.' And indeed we can show that all the sciences on his list
here – 'Mechanics, Hydrostatics, Optics, and Astronomy, Botany,
Metallurgy, Fossilism, Chemistry, Geology, Anatomy, Medicine'
– formed part of his reading. He must be one of few English
poets who have read and annotated Newton's *Optics* in its

original form.[20] As to 'the mind of man – then the minds of men', over a lifetime Coleridge's minute and unflinching analysis in his notebooks and letters, both of his own mind and of those around him, has anticipated a great deal of modern psychology. His immediate programme for discovering 'the minds of men – in all Travels, Voyages and Histories' was at this date already underway. As Livingston Lowes has demonstrated, Coleridge was reading, absorbing, remembering and re-imagining almost every story of travel, sea-voyage, sea-discovery and shipwreck that was available to him. Presumably all these books available to Coleridge also had many other readers. The difference with Coleridge was that he did not simply remember what he had read. He could take and transform the images he found in his memory, and by the shaping spirit of his imagination mould them into a vessel capable of containing our joys and sorrows as well as his. In this letter, Coleridge speaks of what it would take to write an epic poem. By a careful reading of his notebooks and his own later recollections of this period we can get some idea of the type of poetry, epic or otherwise, that he was considering at this time. The notebooks, sometimes in single jottings, sometimes in whole lists, contain the titles of books and poems Coleridge intended to write and never did. What a library they would have made! Looking back as early as 1795, here are some examples: 'Jonas – a monodrama – vide Hunter's Anatomy of a Whale' and 'Wandering Jew' / a romance'.[21] Both of these unrealised projects may have had some final bearing on *The Mariner*. Certainly, the story of Jonah – the story of a man blamed by the whole crew for the disaster that overtook them, accepting in himself both guilt and punishment yet saved and set ashore again by a strange providence – has resonances with *The Mariner*. In the case of the 'Wandering Jew: a romance', we can be more certain of the links. The legend of the Wandering Jew, of a person who does not die but lives on generation by generation witnessing the horrors of history and seeking a resolution of his own guilt, goes back to ideas drawn from the 'mark of Cain'; the mark, both a curse and a mercy, that God puts on the brow of Cain to indicate that he should not be slain. Coleridge did indeed plan with William Wordsworth an epic poem on the origin of evil told through the story of the wanderings of Cain but it never got beyond a prose draft.[22] We also know that the motif of the Wandering Jew, the idea of a person travelling around the world and through time as a kind of perpetual witness, was actually in his mind when he composed *The Mariner*. Here is Kathleen Coburn's commentary on this note:

> That the 'romance' became *The Ancient Mariner*, or at least that the Wandering Jew became the old mariner-narrator of the poem as Lowes argued, is borne out by an unpublished scrap of Coleridge's *Table Talk*, recently come to light: 'It is an enormous blunder in these engravings of De Serte [? John Thomas de Serres], brought here by Dr. Aitken, to represent the An. M. as an old man on board ship. He was in my mind the everlasting wandering Jew – had told this story ten thousand times since the voyage, which was in his early youth and 50 years before.[23]

After these two isolated entries, from late in 1796, just before he moved to Nether Stowey, we have a fuller list, ambitiously titled 'My Works', which includes not only the Tragedy and the Work on Godwin he mentioned in the letter to Cottle but also the Epic and a number of other items of real interest. Here is Coleridge's full list of his proposed works as he imagined them in late 1796:

My Works
(a) Imitations of the Modern Latin Poets with an Essay Biog. & Crit. On the Rest. Of Lit. – 2 Vol. Octavo.

(b)   Answer to the System of Nature – 1 ~~Vol~~. Oct.

(c)   The Origin of Evil, an Epic Poem.

(d)   Essay on Bowles

(e)   Strictures on Godwin, Paley &c &c –

(f)   Pantisocracy, or a practical Essay on the abolition of Indiv(id)ual Property.

(g)   Carthon on Opera

(h)   Poems

(i)   Edition of Collins & Gray with preliminary Dissertation.

(j)   A Liturgy On different Sect of Religion & Infidelity – philosophical analysis of their Effect on mind & manners –.

(k)   A Tragedy.[24]

Most of these never saw the light of day, at least not under the titles he gave them here, but of most interest to us is item (c) 'The Origin of Evil – an Epic Poem'. The problem of human evil, the awareness of a deep flaw running through every heart, undermining even our most virtuous endeavours, had been preoccupying Coleridge since the first shocks of the Terror in France, when so many high hopes for liberty and renewal ended in bloodshed. But he was also dimly and intuitively grappling with the problem of evil on a personal level: from the collapse of his Pantisocratic schemes, the sense of betrayal by Southey, to the difficulty he had in being as good a husband or father as he intended, through to the first incipient struggles with opium. So far, Coleridge had taken opium simply as a painkiller, but he was taking it with increasing frequency and the day would come when opium would exert a terrifying and devastating grip on his life. And this problem of the origin of evil, of the way it coexists with our very capacities for good, was to be the subject of the great epic, which would take, in Coleridge's estimation, twenty years of preparation and which he constantly berated himself for not having written. But as we shall see, everything he had hoped to achieve in the unwritten epic was achieved in *The Ancient Mariner*.

A few pages later in the same notebook comes another more extensive list, with some overlap but with some new items.[25] Of greatest interest to us is item 16 in this list of twenty-seven unwritten books: 'Hymns to the Sun, the Moon, and the Elements – six hymns. – In one of them to introduce a dissection of Atheism – particularly the Godwinian System of Pride. Proud of what? An outcast of blind Nature ruled by a fatal Necessity – slave of an ideot Nature!' Again these six 'Hymns' were never written under those titles but, as we shall see, the four elements and the sun and the moon are all given powerful poetic expression and become essential 'characters' within the drama of *The Rime of the Ancient Mariner*, a poem which could also claim to be a dissection of atheism and a challenge to pride. Coleridge was haunted throughout his life by his apparent failure as a poet, specifically his failure to produce these unwritten works and bear the fruit he had imagined and promised. In fact he succeeded, not by writing these twenty-seven unwritten books but by writing *The Mariner*, a poem which proved a far better vehicle for his thoughts than many of those might have been.

There is one more unfinished project from this period on which Coleridge and Wordsworth were working jointly and for which some scraps of poetry in the notebooks were clearly intended: an extensive narrative poem called '*The Brook*'. Here is how Coleridge described the project years later when he came to write the *Biographia Literaria*:

> I sought for a subject, that should give equal room and freedom
> for description, incident, and impassioned reflections on men,
> nature and society, yet supply in itself a natural connection to
> the parts, and unity to the whole. Such a subject I conceived
> myself to have found in a stream, traced from its source in the

hills among the yellow-red moss and conical glass-shaped tufts of bent, to the first break or fall, where its drops become audible, and it begins to form a channel; thence to the peat and turf barn, itself built of the same dark squares as it sheltered; to the sheepfold; to the first cultivated plot of ground; to the lonely cottage and its bleak garden won from the heath; to the hamlet, the villages, the market-town, the manufactories, and the seaport. My walks therefore were almost daily on top of Quantock, and among its sloping combes. With my pencil and memorandum book in my hand, I was *making studies*, as the artists call them, and often moulding my thoughts into verse, with the objects and imagery immediately before my senses. Many circumstances, evil and good, intervened to prevent the completion of the poem, which was to have been entitled 'THE BROOK'.[26]

Like the epic *On the Origin of Evil* and the six hymns, 'The Brook' itself was never written as planned. But just as the thoughts, readings and intentions – the themes and meanings – of those other unwritten poems all found their way into *The Ancient Mariner*, where they perhaps found a better expression than they would have done in a laboured epic, so Coleridge's minute observations of the brooks and streams, the hidden waterfalls in the Quantock Hills, were to flow as tributaries into many other poems, not least into *Kubla Khan*, the great river poem, which arrived almost accidentally and, even by itself, would make Coleridge immortal.

In the short term, however, the 'studies' he and Wordsworth were making for 'The Brook' got them into trouble. Local people suspected that, as notorious radicals and Jacobins, these moonlight wanderers with their notebooks and camp stools might be spying out the way for a French invasion. A government spy was assigned to watch them and report back to the Home Office. The special agent filed a report on 15 August, still in the possession of the Home Office, describing Coleridge, Wordsworth and their friends as 'A Mischievous gang of disaffected Englishmen' and a 'Sett of violent Democrats'.[27] Years later in the *Biographia Literaria* Coleridge would make light of this episode and treat it comically, but at the time it could have had very serious consequences for all of them and did have the consequence that the Wordsworths' lease on Alfoxton was not renewed, hastening their departure to Germany later in 1798, and eventually drawing Coleridge away from the West Country to join the Wordsworths up in the Lake District, a move which had momentous consequences for English poetry and disastrous consequences for Coleridge's domestic life.

Returning to the unwritten 'Brook', we can see a pattern emerging. It seems that Coleridge found it almost impossible to complete, and sometimes even to begin, any task that presented itself as a duty, however much he might actually want to finish it. There was something about the sheer weight of moral obligation that crushed him or at least inhibited his imagination. So he would procrastinate by turning to another task. And for this very reason, like many procrastinators, he was, paradoxically, a very productive person. This meant, though, that what he produced, even when it was work of the very first order, was something he perceived as secondary because it was almost never 'the great unwritten work'.

Coleridge's wide reading stimulated and inspired him, though it also sometimes left him in awe and feeling overshadowed by the great masters of the past, like Milton and Shakespeare. To release him as a writer, the great weight of his learning had to be counterbalanced by stimulus in his own experience, by the conversation of friends, by turning his eye from the page and looking with just that intensity which Wordsworth was now showing him, at the visionary landscape around him.

Even with the stimulus of Wordsworth there was still something wanting for that 'release', and that was financial security, or at least a sure enough expectation of money to keep Coleridge from bartering the time needed to write, just to secure 'Bread and Cheese' (his two words for the necessities of life).

Coleridge had one child already, was from a large family himself, and could foresee that he might well have more. So, constantly weighed in the balance, in the other scale, against all these heady and epic literary ambitions, was the temptation to security and to some job that might provide a steady income. School-mastering beckoned several times – tutoring and taking in lodgers had already proved too fraught and insecure – but the other and more tempting possibility was Christian ministry. Coleridge had already ruled out the Church of England but he was widely known and approved of in radical dissenting circles, particularly among the Unitarians, because of his vigorous campaign against the slave trade and his generally radical stance in *The Watchman*. On the tour to raise subscriptions to *The Watchman* he had often been invited to preach in Unitarian pulpits. With an eye to a growing family and to Sara's anxiety about having a secure and dependable income, he accepted an invitation to preach to the Unitarian congregation at Shrewsbury with a view to becoming their minister. The sermon, which dealt with the pressing political issues of war and peace, was a great success, not least with the teenage son of another local minister, young William Hazlitt, who wrote: 'The preacher launched into his subject like an eagle dallying with the wind . . . I could not have been more delighted if I had heard the music of the spheres. Poetry and Philosophy had met together. Truth and Genius had embraced under the eye, and with the sanction of Religion.'[28]

Coleridge was offered the job and was on the very cusp of accepting, when a letter arrived for him from Tom and Josiah Wedgwood, the wealthy and philanthropic members of the

Wedgwood family who were transforming the pottery industry, to whom he had been introduced by Tom Poole, offering Coleridge 'an annuity of £150 for life, legally secured to me, no condition whatever being annexed'. Hazlitt himself witnessed the moment Coleridge made his choice about this annuity, and his account of it suggests an understanding that the annuity wasn't as entirely without condition as the wording of Wedgwood's letter suggested:

> When I came down to breakfast I found he had just received a letter from his friend, T. Wedgwood, making him an offer of £150 a year if he chose to waive his present pursuit, and devote himself entirely to the study of poetry and philosophy. Coleridge seemed to make up his mind to close with this proposal in the act of tying up one of his shoes.[29]

In one sense, of course, this was the moment of liberation. Coleridge was free to return to the Quantocks and Wordsworth and continue their work together. Without this freedom and release from anxiety that the annuity brought, the ensuing *annus mirabilis* might never have happened. But the annuity was not quite string-free. It's clear from Coleridge's later correspondence with Tom Wedgwood that this annuity carried a huge burden of expectation: that Coleridge would be the man of genius, the new Milton who would give the modern age the all-synthesising epic reconciling science and religion, philosophy and poetry, tradition and innovation. This was no small burden to lay on someone's shoulders! Further, the terms Hazlitt discerned in the offer, not written, but presumably reflecting the way Coleridge explained it to him at the time, and therefore giving us an insight into what Coleridge thought the expectations were, are 'the *study* of poetry and philosophy'. Coleridge laid that notion of *study* to heart: soon he would spend and overspend the annuity on a trip to Germany and persuade himself that a long slow prose Life of the

German dramatist G.E. Lessing, or a full history of German literature, was what was expected. Neither of these learned works
was ever written but who knows what great poetry was never
written because Coleridge diverted so much time to these barren
tasks. But that was all to come. And as Coleridge rose from tying
his shoe on that January day, the annuity meant nothing but
liberty and a new burst of song.

A view of Porlock Bay: 'the hilly fields, the meadows and the sea' – a visionary landscape

CHAPTER FIVE

A Visionary Landscape

Though we generally read the great works of the past somewhere comfortably indoors, in a library or a living room, we must not imagine the conversations which inspired *Lyrical Ballads*, and the whole Romantic Movement in literature which took root from that book, as having taken place in such quiet and studious surroundings. Wordsworth and Coleridge were inveterate walkers, indeed Coleridge has been credited with inventing the pastime of fell walking.[1] We must imagine them not as two poetical theorists concocting a new school in some entirely intellectual way but as men of both heart and head, newly awakened by the revolutionary hopes that stirred the age they lived in, and turning to one another and to the world around them in a three-way conversation through which new meanings were constantly being uncovered. The poetry itself arose and took its very rhythms as well as its subject from the physical act of walking, as William Hazlitt, who visited the poets as they worked and walked together in this magical summer, accurately observed:

> There is a chaunt in the recitation both of Coleridge and Wordsworth, which acts as a spell upon the hearer, and disarms the judgment. Perhaps they have deceived themselves by making habitual use of this more ambiguous accompaniment. Coleridge's manner is more full, animated, and varied; Wordsworth's more equable, sustained, and internal. The one might be termed more dramatic, the other more lyrical. Coleridge has told me that he himself liked to compose in walking over uneven ground, or

breaking through the straggling branches of a copse-wood;
whereas Wordsworth always wrote (if he could) walking up and
down a straight gravel-walk, or in some spot where the continuity of his verse met with no collateral interruption.[2]

Hazlitt is a useful witness to these formative months, though it
should be remembered that much of what he wrote was written a
long time afterwards when he felt that these two idols of his youth
had betrayed the radical cause and become part of an establishment he despised. We always hear two voices in Hazlitt's accounts
of Coleridge: that of the ardent hero-worshipper and that of the
bitter cynic. The two voices unite in a word like 'spell' or 'enchant',
the one delighting in the spell and the other renouncing it as a
deception, so here 'chaunt' acts as a spell on the hearer, but the
phrase 'disarms the judgment' and the further comment 'perhaps
they have deceived themselves' suggest that the spell was a delusion and not great poetry. Hazlitt refers to the 'chaunt' in recitation as 'an ambiguous accompaniment' – but the real ambiguity
is in Hazlitt's own commentary.

Perhaps the best description of one of these walks and of the
moments of transfigured vision that accompanied them comes
from Coleridge himself, though ironically it is the description of
a walk from which Coleridge was forcibly absent. In early July of
1797, Coleridge's oldest friend, Charles Lamb, came up from
London to see them, and it was planned that Lamb, Coleridge
and the Wordsworths would make their favourite walk together
up from Nether Stowey along the hilltop edge and to the secret
waterfall that Coleridge and Wordsworth had discovered at
Holford. But as Coleridge put it, in the note which accompanied
this poem, when it was published 'on the morning of their arrival,
he met with an accident, which disabled him from walking during
the whole time of their stay. One evening, when they had left him
for a few hours, he composed the following lines in the

Garden-Bower.'³ The accident had been Sara spilling a skillet of
boiling milk on Coleridge's foot, an incident which gives us a
glimpse of the crowded little cottage and perhaps the penchant
Coleridge and his friends had for getting in the way! As he sat
recuperating in Tom Poole's lime-tree bower he turned the frus-
tration of being held back from the walk into great poetry. The
very sense of restriction, of having to do something else instead
of what had been planned, of needing *to imagine* what was
absent, all seemed to have opened the wings of his muse. So the
poem begins with a sense of confinement and loss:

> Well, they are gone, and here must I remain,
> This Lime-Tree Bower my Prison! I have lost
> Beauties and Feelings, such as would have been
> Most sweet to my remembrance even when age
> Had dimmed mine eyes to blindness!⁴

But the poet, however much he may remain physically imprisoned
in the lime-tree bower, does not remain in the little prison of his
own feelings and frustrations. From the end of line 5, the poem
turns outwards to an imagined view of the walkers.

> They, meanwhile,
> Friends, whom I never more may meet again,
> On springy heath, along the hill-top edge,
> Wander in gladness, and wind down, perchance,
> To that still roaring dell, of which I told;
> The roaring dell, o'erwooded, narrow, deep,
> And only speckled by the mid-day Sun;
> Where its slim trunk the Ash from rock to rock
> Flings arching like a bridge;—that branchless Ash,
> Unsunn'd and damp, whose few poor yellow leaves
> Ne'er tremble in the gale, yet tremble still,

Fann'd by the water-fall! and there my friends
Behold the dark green file of long lank weeds,
That all at once (a most fantastic sight!)
Still nod and drip beneath the dripping edge
Of the blue clay-stone.[5]

Coleridge has, of course, made this walk many times before with
William Wordsworth and it is memory which helps him to write
in such detail about what his friends are now seeing, but because
they are doing it *now*, even as he writes, the memory itself is not
something looked back to in nostalgia, but something vividly
imagined and realised in the present.

The next section of the poem, in which Coleridge imagines his
friends emerging from the dripping stillness of Holford Dell out
into the open 'beneath the wide, wide heaven' also brings in a new
phase in Coleridge's vicarious participation in the walk.

At first he was simply observing his friends on their walk, as he
imagined it, but now he turns to address Charles Lamb directly, to
bless and to encourage, then finally he moves from addressing
Charles to addressing the very clouds, flowers, sun and ocean
which he imagines Charles seeing.

> Now, my friends emerge
> Beneath the wide wide Heaven—and view again
> The many-steepled tract magnificent
> Of hilly fields and meadows, and the sea,
> With some fair bark, perhaps, whose sails light up
> The slip of smooth clear blue betwixt two Isles
> Of purple shadow! Yes! they wander on
> In gladness all; but thou, methinks, most glad,
> My gentle-hearted Charles! for thou hast pined
> And hunger'd after Nature, many a year,
> In the great City pent, winning thy way

With sad yet patient soul, through evil and pain
And strange calamity! Ah! slowly sink
Behind the western ridge, thou glorious Sun!
Shine in the slant beams of the sinking orb,
Ye purple heath-flowers! richlier burn, ye clouds!
Live in the yellow light, ye distant groves!
And kindle, thou blue Ocean![6]

It is almost as though the first imaginative out-going from himself, in which Coleridge visualised the physical details of the walk, here opened and allowed a second imaginative out-going, this time setting aside his own troubles and entering into complete empathy with his friend. Charles Lamb worked in London at a dull desk job in the East India Company and Coleridge begins with the thought of how he 'hungers after nature' in the 'great city pent'. But there was another more urgent reason why Coleridge had invited Lamb to Nether Stowey, to which Coleridge alludes in a veiled way in the lines 'winning thy way / With sad yet patient soul, through evil and pain / and strange calamity'. The 'strange calamity' was a sudden episode of mental illness afflicting Charles' sister Mary, during the throes of which she had killed their mother. Lamb wrote immediately to Coleridge and asked for 'as religious a letter as possible'.[7] This was an unusual request as Lamb disliked any form of religious cant and asked others not to write to him in religious terms, but he knew that Coleridge was different, for Coleridge never dealt out pious clichés but wrote from the heart with a combination of deep feeling and clear thought. Coleridge wrote a powerful, prayerful and empathetic letter in reply to this invitation, asking Lamb to come and see him as quickly as possible but also offering deep counsel, which Lamb kept and treasured all the rest of his life.

Perhaps this poem itself was written for and offered to Charles as part of his healing; we know that on receiving the poem Charles had, under the stimulus of Coleridge's ebullient friendship, recovered enough of the old humour they shared together to write back and say it sounded a bit limp to be called 'gentle-hearted Charles' and suggesting to Coleridge a series of alternative epithets: 'Drunken-dog, ragged-head, seld-shaven, odd-ey'd, stuttering, or any other epithet which truly and properly belongs.'[8]

Returning to the poem we come to the third phase in the narrative arc, a renewal and transfiguration of vision:

> So my Friend
> Struck with deep joy may stand, as I have stood,
> Silent with swimming sense; yea, gazing round
> On the wide landscape, gaze till all doth seem
> Less gross than bodily; and of such hues
> As veil the Almighty Spirit, when yet he makes
> Spirits perceive his presence.[9]

Now we see what the address to the sun and the clouds and the ocean (in lines 31–7) had been leading up to; Coleridge addresses them almost as persons, rather than things, because of his deepening intuition that there is something personal behind all phenomena. He brings us to the brink of a spiritual awareness which does not seek the holy and numinous by rejecting or denigrating the world and fleeing beyond it, but paradoxically by attending to it, in its minutest detail, by gazing upon it with the concentration of every faculty. He finds that this affirmed and un-rejected world has become for a moment the veil of something even greater beyond it. In the very act of wishing that Charles might have such a vision, even in that moment of self-forgetfulness, Coleridge renews his own vision, and so at this point the focus of the poem returns to Coleridge himself, but it is to a transfigured and liberated self, and for that reason the lime-tree bower itself is transfigured and is no longer a prison. The imagined vision he wished to bestow on

Charles has itself given rise to real vision in the bower where
Coleridge sits.

> A delight
> Comes sudden on my heart, and I am glad
> As I myself were there! Nor in this bower,
> This little lime-tree bower, have I not mark'd
> Much that has sooth'd me. Pale beneath the blaze
> Hung the transparent foliage; and I watch'd
> Some broad and sunny leaf, and lov'd to see
> The shadow of the leaf and stem above
> Dappling its sunshine! And that Walnut-tree
> Was richly ting'd, and a deep radiance lay
> Full on the ancient Ivy, which usurps
> Those fronting elms, and now, with blackest mass
> Makes their dark branches gleam a lighter hue
> Through the late twilight: and though now the Bat
> Wheels silent by, and not a Swallow twitters,
> Yet still the solitary humble-bee
> Sings in the bean-flower![10]

As he moves towards the poem's conclusion, Coleridge general-
ises from this experience.

> Henceforth I shall know
> That Nature ne'er deserts the wise and pure;
> No Plot so narrow, be but Nature there,
> No waste so vacant, but may well employ
> Each faculty of sense, and keep the heart
> Awake to Love and Beauty! and sometimes
> 'Tis well to be bereft of promised good,
> That we may lift the Soul, and contemplate
> With lively joy the joys we cannot share.[11]

The poem finishes with the image of a bird in flight, 'the last rook', which 'beat its straight path along the dusky air' and becomes itself an emblem of the link between the poet, his friend, and in the final line, Life itself.

> My gentle-hearted Charles! when the last Rook
> Beat its straight path along the dusky air
> Homewards, I blest it! deeming its black wing
> (Now a dim speck, now vanishing in light)
> Had cross'd the mighty Orb's dilated glory,
> While thou stood'st gazing; or, when all was still,
> Flew creeking o'er thy head, and had a charm
> For thee, my gentle-hearted Charles, to whom
> No sound is dissonant which tells of Life.[12]

The narrative arc of this poem, its movement from a person who is imprisoned in their own self-concern through to a conscious act of empathy for another, accompanied by a transfigured vision of nature, which leads from that particular blessing to an empathy and blessing on all of life – this all foreshadows the great narrative arc and meaning of *The Rime of the Ancient Mariner*.

This Lime-Tree Bower My Prison was the first of the three great visionary poems that framed and nurtured the composition of *The Rime of the Ancient Mariner. Kubla Khan: Or a Vision in a Dream*, probably composed in the October of that year,[13] was the second. The poem itself wasn't published until 1816, when Coleridge included it, along with 'The Pains of Sleep', in the little volume *Christabel* at the request of Lord Byron. Published by John Murray, Byron's publisher, this was a popular book, which went through three editions in that year. But as it contained two unfinished 'fragments' and various opium references, it unfortunately served to confirm a popular image of Coleridge as an opium-fuelled dreamer who had not achieved his promise. This is a terrible irony, as 1816 was the very year in which, with the help of Dr Gillman, Coleridge began to bring his opium dependence under control. That first publication of *Kubla Khan* contained the famous note in which Coleridge linked its composition with the effects of opium.

The Author ... had retired to a lonely farm-house between Porlock and Linton, on the Exmoor confines of Somerset and Devonshire. In consequence of a slight indisposition, an anodyne had been prescribed, from the effect of which he fell asleep in his chair at the moment he was reading the following sentence, or words of the same substance, in 'Purchas's Pilgrimage:' 'Here the Khan Kubla commanded a palace to be built, and a stately garden thereunto; and thus ten miles of fertile ground were inclosed [sic] with a wall.' The author continued for about three hours in a profound sleep, at least of the external senses, during which time he has the most vivid confidence, that he could not have composed less than from two to three hundred lines, if that indeed can be called composition in which all the images rose up before him as *things*, with a parallel production of the correspondent expressions, without any sensation or consciousness of effort. On awakening he appeared to himself to have a distinct recollection of the whole, and taking his pen, ink and paper, instantly and eagerly wrote down the lines that are here preserved. At this moment he was unfortunately called out by a person on business from Porlock, and detained by him above an hour, and on his return to his room, found, to his no small surprise and mortification, that though he still retained some vague and dim recollection of the general purport of the vision, yet, with the exception of some eight or ten scattered lines and images, all the rest had passed away like the images on the surface of a stream into which a stone had been cast, but alas! without the after restoration of the latter.[14]

There has been some dispute about the accuracy and even the main substance of this story as Coleridge told it in 1816, partly grounded on the observation that the poem, as we read it, does not in fact read or feel like a fragment. It has such artistic unity, such subtle relations in all its parts, its beginning and its end, that some people have suggested that Coleridge employed some artistic licence in bestowing on it the status of a fragment. To make a work that is deliberately fragmentary, that was intended from the outset to be a suggestive ruin, is part of the larger Romantic trope which exploits the open-ended possibilities of the unfinished, the fragmentary and the ruined. Indeed, some critics see the same technique at work in the deliberately unfinished work in chapter 13 of the *Biographia Literaria*, which of course shares *Kubla Khan*'s theme: the creative power of the imagination. Furthermore, the poetic structure and technique of *Kubla Khan* is so rich and delicate, and its web of literary allusion so carefully wrought, that some critics have doubted that it could have been composed in a dream or with anything less than full poetic concentration. However, there is support for Coleridge's prefatory note in 1816 from the Crewe Manuscript, which only emerged in the twentieth century and reads: 'This fragment was a good deal more, not recoverable, composed, in a sort of Reverie brought on by two grains of Opium, taken to check a dysentery, at a Farm House between Porlock & Linton, a quarter of a mile from Culbone Church, in the fall of the year, 1797. S. T. Coleridge.'[15] So it would seem that whatever subsequent polishing he may have done, the poem arrived with him or surfaced from his unconscious as a kind of gift.

In the Crewe Manuscript note, Coleridge insists that the opium was taken for medicinal purposes and not as a stimulus to composition. But much later in 1810, when he had begun to face his opium addiction with more honesty, Coleridge looked back on the autumn of 1797, in a long note giving an agonised retrospective on his life since this golden year and on the losses and misunderstandings that followed it, including a little detail in which he remembers that 'the retirement between Linton and Porlock was the first occasion of my having recourse to opium'.[16] Coleridge had certainly been prescribed opium and used it on many occasions before this, because it was commonly used to dull pain, so the phrase 'having recourse to opium' may be intended to mean that this was the first time he had chosen to use it as a stimulus or a psychological prop. For the note says that he was suffering from the ill effects of a terrible argument with Charles Lloyd, the unstable young man who was his lodger and whom he had been trying to help, and that he had retreated to the farmhouse both to recover emotionally and to try and compose poetry. There is nothing in this notebook entry to suggest he was ill when he took the opium. But if indeed this was the first time he had 'recourse' to opium in this particular sense, then it is indeed a significant and sinister occasion, and looking back years later, Coleridge would have perceived the dreadful irony that even as he received and composed one of his greatest poems he was setting out on a self-destructive course with a drug which, far from inspiring him, would ultimately corrupt and freeze the well-springs of his inspiration.

If he had begun to flirt with the drug as more than 'an anodyne' in that autumn, he was still in what drug users call the 'honeymoon' period and his great powers were intact and un-interfered with. For what welled up within Coleridge on that October evening was itself a great river poem, a poem which would embody implicit truths about the imagination that Coleridge, himself, would not make explicit until many years later.

Kubla Khan
Or, a vision in a dream. A Fragment.

In Xanadu did KUBLA KHAN
A stately pleasure-dome decree:

Where ALPH, the sacred river, ran
Through caverns measureless to man
    Down to a sunless sea.
So twice five miles of fertile ground
With walls and towers were girdled round;
And there were gardens bright with sinuous rills,
Where blossomed many an incense-bearing tree;
And here were forests ancient as the hills,
Enfolding sunny spots of greenery.

But oh that deep romantic chasm which slanted
Down the green hill athwart a cedarn cover!
A savage place! as holy and inchanted
As e'er beneath a waning moon was haunted
By woman wailing for her demon-lover!
And from this chasm, with ceaseless turmoil seething,
As if this earth in fast thick pants were breathing,
A mighty fountain momently was forced:
Amid whose swift half-intermitted Burst
Huge fragments vaulted like rebounding hail,
Or chaffy grain beneath the thresher's flail:
And mid these dancing rocks at once and ever
It flung up momently the sacred river.
Five miles meandering with a mazy motion
Through wood and dale the sacred river ran,
Then reached the caverns measureless to man,
And sank in tumult to a lifeless ocean;
And 'mid this tumult Kubla heard from far
Ancestral voices prophesying war!

    The shadow of the dome of pleasure
    Floated midway on the waves;

Where was heard the mingled measure
From the fountain and the caves.
It was a miracle of rare device,
A sunny pleasure-dome with caves of ice!

A damsel with a dulcimer
In a vision once I saw:
It was an Abyssinian maid
And on her dulcimer she play'd,
Singing of Mount Abora.
Could I revive within me
Her symphony and song,
To such a deep delight 'twould win me,
That with music loud and long,
I would build that dome in air,
That sunny dome! those caves of ice!
And all who heard should see them there,
And all should cry, Beware! Beware!
His flashing eyes, his floating hair!
Weave a circle round him thrice,
And close your eyes with holy dread:
For he on honey-dew hath fed,
And drunk the milk of Paradise.[17]

Were someone at last to master the whole of what Coleridge has said about God as the source, both of the world and of the human imagination which apprehends that world, they might at the end of their endeavour look back to this little poem written in distraction and fever by the young Coleridge, and find that everything had already been said here; not in technical, theological language, but in what Coleridge called the language of living symbols. The river that rises and runs through this poem is not only a 'sacred river', but is significantly called 'Alph', a name summoning both the Hebrew Aleph and Greek Alpha, and, therefore, the title of Christ the *Logos*, as Alpha and Omega. This river with its beauty, its dancing imagery, emerges from invisibility into visibility, and then dives deeply again to depths we cannot measure.

It is this sacred river which makes our ground fertile. Like *Kubla*, we can measure and fence, cultivate and build, have our art and our life, cultivate our garden on the side of the river, our 'twice five miles of fertile ground', and our 'gardens bright with sinuous rills'. But the river itself, we cannot contain; its source is beyond us, and so is the sea to which it flows. All our art, beautiful as it may be, rightly as it may be called 'a miracle of rare device', is, in comparison with the life of the sacred river on whose sides we are camping, no more than the shadow of the dome of pleasure floating mid-way on the waves. And yet the second movement of the poem closes with an intimation that we ourselves come from the source of that river, flowing out of Paradise, and that we are called to find that again. This intimation is given through the final image of the inspired poet acknowledging the source of his inspiration:

Weave a circle round him thrice,
And close your eyes with holy dread:
For he on honeydew hath fed,
And drunk the milk of Paradise.[18]

The river is both the river of Imagination and the river of Being, arising from the same source; and Coleridge's own account of writing the poem begins with the image of a river rising from its source and finishes with the image of reflections on the surface of a stream. 'All the images rose up . . . as things with a parallel production of the correspondent expressions without any sensation of consciousness or effort . . .' and, 'All the rest had passed away like images on the surface of a stream onto which a stone has been cast.'

If writing *Kubla Khan* had been the experience of the twin streams of Being and Imagination, flowing through Coleridge's mind from their unknowable and unimagined Source in 'caverns measureless to man', then much of his later prose writing was done in the effort to follow these twin streams back to their sacred source. As Coleridge himself wrote in a notebook of 1814:

> I have read of two rivers passing through the same lake, yet all the way preserving their streams visibly distinct. In a far finer distinction, yet in a subtler union, such, for the contemplative mind, are the streams of knowing and being. The lake is formed by the two streams in man and nature as it exists in and for man; and up this lake the philosopher sails on the junction-line of the constituent streams, still pushing upward and sounding as he goes, towards the common fountain-head of both, the mysterious source whose being is knowledge, whose knowledge is being – the adorable I AM IN THAT I AM.[19]

Whatever he subsequently came to feel about this poem, and whatever made him hold back until he finally published it at Byron's instigation in 1816, simply to have composed it at all must have given Coleridge some lift and confidence. He had seen the mysterious river of his own creative imagination emerge suddenly and powerfully into the light; he had indeed, for himself and for his readers, 'built that dome in air'; he had in some sense both inwardly and outwardly confirmed his vocation as a poet, as that mysterious, perhaps dangerous figure with flashing eyes and floating hair who appears at the end of *Kubla Khan*. The same figure would emerge in the wild looks, the glittering eye, at the beginning of *The Ancient Mariner*.

A few weeks after the composition of *Kubla Khan*, Coleridge and both of the Wordsworths set out together on a walking tour, the first leg of which would cover the same ground between

Porlock and Linton that Coleridge had covered the month before
with such momentous consequences. They set out from Alfoxton
at 4.30 on a wintry afternoon on 13 November, and the light
must already have been beginning to fail. As they walked, it
occurred to them that they might between them quickly compose
a racy poem telling some supernatural or gothic tale in ballad
form, which they felt confident they could sell to the *Monthly
Magazine* for £5 and so defray the expenses of their walking
tour. Coleridge remembered that John Cruickshank, a Stowey
friend and neighbour, had recently told him about a disturbing
dream in which he had seen a spectral ship. Both Coleridge and
Wordsworth had recently been reading books of voyages and
discoveries to stock their minds with poetic images. Soon the
outline of a story, to be told by an ancient mariner, began to form
in their minds. This is how Wordsworth recollected it forty years
later:

> For example, some crime was to be committed which would
> bring upon the Old Navigator, as Coleridge afterwards delighted
> to call him, the spectral persecution . . . and his own wanderings.
> I had been reading in Shelvocke's Voyages, a day or two before,
> that, while doubling Cape Horn, they frequently saw albatrosses
> in that latitude, the largest sort of sea-fowl . . . 'Suppose,' said I,
> 'you represent him as having killed one of these birds on entering
> the South Sea, and that the tutelary spirits of these regions take
> upon them to avenge the crime.' The incident was thought fit for
> the purpose and adopted accordingly.[20]

As Wordsworth remarked many years later, 'The Ancient Mariner,
grew and grew until it became too important for our first object
and we began to think of a volume . . .'[21] That volume was the
Lyrical Ballads of which *The Ancient Mariner* was the first poem
in the first edition. By the time the poets returned from this brief

tour, the poem was a ballad of some 300 lines, but it is clear that, by this time, Coleridge's imagination was fully engaged and the deepest springs of his inspiration were open and flowing. He took the poem back with him to Nether Stowey and worked on it throughout the end of that year, through the New Year and into the first days of spring, until four months later on 23 March 1798 he would read to William and Dorothy a poem of over 600 lines, which was the whole of *The Ancient Mariner*, substantially as we have it, though he would continue to revise and refine this poem for the rest of his life. Even the version in *Poetical Works* of 1834, the year of his death, has minor revisions. And of course, the publication of the poem in *Sibylline Leaves* of 1817, whose 200th anniversary this book celebrates, added the famous gloss which brings out some of the depths in the poem that Coleridge himself only saw as he began to live them.

We will turn to the full text of *The Mariner* in Part II of this book. But to conclude this Prelude to *The Mariner* we will consider *Frost at Midnight*, the third, great and formative poem, composed in February of 1798, while Coleridge was still working on and revising *The Mariner*. We touched on *Frost at Midnight* in chapter 1 – a passage that evoked Coleridge's childhood memories of hearing the church bells in the village of Ottery St Mary – but it is worth looking at the whole poem and its setting in the domestic hearth of Nether Stowey before we embark with Coleridge and his mariner on a darker voyage.

Frost at Midnight is a poem that explores the relationship between the inner world of our consciousness and the outer world we inhabit, between the images with which we clothe and express our inner thoughts and the images of the world around us, which also seem to express our minds. The poem has a deceptive simplicity; it opens with the poet sitting up late at night in front of the dying embers of the fire in the Nether Stowey cottage, in quiet and solitude, with his infant son Hartley slumbering beside him. And a stream of association, partly mediated through the image of the fire dying in the grate, leads him back first to memories of his own childhood, then forwards and out to an imagined future for his own child, and then finally, back again to the cottage.

The images in this poem are beautifully realised with great fidelity to nature as Coleridge has observed it. There is no straining to introduce symbolism, or to reduce the things he observes in nature to the status of mere ciphers or allegories. He is not trying to seize upon an image in order to make a point, and indeed he would regard it as an infidelity to nature to do so. In discussing the work of Bowles, a contemporary whom he otherwise admired he wrote:

> 'There reigns thro' all the blank-verse poems such a perpetual trick of *moralizing* every thing – which is very well, occasionally – but never to see or describe any interesting appearance in nature, without connecting it by dim analogies with the moral world, proves faintness of Impression. Nature has her proper interest; & he will know what it is, who believes & feels, that every Thing has a Life of it's [*sic*] own, & that we are all *one Life*. A Poet's *Heart & Intellect* should be *combined*, *intimately* combined & *unified*, with the great appearances in Nature – & not merely held in solution & loose mixture with them, in the shape of formal Similies.'[22]

Nevertheless, we have the sense throughout this poem that as well as giving us these beautiful descriptions, Coleridge's mind is communing through the appearances of nature he describes, through the seas and hills, the fire, frost and moonlight, with the mind behind nature. Nature herself, celebrated for her own beauties, becomes in the course of this poem both the medium and the language of that communion. So the poem opens:

> The Frost performs its secret ministry,
> Unhelped by any wind. The owlet's cry
> Came loud—and hark, again! loud as before.[23]

Coleridge is opening his heart and speaking directly to us in the present continuous, his request that we 'hark again' to the owlet's cry that he is hearing gives us a sense of immediacy and presence with him. This is one of the poem's many paradoxes: it is a poem in some senses about solitude, and yet we are invited vividly and presently into the intimacy of that solitude.

> The inmates of my cottage, all at rest,
> Have left me to that solitude, which suits
> Abstruser musings: save that at my side
> My cradled infant slumbers peacefully.
> 'Tis calm indeed! so calm, that it disturbs
> And vexes meditation with its strange
> And extreme silentness.[24]

Before the reflections and echoes between the inner and the outer, which form the poem's main theme, Coleridge draws a contrast between the hush of nature and the disquieting sense of movement and restlessness in his own mind, which is what has kept him awake.

> Sea, hill, and wood,
> This populous village! Sea, and hill, and wood,
> With all the numberless goings on of life,
> Inaudible as dreams![25]

This is simply a beautiful evocation of the sleeping village of Nether Stowey, in its setting among the hills by the sea. But also it introduces subtly to our minds the notion of the potential for speech hidden in silence. The 'sea, and hill, and wood' are all for the present inaudible, but there is a distinct suggestion that they could speak had we but ears to hear them; that they have about them the intimations of a deeper meaning that adheres to the imagery of dreams.

So Coleridge continues:

> the thin blue flame
> Lies on my low burnt fire, and quivers not;
> Only that film, which fluttered on the grate,
> Still flutters there, the sole unquiet thing.
> Methinks, its motion in this hush of nature
> Gives it dim sympathies with me who live,
> Making it a companionable form,
> Whose puny flaps and freaks the idling Spirit
> By its own moods interprets, every where
> Echo or mirror seeking of itself,
> And makes a toy of Thought.[26]

Now he introduces for the first time the notion of a direct reflection between the inner and the outer. He begins with the first, perhaps the easiest; one might say the lowest level of that sympathy or connection, which is the one that we make in fancy for ourselves. We see something exterior and seize upon it, and our imagination shapes it and turns it to a symbol for that which is within. Coleridge frankly admits that the symbol he makes out of the little film of ash fluttering in the grate is entirely his own: 'Methinks, its motion . . . / Gives it dim sympathies with me . . .'

And yet he introduces the idea that there is something within us which is not content to look at the mere surface of nature, something which looks out and beyond, and seeks in nature the 'echo or mirror' of the stirrings it feels within itself. Then comes that experience we all have when an outward and visible object becomes the gateway or the window through which the mind is drawn, either out into the imaginary world or back through memory to other times. In this case the object that becomes the gateway to Coleridge's past is the fire in the grate. The poem begins in the present, with Coleridge, a young father, gazing at the last embers of the fire through the grate, and shifts back to Coleridge the schoolboy, staring at the schoolroom fire, remembering the stories he had been told as a still-younger boy, at home in the rural vicarage, of how the fluttering back and forth of the last little film of ash on the fire, knocking at the grate, presaged the arrival of a stranger knocking at the cottage door, which was why the country people called that last flapping film of ash, the 'stranger'. So Coleridge writes:

> But O! how oft,
> How oft, at school, with most believing mind,
> Presageful, have I gazed upon the bars,
> To watch that fluttering stranger ! and as oft
> With unclosed lids, already had I dreamt
> Of my sweet birth-place, and the old church-tower,
> Whose bells, the poor man's only music, rang
> From morn to evening, all the hot Fair-day,
> So sweetly, that they stirred and haunted me
> With a wild pleasure, falling on mine ear
> Most like articulate sounds of things to come![27]

Thus Coleridge in the cottage at Stowey is reminded, as he looks at the fire, of Coleridge the schoolboy. But in turn, he's reminded of Coleridge the schoolboy at that very time also being reminded by the fire to look further back. It is as though we have not so much a double vision as a triple vision; he is remembering himself remembering.

The boy, unhappy at school, looks at the fire and thinks of visitors, home and holidays, and of his early childhood growing up in the little vicarage of Ottery St Mary: 'I dreamt / Of my sweet birth-place, and the old church-tower'. And that memory itself triggers another memory: that of a young child, of hearing the bells ring in the church, 'Whose bells, the poor man's only music, rang / From morn to evening, all the hot Fair-day, / So sweetly'. And then these remembered bells themselves seem to be stirring in his imagination, and speaking of something beyond themselves, 'So sweetly, that they stirred and haunted me / With a wild pleasure, falling on mine ear / Most like articulate sounds of things to come!' It is as though we pass through one layer after another; each layer seems to beckon us to the one beyond it. The passage thus far has been backwards, taking us closer and closer to the source of things in Coleridge's childhood.

When Coleridge, the schoolboy, wakes guiltily from his reverie he takes comfort from the country superstition that the knocking of the last ash in the fire, 'the stranger', might prophesy a knock upon the door that would really set him free from the schoolroom and take him back in fact, not just in fancy, to his childhood home.

And so I brooded all the following morn,
Awed by the stern preceptor's face, mine eye
Fixed with mock study on my swimming book:
Save if the door half opened, and I snatched
A hasty glance, and still my heart leaped up,
For still I hoped to see the *stranger's* face,[28]

This is a particular childhood memory, and yet in the gathering symbolism of the poem, it becomes much more. For in one sense, the whole poem is about listening for a knock from behind the door of nature; it's about hoping to find that the world around us is not a blank wall, but a door or a window. It is about hoping that we might glimpse that face which is behind nature. In a sense, Coleridge is saying of the whole cosmos what he says of the schoolroom door: 'A hasty glance, and still my heart leaped up, / For still I hoped to see the stranger's face'.

Then he returns us to the present. He looks down at his sleeping child, and realises that now, he, Samuel Taylor Coleridge, is no longer a child, but an adult, with the care of a child himself. And so he speaks to Hartley:

> Dear Babe, that sleepest cradled by my side,
> Whose gentle breathings, heard in this deep calm,
> Fill up the interspersed vacancies
> And momentary pauses of the thought!
> My babe so beautiful! it thrills my heart
> With tender gladness, thus to look at thee,
> And think that thou shalt learn far other lore,
> And in far other scenes![29]

Coleridge goes on to contrast the childhood he hopes he can provide for Hartley with his own devastating experience of having been taken from the bliss of his early days at Ottery St Mary, to be pent up in the grime of London as a schoolboy at Christ's Hospital. Coleridge remembers how the stars were the one thing unsmudged by the dirt of the city, the one living link with the memories of his childhood and the beauties of nature:

> For I was reared
> In the great city, pent 'mid cloisters dim,
> And saw nought lovely but the sky and stars.[30]

So, in *Frost at Midnight*, Coleridge moves from the memory of himself as a child on the roof of Christ's Hospital watching the stars, to think of how his own child might be brought up.

But *thou*, my babe! shalt wander like a breeze
By lakes and sandy shores, beneath the crags
Of ancient mountain, and beneath the clouds,
Which image in their bulk both lakes and shores
And mountain crags: so shalt thou see and hear
The lovely shapes and sounds intelligible
Of that eternal language, which thy God
Utters, who from eternity doth teach
Himself in all, and all things in himself.
Great universal Teacher! he shall mould
Thy spirit, and by giving make it ask.[31]

In this passage, Coleridge approaches the heart of what he has to say in his poem. He prepares our mind for the notion that the beauties, the shapes and sounds, of nature might be themselves and yet be more than themselves, by beginning first at the level of analogy. He compares the wanderings of his boy as he grows up to a wandering breeze. Then he introduces the word 'image', which he uses, not in its usual sense as a noun, but in a new sense, as a verb, and he suggests that one part of nature images another part of nature: 'by lakes and sandy shores, beneath the clouds / Which image in their bulk both lakes and shores / And mountain crags'. Here, the cloud-mountains correspond to the physical mountains, which in turn are reflected in the lakes. All these examples of one thing *imaging* and referring to another prepare the imagination to receive the more explicit teaching: that nature herself may be imaging that which is beyond nature: that nature may be not only a distinct series of opaque objects, but also a language of symbols.

The lovely shapes and sounds intelligible
Of that eternal language, which thy God
Utters,

136

This is one of Coleridge's most important insights. He never ceased to be amazed by the fact that nature is intelligible: that we not only perceive it in a coherent and ordered way, but its very coherence and order provides us with a vocabulary of symbols with which to explore a similar coherence and order both within ourselves, and beyond or through the veil of nature. Throughout his life, he tried to build a coherent system of thought on the foundation of this insight. In this system, the analogy of language is crucial. In his later prose he works out the foundations and structure of such a system in a rigorous and rational way. But in one sense, the heart of it had already been disclosed to him intuitively in this poem. As often happens, imagination was the forerunner of reason. In this poem, he expresses the intuition that the world in which we find ourselves, and all its contents – its lakes, its mountains, the shining stars – are themselves words, within an 'eternal language which God utters'. And what is taught in that language? It is not the accumulation of observations and statistics which passes for science, but rather the language of the cosmos which, rightly heard, teaches, or perhaps reaches towards, the hidden speaker of that language: the One 'who from eternity doth teach / Himself in all, and all things in himself. / Great universal Teacher!'

The poem then returns from the speculation about Hartley growing up, back to its point of origin; the midnight hush in the cottage in Nether Stowey, and we return with it; but we return changed by our journey through these images. We come back to the first image with which the poem began, but in a sense we understand it for the first time. So Coleridge continues,

> Therefore all seasons shall be sweet to thee,
> Whether the summer clothe the general earth
> With greenness, or the redbreast sit and sing
> Betwixt the tufts of snow on the bare branch

Of mossy apple-tree, while the nigh thatch
Smokes in the sun-thaw; whether the eave-drops fall
Heard only in the trances of the blast,
Or if the secret ministry of frost
Shall hang them up in silent icicles,
Quietly shining to the quiet Moon.[32]

When we began the poem, we might have read the words, 'The frost Performs its secret ministry / Unhelped by any wind' simply as an analogy. We might have thought it a quaint poeticism to suggest that frost had in any sense a ministry or service, let alone any of the aura that surrounds a word like 'ministry': the aura of priesthood, the suggestion that in some sense the minister is concerned with sacraments, with gateways to God. By the time we've finished the poem and grasped that the frost and the moon-light are part of those 'lovely shapes and sounds intelligible / Of that eternal language' uttered by God, we can understand, at last, the full weight of meaning concealed in the poem's opening line, 'The Frost performs its secret *ministry*'. It is as though Coleridge is saying, 'hark! and hark again' – when we hear the word 'minis-try' in the opening line, we do not know what to make of it; but when 'we hark again' to the closing lines of the poem, we have a completely new understanding of what it might mean to speak of the 'secret ministry of frost'. This in turn opens our imagination to receive the final image of the 'quiet moon' as the image of one who is also a minister of God.

This final picture of the quiet moon at the end of *Frost at Midnight* is an apt image to finish the first part of this book. In Part II, we shall see how the rise of the moon and the transfigur-ing power of its reflected light open the way for a personal recov-ery and renewal of vision for the mariner in his darkest hour. This would prove true for Coleridge too. During this miraculous year at Nether Stowey, it seems he could always hear and discern the glory and meaning in all things; 'the lovely shapes and sounds' of the Quantock landscape were, indeed, an intelligible and eternal language which Coleridge could read and translate for us. But the time would come, not many years hence, when the world would become opaque to him, when he would 'see, not feel'[33] the beauty around him. Strangely, *The Ancient Mariner*, the poem he completed a month after the radiance and vision of *Frost at Midnight*, tells the story of that loss, darkness and desolation before it happened, but it also holds out the promise of recovery. It is to that poem that we now turn.

Part II

The Mariner's Tale

'Strangely, perversely, suddenly, he was shooting a deadly bolt into the heart of his marriage and, indeed, into the heart of the woman he loved, just as suddenly and irrevocably as the mariner shot his albatross.'

CHAPTER SIX

The Ship Was Cheered

An ancient Mariner meeteth three Gallants bidden to a wedding-feast, and detaineth one	It is an ancient Mariner, And he stoppeth one of three. "By thy long grey beard and glittering eye, Now wherefore stopp'st thou me?" *(Lines 1–4 with gloss)*

We turn now to *The Rime of the Ancient Mariner* itself, the tale that Coleridge imagined his mariner telling to a hapless wedding guest; in some ways it is impossible not to become a little like the wedding guest himself as we hear it, at once enthralled and appalled.

'Now wherefore stopp'st thou me?' asks the guest, in the very first verse. With him, we need to keep asking ourselves as we read the question: Why am *I* hearing this? We empathise with the poor wedding guest who wonders why he should be the unlucky one picked out by this embarrassing 'grey beard loon' while his two friends go merrily off to the festivities. The first time he and we ask this question 'why me?' it is at the most trivial and resentful level that such a question can be asked. But even as the water deepens under the keel of a mysterious ship, so the question 'why me?', 'Wherefore stopps't thou me?' deepens for the wedding guest and for us. It is only towards the very end of the poem that the mariner reveals that this meeting, this stopping one of three, is not in the least random, for he knows intuitively who needs to hear his story, who it is for whom the experience of hearing his story will turn out to be a turning point in their story.

143

As we read through each part of this poem and open out its meaning, we will be asking and answering this 'wherefore' question, for ourselves in our own age, and also for Coleridge. The task of writing this poem came to Coleridge rather as the mariner comes to the guest: as an unexpected interruption, a compelling diversion from his main agenda, but in the end, as much for the poet as for the wedding guest, the experience of the poem became so personal that it changed everything.

So the mariner holds the wedding guest spellbound with his 'glittering eye' and commences his tale. The start of the voyage seems auspicious enough: the ship is cheered, sets off in bright sunlight to sail south. In a couple of stanzas, Coleridge has already brought us right down to the equator, the 'Line' as he calls it in the gloss, indicated by the phrase in the poem that the sun is 'over the mast at noon'.

The Mariner tells how the ship sailed southward with a good wind and fair weather, till it reached the line.

The Sun came up upon the left,
Out of the sea came he!
And he shone bright, and on the right
Went down into the sea.

Higher and higher every day,
Till over the mast at noon—

(Lines 25–30)

And here, with the ship poised between the hemispheres, about to cross an invisible line, towards, in every sense, a different polarity, the mariner's narrative suddenly breaks off and we are reminded of the guest still desperate to get to the wedding, as we are given a glimpse of the bride arriving. But the mariner still casts his spell and the wedding guest 'cannot choose but hear'. We are plunged back into the story and as we cross the line, the whole tone changes; we leave all that is familiar, and voyage into the unknown. We also become aware at this point of the way in which, as the mariner tells his story, all the elements of nature are personal and are perceived quite literally as persons:

The ship driven by a storm toward the south pole.

And now the storm-blast came, and he
Was tyrannous and strong:
He struck with his o'ertaking wings,
And chased us south along.

(*Lines 41–4 with gloss*)

Indeed, the way the ship herself becomes a terrified person:

With sloping masts and dipping prow,
As who pursued with yell and blow
Still treads the shadow of his foe,
And forward bends his head,
The ship drove fast, loud roar'd the blast,
The southward aye we fled.

(*Lines 45–50*)

So here we have the image of fleeing *from* the shadow of some unknown foe, and as we shall see in the poem the ship is driven towards a profound confrontation in strange waters *with* the unknown. What lies ahead of her is more fearful than the shadow from which she flees, but so it often is with us, and so it proved to be with Coleridge.

Then the tone and feel of the poem changes again. After the swift driving rhythms of the extended six-line stanza about the storm, we emerge back into the poem's more regular four-line verse and have a moment of calm and leisure to observe the strange place to which we have been driven; a place of extremity, of beauty and of loneliness.

The land of ice, and of fearful sounds where no living thing was to be seen. And now there came both mist and snow,
And it grew wondrous cold:
And ice, mast-high, came floating by,
As green as emerald.

And through the drifts the snowy clifts
Did send a dismal sheen:
Nor shapes of men nor beasts we ken—
The ice was all between.

(Lines 51–8 with gloss)

This sense of being in a place utterly bereft of life is an essential prelude to the arrival of the albatross. As the sole living thing in this icy region, the albatross will carry in itself, as though in a sacred vessel, all that *life* means, its very essence, shared by all living things. It represents all that Coleridge had meant by his phrase 'the one Life', in *The Eolian Harp*:

O the one Life within us and abroad,
Which meets all motion and becomes its soul,
A light in sound, a sound-like power in light,
Rhythm in all thought, and joyance every where—
Methinks, it should have been impossible
Not to love all things in a world so filled.[1]

But before the albatross arrives we have the eerie 'unlife' of the ice itself, and its threatening sounds.

The ice was here, the ice was there,
The ice was all around:
It cracked and growled, and roar'd and howl'd,
Like noises in a swound!

(Lines 59–62)

The line 'Like noises in a swound' is very important. The intentionally archaic word 'swound' means a 'faint' or trance and is related to the more modern word swoon. In one sense there is a brilliant accuracy to this simile: the strange sounds coming and going all around and the groaning of the ice are like the strange interior sounds that people may hear when losing or recovering consciousness. But this simile is here for more than surface accuracy; it also affects the way we will read the poem, and particularly the coming section, by its power of suggestion or association. A swoon or 'swound' is an involuntary transition from one form of consciousness to another, from the surfaces of waking to the depths of dreaming. To suggest to us the experience of a 'swound' just at the moment when Coleridge is about to introduce the all-important figure of the albatross into the poem allows us to perceive the bird at both levels: the living creature perceived by the waking mind, and the deeper symbol of the dream.

Till a great sea-bird, called the Albatross, came through the snow-fog, and was received with great joy and hospitality.

At length did cross an Albatross,
Thorough the fog it came;
As if it had been a Christian soul,
We hailed it in God's name.

(Lines 60–3 with gloss)

It is at this freezing zero point of complete isolation that the albatross appears, glimmering out of the fog. The bird emerges into the poem surrounded and haloed by words that carry numinous and specifically Christian associations, 'Christian Soul' and 'God's Name', but also, though at this point by means of wordplay, 'Cross'. The internal rhyme of *cross* and *albatross* in the first line of the bird's appearance prepares us for the much more sustained and deliberate association of the cross with the albatross later in the poem, culminating in the lines 'instead of the cross the albatross / about my neck was hung'. ✓ ⌄

(*Swound means faint*)

The appearance of the albatross at this stage in the story had always been intended as a turning point in the plot, even when this was first conceived as a much lighter popular-gothic ballad. As Martin Gardner comments, in his *Annotated Ancient Mariner*,

> It was Wordsworth who proposed to Coleridge that an albatross be brought into his ballad and that the shooting of the bird provide the Mariner's "crime". The idea had been suggested to Wordsworth by his reading of *A Voyage Round the World by the Way of the Great South Sea*, by Captain George Shelvocke, London, 1726. Shelvocke speaks of a "disconsolate black albatross" . . . that followed the ship for several days "hovering about us as if he had lost himself, till Hatley, (my second captain) observing, in one of his melancholy fits, that this bird was always hovering near us, imagined, from his color, that it might be some ill omen. That which, I suppose, induced him the more to encourage his superstition, was the continued series of contrary tempestuous winds, which had oppressed us ever since we had got into the sea. But be that as it would, he, after some fruitless attempts, at length, shot the albatross, not doubting (perhaps) that we should have a fair wind after it.[2]

But as we have seen, although Coleridge draws many elements from Shelvocke – the shooting itself and the sailors' superstitions, indeed their notion that the bird should be instrumental to their purposes and they could shoot it for better weather – he also changes and enhances this material. There is no suggestion in Shelvocke of the numinous aura with which Coleridge surrounds the albatross, nor is there any evocation of the sacred laws of hospitality. Although Coleridge later refers to the superstitions about the bird bringing contrary weather, it is important to note that unlike Shelvocke he does not make that the motive for shooting the bird. Indeed, at no point is any motive ascribed to the mariner's sudden murderous action, with all its huge implications; it is the sense of mystery, intensified by this omission, that allows the shooting of the albatross to carry the symbolic weight of 'the fall' in the deepest theological sense: the mystery of human evil itself.

If we look back to Shelvocke as a source for this episode in the poem, it is also worth looking forward to Coleridge's contemporaries and successors in the nineteenth century for other accounts of encounters with albatrosses, to get a sense of their impact. Of particular interest, is the passage in chapter 42 in *Moby Dick*, in which Melville's narrator describes an albatross in very Coleridgean terms, and even evokes Coleridge's name, though claiming at the same time that he was not influenced by Coleridge's description. 'Bethink thee of the albatross, whence come those clouds of spiritual wonderment and pale dread, in which that white phantom sails in all imaginations? Not Coleridge first threw that spell; but God's great, unflattering laureate, Nature.'[3]

The association of the albatross with the regal and the divine is made even clearer in a fascinating note appended to this sentence describing the first time Melville himself saw an albatross:

I remember the first albatross I ever saw. It was during a prolonged gale, in waters hard upon the Antarctic seas. From my forenoon watch below, I ascended to the overclouded deck; and there, dashed upon the main hatches, I saw a regal, feathery thing of unspotted whiteness, and with a hooked, Roman bill sublime. At intervals, it arched forth its vast archangel wings, as if to embrace some holy ark. Wondrous flutterings and throbbings shook it. Though bodily unharmed, it uttered cries, as some king's ghost in supernatural distress. Through its inexpressible, strange eyes, methought I peeped to secrets which took hold of God. As Abraham before the angels, I bowed myself; the white thing was

Coleridge was a source for Moby Dick albatross

so white, its wings so wide, and in those for ever exiled waters, I had lost the miserable warping memories of traditions and of towns. Long I gazed at that prodigy of plumage. I cannot tell, can only hint, the things that darted through me then.

Later in this same note Melville specifically asserts:

So that by no possibility could Coleridge's wild Rhyme have had aught to do with those mystical impressions which were mine, when I saw that bird upon our deck. For neither had I then read the Rhyme, nor knew the bird to be an albatross. Yet, in saying this, I do but indirectly burnish a little brighter the noble merit of the poem and the poet.

Of course, it is in the very nature of poetry, as Coleridge asserted, that it should awaken the mind's attention and restore to it a sense of wonder, of feelings 'analogous to the supernatural'. Whether or not Melville's subsequent description of this first sighting is intensified by the encounter with Coleridge, there can be no doubt that Coleridge intends us, as his readers, to have this intense apprehension of the bird as bodying forth a spiritual power and meaning.

The welcome bestowed on the albatross by the ship's crew is set not only in a human, but in a sacral frame: 'as if it had been a Christian soul, we hailed it in God's name'. The gloss expands on this further, telling us that the bird was 'received with great joy and hospitality'. Given this sacral framing, the sharing of food with the albatross also takes on a potentially sacramental meaning.

'At length did cross an albatross': the albatross also appears at a crossing place or a turning point in both the narrative and the voyage. Before the albatross arrives they are still heading southwards into an impasse, into iciness and death, but the appearance of the bird and its guidance turns everything around, including the direction of the ship.

> It ate the food it ne'er had eat,
> And round and round it flew.
> The ice did split with a thunder-fit;
> The helmsman steer'd us through!

And lo! the Albatross proveth a bird of good omen, and followeth the ship as it returned northward through fog and floating ice.

> And a good south wind sprung up behind;
> The Albatross did follow,
> And every day, for food or play,
> Came to the Mariner's hollo!
>
> *(Lines 67–74 with gloss)*

Again the gloss makes this change of direction clearer as well as heightening the numinous or supernatural significance of the albatross. Now the relationship between the ship's company and the bird, already made sacred by shared hospitality and the invocation of God's name, is given a further association with *vespers*, the last prayers at night, and with the moonlight, which will prove so redemptive for the mariner later in the poem.

> In mist or cloud, on mast or shroud,
> It perch'd for vespers nine;
> Whiles all the night, through fog-smoke white,
> Glimmered the white Moon-shine.
>
> *(Lines 75–8)*

It is just at this point – when a crisis has been averted, a turning point achieved, the ship has been steered through the ice barriers, which open before the bird, and she is on her way north again – that Coleridge suddenly breaks the mariner's narrative, brings us back into the 'present' where the mariner stands speaking to the wedding guest, and in the dramatic climax to this first part of the poem, gives us the guest's view of the mariner as he makes his horrifying confession:

The ancient Mariner inhospitably killeth the pious bird of good omen.

"God save thee, ancient Mariner!
From the fiends, that plague thee thus!—
Why look'st thou so?"—"With my cross-bow
I shot the Albatross."

(Lines 79–82 with gloss)

In one way nothing could be plainer or clearer than the mariner's blunt statement 'with my cross-bow / I shot the Albatross'. It has the irrefutable finality of sentences like 'and they crucified him' in the Gospels; the dreadful thing is done and cannot be undone. The wedding guest, with his reference to 'fiends' frames the horror in the wider context of devils and angels, of a spiritual struggle between good and evil, but the mariner himself offers neither motivation nor excuse, and in some ways this makes his confession far more stark, powerful and universal. If there is a mystery in goodness, there is also a mystery in human evil, something unfathomable and inexplicable in the perversity of the human world, in our propensity to make havoc of things when they are at their best and to destroy our own happiness when it is at its height. Many years later in 1830, within four years of his death, Coleridge composed for his own use a nightly prayer in which he made his own confession: 'When I fell from thee, into the mystery of the false and evil will [thou] did'st not abandon me, poor self-lost creature, but in thy . . . mercy did'st provide an access and return to thyself'.[4] As this later prayer suggests, Coleridge recognised that evil, in himself and in others, is itself something of a mystery. He spent a lifetime discovering how this poem presaged and interpreted his own life, not least the mysteries of our inner lives and

Turning point of albatross

choices. So let us consider now what became of Coleridge himself in the first years after writing this poem.

At the time he wrote *The Ancient Mariner*, Coleridge had never set foot on board a ship. In his days as a young radical in Bristol, a major seaport, he would have seen the great ships coming and going and, doubtless, have talked with the sea captains, not least as he gathered material first hand for his lectures against the slave trade. But most of the circumstantial details about seafaring in *The Ancient Mariner* were drawn from his voluminous reading of the many books of exploration and adventure available to him.

However, not long after he finished *The Ancient Mariner*, and before it was published in *Lyrical Ballads*, as though impelled by the spell of his own poem, Coleridge himself was to become a mariner.

The spring and summer of 1797, immediately following the completion of the poem, saw more of the heady conversation with Wordsworth that was bringing out the best in both poets, and also the planning and preparation for *Lyrical Ballads*. But there was more afoot. The Wedgwood annuity meant that Coleridge no longer needed to be tied to finding employment as a Unitarian preacher or a schoolmaster, his two previous plans, and he felt strongly that he must complete his unfinished education (for he had taken no degree at Cambridge) as part of his intellectual preparation for a future as an epic poet and philosopher. He hatched a plan to travel for a few months to Germany, to learn the language, go to the universities and imbibe something of the rich philosophical and cultural ferment that was going on there. The Wordsworths' lease on Alfoxton House was running out and would not be renewed, thanks to the suspicion under which they had all fallen.[5] Coleridge was desperate not to lose their company and Wordsworth, in turn, had begun to realise he also needed Coleridge as adviser and ideal reader for *The Recluse*, the philosophical poem he was planning. Soon the Wordsworths were swept up in Coleridge's plans and agreed that they would go to Germany too. Originally Sara Coleridge had also been included in these plans, as Coleridge only intended to be in Germany for a few months and hoped they might somehow manage the travel with the young children; another baby, Berkeley, had been added to the family. But little Berkeley's health was fragile and they changed their minds. Sara would stay behind with the children and Tom Poole promised to look after them. In the light of what was to follow, this proved to be a very bad decision. Not only because Coleridge's separation from his wife at a time of rich intellectual ferment and development in his own mind and spirit meant that they were less and less able to share with each other on an equal footing when he returned, but also because it meant that Coleridge was absent when Sara went through the harrowing experiences of Berkeley's illness and death. Unable to share that pain with the husband she deeply loved, and badly advised by Tom Poole not even to show her grief in letters, it meant that when Coleridge returned there was a gulf between them that in the end neither of them could bridge. So, although 'The ship was cheered, the harbour cleared' and the poets set off merrily enough, Coleridge was, like his mariner, setting off on a journey towards disaster which he could not foresee.

When it came to it, Coleridge proved, in the most practical sense, to be a very good mariner, and to find his sea legs almost at once, unlike the Wordsworths, who retired below decks and were wretchedly seasick, almost all the way from Yarmouth to Hamburg. We know a great deal of circumstantial detail about this German trip, which in the end lasted much longer than the three or four months originally envisaged, because Coleridge wrote a series of vivid and tender journal letters back to Sara, perhaps aware of how left out she was feeling and how important it would be to share everything with her – although in the end letters proved to be not enough.

Coleridge had bought a magnificent greatcoat, in lieu of a blanket, with a collar so wide it could be pulled over and cover his head, and he must have been an extraordinary figure, pacing the deck in it, delighting in the night stars and keeping up a spirited conversation with several Germans and a Dane about politics, philosophy and religion. His letters to Sara give us some wonderful details: as in the moment when all familiar land 'the kirk, the hill, the light-house top' have dropped away below the horizon. 'When we lost sight of land, the moment that we quite lost sight of it, & the heavens all round me rested upon the waters, my dear Babies came upon me like a flash of lightning – I saw their faces so distinctly!'[6]

A little later in the same letter Coleridge sees for himself the very phosphorescent 'stars' that play such an important part in the imagery of *The Mariner*:

The Ocean is a noble Thing by night; a beautiful white cloud of foam at momently intervals roars & rushes by the side of the Vessel, and Stars of Flame dance & sparkle & go out in it – & every now and then light Detachments of Foam dart away from the Vessel's side with their galaxies of stars, & scour out of sight, like a Tartar Troup over a Wilderness! – What these Stars are, I cannot say – the sailors say, that they are the Fish Spawn which is phosphorescent.[7]

The next letter to Sara, beginning 'my dearest love' returns at greater length to this first night at sea. Coleridge stayed up most of the night, having a vigorous philosophico-poetic conversation with a slightly drunken Dane. It was clear they shared the same radical politics, but interestingly, when the Dane assumed this would make Coleridge a sceptic in religion, he was brought up short with a Coleridgean riposte:

After this the Dane talked about Religion, and supposing me to be in *the continental sense* of the expression what I had called myself – 'Un Philosophe', – he talked of Deity in a declamatory style very much resembling some Parts of Payne's devotional Rants in the Age of Reason – & then said, 'what damn'd *Hypocrism* all Jesus Christ's Business was, and ran on in the commonplace style about Christianity – and appeared withered when I professed myself a Christian. I sunk 50 fathoms immediately in his Graces – however I turned the conversation from a subject on which I never think myself allowed not to be in earnest . . .'[8]

After the Dane retires to his cabin, Coleridge stays up half dozing in the lifeboat and gazing out to sea. Here is the glimpse of himself he gives to Sara:

The Dane retired to the Cabin, and I wrapped myself up in my great Coat, lay in the Boat, and looked at the water, the foam of which, that beat against the Ship & coursed along by its sides, & darted off over the Sea, was full of stars of flame . . . I found reason to rejoice in my great Coat, which I bought in London and gave 28 shillings for – a weighty, long, high caped, respectable rug – The Collar will serve for a night Cap, turning my head – I amused myself with two or three bright stars that oscillated with the motion of the sails.[9]

The visit to Germany was originally planned as three months' absence. In the end, Coleridge was away for ten months, an extension of his time away from his family that proved ill fated. Things began well enough, with Coleridge finding good lodgings with a Protestant pastor in Ratzeburg, but quite early on in their time the Wordsworths decided to part company with Coleridge and spend some time on their own. This was initially because they couldn't find lodgings cheap enough in Ratzeburg, for at this stage Coleridge's Wedgwood annuity allowed him more leeway than Wordsworth's allowance. But there were other reasons. Coleridge's entire purpose in going was to learn German, immerse himself in German culture and gain some kind of entry to German university circles, so effectively to complete his education which had been broken off at Cambridge. This plan was perfectly suited to Coleridge's extrovert sociability, his innate gift for languages, and his fascination with the new movements in philosophy and literary criticism. By contrast, Wordsworth, naturally more introverted, was entering a deep period of poetic creativity and needed to be alone with Dorothy, who was effectively his muse and carried the keys to his childhood memories, to think, compose and write in English. Perhaps, the very absence from England focused his thoughts and memories back on the Lakes even more clearly, and ironically what he wrote during his absence from Coleridge was large sections of the poem Wordsworth always referred to 'as the poem to Coleridge' but which we know as *The Prelude*.

Coleridge's loyal friend Tom Poole, for one, and probably Sara Coleridge too, were both pleased at this temporary separation from the Wordsworths and felt it would help Coleridge to enlarge his own mind and to become firmer in his own purposes. For Poole already perceived that Coleridge's hero-worship of Wordsworth might shadow and cramp his own poetic genius. Unfortunately, Poole also thought that it would be a bad thing and a distraction for Coleridge to attempt poetry while he was in Germany, because it would somehow dilute the fullness of his immersion in the German language. This meant that when Coleridge met with Wordsworth again, Wordsworth had a trove of really great poetry and Coleridge had comparatively little, thus confirming Coleridge's sense of inferiority, which Poole was trying to mitigate. But if Coleridge's poetic wings were clipped, his prose, itself composed with much poetic vision, became all the more burnished and vivid. Some of the journals he kept and the journal letters he wrote, he gathered together and published much later in his journal *The Friend* and the *Biographia Literaria*. As we shall see, when one reads these, one often has the uncanny sense of Coleridge experiencing for himself, in image after image, so much of what he had previously only imagined for his mariner.

Autumn deepened into the coldest winter that Germany had experienced for a hundred years. The lake at Ratzeburg froze. Coleridge went skating on it, and sent descriptions to Wordsworth. Some phrases from that description eventually made their way into the famous skating episode in *The Prelude*, but Coleridge found himself fascinated by the ice itself: by the sounds it made, and the extraordinary effects of colour when the light struck it.

Yester-morning I saw the lesser Lake completely hidden by Mist; but the moment the Sun peeped over the Hill, the mist broke in the middle, and in a few seconds stood divided, leaving a broad road all across the Lake; and between these two Walls of mist the sunlight burnt upon the ice, forming a road of golden fire, intolerably bright! and the mist-walls themselves partook of the blaze in a multitude of shining colours. This is our second Frost. About a month ago, before the Thaw came on, there was a storm of wind; during the whole night, such were the thunders and howlings of the breaking ice, that they have left a conviction on my mind, that there are Sounds more sublime than any Sight can be, more absolutely suspending the power of comparison, and more utterly absorbing the mind's self-consciousness in its total attention to the object working upon it. Part of the ice which the vehemence of the wind had shattered, was driven shore-ward and froze anew. On the evening of the next day, at sun-set, the shattered ice thus frozen, appeared of a deep blue, and in shape like an agitated sea; beyond this, the water, that ran up between the great Islands of ice which had preserved their masses entire and smooth, shone of a yellow green; but all these scattered Ice-islands, themselves, were of an intensely bright blood colour – they seemed blood and light in union![10]

One wonders how conscious Coleridge was, both when he saw these things, and when he came to describe them, of how close the experience was to his description of the ice in *The Ancient Mariner*. The shining yellow-green, the same word for the sounds of the ice and its howlings. Certainly, this passage draws out the sense of the sublime, which many readers of the poem feel in the first description of the ice floes of the Antarctic.

For Coleridge that sense of the sublime was also caught up with a sense of awe, of danger and, paradoxically, of a kind of transfigured loneliness; the observer must be alone in order to absorb the scene with complete concentration, and yet in that concentration on the utterly other, in that receiving into the soul of sublime images from beyond itself, the loneliness, which was the condition of such concentration, can suddenly be transfigured into a sense of communion and connection with the vast and sublime and, more deeply still, with life itself. Coleridge expressed these things in a letter to Thomas Wedgwood, three years after his return from Germany, describing not his expedition to the Hartz Mountains, but his great feats of fell walking in the English Lakes.

In simple earnest, I never find myself alone within the embracement of rocks & hills, a travel up an alpine road, but my spirit courses, drives, and eddies, like a Leaf in Autumn: a wild activity, of thoughts, imaginations, feelings, and that blows to no point of the compass, & comes from I know not whence, but agitates the whole of me; my whole Being is filled with waves, as it were, that roll & stumble, one this way, & one that way, like things that have no common master. I think, that my soul must have pre-existed in the body of a Chamois-chaser; feelings & impulsive habits, & incipient actions, are in me, & the old scenery awakens them. The farther I ascend from animated Nature, from men, and cattle, & the common birds of the woods, & fields, the greater becomes in me the Intensity of the feeling of Life; Life seems to me then a universal spirit, that neither has, nor can have, an opposite. God is every where . . .[11]

Just as the mariner finds himself in a new hemisphere, leaving behind the familiar, 'Nor shapes of men nor beasts we ken— / The ice was all between', so Coleridge, both outwardly in the extremities of the German winter, and inwardly in the adventures of his mind and soul, was beginning in his own phrase to 'ascend from animated Nature, from men, and cattle, & the common birds'. For it was in Germany that he began his 'metaphysical' mountain climbing, particularly in reading Kant and trying to ascend mentally beyond the *phenomena*, the world of familiar shapes and appearances, to penetrate what Kant called the *noumena*; those underlying and over-arching realities, pre-existent categories, shapes of the mind itself, which give rise to our ordinary experience, that always exist just beyond or below them. Coleridge's lifelong passion for metaphysics was, at one level, part of his never-appeased desire for truth and meaning, but it also became a retreat, a withdrawal, a refusal of the inconvenient demands of the present: another kind of opium.

Meanwhile, this same severe winter was playing havoc with communications between England and the Continent. Coleridge's long, loving letters were not getting through to Sara, nor were her increasingly anxious and desperate letters to him. When the letters did arrive the months of delay often meant that there was no way for either to respond, as needed, to a crisis. Coleridge, in all his journal letters, always asked tenderly after the children and hoped that all was well: but it was not.

Only three weeks after Coleridge had left for Germany, just as he was beginning to settle at Ratzeburg, disaster struck at Nether Stowey. A faulty batch of an inoculation against smallpox had been administered to a number of the children in the district, including baby Berkeley, who soon developed the disease, the symptoms of which were horrific. Sara put it all in a vivid letter to Coleridge dated 1 November 1798, written in response to his first cheerful letter about his adventures with the Dane on board ship. She wrote:

> . . . my dear baby [Berkeley] on the eighth day began to droop, on the ninth he was very ill and on the tenth the Pustles began to appear in the skin by hundreds.
>
> He lay on my lap like a dead child, burning like fire and all over he was red as scarlet; after I had counted about two hundred I could almost see them coming out and every one that appeared after that, seemed to me a little ugly messenger come bid me prepare for his death! By the thirteenth day every part of his face and body was covered except the pit of his stomach. I was almost distracted! Lewis [the doctor] was frightened – he came six *or eight times a day* – the ladies of Stowey also visited me and wept over this little victim, affected by my complaints, and the miserable plight of the child! What I felt is impossible to write – I had no husband to comfort me and share my grief – perhaps the boy would die, and he [Coleridge] far away! All the responsibility of the infant's life was upon me and it was a weight that dragged me to the earth! He was blind – his nose was clogged that he could not suck and his dear gums and tongue were covered and he so hoarse that he could not cry; but he made a *horrid noise in his throat* which when he dozed for a minute I always heard in my dreams.[12]

Thomas Poole, desperate that Coleridge should not be unnecessarily alarmed or disturbed in case he might break off his essential German education, counselled Sara not to send this letter, but she was so desperate for Coleridge to know what she was going through that she posted it anyway. Unfortunately, it was sent without the right postage and it was stopped at Yarmouth and eventually returned to her. There was a brief period of hope when Berkeley apparently made a recovery and Sara took him to Bristol to be with her own mother and family, thinking the change of air might do him good; but Berkeley had not fully regained his strength and had a convulsion from which he died on 11 February 1799.

Thomas Poole took it upon himself to break the news to Coleridge. In this he doubtless thought he had both Sara's and Coleridge's best interests at heart. Sara, utterly distraught in Bristol where Berkeley had died, might not be expected to write immediately, so Poole undertook to write himself. He felt Coleridge must always be protected from sudden shocks and extremities of feeling, which might upset the delicate balance he seemed to have found and which was enabling him to work so hard on his essentially academic projects in Germany. But, whatever Poole's good intentions, the results of his action were disastrous. He wrote a brisk, seemingly matter-of-fact letter that gave Coleridge a completely false picture of how things really were. Poole began by telling Coleridge that Sara was very well and then went on to say:

> even by reading so far, you *feel the reason* for my wishing to write to you before Mrs Coleridge. I suspect you feel it by the anticipations in your last letter. You say there that you have serious misgivings concerning Berkeley – well – you now, my dear Col., know the worst. I thus give you to understand the catastrophe of the drama, without heightening it by first narrating the circumstances which led to it; but, as you will hear by and by, those

Thomas Poole
tells Coleridge
his baby is sick

circumstances which purely natural, and such as probably no human conduct or foresight could have averted . . . On examination it was found that he died of consumption. Mrs Coleridge was much fatigued during the child's illness, but her health was very good, and she very wisely kept up her spirits . . .

I have thus, my dear Col., informed you of the whole truth. It was long contrary to my opinion to let you know of the child's death before your arrival in England. And I thought, and still think myself justified in the notion, by the OVER-anxiety you expressed in your former letters concerning the children. Doubtless the affection found to exist between parents and *infant* children is a wise law of nature, a mere instinct to preserve Man in his infant state . . . But the moment you make this affection the creature of reason, you degrade reason. When the infant becomes a reasonable being, then let the affection be a thing of reason, not before. Brutes can only have an instinctive affection. Hence, when that ceases to be necessary, all affection ceases. This seems to me to be a great line of demarcation between Men and Beasts, between Reason and Instinct. If then the love of infants be a mere instinct, it is extraordinary particularly when the end of that action, if I may so speak, becomes a nullity . . . Don't conjure up any scenes of distress which never happened. Mrs Coleridge felt as a mother . . . and, in an exemplary manner, did all a mother could do. But she never forgot herself. She is now perfectly well, and does not make herself miserable by recalling the, engaging, though, remember, mere instinctive attractions of an infant a few months old. Heaven and Earth! I have myself within the last month experienced disappointments more weighty than the death of ten infants . . . Let us hear from you circumstantially, let us hear that you are happy . . . We long to see you. But still I say, don't come till you have done your business . . . Heaven bless you, Thos. Poole[13]

Poole sent this letter to Bristol for Sara to see before he posted it and one can only imagine what she felt inwardly on reading this complete travesty of the truth and utter dismissal of her own feelings and the real value of the baby she had lost. She was, perhaps, too prostrate and distraught to gainsay Poole's strong, if misguided, advice and allowed it to be sent. Finally, on Easter Sunday (24 March 1799) she wrote the letter that should have been sent and which Coleridge should have received first.

My darling infant left his wretched Mother on the tenth of February, and tho' the leisure that followed was intolerable to me, yet I could not employ myself in reading or writing, or in any way that prevented my thoughts from resting on him – this parting was the severest trial that I have ever yet undergone and I pray to God that I may never live to behold the death of another child for O my dear Samuel! it is a suffering beyond your conception! You will feel, and lament, the death of your child, but you will only recollect him a baby of fourteen weeks, but I am his Mother, and have carried him in my arms and have fed him at my bosom, and have watched over him by day and night for nine months; I have seen him twice on the brink of the grave but he has returned, and recovered and smiled upon me like an angel – and now I am lamenting that he is gone! . . .

. . . and now my dear Samuel I hope you will be perfectly satisfied that every thing was done for the dear babe that was likely to restore him and endeavour to forget your own loss in contemplating mine. I cannot express how ardently I long for your return, or how much I shall be disappointed if I do not see you in May; I expect a letter from you daily, and am much surprised that you have not written from Gottingen; your last is dated Jan. the 5th and in it you say you will write again immediately – now

this is Easter Sunday March the 24th. You will write once probably after you receive this, from Germany – and I wish you would
be so good as to write me a few lines from London that I may
know the very day when I may see you; . . .

I am much pleased to see you wrote that you "languish to be at
home". O God! I hope you never more will quit it! . . .

God almighty bless you my dearest Love! Sara C–[14]

Both of these letters, of course, took a long time to reach Coleridge
so there was no possibility of the immediate response that Sara so
needed, especially after Poole's letter, with its false assurance of
Sara's wellbeing, arrived first. It was in response, therefore, to
Poole's letter that Coleridge first wrote to Sara on 18 April, falsely
assuming that she had taken these events in her stride. He begins
that letter by putting his finger on the problem: the delay in their
correspondence:

It is one of the discomforts of my absence, my dearest Love!
that we feel the same calamities at different times – I would fain
write words of consolation to you; yet I know that shall only
fan into new activity the pang which was growing dead and dull
in your heart – Dear little Being! – he had existed to me for so
many months only in dreams and reveries, but in them existed
and still exists so livelily, so like a real Thing, that although I
know of his Death, yet when I am not alone and have been long
silent, it seems to me as if I did not understand it. – Methinks,
there is something awful in the thought, what an unknown
Being one's own Infant is to one! – a fit of sound – a flash of
light – a summer gust, that is as it were *created* in the bosom of
the calm Air, that rises up we know not how, and goes we know
not wither! – But we say well; it goes! It is gone! . . . I will not

believe that it ceases – in this moving stirring and harmonious Universe I cannot believe it! – Can cold and darkness come from the Sun? where the Sun is not – there is cold and darkness! – But the living God is every where, & works every where – and where is there room for Death? – To look back on the life of my Baby, how short it seems! – but consider it referently to non-existence, and what a manifold and majestic Thing does it not become? – What a multitude of admirable actions, what a multitude of habits of actions it learnt even before it saw the light! And its hopes and fears, & joys and pains, & desires . . . from the moment of its birth to the moment when the Glass through which we saw him darkly, was broken and he became suddenly invisible to us . . . But Jesus has declared that *all* who are in the grave shall arise – and that those who should arise to perceptible progression must be ever as the Infant which he held in his Arms and blessed . . . When I return indeed, and see the vacancy that has been made – when no where any thing corresponds to the form which will perhaps for ever dwell on my mind, then it is possible that a keener pang will come upon me – Yet I trust, my Love! – I trust, my dear Sara! That this event which has forced us to think of the Death of what is most dear to us, as at all times probable, will in many and various ways be good for us – To have shared – nay, I should say – to have divided with any human Being any one deep Sensation of Joy or of Sorrow, sinks deep the foundations of a lasting love – When in Moments of fretfulness and Imbecility I am disposed to anger or reproach, it will, I trust, be always a restoring thought – 'We have wept over the same little one – & with whom am I angry? – with her who so patiently and unweariedly sustained my poor and sickly Infant through his long Pains – with her – who, if I too should be called away, would stay in the deep anguish over my death-pillow! – who would never forget me!' – Ah, my poor Berkley . . .

On an infant, who died before it's Christening –
  Be rather than be *call'd* a Child of God!
  Death whisper'd. With assenting Nod
  It's head upon the Mother's breast
  The baby bow'd, and sent without demur,
  Of the Kingdom of the blest
  Possessor, not Inheritor! – . . .

Your affectionate & faithful Husband
S T Coleridge[15]

While there are moments of tenderness and affection, and keen insights into the mystery and sorrow of death, together with a deep affirmation of a life beyond its gates, there is nevertheless something abstract and abstracted about this letter. It is almost as though Coleridge was using his easy flow of words to cover and distance himself from the calamity, to numb himself rather than come to the quick of it, engaged and exposed. But, at this stage he had only Poole's letter to go on. Finally, he received Sara's own letter and wrote to her again on 23 April 1799. And here we come to a mystery. It seems inconceivable that a man of Coleridge's love and sensitivity on receiving such a letter could have done anything but pack his bags and return. Instead he persuaded himself that it was his duty to stay, even refusing the opportunity provided by the sudden appearance of the Wordsworths on their way back to England and eager for him to travel with them. Strangely, perversely, suddenly, he was shooting a deadly bolt into the heart of his marriage and, indeed, into the heart of the woman he loved, just as suddenly and irrevocably as the mariner shot his albatross:

My dear Sara
Surely it is unnecessary for me to say, how infinitely I languish to be in my native Country & with how many struggles I have

167

remained even so long in Germany! – I received your affecting
letter, dated Easter Sunday; and had I followed my impulses, I
should have packed up & gone with Wordsworth & his Sister,
who passed thro', & only passed thro', this place, two or three
days ago. – If they burn with such impatience to return to their
native Country, they who are all to each other, what must *I* feel,
with every thing pleasant & every thing valuable, & every thing
dear to me at a distance – here, where I may truly say, my only
amusement is – to labour! –. But it is in the strictest sense of the
word impossible that I can collect what I have to collect, in less
than six weeks from this day; yet I read & transcribe from 8 to
10 hours every day. Nothing could support me but the knowledge that if I return now, we shall be embarrassed & in debt; &
the moral certainty that having done what I am doing, we shall
be more than *cleared*: / not to add that so large a work with so
great a variety of information from sources so scattered, & so
little known even in Germany, will, of course, establish my
character – for industry & erudition, certainly; & I would fain
hope, for reflection & genius. – This day in June I hope, &
trust, that I shall be in England –! – O that the Vessel could but
land at Shurton Bars! – Not that I should wish to see you &
Poole immediately on my Landing – No! – the sight, the touch
of my native Country were sufficient for one *whole Feeling* –
one most deep unmingled Emotion! But then & after a lonely
walk of the three miles – then, first of all whom I knew, to see
you, & my *Friend*! – It lessens the delight of the thought of my
Return, that I must get at you thro' a tribe of *acquaintances*,
damping the freshness of one's Joy! – My poor little Baby! – at
this moment I see the corner of the Room where his cradle
stood – & his cradle too – and I cannot help seeing *him* in the
cradle. Little lamb! & the snow would not melt on his limbs! – I
have some faint recollection that he had that difficulty of
breathing once before I left England – or was it Hartley? – / – 'A

child! a child! is born, and the fond heart Dances: and yet the childless are more happy!'[16]

This extraordinary letter must have been devastating for Sara to receive; he '*languishes*' to be home he says and then dismisses that desire as 'mere impulses' and says it is his duty to stay. To stay and do what? 'read and transcribe' from eight to ten hours each day in a German library. Telling her that he had the opportunity to return with the Wordsworths, only to refuse them, must have made it even worse. Nor does the return to tenderness in the section starting 'My poor little Baby' help. No sooner has he described the vision of Berkeley still in the cradle, which must have been agony for Sara to read, than he says he is confused and can't remember which of the children he is remembering. Coleridge continues this letter over two or three pages with a vivid description of a family Christmas he has shared in Germany with all the children clustered around their parents, as though this would be a comfort to a woman who has just lost her child. The letter finishes with a rather weak little ditty saying that he 'flies to her in his thoughts and in his sleep' but still coldly affirming that he will stay where he is:

If I had but two little wings
And were a little feath'ry Bird,
    To *you* I'd fly, my Dear!
But Thoughts, like these, are idle Things –
    And I stay here. . . .

God bless you, my dear wife, & believe me with eagerness to clasp you to my heart, your faithful Husband
S T Coleridge[17]

Coleridge must soon have come to realise how crass and insensitive this letter was and what a mistake he had made in staying, but that very realisation just added to the many self-recriminations which always seemed to paralyse him rather than stir him into action. The more he delayed, the more reluctant he would be to face Sara and the truths he had been evading, and so the more likely he was, weakly, to delay his return even further. Southey, not always so perspicacious, but who had witnessed Sara's agony at first hand, and would later be the man who covered for Coleridge's much longer absences, put his finger on the nub of things when he wrote of Coleridge's 'pattern of absences and silences': 'Never I believe did any other man for the sake of sparing immediate pain to himself inflict so much upon all who were connected with him, and lay up so heavy and unendurable burthen of self condemnation.'[18] This is not to say that Coleridge did not deeply feel the loss and deeply intuit Sara's pain. It is not to say that he didn't love her, for he did; but somehow he allowed a misplaced sense of duty to pervert and ruin the course of his own actions. He did have a duty to study, to develop his mind, to make the most of the Wedgwood annuity for which he felt a sense of gratitude and obligation. But his duties as a husband and father were surely greater. He allowed himself to misconstrue these greater duties as mere 'impulses' and persuaded himself that the very strength of his natural desires and feelings in wanting to return home were something he had forever, painfully, to resist. Thus he inflicted great and unnecessary wounds not only on Sara but also on himself.

Eventually, after an absence of nearly ten months, he returned home, but home had changed. In her distress Sara had naturally looked to her own family and to her brother-in-law, Coleridge's old but now estranged friend, Robert Southey, for dependable support. One of the first things on which Sara insisted when he returned was a reconciliation between Coleridge and Southey, which did indeed take place, and soon the two men were planning projects and even writing poetry together, but at a deeper level things were not the same. Sara had, understandably, given

Coleridge a cold reception and he himself was strangely restless and brooding, veering back and forth with every wind. Somehow he knew there was no simple return, no going back; like his mariner he had crossed an invisible line and would have to take whatever adventures came in a new hemisphere.

Coleridge finally returned home feeling unwelcome

'And I had done a hellish thing': the mariner and the poet, cruciform in their
agony

CHAPTER SEVEN

Instead of the Cross, the Albatross

The Sun now rose upon the right:
Out of the sea came he,
Still hid in mist, and on the left
Went down into the sea.

(Lines 83–6)

As Coleridge continues with the tale of the mariner in this opening verse of Part II, our first impression is that we see nature continuing in her courses, as though nothing had happened and, of course, neither we nor the mariner have at this stage any inkling of the huge implications and consequences of the 'hellish thing' that he had done.

As this part begins with the sun rising, it is worth reflecting here on the rich symbolic importance of the sun and the moon in this poem. At one level, when Coleridge tells us that 'the sun now rose upon the right' he is simply telling us, in a kind of poetic ellipsis, that the ship has changed direction, for the albatross had guided them through the impasse of the ice, she has rounded Cape Horn and is heading north into the Pacific.

The first four lines of Part II deliberately echo the description of the ship when she set off merrily southward in Part I:

The Mariner tells The Sun came up upon the left,
how the ship
sailed southward Out of the sea came he!
with a good
wind and fair And he shone bright, and on the right
weather, till it
reached the Line. Went down into the sea.

(Lines 25–8 with gloss)

So the sun is always the witness and the measure of their direction, but there is something more, for the sun has a personal pronoun – 'out of the sea came *he*' – and all the great appearances of nature in this poem seem to look upon and bear witness to the story with a kind of personal consciousness. This is more than Coleridge deliberately 'archaising' to create the effect of a medieval ballad; it is essential to the whole vision of human beings and their relation to nature, which is embodied and expressed in this poem. The ground and the frame of the poem is a covenanted and personal relationship between people and the world around them, a mutual courtesy and hospitality. It is this essential courtesy that the mariner has broken when, as the gloss told us at the end of Part I, he '*inhospitably* killeth the pious bird of good omen'.

At first, the ship's company continue as if nothing has happened and the second stanza begins cheerfully enough: 'And the good South Wind still blew behind'. But as soon as the fitful weather changes, and the mist and fog mentioned in the first stanza of this section return, then the other mariners, still feeling cursed by ill luck in the weather, turn on the mariner and lay the whole blame on him.

His shipmates cry out against the ancient Mariner, for killing the bird of good luck.	And I had done an hellish thing, And it would work 'em woe: For all averred, I had killed the bird That made the breeze to blow. Ah wretch! said they, the bird to slay, That made the breeze to blow!

(Lines 91–6 with gloss)

This turn of events, rooted in the superstition of the sailors, was one of the starting points for the poem, as Wordsworth and Coleridge had first envisaged it on that November walk to Watchet.

As Lowes has shown, Shelvocke is clearly the source for this stanza in the poem, but Coleridge has done something extraordinary with his source. In Shelvocke, the shooting of the albatross is just a passing episode with no consequences: in *The Ancient Mariner* it is the turning point of the whole story, and, more than that, it gathers weight and consequence and becomes a sign and emblem of the whole mystery of evil and the strange self-destructing nature of fallen humanity. When the mariner says 'And I had done an hellish thing' you feel that he owns up to something even deeper than the accusations of his fellow mariners. The other significant change Coleridge brings to Shelvocke's account is the almost immediate *volte-face* on the part of the crew, when the weather changes again. This time, instead of condemning the mariner they applaud him in the very next stanza, only to condemn him yet again much later, when the ship is becalmed.

> *But when the fog cleared off, they justify the same, and thus make themselves accomplices in the crime.*
>
> Nor dim nor red, like God's own head,
> The glorious Sun uprist:
> Then all averred, I had killed the bird
> That brought the fog and mist.
> 'Twas right, said they, such birds to slay,
> That bring the fog and mist.
>
> *(Lines 97–102 with gloss)*

At the narrative level, this stanza is perfectly clear and simple: as soon as the fog clears and the sun rises the next day, the other crew members change their minds and approve of the mariner's slaying of the albatross, this time concluding that it must have been a bird of ill omen rather than good omen. The striking parallels in phrasing between these two stanzas placed next to each other makes the sudden *volte-face* of the entire crew even clearer and more absurd:

For all averred, I had killed the bird
That made the breeze to blow.
Ah wretch! said they, the bird to slay,
That made the breeze to blow!

(Lines 93–6)

Then all averred, I had killed the bird
That brought the fog and mist.
'Twas right, said they, such birds to slay,
That bring the fog and mist.

(Lines 99–102)

The 'gloss', however, adds a detail, or rather a conclusion, that we could not have drawn from the poem and that was a direct response from Coleridge to complaints about his poem after its first publication that it was unfair for the other sailors to be punished for the mariner's deed. The 'gloss' reads

His shipmates cry out against the ancient Mariner, for killing
the bird of good luck.
But when the fog cleared off, they justify the same, and thus
make themselves accomplices in the crime.

In fact, this 'gloss' takes us straight to one of the most important questions that Coleridge is raising in this poem: 'what is our proper relation to the natural world?' Is it a sacred web of exchange of which we are only one small part, or is it simply an agglomeration of 'stuff', which we can use at will for our own purposes? At this point, the whole ship's crew and, perhaps, the mariner himself, have taken an *instrumental* rather than a *sacral* view of nature. The albatross is not considered to have an intrinsic value, or rights, in itself, but is merely an instrument that might assist human beings for their own ends. If the bird was useful for the human agenda then it would be right to preserve it: <u>but if it hinders an immediate human goal then it is right to kill it</u>. In one sense, the terrible curse that falls on the ship and its crew and the dreadful experience of loneliness and alienation suffered by the mariner are a consequence of this instrumental view of nature, <u>but in a deeper sense the instrumental view is, itself, the curse</u>, and there can be no blessing or release until the mariner experiences a radical conversion of heart and mind in which he can look out from the deck of the ship at the other living things around him and simply bless them and love them for themselves, without any reference to a private or even purely human agenda. This transformation, which occurs in Part IV of the poem, is still to come, and until then we will see the terrible outworkings of this instrumentalism at both an emotional and a spiritual level. The instrumental view taken by the sailors is contrasted with, and so highlighted by, the personal and sacramental view of the poem's narrative voice, which is the voice of the mariner himself after his conversion. So in this very stanza we return to a 'powerful' 'personal' understanding of the sun:

Nor dim nor red, like God's own head,
The glorious Sun uprist:

(Lines 97–8)

Here the sun is more even than mythologically personal, a Phoebus or Apollo, but is compared to God himself. Readers of the first edition of the *Lyrical Ballads* found this analogy shocking; as Gardner remarks in *The Annotated Mariner*: 'the likening of the sun to the head of God offended at least one contemporary reviewer; he wrote that the simile "makes a reader shudder, not with poetic feeling but with religious disapprobation"'.[1] For this reason, Coleridge was persuaded to amend the line for the 1800 edition to 'like an angel's head' but in the 1802 and all subsequent editions, he changed it back, and with good reason.

'The glorious Sun' was a phrase Coleridge had already used in his poetry and would use again after *The Ancient Mariner*. From the outset, in Coleridge's luminous reading of nature as divine language, the sun was always the great symbol of God himself. Indeed, seeing the glory as well as the physical light was the very mark of that sacramental view of nature, without which the mariner could never be redeemed from his curse. Coleridge, like his mariner, would lose this sacramental vision, and then, like his mariner, eventually recover it. Many years later, when he had recovered from the agonies of his middle years, Coleridge met William Blake and they recognised one another's visions, for Blake had written: 'What it will be Question'd, "when the Sun rises, do you not see a round disk of fire somewhat like a Guinea?" O no, no, I see an Innumerable company of the Heavenly host crying, Holy, Holy, Holy is the Lord God Almighty' (see also below, chapter 12, pages 407–8).[2]

It is worth looking at the two other places where Coleridge uses the phrase 'glorious Sun', which 'bookend' its use in *The Rime of the Ancient Mariner*. The first we have already seen, in *This Lime-Tree Bower My Prison*. It will be remembered that Coleridge, imprisoned in his lime-tree bower, imagines Charles Lamb and the others emerging from the dell at Holford out into the light and the view of the sea, and then he turns to address the sun, specifically so that its light might heal Charles, who has been winning his way 'through evil pain and strange calamity',[3] the very things that will happen to the mariner. So Coleridge wrote:

> Ah! slowly sink
> Behind the western ridge, thou glorious Sun! . . .

> So my Friend
> Struck with deep joy may stand, as I have stood,
> Silent with swimming sense; yea, gazing round

On the wide landscape, gaze till all doth seem
Less gross than bodily; and of such hues
As veil the Almighty Spirit, when yet he makes
Spirits perceive his presence.[4]

The tragedy, for the mariner, is that in his fallen state, he cannot pierce the veil or perceive the presence. Not long afterwards, this would be Coleridge's tragedy too.

The second poem in which Coleridge speaks of 'the glorious sun' is *Fears in Solitude*, written April 1798, the month after he finished *The Ancient Mariner*. In this long 'conversation poem' Coleridge is again considering the power of nature suddenly to suggest a holy transcendence, but he does so in the context of the fear of French invasion, a fear which prompts him to review the shortcomings of his own society. The poem starts with the image of the sun as a glimmering and healing blessing, shining through half-transparent stalks:

When, through its half-transparent stalks, at eve,
The level sunshine glimmers with green light.
Oh! 'tis a quiet spirit-healing nook![5]

Then the tone changes and Coleridge reviews the confusions and corruptions of the English Church and State. He recognises that the Church in his day is so compromised that the Bible, on which so many are obliged to swear false oaths, is cheapened and brought into disrepute. It is scarcely surprising, he argues, that this cheapening gives rise to atheism:

That faith doth reel; the very name of God
Sounds like a juggler's charm; and, bold with joy,
Forth from his dark and lonely hiding-place
(Portentous sight!) the owlet ATHEISM

Sailing on obscene wings athwart the noon,
Drops his blue-fringed lids, and holds them close,
And hooting at the glorious sun in Heaven,
Cries out, 'Where is it?'[6]

We will return later to this paradox, in which one cannot see the
sun for its very brightness, when we come to consider some of the
Platonic and Neo-Platonic ideas about the meaning of the sun
and moon which Coleridge wove into later passages of this poem,
but here it is worth noticing that the phrase 'nor dim nor red' even
as it asserts that this glorious sunrise was neither dim nor red, is
in fact subtly preparing us for the vivid image of 'the bloody sun
at noon' which is shortly to follow. For now however, all seems to
be going well:

The fair breeze   The fair breeze blew, the white foam flew,
continues; the
ship enters the   The furrow followed free:
Pacific Ocean,
and sails north-   We were the first that ever burst
ward, even till it   Into that silent sea.
reaches the
Line.

                                             (Lines 103–6)

Once more Coleridge opens out this verse with a gloss that adds
information we can't find in the verse. This gloss explains why in
the following verse we are suddenly in equatorial heat when only
a stanza ago we had rounded Cape Horn in Antarctic seas. 'the
ship . . . sails northward, even till it reaches the Line'. 'The Line',
that is to say the equator, is, as we have seen, highly significant.
The mariner has left his familiar world and is now, doubly, in
strange hemispheres. He and his crew are the first Europeans in
the Pacific ('We were the first that ever burst / Into the silent sea'
– thus Coleridge implicitly sets his story before 1520 when
Magellan entered the Pacific) and in the southern hemisphere. In
that hemisphere he is subject, so he is to discover, to the 'Polar

Instead of the Cross, the Albatross

Spirit' of that hemisphere and he cannot return to his own sphere until the wrongs committed in this other sphere have been addressed. Indeed, for all the subsequent adventures and the movement of the ship, she will not be released from the Polar Spirit's grip and freed to re-cross the line and return home until Part V of the poem, when we hear the two voices and understand how both judgement and mercy have reached the mariner.

So now the ship is becalmed in the equatorial 'doldrums':

The ship hath been suddenly becalmed.
Down dropt the breeze, the sails dropt down,
'Twas sad as sad could be;
And we did speak only to break
The silence of the sea!

All in a hot and copper sky,
The bloody Sun, at noon,
Right up above the mast did stand,
No bigger than the Moon.

(Lines 107–14 with gloss)

After the free-flowing stanza about the breeze and the furrow there is a subtle change in the very feel and rhythm of the verse, which itself slows down to reflect the feel of the becalmed ship, the silence, the heat, the sense of waste and futility, but key to it all is the image of 'the bloody Sun' 'Right up above the mast'. The fact that it is directly above the mast at noon again indicates that they have reached the equator, but far more significant is the image of the diminished and *bloody* sun.

How is it that the sun, so glorious when it rose in those Antarctic seas, so glorious in much of Coleridge's visionary writing, should now be threatening, bloody, remote? To answer that question we need to remind ourselves of two things we have already touched upon: Coleridge's deep debt to Neo-Platonic and mystical writers, and his own distinct ideas about the relation of the outer images of nature to the inner states of the human soul. In the tradition of Platonic and Neo-Platonic thinking, in which Coleridge participated, the sun in all its naked glory symbolises the absolute truth in itself, which cannot be apprehended directly by fallen man any more than the naked eye can endure to look directly at the sun. The whole world is revealed to us in a light at the source of which we may not gaze. And there is a further nuance, which concerns both our common 'fallenness' and also those specific states of sin and alienation in which we have offended against the natural order and wounded our own inner light or eye of reason. In such a specific state of sin we can only experience the beneficent as itself darkened and wrathful. The mystic who developed that idea most clearly is Jacob Boehme (also a key influence on Blake), whom Coleridge had read and closely annotated by the time he came to write *The Mariner*. John Beer has summarised Boehme's writing and its influence on this passage in *The Mariner* very succinctly:

> The heat of the sun is as we have seen an essential element in the speculations of Jacob Boehme. Boehme's insistence on the benevolence of God led him to the doctrine that if God sometimes seems angry, this was no more than an appearance engendered by the diseased imagination of fallen man. Cut off from the light of God, he could experience only the heat of his presence: and any exposure to his full glory would therefore be felt as nothing less than exposure to unendurable fire.[7]

That heat and unendurable thirst is, of course, exactly what the mariner and the rest of the ship's company are about to experience. The image of blood in the sun is also important here; there is an evocation of primal guilt, of the spilt blood of Abel crying to God for vengeance, which runs throughout this poem, especially when we remember that it was written instead of the unfinished 'Wanderings of Cain'. The mariner's continuing sense of blood-guilt is vividly expressed on his return when he longs to be shriven and says of the hermit that, when he meets him

> He'll shrieve my soul, he'll wash away
> The Albatross's blood.
>
> *(Lines 512–13)*

But here, just before the gloss tells us that 'the Albatross begins to be avenged', we see the blood-guilt written in the heavens, in the very appearance of the sun.

Throughout this poem the inner states of the protagonists are expressed in and through the 'outer imagery' and all the images in turn speak into the depth of the soul. This is entirely in keeping with Coleridge's whole vision of what poetry is for and how it works, which he later expressed in his brilliant essay 'On Poesy':

> In the objects of nature are presented, as in a mirror, all the possible elements, steps and processes of intellect antecedent to consciousness, and therefore to the full development of the intelligential act; and man's mind is the very focus of all the rays of intellect which are scattered throughout the images of nature. Now so to place these images, totalized, and fitted to the limits of the human mind, as to elicit from, and to superinduce upon, the forms themselves the moral reflexions to which they approximate, to make the external internal, the internal external, to make nature thought, and thought nature – this is the mystery of genius in the Fine Arts . . .[8]

This essay clearly implies that the link between the outer and inner which poetry brings into focus is not an arbitrary one created by the poet, but expresses a genuine correspondence

which arises from the fact that the inner soul and the outer appearances of nature both have the same divine origin. Coleridge would
have to voyage much further, both into agony and redemption,
before he came to see the full implications of these insights, but
they are already foreshadowed and at work in *The Ancient
Mariner*.

*And the
Albatross
begins to be
avenged.*

Day after day, day after day,
We stuck, nor breath nor motion,
As idle as a painted ship
Upon a painted ocean.

Water, water, every where,
And all the boards did shrink;
Water, water, every where,
Nor any drop to drink.

(Lines 115–22)

These stanzas take us into that lassitude and helplessness, that
sense of meaningless repetition, which is both the outer doldrums
of the becalmed ship and the inner state of the mariners and the
crew. They include perhaps the most famous, certainly the most
quoted (and frequently misquoted) lines of the poem:

Water, water, every where,
Nor any drop to drink.

Of course, at the literal level, this refers to the agony of being
surrounded by undrinkable salt water without any fresh water to
drink, but it also means much more than that, and the many
contexts in which it is quoted make that clear. You can be in a
state of mind and soul where you may be surrounded by plenty
but it does you no good, where the more you consume, the less

satisfied you are, where you pursue an addiction until the very means of satisfying it becomes a poison that prolongs rather than relieves the agony of craving. We will be looking in the second part of this chapter at how Coleridge began to find this true in the specific arena of his addiction to opiates, but as we consider the poem itself and our reading of it now, we are bound to reflect on the way these lines are prophetic of the current crisis in the Western culture of consumerism:

> Water, water, every where,
> Nor any drop to drink.

Never has every whim of so many people been so completely catered to, so many needs at once stimulated and 'satisfied', and yet, far from being made happy by all these little satisfactions of impulse and appetite, we find a growing discontent and anomie in all Western consumer societies, until we are forced at last to make a distinction between 'standard of living' and 'quality of life'. It is particularly telling that a poem whose overarching meaning is so prophetic of the current ecological crisis should also so acutely express the hollow centre of the consumerism which has itself led to that ecological catastrophe. Like the mariner we have disturbed a delicate polar balance and unleashed forces beyond our comprehension which are quite likely to destroy us, and like the mariner, we do not even experience an interim satisfaction as a consequence of our actions, merely emptiness and thirst in the midst of plenty.

Then comes the moment when in this fallen state the mariner looks beyond the ship, and experiences disgust and loathing at all the life he sees there:

> The very deep did rot: O Christ!
> That ever this should be!

Yea, slimy things did crawl with legs
Upon the slimy sea.

(Lines 123–6)

Lowes has discovered the various places in the books of sea
voyages and mariners' tales which Coleridge had read, from
which he has drawn some of the imagery and phrasing of this
passage and the later passages in which he sees these same creatures in a new light, but once again it is not the sources, but what
Coleridge does with them, that makes for meaning in the poem.
When we first read this stanza we experience the disgust experienced by the mariner as he was then, particularly with the repetition of the word 'slimy' and the preternatural idea of something 'crawling with legs' upon the sea. And this outwardly
disgusting image bodies forth the inner sense of defilement and
corruption which is fast growing on the guilty mariner and
indeed the whole ship's company. But, as with their perception
of the sun, we are learning more about their own inner state
than about the creatures they are actually seeing. Having
fallen from the 'sacral' to the 'instrumental' view of nature, they
are now experiencing just that sense of alienation from and
disgust at life itself which has characterised so much post-
Enlightenment thinking. The disgust they see is in themselves,
not in the nature they are looking at, and when we read the
poem a second time, with the whole of it in our minds, we are
aware that these same 'slimy things' are referred to later as
'God's Creatures of the great calm' and they are in their own
way beautiful! Recognising their beauty and blessing, rather
than cursing them, becomes an essential part of the mariner's
redemption; but he has much to go through before he can reach
that insight. In fact, Coleridge's source in Captain Cook's
descriptions of protozoa in a phosphorescent sea has elements

186

of both responses – the slime we see here and the beautiful light which is to come – but Coleridge has separated them out so as better to express the transfiguration of vision and transformation of the mariner to come:

> *During a calm* . . . some parts of the sea seemed *covered with a kind of slime*; and some small sea animals were swimming about . . . that had a white, or shining appearance . . . When they began to swim about, which they did, with equal ease, upon their back, sides, or belly, they emitted the brightest colours of the most precious gems . . . Sometimes they . . . assum[ed] various tints of *blue* . . . But . . . the colour was, chiefly, a beautiful, pale *green*, tinged with a burnished gloss; and, in the dark, it had a faint appearance of glowing fire. They proved to be . . . probably, an animal which has a share of producing . . . *that lucid appearance, often observed near ships at sea, in the night.*[9]

This passage is a possible source for three quite distinct phases in the account of what the mariner sees: the slimy seas already discussed, the water burning like a witch's oils which we will look at next, and the transforming beauty of the 'elvish light' which we will discuss when we come to Part IV of the poem. Part of Coleridge's genius and originality as a poet is the distinctive uses to which he puts the same source; images in different parts of his poem each subtly changed and enhanced in atmosphere to work with the deeper purposes of Coleridge's own narrative.

> About, about, in reel and rout
> The death-fires danced at night;
> The water, like a witch's oils,
> Burnt green, and blue, and white.

> *(Lines 127–30)*

"Slimy things" will later be part of his redemption

This passage, while picking up some of the details of colour in it from Cook's account, also draws on other voyage narratives, as Lowes has shown, particularly on the account of the second, ill-fated voyage of John Davis in 1604, which Coleridge found in *Purchas his Pilgrimage*. The same book that had given him the starting point for *Kubla Kahn* now gave Coleridge the paradoxical and uncanny image of water burning:

> at night, I thinke I saw the strangest Sea, that ever was seene: which was, That the *burning* or glittering light of the Sea did shew to us, *as though all the Sea over had beene burning flames of fire*, and all the night long, the Moone being downe, you might see to read in any booke by the light thereof.[10]

It's worth knowing this source because it's important to know that, at this point, in describing what the mariner sees in his fallen state, Coleridge is not yet drawing on the supernatural – that will come shortly with the advent of the 'Polar Spirit' – but rather conveying the sense of revulsion and horror which the mariner's guilt and alienation projects onto the natural phenomena around him. There are no witches here, but the association with witchcraft and damnable arts is a continual outworking of the mariner's earlier realisation that he has 'done a hellish thing'.

So Coleridge takes this natural, if uncanny, image of the oily burning water with its coloured flames and stirs it, as though in the witches' cauldron, with a summoned echo, in our auditory imagination, of the witches in *Macbeth*. His verse here deliberately echoes:

> The Weird sisters hand in hand
> Posters of the sea and land
> Thus do go about, about.[11]

So Davis's 'fires' have become death-fires, and the oily water 'like a witch's oils'. The echoes of *Macbeth* deepen the ballad as a tragedy about an entirely human choice which is nevertheless set in a supernatural frame, a tragedy therefore in which the human choices have more than human consequences, exactly as in the story of Macbeth. Both Macbeth and Banquo encounter the witches, but only Macbeth makes the 'bloody' choice. There is a further, and in its own way uncanny, link here between Shakespeare's masterpiece and Coleridge's. If one reads further into the account in *Purchas*, one cannot help being struck by the name of Davis's ship; he was in fact 'the Master of the *Tiger*'. Act 1, scene 3 of *Macbeth* goes on to detail the fate of that ship's master, again with striking parallels to the mariner's:

> Her husband's to Aleppo gone, master o' the *Tiger*:
> But in a sieve I'll thither sail,
> And, like a rat without a tail,
> I'll do, I'll do, and I'll do.[12]

> I will drain him dry as hay:
> Sleep shall neither night nor day
> Hang upon his pent-house lid;
> He shall live a man forbid:
> Weary se'n nights nine times nine
> Shall he dwindle, peak and pine:
> Though his bark cannot be lost,
> Yet it shall be tempest-tost.[13]

Of course, there were a number of vessels from mid-sixteenth-century onwards named the *Tiger* whose voyages are recorded, but, as Nicholas Brooke argues in his Oxford Shakespeare edition of *Macbeth*, there is very strong evidence suggesting that Shakespeare had this voyage in mind and had read this account, not least that when the *Tiger* limped back into Milford Haven on 27 June 1606, 'they had been absent for 567 days which equals 7 × 9 × 9. Exactly as in the Sisters' magical chant.'[14]

So Coleridge was not simply echoing Shakespeare but also drawing inspiration and imagery from the very source that Shakespeare himself had used. This whole stanza also subtly prepares us for the appearance in the next section of the poem of the spectre-ship and the witch-like figure of the Night-mare Life-in-Death. It is at this point of heightened awareness of the supernatural frame or architecture within which the mariner's story is set that Coleridge first introduces the Polar Spirit, whose nature and role is key to our understanding of the whole poem:

> And some in dreams assured were
> Of the spirit that plagued us so:
> Nine fathom deep he had followed us
> From the land of mist and snow.

> *(Lines 131–40)*

Here we learn that the destruction of the bird in the heights has also stirred and disturbed something in the depths. Much later in the poem we will learn of the true link between the spirit, the bird, and the mariner himself, but for now we have the first intuition and presentiment, in a dream, given, not to the mariner, but to those around him. This is also one of those occasions when the gloss, composed when Coleridge himself had a much deeper understanding of what was happening in the poem, tells us more than the text of the poem itself, and reflects back on it in a most helpful way. The gloss reads:

> A Spirit had followed them; one of the invisible inhabitants of this planet, neither departed souls nor angels; concerning whom

the learned Jew, Josephus, and the Platonic Constantinopolitan, Michael Psellus, may be consulted. They are very numerous, and there is no climate or element without one or more.

(Gloss to lines 131–40)

This passage is extraordinary and helpful in a variety of ways. First, it reminds us of Coleridge's wide and deep reading and especially of his interest, already noted, in the Neo-Platonic spiritual tradition. In November 1796, almost exactly a year before he began to compose *The Mariner*, he had written to Thelwall in these terms: 'I am and ever have been a great reader . . . almost always reading.'[15]

This letter ends with a request for Thelwall to obtain for him, in a London sale, a list of books which represent the very heart of the Neo-Platonist tradition and on which he drew extensively all his life, and many of which cite Psellus and Josephus as mentioned in the gloss. A common strand in all these works is the idea of the Dæmon (not 'Demon'!). Dæmons are beings that are neither angels in heaven, nor fallen angels, but spirits who occupy a middle position and inhabit, and indeed animate, the four elements that were believed to make up the earth. Some of them are deemed to have important roles in relation to the human beings with whom they share the world. Socrates, for example, speaks of his 'dæmon' who helps and inspires him and encourages him to 'sing'. The term came to be translated into Latin as 'Genius' and, to begin with, people spoke of a person *having* a genius rather than '*being* a genius'.[16] The English Neo-Platonist Taylor, whom Coleridge specifically mentions in the letter to Thelwall, says in his commentary on Plato's *Phaedrus* that there is another role for these dæmons of direct relevance to the frame of *The Ancient Mariner*: 'But there are other Dæmons transcending these, who are the punishers of souls, converting them to a more perfect and elevated life.'[17]

Coleridge has fused many of these ideas in his own conception of the Polar Spirit, and three elements seem to emerge. First, it is a spirit of place, an animator and guardian of the whole South Polar region, the carer and protector of all its life, and it therefore seeks to avenge the death of the albatross which, we are told later, it loved. But second, it is in some sense beneficent, an agent of providence, as Taylor here suggests, and its pursuit of the mariner and insistence on his penance is ultimately a blessing and restoration for the mariner himself, even though the process takes him on a very dark path. Third, it is in some sense part of the being or 'genius' of the mariner/poet as narrator, or even more particularly of Coleridge himself. By the time Coleridge came to write the gloss he had not only identified himself with the mariner but had also begun to feel that the imagination itself, the power and genius or Spirit of creativity, and specifically his own imagination, could only be expressed in terms of both height and depth of a deep, complementary and (his favourite term) 'polar' relation between conscious and sub-conscious. Indeed it was Coleridge, long before Freud and Jung, who pioneered the idea of a sub-conscious or unconscious element to our being, most famously when he was reflecting on Shakespeare's gifts and genius and said that Shakespeare was 'a genial understanding directing self-consciously a power and a[n] implicit wisdom deeper than consciousness'.[18]

But this is to anticipate; at this stage in the story all these apprehensions of the supernatural, which might later mean grace, can only be interpreted by the 'fallen' mariner and crew in terms of blame and vengeance.

The shipmates, in their sore distress, would fain throw the whole guilt on the ancient Mariner: in sign whereof they hang the dead sea-bird round his neck.

Ah! well a-day! what evil looks
Had I from old and young!
Instead of the cross, the Albatross
About my neck was hung.

(Lines 139–42 *with gloss*)

Here we come once more to one of those moments when an image or episode from this poem has entered common parlance, for we all know what it is to speak of 'having an Albatross round one's neck' – a phrase used to suggest that one is carrying a debilitating and unnecessary burden which is a hindrance to getting on with life. In its original context, however, it means rather more than that.

In the gloss, Coleridge is tapping into the dark and ancient tropes of the scapegoat and the ship's 'Jonah', the one figure who must take the blame and suffer vicariously for all. Both Jonah and the scapegoat are of course biblical types or anticipations of Christ; indeed, Christ offers 'the sign of Jonah' as a sign of who he is, as Coleridge well knew, and this link is deepened by the mention of the cross in this verse. At one level there is an ironic negation of that divine substitution:

> *Instead* of the cross, the Albatross
> About my neck was hung.
>
> *(Lines 141–2)*

One of the many mysteries of the cross is the mystery of substitution: it is Jesus suffering instead of us. So to take that cross away and substitute the albatross is, on the part of the ship-mates, a deliberate substitution of blame and vengeance for grace, instead of the other way round, and one way at least of interpreting the fate of the crew, as opposed to that of the mariner, is to read it through Christ's sayings about judgement: 'Judge not, that ye be not judged. For with what judgment ye judge, ye shall be judged: and with what measure ye mete, it shall be measured to you again'[19] (Matt. 7:1–2). If we forgive we are forgiven; if we cry for judgement and vengeance on another then that is what falls on us.

But turning to the mariner himself we may see things from a different perspective. The dead bird certainly represents his guilt, but later in the poem we learn that the bird 'loved the man who shot him with his bow'. From the outset the bird has been associated with the cross, and it has already achieved the 'deliverance' of the whole ship and its crew when it guided them out of their ice-bound fastness and into this new sea. Perhaps there is a secret promise of grace hidden even in this emblem of guilt and burden. In that case the Albatross would, for a while, be 'instead of the cross' in a quite different sense: it would be standing in for, and doing the work of, the cross.

A great deal of ink has been spilt by commentators worrying and puzzling over how it was physically possible to hang around a man's neck an albatross whose wingspan, as Wordsworth observed, and Coleridge certainly knew, can be twelve or thirteen feet. Perhaps, they suggest, it was the smaller black albatross, also mentioned in Shelvocke, that Coleridge had in mind. This is entirely to miss the point. This ritual and emblematic 'shaming' of the mariner is not meant to fit, and work! It's meant to be uncomfortable, ungainly and difficult. This is especially true, at the deeper symbolic level, if we consider the albatross in all the glory of its flight as an emblem of the joy and power of the poet in full flight, the potential height in all of us to which the Dæmon beneath the keel is the corresponding depth. Here it is artists and poets, rather than learned commentators, who are best able to catch the essence of what these episodes and images mean. Mervyn Peake's engraving of this moment in the poem is especially powerful.[20] In that image the albatross itself seems fused with the mariner, its ungainly wings spreading out from his midriff and drooping to the deck as he himself falls to his knees.

When we first encountered the Albatross we recalled Melville's beautiful evocation of it in the notes to *Moby Dick*; as we contemplate the fallen bird, its wings a crippling encumbrance to the one around whose neck it is hung, we can call to our aid another poet

who has seen in the albatross an emblem of both the glory and
the burden of the poetic vocation. Consider Baudelaire's poem
'The Albatross', translated here by George Dillon:

Sometimes, to entertain themselves, the men of the crew
Lure upon deck an unlucky albatross, one of those vast
Birds of the sea that follow unwearied the voyage through,
Flying in slow and elegant circles above the mast.

No sooner have they disentangled him from their nets
Than this aerial colossus, shorn of his pride,
Goes hobbling pitiably across the planks and lets
His great wings hang like heavy, useless oars at his side.

How droll is the poor floundering creature, how limp and weak –
He, but a moment past so lordly, flying in state!
They tease him: One of them tries to stick a pipe in his beak;
Another mimics with laughter his odd lurching gait.

The Poet is like that wild inheritor of the cloud,
A rider of storms, above the range of arrows and slings;
Exiled on earth, at bay amid the jeering crowd,
He cannot walk for his unmanageable wings.[21]

We don't know whether Charles Baudelaire had read *The Rime
of the Ancient Mariner* by the time he published *L'Albatros* in
1859, but he has certainly intuited the meaning of the albatross
for the poet, with his insight that it is the very wings that lift the
poet in flight, his capacities for empathy and imagination, which
become in ordinary life something unmanageable and crippling.
This was certainly the case with Coleridge, to whom we shall
shortly return, as the pattern of his poem continues to unfold in
his life.

Before we leave this image of the dead albatross that speaks so much of the mariner's own condition, we must ask what an emblem like this might mean for us. If we are to interpret the dead body of the albatross as an emblem of the deeper guilt incurred by the mariner and his crew, the guilt of having broken the laws of hospitality, sheared the web of life, and disturbed the polar balance, then that image has a strange and terrible resonance for us today. Readers may be familiar with the story of Midway Island and with the eerie and unforgettable photographs taken by the artist Chris Jordan of the albatrosses dying there (see picture section). The seas of the world, even these remote southern waters, have been so filled and polluted with the throwaway plastic detritus of our consumer society – empty plastic bottles and containers and so forth – that the albatross which fish these waters have been scooping up this plastic flotsam and feeding it to their young. As a result of swallowing so much plastic-coated emptiness, which their digestive systems cannot process, the young birds find their stomachs are so full that there is no room left for real sustenance. Full of nothing, they starve to death in the midst of plenty. Jordan's photographs show the skeletal and feathered outlines of the birds, and where the stomach should be, a scatter of our discarded plastic.

What Jordan presents are images of such dark beauty and strange irony that Coleridge would have responded to them with his whole soul. He would certainly have seen an emblem here of our whole culture and its crisis, an apotheosis of our 'instrumental' attitude to nature and its consequence. As surely as the fallen albatross was an emblem of the mariner's wounded soul, so these dead albatrosses on Midway Island show us who we are: bloated with emptiness, dying of excess, visiting destruction on our fellow creatures in the pursuit of what we ourselves can only discard.

We return now from our voyage through the poem to the voyage of Coleridge's own life. Like the mariner, at the beginning of Part

A Ualtruss is an emblem of deeper guilt of crew & mariner

II of his poem, Coleridge may have thought he was sailing with a good wind behind him, into clearer and calmer seas, but he would soon find that this was not so, and within months of his return he was veering ineffectually back and forth, round all points of the compass, but still 'as idle as a painted ship', not getting anywhere. He had made a terrible mistake in delaying his return, but he still very much loved his wife and, as we saw in the last chapter, had written to her, even as he travelled back, about his eagerness to see her, that he wanted nothing to be '*damping* the freshness of one's joy'.[22]

But if there was any freshness of joy, it was not long lasting. It was clear that, for many reasons, life could not go on as it had done in the tiny cottage at Nether Stowey. On his return, Coleridge renewed his friendship with Poole but, of course, desperately missed the Wordsworths, who had gone up to stay with friends and family at Sockburn in Teesdale, while prospecting for a place of their own in their beloved Lake country, a place they eventually found and made famous, as Dove Cottage. Once back in his own deeply nurturing rootedness in the North, Wordsworth was becoming surer of his vocation and more and more certain of his range and power as a poet. By contrast, Coleridge was pulled in all directions: Wordsworth urged him to come North with his family; he countered in his letters and begged the Wordsworths to return to the West Country, each poet perhaps secretly knowing that they could only flourish best in their own place. If so, it was a tug of war which Coleridge would lose.

Meanwhile, Daniel Stuart, Coleridge's friend and contact in the London newspaper world, who ran the *Morning Post* and rightly discerned that Coleridge would make a brilliant political feature writer and cultural commentator, was wooing him to come to London and work there. Poole was pressing Coleridge to stay in Nether Stowey and Tom Wedgwood – whose annuity to

Coleridge had first been proffered with 'no strings attached', and who had fallen ill with a combination of depression, what may have been the early onset of cancer and a deepening opium use – was pressing Coleridge to accompany him as a kind of travelling companion and unofficial tutor on a series of desperate journeys in search of relief and health. For a while Coleridge – who once confessed: 'Of all words I find it most difficult to say "No"'[23] – tried to do all these things at once, of course without success. As a result he was still often away from the household to which he had said he was so anxious to return. It was an unsettled and confusing summer, and when autumn came Coleridge was really no further forward with any of his various and conflicting plans for the future. He and Sara had visited his family in Devon, in the hope of finding a place to live there, but without success. In September Hartley became ill with scabies so their little cottage had to be fumigated with sulphur and then, to make matters worse, the cottage flooded in the heavy rains of that autumn. Coleridge wrote to Southey:

> Our little Hovel is almost afloat – poor Sara tired off her legs with servanting – the young one fretful & noisy from confine-ment exerts his activities on all forbidden Things – the house stinks of Sulphur – I however, sunk in Spinoza, remain as undis-turbed as a Toad in a Rock / that is to say, when my rheumatic pains are asleep.[24]

There is more to this last remark than meets the eye, and it marks an ominous development. Rheumatic pains had been a constant in Coleridge's life from the time he had rheumatic fever as a child, and had been the occasion, even while he was at Christ's Hospital, of his being dosed with laudanum. That last image of being sunk in Spinoza and undisturbed as a toad in the rock, suggests a retreat against pain into a combination of opium and metaphysics. It was this combination which Coleridge himself later diagnosed as having been both what killed his poetic spirit and what ultimately rendered him an addict. For now, these were only brief bouts of withdrawal, though it can hardly have been helpful to Sara, having waited so long for his return, to find him in the midst of a crisis retreating into reading and opium. It should also be said, though, that the rheumatic fever was a very real thing, genuinely agonising, which led him later to crippling pains in his joints, especially his knees, to swollen legs and to an atrial fibrillation and enlarging of the heart which eventually killed him.[25]

When Coleridge recovered from this particular bout, which was in fact a combination of the long-term rheumatic pains and pneumonia, he got into a panic about the arrival of the precious box of books from Germany, on which he had spent (Sara might have said wasted) so much of the Wedgwood annuity that he was now in debt to them, having drawn an advance on what should have been due to him the following year. He set off to Bristol to investigate along the seaport warehouses and see if they had arrived there. It was a real reason for going, but at another level Coleridge was 'bolting', as he had done as a child running out from the house in Ottery and as a student running away from Jesus College and enlisting in the Dragoons. Needless to say, the books arrived quite safely in Nether Stowey two days after Coleridge had left. Sara sent letters after him, but it was too late; Coleridge had heard in Bristol that Wordsworth was ill and depressed in the North and needed him. The news came from their publisher, Joseph Cottle, and on 22 October Coleridge was racing north to Sockburn with Cottle in the latter's private coach. Sara would not see him again for six weeks, but she seems to have made the best she could of it and taken herself and little Hartley out of the stinking, and now damp, cottage for a holiday at Kilve.

Coleridge becomes an addict

It is, in its own way, understandable that Coleridge would have responded so swiftly and decisively to what he believed was Wordsworth's real need. He knew, in his heart, how completely each had brought out the other's gifts and at this point he knew, even more than Wordsworth himself, how great Wordsworth could be. He also knew he had a part to play in that greatness: it was Coleridge himself who could convey the wider vision and the philosophical depth and undergirding which they both knew Wordsworth would need for a great and sustained poem. Even as the floodwaters had been rising in Stowey earlier that September, Coleridge had written to Wordsworth:

> My dear friend, I do entreat you go on with "The Recluse"; and I wish you would write a poem, in blank verse, addressed to those, who, in consequence of the complete failure of the French Revolution, have thrown up all hopes of the ameliora-tion of mankind, and are sinking into an almost epicurean self-ishness, disguising the same under the soft titles of domestic attachment and contempt for visionary *philosophes*. It would do great good, and might form a part of "The Recluse", for in my present mood I am wholly against the publication of any small poems.[26]

Coleridge arrived at Sockburn where the Wordsworths were stay-ing in a farmhouse belonging to their friends the Hutchinsons, on 26 October. It was a visit that would change everything for all of them.

Wordsworth, who proved to be in perfectly good health, was staying with the Hutchinson family consisting of Tom, a farmer and his three sisters, Mary, Sara and Joanna. Of course they had all been told about the 'wonderful Coleridge', so Coleridge found the whole place emotionally warmed and ready to receive him, and enjoyed a doubtless delicious transition from the constant stress, criticism and anxiety of life at Nether Stowey, to a household full of people who were enthusiastic and ready to be charmed – and charm them he did. But the attractions were mutual. Both poets had their ideal audience, for even now Wordsworth was perhaps beginning to fall in love with Mary Hutchinson, his sister Dorothy's best friend, whom he would eventually marry, and Dorothy was delighted to show off Coleridge to both Mary and Sara. But Wordsworth had more than new friendships in mind. He was longing to show Coleridge the deep and magic kingdom of his childhood and to share with him, if he could, the sense of sublimity, suggestion and transfiguration, the sense of an outward expression in landscape of the inner glories of the soul, which he was discerning more and more deeply in the beauty of the Lake District. Within two days the poets were off on a walking tour together, rekindling the glory days of the Quantocks, but this time on Wordsworth's native ground. Coleridge, as Wordsworth hoped, had eyes and ears for everything and filled his notebooks with observations, which would later emerge in both of their poetry. He was especially drawn, as one would have expected, to the sights and sounds of streams and running waters, the contrasts of motion and stillness, and the way old walls and ruins suggested so much of the paradox of permanence and impermanence in the midst of which we live, as for example in this passage from a notebook:

here struck and astonished with the *rush* of Sound which came upon the ear at each opening – till at last we look up the River & behold it pouring itself down thro' a steep bed of rocks, with a wall of woods on each – & again over the other wall of the Bridge the same scene in a long vista except that here instead of rapid a deep-solemn pool of still water, which ends in a rapid only in the far distance. – The grey ruin faces you on the one side – over the other in contrast of this still pool with a soft murmur of the other distant rapid – & a handsome Gentleman's house in the distance – rocks rising stepwise – The Banks & [?mirror/murmur] pained to look up –

    Castle – Star over the Tower –

    Twinkling behind the motionless fragment.[27]

We have a very good account of this tour and of the impressions it made on both men because together they wrote a journal-letter to Dorothy describing it. We don't have the whole thing but Mary Wordsworth later transcribed most of it, and it is among the treasures at Dove Cottage. If Wordsworth was trying to cast the spell that would eventually draw Coleridge northward, then he succeeded. Coleridge wrote to Dorothy:

> You can feel what I cannot express for myself—how deeply I have been impressed by a world of scenery absolutely new to me. At Rydal & Grasmere I recd, I think, the deepest delight, yet Hawes Water, thro' many a varying view, kept my eyes dim with tears, and, the evening approaching, Derwentwater in diversity of harmonious features, in the majesty of its beauties, and in the beauty of its majesty . . . & the Black Crags close under the snowy mountains, whose snows were pinkish with the setting sun, & the reflections from the rich Clouds that floated over some and rested upon others!. It was to me a vision of a fair Country.

Coleridge must surely have felt some tugging of conscience to turn back, for Sara had no idea where he was, but there was so much to keep him. Knowing his passionate advocacy of the abolition of the slave trade Wordsworth introduced him to Thomas Clarkson, who was then staying in the Lake District to recover his nerves and strength in the long and seemingly fruitless campaign. So here at last was a meeting with the man whose work had so inspired Coleridge's undergraduate prize essay, and who had himself been radicalised by writing for such a prize. They must have had a great deal to say to one another and they formed a fast friendship, for later, when both men were themselves in a deep crisis of depression and opium, struggling for their own inner freedom as they had struggled for the outer freedom of others, Clarkson would write to Coleridge for help with his faltering faith and Coleridge would reply to Clarkson with some of the most profound and liberating theology that ever flowed from his pen.

But Coleridge would make one more visit before he returned home and this one proved fatal, at once providing the lift for, and ensuring the downfall of, all the imaginative and personal hopes that this northern visit had inspired. Coleridge finally left Wordsworth on 18 November, but instead of going the short way home he recrossed the Pennines and returned to the farmhouse at Sockburn, where that enchanting trio of Dorothy, Mary and Sara were ready to welcome their wonderful poet.

And so he passed a few delicious days in their company, mildly flirtatious perhaps with them all, but something rather deeper than that was beginning to kindle between Coleridge and Sara Hutchinson. Sara was a kind, quick, humorous and sympathetic woman, not by most accounts especially glamorous, but intelligent, capable of great empathy and with beautiful auburn hair, bright eyes, and a kind of comfortable and motherly warmth about her. Coleridge loved all the Hutchinsons' company but something about Sara seemed to rekindle his dormant poetic gifts and while he was there he began a beautiful ballad called 'Love', which proved, in the coming century, to be one of his most enduringly popular poems. It tells the story of a minstrel poet who himself tells a story of hopeless love to the girl with whom he is himself hopelessly in love. Even as she hears the poem, she falls in love with the poet! Perhaps this was all gentle game playing on both their parts, but the poem's famous opening verse speaks of how all kinds of thought and delight can feed the flame of love:

All thoughts, all passions, all delights,
Whatever stirs this mortal frame,
All are but ministers of Love,
    And feed his sacred flame.[28]

The single notebook entry for this time – 'The long Entrancement of a true-love's kiss'[29] – may just be a playful working on another verse, it may be wishful thinking, or it may record something that actually happened. At the time, with all of them entranced by youth and poetry, but also all in company together, there was a mantle of innocence over all things, even an unexpected kiss. But when Coleridge looked back three years later at one particular evening on this stay, he knew that something life changing had happened. Three years later, when his love for Sara Hutchinson had deepened, indeed become so deep that it had to be renounced, Coleridge acknowledged that somehow it had all started here. In 1802, looking back to this day in 1799 he wrote: 'Conundrums & puns & stories & laughter – with Jack Hutchinson – Stood up round the Fire et Sarae manum a tergo longum in tempus prensebam . . .' A translation of the secret Latin passage in this entry runs: 'and pressed Sara's hand for a long time behind her back and then, then for the first time love pricked me with its light arrow, poisoned alas! and hopeless.'[30] This is not to say that on that November day in 1799 he was, or knew himself to be, so deeply in love, but that gradually he came to realise that this is where it began. At this moment and for some while to come there is no doubt that in Sara Hutchinson's company his heart lifted, his imagination kindled, and he could spread his wings not only to her delight but also to the delight of all around him. It was only later that, faced with all its impossibilities and contradictions, they both saw the need to renounce this love. Then, of course, the very force that had lifted him up brought him crashing down, then the lively became deadly. And perhaps, as he reached for the metaphor of an envenomed arrow, it was not just the traditional image of blind cupid that stirred in him but the powerful emblem of his own creation: the bolt from the cross-bow, and the white-winged albatross falling towards the deck, soon to shame and encumber the mariner.

'The Night-mare Life-in-Death was she
Who thicks man's blood with cold...'
Coleridge's poetry embodies the nightmare he was yet to live through

CHAPTER EIGHT

The Night-mare Life-in-Death

In this third section of the poem we encounter a ghost ship, the skeletal figure of death and the even more frightening figure of the 'night-mare life-in-death', some of the classic motifs and images of the gothic horror genre on the one hand, and of sailors' tales of the supernatural on the other. But Coleridge is doing much more than recycling the standard fare of a gothic ballad. In this poem all these images are subtly transformed from their various sources. In Coleridge's hands they are more than the passing images of stock hair-raising gothic imagery, or standard *Flying Dutchman*-type narratives but become much deeper emblems of the experiences of alienation and dread so familiar to our own age – experiences which Coleridge himself was about to enter.

> There passed a weary time. Each throat
> Was parched, and glazed each eye.
> A weary time! a weary time!
> How glazed each weary eye,
> When looking westward, I beheld
> A something in the sky.
>
> *(Lines 143–8)*

This opening stanza for Part III was not included in the poem when it was first published in 1798 but was added by Coleridge, like the gloss, to the *Sibylline Leaves* edition of 1817. The original version of Part III launched in with the line 'I saw a something in the sky' and took us immediately to the frightening apparition of the spectre-ship. By 1817 Coleridge knew better. He knew that the long periods of slackness, doldrums, inaction and sheer weariness are as much a part of the suffering and woundedness of our nature which he was seeking to evoke, as are the sudden or decisive moments of revelation and action, whether for good or ill. We are to imagine the whole crew, day after day enduring their increasing thirst, their enforced idleness, their growing fear for their own survival. But in addition we are to imagine the mariner isolated and ostracised, the emblem of his crime and shame hung round his neck, exiled from community even by his kith and kin (for we learn later in the poem that his nephew is among the crew). Yet even thus ostracised, it is still the mariner who takes the lead in pointing out the spectre-ship:

The ancient Mariner beholdeth a sign in the element afar off.

At first it seemed a little speck,
And then it seem'd a mist:
It moved and moved, and took at last
A certain shape, I wist.

A speck, a mist, a shape, I wist!
And still it near'd and near'd:
As if it dodged a water-sprite,
It plunged and tacked and veered.

(*Lines 149–56 with gloss*)

The gradual discernment of the ship from being a mere speck, to taking a shape, and then the fleeting joy of seeing a sail, is beautifully expressed in the movement of the next two verses and their linked temporal phrases: 'At first . . . and then . . . at last . . . and still'. Even before the full revelation of what this approaching object is, there is perhaps a sense of the uncanny implied in 'plunged' and 'veered' and the mention of a water-sprite, though this does not extinguish or preclude what the gloss calls the 'flash of joy' as the sailors are allowed to think for a moment that this ship might mean them some good, that they might be rescued.

> *At its nearer approach, it seemeth him to be a ship; and at a dear ransom he freeth his speech from the bonds of thirst.*
>
> With throats unslaked, with black lips baked,
> We could nor laugh nor wail;
> Through utter drought all dumb we stood!
> I bit my arm, I sucked the blood,
> And cried, A sail! a sail!
>
> *(Lines 157–61 with gloss)*

The graphic detail of the mariner's throat being so dry that he must bite his own arm and suck the blood in order to have moisture enough to speak is also worthy of comment. It adds to the undercurrent or theme of blood and blood-guilt, and it anticipates the chilling lines to come: 'Fear at my heart, as at a cup / My life-blood seemed to sip', but as so often it is the gloss which comments on and suggests the deeper sacral framing of the poem.

Given the deep associations which the poem is gradually building between the albatross and the cross, and the invocations later of 'him who died on cross', we should note the inclusion here of theologically loaded language: 'dear ransom' and 'freeth . . . from bonds'. At this point, though, in the story, no ransom of course has been paid and no freedom is on offer, for the mariner cannot ransom himself by shedding his own blood. Indeed, we can see in this sudden extravagant gesture a kind of self-harming which is so much the expression of people's sense of desolation, of guilt, and of the implicit or explicit accusation of others.

So comes the false comfort, the delusive 'flash of joy':

> With throats unslaked, with black lips baked,
> Agape they heard me call:
> *A flash of joy.* Gramercy! they for joy did grin,
> And all at once their breath drew in,
> As they were drinking all.

And horror follows. For can it be a ship that comes onward without wind or tide?

See! see! (I cried) she tacks no more!
Hither to work us weal;
Without a breeze, without a tide,
She steadies with upright keel!

The western wave was all a-flame.
The day was well nigh done!
Almost upon the western wave
Rested the broad bright Sun;
When that strange shape drove suddenly
Betwixt us and the Sun.

(Lines 167–76 with gloss)

There is an irony in the expression 'Gramercy', a shortening for 'Grant mercy' or 'Mercy on us', in light of what this ship turns out to be.

One of the most striking and dramatic effects in the whole poem is the way the ship comes towards them, uncannily moving against wind and tide on upright keel. Coleridge gives us an unforgettable image of the ship coming 'betwixt us and the Sun' and of the sun, still that personalised, semi-divine presence, suddenly being barred out or away from them:

It seemeth him but the skeleton of a ship.

And straight the Sun was flecked with bars,
(Heaven's Mother send us grace!)
As if through a dungeon-grate he peer'd
With broad and burning face.

(Lines 177–80 with gloss)

This stanza has a double effect: it certainly gives us, as the gloss emphasises, the horrific image of the 'skeleton of a ship', its 'ribs' missing their planks, anticipating the skeletal figure of Death whom we will shortly meet, but, given the huge significance of the sun and moon in this narrative, it also deepens the sense of alienation from the Good which is building throughout this part of the poem. It is left, I think, deliberately ambiguous whether we are to imagine the sun himself and all he represents as somehow imprisoned in a dungeon by this apparition of evil, or whether it is the mariners and their whole world which has become as it were a self-imposed dungeon through the grate of which God himself can only peer.

Then comes the incomparable description of the ship herself and her crew.

The spectre-ship itself may have many original sources, not least in the oral tradition of the Bristol Docks where Coleridge spent so much time, where he would have heard the many local superstitions and stories about ghost ships with their undead crews sailing on against the wind. Wordsworth tells us, though, that it was a nightmare experienced by Coleridge's friend John Cruickshank that first set this ghost ship sailing into the poem. In the dream, Cruickshank, according to Wordsworth's later account, 'saw a skeleton ship with figures in it'.[1] To this first hint it is almost certain that Coleridge added details from a Dutch story of a man called Falkenberg:

> who, for murder done, is doomed to wander forever on the sea, accompanied by two spectral forms, one white, one black ('eine weisse . . . und eine schwarze'). And in a ship with all sails set the two forms play at dice for the wanderer's soul.
>
> Six hundred years has that ship been sailing without either helm or helmsman, and so long have the two been playing for Reginald's soul. Their game will last till the last day. Mariners that sail on the North Sea often meet with the infernal vessel.[2]

Coleridge takes these initial elements and ideas and makes something new out of them; his description of the spectre-bark is made all the more vivid as it is evoked for us or in us not by a series of delimiting statements but by a series of open questions:

And its ribs are seen as bars on the face of the setting Sun.

Alas! (thought I, and my heart beat loud)
How fast she nears and nears!
Are those *her* sails that glance in the Sun,
Like restless gossameres!

The Spectre-Woman and her Death-mate, and no other on board the skeleton ship.

And those *her* ribs through which the Sun
Did peer, as through a grate?
And is that Woman all her crew?
Is that a Death? and are there two?
Is Death that woman's mate?

(Lines 181–9)

There is considerable change and improvement in this later version from the original publication in *Lyrical Ballads*, change which indicates Coleridge's move away from the mere gothic sensationalism of the original plan to something much deeper.

In the earlier version there was an extra verse at this point and the verse following that also read slightly differently. The first version has:

His bones were black with many a crack,
    All black and bare, I ween;
Jet-black and bare, save where with rust
Of mouldy damps and charnel crust
    They're patch'd with purple and green.

Her lips are red, *her* looks are free,
    Her locks are yellow as gold:

> Her skin is as white as leprosy,
> And she is far liker Death than he;
> Her flesh makes the still air cold.[3]

He was right to withdraw this rather sensationalist description of the blackened mouldy bones of the skeleton, though it does contrast well with the leprous white skin of the woman, because such vivid detail about this particular skeleton weakens the more ✓ important sense that we are encountering Death himself, and not just one particular skeleton. The really significant change is to the end of the second stanza above, which now reads:

Like vessel, like crew!

> Her lips were red, her looks were free,
> Her locks were yellow as gold:
> Her skin was as white as leprosy,
> The Night-mare Life-in-Death was she,
> Who thicks man's blood with cold.

(Lines 190–4 with gloss)

The opening three lines, which he left comparatively unchanged, are effective because, like the earlier stanzas when the mariners experience a flash of joy when they first see the ship only to have it turned to horror as the ship nears, so here the first two lines lure us into feeling that, in contrast to death, we are seeing life and beauty.

> Her lips were red, her looks were free,
> Her locks were yellow as gold:
> Her skin was as white . . .

(Lines 190–2)

These two and a half lines could have come in any ballad describing some minstrel's fair love; it is only as we get to the image of

213

leprosy that everything has to be revisited and the apparent beauty becomes all the more horrific because of the nightmare anti-life it brings. For this reason the change in the last two lines is a real improvement. 'She is far liker death than he' blurs rather than heightens the distinction between the two figures, whereas 'the Night-mare Life-in-Death' is a brilliant coinage, summoning up not only the metaphorical sense of nightmare as a hideous or frightening dream, but the literal sense from which the metaphor was drawn, as the OED defines it 'A female spirit or monster supposed to beset people or animals by night, settling upon them whilst they are asleep and producing a feeling of suffocation by its weight.' As we shall see, Coleridge was beset by nightmares as a direct consequence not so much of his opium addiction as of his attempts to withdraw from it, but there was also another sense in which the dreamlike and beautiful, particularly in his images of and relations to women, eventually became tragically shadowed and nightmarish.

And what are we to make of her name, capitalised in the poem: LIFE-IN-DEATH? Certainly it sums up the mariner's fate for the next part of the poem. The others die but he remains alive, every moment wishing for death but unable to achieve it, condemned to a life which is death-like and yet which still envies death, a life in which all that should be a sign of goodness, those fair colours, red and yellow and gold and white, all spell a curse rather than a blessing. Moreover, for us in our contemporary reading of the poem, they connect with and amplify those earlier and more famous lines 'Water, water every where / Nor any drop to drink'.

What if we have life, and all the means of life, but we can make nothing of it, get no good from it? What if the endless iteration of images of beauty and of 'the good life', the pointing and beckoning bright young things that fill the ads, the posters, the repetitions of the internet, the red lips, the yellow hair, the free looks

– what if all of those become so empty, so meaningless, so utterly contrasted with our real states, our real circumstances and lives, that they become, not an enhancing beauty, but a nightmare collage of triviality and emptiness? Something of that seems suggested and embodied in the figure of the Night-mare Life-in-Death, something brought out in her twentieth-century illustrators, particularly Mervyn Peake and David Jones.

In his ballad Coleridge continued the intense realisation and fusion of his sources in another chilling verse:

Death and Life-in-Death have diced for the ship's crew, and she (the latter) winneth the ancient Mariner.

The naked hulk alongside came,
And the twain were casting dice;
"The game is done! I've won! I've won!"
Quoth she, and whistles thrice.

What are we to make of this game of dice? Clearly the detail itself came from the tale of Faulkenberg we cited earlier, but what is its function in Coleridge's poem; indeed, what is the function of the whole episode of the spectre-bark, which appears so dramatically at this point in the poem, disappears equally suddenly and is never heard of again?

At one level Coleridge's helpful gloss gives us an answer: the crew are death's prize, and so they die; the mariner has been won by the nightmare and so he lives, but lives a life-in-death. But in a way this gets us no further forward. How have Death and Life-in-Death appeared? How is it that the prize of the ship's crew and the mariner were at their disposal to divide at the throw of the dice? The fact that no explanation is given deepens our growing sense that by entering these waters – and by the mariner's rash and unprovoked slaying of the bird that had guided them – the ship and crew had themselves been dicing with the unknown and unknowable. Arrogantly, they had assumed that they were the ones with the rights of life and death, they could choose whether

215

The crew are death's prize

or not the albatross lived or died, and even though it was the mariner who had done the actual shooting, the crew in concluding that it was 'right such birds to slay' had, as the earlier gloss tells us, made 'themselves accomplices in the crime'. Now they themselves are at the disposal of, and subject to, the forces they have unleashed.

For modern readers the game of dice poses a deeper question still: the question of 'moral luck'. The philosopher Bernard Williams first introduced this phrase in a book of that title in 1981,[4] and asserts that when he did so he assumed he was introducing an oxymoron, since Kant and others had claimed that there is no 'luck' in either moral judgement or moral responsibility – otherwise it would be *random* and not *moral*. In those terms: if two people each choose to take out their car one evening, each knowing that the brakes might be faulty because they have not been checked or serviced, and a child runs in front of one of them and is killed because the car can't stop in time, but the other, on this occasion, makes their journey without killing anyone, then strictly speaking both parties are equally guilty of dangerous negligence, it's just that one of them had the luck not to have their negligence exposed. But in fact we respond with greater horror to the one whose trip resulted in a fatality. The concept of moral luck raises very real questions about the nature of moral judgement and indeed about what we mean by the random, as contrasted with the meaningful or even the providential. If we espouse an entirely material/mechanical view of all causation, including the physical causation of those events within the brain that appear to us as moral choices, we may end up removing any ground for morality in the world at all and have to suspend all judgements. If on the other hand we say that there is always a clear relationship between moral choice and its consequences, we are confronted at every turn with manifest unfairness, which we then have to 'explain away'. Most philosophers who have considered this, and indeed most ordinary people, end up with a kind of 'mixed econ-omy' on this issue, recognising that we must each be responsible for our choices and that such responsibility involves thinking through the likely consequences of our choices, but equally recog-nising that many consequences of our actions are unpredictable and seemingly random.

Here the mariner in particular and then the whole crew have put themselves in hazard, through the mariner's action and their approval of it, and yet it seems, if we are to believe the dice, that the outcome of how the effects of the hazard are distributed is random. But this apparently random element in the poem, as to the different fates of the mariner and the crew, is counterbalanced by the overarching and undergirding symbolic and spiritual struc-ture of the poem, which is not random at all but full of meaning and coherence. The Polar Spirit, who loves the bird, the albatross who loves the mariner, the two voices of the good 'dæmons' whom we meet later and who discuss his fate and its meaning, the 'guard-ian saint in heaven' and the troop of angels whom the spirit sends, are all moral agents. Even though they sometimes represent opposing judgements or views, they all work together for the mariner's redemption, restoring the balance of love and beauty against which he has offended, and enabling him in turn to kindle and enable love in others and to bring them, including the wedding guest (and so by implication the reader – for he is our proxy) to a place of redemption and renewal.

Indeed, one might say that the appearance of the spectre-bark is just that: an appearance and no more. It is not so much a direct cause of what happens as an outward and visible showing of what has happened and what will happen as a result of the mariner's own free will. There is a sense in which the mariner and his own vessel later become themselves the spectre-ship of his own vision, for when the hermit first sees the mariner's ship he describes it in terms very reminiscent of the spectral ship:

This is random, unlike the rest of the poem

The planks look warped! and see those sails,
How thin they are and sere!
I never saw aught like to them,
Unless perchance it were

Brown skeletons of leaves . . .

(Lines 529–33)

Indeed, no sooner has Coleridge introduced this chilling vignette of the spectre-ship and its two inhabitants black against the setting sun, as a kind of vivid emblem, than he dismisses it and plunges us all into absolute darkness:

No twilight within the courts of the Sun.

The Sun's rim dips; the stars rush out:
At one stride comes the dark;
With far-heard whisper, o'er the sea,
Off shot the spectre-bark.

(Lines 199–202 with gloss)

It is wonderful how the sound of those last two lines themselves make an eerie whispering sound, like the spectre-bark itself disappearing into the silence of the night seas. Then, in that utter blackness, we begin to experience the outworking of what we have glimpsed in the spectre-bark. Coleridge sets the scene in an unforgettable verse which he added to the 1817 version, a verse which drew directly on his second experience as a mariner himself, in the voyage to Malta,[5] which we shall be discussing in the next chapter:

At the rising of the Moon,

We listen'd and look'd sideways up!
Fear at my heart, as at a cup,
My life-blood seemed to sip!
The stars were dim, and thick the night,

218

The steerman's face by his lamp gleam'd white;
From the sails the dew did drip—
Till clomb above the eastern bar
The horned Moon, with one bright star
Within the nether tip.

(Lines 203–11)

Looking sideways up does so much to convey the fear in their faces but the truly chilling image returns to the theme of life-blood:

Fear at my heart, as at a cup,
My life-blood seemed to sip!

(Lines 204–5)

This sense of being slowly drained, sip by sip, of life itself by fear, as though by the leprous white Night-mare Life-in-Death herself, is unforgettable and it carries with it a subtle and horrific inversion of the redemptive/sacramental frame of the whole poem. For what we see here is an eerie anti-communion: instead of sipping from the chalice the freely given wine that is the life-blood of his redeemer, 'him who died on cross', the mariner has his own life-blood drained away. The detail of the steersman's face gleaming white in the lamplight, drawn from his Malta voyage notebooks, adds to the sense of the deathly pale and reminds us again of the leprous white skin of the Night-mare Life-in-Death.

Then the moon, which is to be so beneficent in the next part of the poem, rises but is star-dogged for the mariner, at this stage, with the eerie impossibility of a star 'within the nether tip'.[6]

Then comes the act in which, with their last look, each member of the crew curses the mariner with his eye. This is again an inversion of something else that is beneficent, if still eerie, in the poem:

the mariner's own 'glittering eye'. He holds the wedding guest against his will with this glittering eye, not to curse, but to bless; and this ritual reversal of what was done to him is part of his penance, part of his healing, as well as that of the wedding guest's.

Coleridge brings this section of the poem to a masterly close with a return, as he does at the end of each section, to the image of the cross-bow and the slaying of the albatross:

But Life-in-Death begins her work on the ancient Mariner.
The souls did from their bodies fly,—
They fled to bliss or woe!
And every soul, it passed me by,
Like the whizz of my cross-bow!

(Lines 220–3 with gloss)

In this third section of the ballad the mariner is languishing, tied down and burdened by the body of a bird that had once soared. As Coleridge returned from his northern expedition, still elated by his dalliance in the charmed circle of the Wordsworths and their friends, he had little presentiment of how soon that image from *The Mariner* would be an emblem of his own situation. It is true that three years later he had marked that fire-lit evening in November as the moment the shaft pierced him 'poisoned and alas incurable', but if it was envenomed, then the poison was slow working; and travelling south again, Coleridge still imagined he had everything under control. He had plans for a productive new phase of life, gathering his family around him, this time in London. Coleridge's brilliant if unprofitable flights into journalism in *The Watchman* and in occasional articles for other publications had not gone unnoticed and at Bristol, on the way north, he had been introduced to Daniel Stuart, the proprietor of the *Morning Post*, a paper that had already taken a number of Coleridge's poems. Stuart recognised Coleridge's wayward genius and seized his chance, offering Coleridge work in writing leading articles and opinion pieces on current affairs and politics, but also a platform for publishing his poetry to a wide audience, whether it was topical or not. Stuart offered Coleridge an initial six-month contract which would help him deal with his immediate debts and take lodgings with his family in London (they still had nowhere to live, other than the flooded cottage at Stowey). Coleridge, returning back from his northern reverie, was determined at this point to shake off these northern fantasies, make a new effort in his marriage and family life, and take the opportunity that was offered.

Coleridge did not even return to Stowey; he went straight to London from Sockburn and took lodgings in Buckingham Street, where Sara and Hartley came down to join him. For a while all seemed set fair. Though Coleridge often berated himself for indolence, he was in fact capable of bouts of intense hard work, writing under pressure at a level of sustained brilliance. In this first burst of official and commissioned journalism he wrote seventy-six articles in five months. All this was to pay off the debt to the Wedgwood annuity he had accrued in advances, and to demonstrate to Sara that he wanted to be an industrious breadwinner like Southey, the brother-in-law with whom she so often unfavourably compared him. The chill that had greeted him on his return to Stowey had clearly thawed, and there was some kind of renewal in the relationship. Sara enjoyed London life, Hartley's health recovered and Sara became pregnant again. In some ways London life also suited Coleridge. He was a brilliant talker and always in demand, and had the satisfaction of seeing his ideas taken up by thousands of readers, helping to form a significant strand of public opinion.

One position he took was that England could and should resist the growing tyranny of Napoleon without herself capitulating to a reactionary and conservative dismissal of all that the French

Revolution had once meant. That ideas of liberty, equality and fraternity had thrown up a tyrant in France did not mean that the search for a fairer and more equal society should be abandoned at home. On the contrary, without a real liberalisation of law, and amelioration of the lives of the poor, England would herself be bound to fall sway to the extremes of France.

London also restored to Coleridge the stimulating company of good friends who, like Wordsworth, could bring out the best in him, but who, unlike Wordsworth, didn't lead him to feel himself a lesser man, or a less worthy poet. He renewed and deepened his friendship with Charles Lamb and began a long series of important conversations with the anarchist philosopher William Godwin, seeking to draw Godwin out of his atheism and towards some acknowledgement of the divine.

But of course, like Yeats after him, Coleridge, treading the 'pavements grey', could always 'hear lake water lapping' and knew that somewhere 'in the deep heart's core' there was a call back to the mountains and lakes, with their 'lovely shapes and sounds intelligible'. Nor had he entirely forgotten his Pantisocratic dreams, and his letters of this period are full of wild schemes to gather his friends and go and live somewhere in a kind of combined artistic and scientific colony where they could make a new world together. Nothing came of any of these plans but already Coleridge's compass was veering wildly round all quarters.

Looking back a little later on these six months of intense work in London, Coleridge sent a 'progress report' to his patron Josiah Wedgwood. He concluded it with an image of a bird trying to struggle free from the limed branches intended to trap it: 'But with all this I have learnt that I have Industry & Perseverance – and before the end of the year, if God grant me health, I shall have my wings wholly unbirdlimed.' His letters to Wedgwood are all like this, long lists of all that entangles him, concluding with a devout hope that he will soon be disentangled. These letters often draw, at this stage I think unconsciously, on images from *The Ancient Mariner*. So when, later that summer, he did arrive at the Lakes, 'unbirdlimed' as he thought, he wrote, waiving the offer of £20, 'I trust I shall be able to sail smoothly without it.'[8] Alas, his wings were soon to be even more deeply netted and cramped, and he had as little chance of a fair breeze as his becalmed and bird-encumbered mariner.

As winter turned slowly to spring in that last year of the eighteenth century he felt the needle point north again, and leaving the family safely ensconced in London set off on 2 April 1800 to see Wordsworth. Wordsworth seized his opportunity and unfolded to Coleridge his plans for a second expanded edition of the *Lyrical Ballads*, with a revised introduction setting out more clearly their joint ideas about poetry – having now reached real maturity – and expanding the range of poetry in the book, inviting Coleridge to be a part of all of this. Dorothy, and Mary and Sara, were all hovering in the wings. How could Coleridge resist? The Wordsworths had already found and rented Dove Cottage, in an idyllic spot by Grasmere, and it was on this trip that Wordsworth showed Coleridge his first glimpse of Greta Hall, the beautiful white house just outside Keswick and nestling near the shores of Derwentwater, which would be Coleridge's home for the next four years.

Did anything happen on that April trip to rekindle the feelings for Sara Hutchinson that had first stirred into life the previous November? We don't know, but there is one notebook entry from around this time that suggests something may have transpired: '– a little of Sara's hair in this pocket'.[9]

Coleridge returned to his own Sara and Hartley at the beginning of May and though they did look, at her insistence and Tom Poole's, for somewhere they might settle in the West Country, nothing came of it. Coleridge's whole being was straining northwards and he began to persuade himself, his family and friends that their West Country friends might follow them there, that perhaps even Humphry Davy, Godwin and Charles Lamb would be tempted up from London, that perhaps even at that distance he could pay the bills through writing for the London papers, but still have time for poetry and the Wordsworths. Sara, expecting a child in September, needed to be settled somewhere. Wordsworth, who had secured a lease of Greta Hall on good terms, was holding out certainties, and Coleridge, with all his famous eloquence and powers of persuasion, was painting glowing pictures. The die was cast and they moved. It was only years later, pondering again his own mariner, that Coleridge might have wondered from whose hands the dice were being cast.

After a brief sojourn in Bristol, where Coleridge renewed his friendship with Humphry Davy, who was to become one of the great scientists of his day and a luminary of the Royal Society, they headed north and arrived at Grasmere to stay with the Wordsworths for a month until, on the 24 July, they settled in their own place at Greta Hall. The move must have been a wrench for Sara Coleridge, whose family and friends were all in or near Bristol, as it was, in its own way, for Coleridge, who was especially torn by leaving his good friend Tom Poole in Nether Stowey. But in the first few months of that lovely summer there was much to compensate and distract them. While they were staying with the Wordsworths, Coleridge abandoned or set back his own writing projects including 'The Life of Lessing' and the translation of Schiller's *Wallenstein*, which were meant to be the great fruits of his German trip, to throw himself into helping Wordsworth order and edit the expanded second edition of the *Lyrical Ballads*, and most importantly, to write a new preface. This would be something of a manifesto of the new poetry with which both men were now associated: free, natural, lucid, unforced, drawn to discover the beautiful in what is close and everyday as well as what is remote, but equally committed to finding in folktale, superstition and myth, emblems of our own inner nature and deeper truths about the human heart.

It was this latter aim that was dear to Coleridge, touching as it did on what he had achieved in *The Rime of the Ancient Mariner*, and what he hoped to achieve in a new poem he was struggling to complete in the midst of all the editorial and emotional help he was offering Wordsworth – a poem which at this stage they both intended to be a vital part of the new *Lyrical Ballads*. This poem was *Christabel*. Coleridge had in fact begun it in the same *annus mirabilis* which produced *The Rime of the Ancient Mariner* and *Kubla Khan*, while they were at Nether Stowey, and had completed 'Part I', but the tale was incomplete and now in these summer months, first at Grasmere and then at Greta Hall, Coleridge was writing Part II.

Christabel is a powerful, almost hypnotic poem with a driving, incantatory four-stress line, which Coleridge developed and perfected specifically for this poem but which became immensely popular with later writers, particularly Walter Scott, then known chiefly as a poet, who had immense success with this meter in his hugely popular long poem *The Lay of the Last Minstrel*, a poem which draws also on a number of other features, images and even lines to be found in *Christabel*. Whereas *The Mariner* makes the most of the heights and depths, of sea and sky, the lights of heaven and their watery reflections, and the superstitions and visionary glimpses of seamen, to weave a poetry that is emblematic of our own heights and depths, *Christabel* uses the suggestive shape and feel of landscape and weather, and the old traditions of the border ballads, of the barons' courts, each with their knights, their chapel and their bard, sometimes linked in friendship, sometimes divided in rivalry, as a setting and a series of emblems with which to explore the complexities of the human heart: our desires, our trustfulness or suspicion, our capacities for love and betrayal.

The two chief figures in *Christabel*, constantly compared and contrasted, are the heroine Christabel, and Geraldine the bewitching interloper. Christabel is the daughter of Sir Leoline, a baron. She is a figure of great innocence and beauty, loved and protected by the spirit and last wishes of her mother, who died in childbirth. Geraldine, whom Christabel meets at night in the woods outside the castle, presents herself to Christabel as a damsel in distress fleeing the depredations of marauding robbers. Christabel has compassion on her, takes her into the castle and to her own room. In all innocence, as far as Christabel is concerned, they spend the night and share Christabel's bed. But a series of uncanny occurrences as the two girls make their way back to the castle, including Geraldine's inability to cross the threshold unaided, gradually unveil to the reader that Geraldine's apparent beauty and innocence conceal a great evil. Finally, Christabel herself sees that Geraldine is a witch and glimpses some unspecified horror about her person as she undresses before bed (there is a hint in Part Two of the poem that beneath the fair form some part of Geraldine is old and withered), but she is cast under a spell and is unable to tell anyone what she has seen. There is certainly a suggestion of vampirism, as Geraldine seems somehow to draw the very life from Christabel, and on the next day she usurps Christabel's place in her father's affections. Only the Bard Bracy, the court poet, seems to be able to tell that something is wrong. Then, frustratingly, the narrative breaks off and the incomplete fragment of the tale ends. Though the poem was left unfinished, it carries deep suggestions that somehow the poet's art, embodied in the Bard Bracy, will itself help to free Christabel, and enable the others to see more clearly and distinguish between the false and the true images of the beautiful and the good. In some ways the figure of

Geraldine seems to be a development of Coleridge's image of 'the Night-mare Life-in-Death'; she is seemingly fair and free, but she too 'thicks men's blood with cold'. In Part I of the poem the landscape of the Quantocks is beautifully evoked, but in Part II, on which he worked during that summer, Coleridge draws freely on the beautiful images and striking place names and folktales of the Lakeland that surrounded him.

As Coleridge worked on the second part of this poem all seemed set fair, especially when he and his family left Grasmere and came to their own place at Greta Hall. Built as a summer 'observatory' (not an astronomical observatory but a place for observing a panorama of 'picturesque' views) it did indeed have commanding views, but was by virtue of that also very exposed to cold and damp – as they would soon discover. For now though, Coleridge was enchanted and, famously, climbed on the roof when he arrived and penned letters to his friends, describing their idyllic situation, and addressing the letters as: 'From the leads of the housetop of Greta Hall, Keswick, Cumberland, at the present time in the occupancy and usufruct-possession of S. T. Coleridge Esq., Gentleman-poet and Philosopher in a mist.'[10] Sara was glad to have the space and also to see how little Hartley flourished and delighted in the

> lakes and sandy shores, beneath the crags
> Of ancient mountain, and beneath the clouds,
> Which image in their bulk both lakes and shores
> And mountain crags.[11]

Just as Coleridge had hoped in *Frost at Midnight*.

Coleridge wrote to Humphry Davy, partly drawing on Davy's discovery of nitrous oxide, or laughing gas, with which he and Coleridge had experimented in Bristol:

Sara desires her kind remembrances – Hartley is a spirit that dances on an aspen leaf – the air, which yonder sallow-faced & yawning Tourist is breathing, is to my Babe a perpetual Nitrous Oxyde. Never was more joyous creature born – Pain with him is so wholly tran-substantiated by the Joys that had rolled on before, & rushed in after,[12]

Coleridge too was lifted and drawn up into the mountains (though not quite as light as an aspen leaf!) and began to explore the fells around him in great circuitous expeditions, setting out in all weathers driven by an almost preternatural energy, observing and recording everything in his increasingly vivid notebooks and describing his wanderings in brilliant letters.

Soon Coleridge finished Part II of *Christabel* and hastened over the high passes to read it to the Wordsworths. It would seem that both William and Dorothy were enchanted and entranced by that reading. The new verses were filled with references to places and stories in Wordsworth's beloved Lakes. Coleridge felt that he was not only recovering his stalled poetic powers but also assimilating himself into Wordsworth's native place, and in the process enhancing Wordsworth's vision and commitment to this particular landscape until it became something really and jointly held. But over the next two months it seems that Wordsworth himself began to have his doubts about the poem. Years later, in the *Biographia Literaria*, Coleridge looked back on what he understood to have been the joint vision of the *Lyrical Ballads* and the particular ways in which he and Wordsworth were to divide the labour:

In this idea originated the plan of the *Lyrical Ballads*; in which it was agreed, that my endeavors should be directed to persons and characters supernatural, or at least romantic; yet so as to transfer from our inward nature a human interest and a semblance of truth sufficient to procure for these shadows of imagination that willing suspension of disbelief for the moment, which constitutes poetic faith. Mr. Wordsworth, on the other hand, was to propose to himself as his object, to give the charm of novelty to things of every day, and to excite a feeling analogous to the supernatural, by awakening the mind's attention to the lethargy of custom, and directing it to the loveliness and the wonders of the world before us; an inexhaustible treasure, but for which, in consequence of the film of familiarity and selfish solicitude, we have eyes, yet see not, ears that hear not, and hearts that neither feel nor understand.[13]

Christabel fitted this scheme perfectly and in some ways even better than *The Ancient Mariner*, the constant flashing back and forth in that poem between the heightened symbolic awareness arising from the magical elements and the vividly realised elements of natural description having just that effect of enabling a rich transfer between the inner and the outer in the reader's imagination – but Wordsworth was beginning to think differently. *The Ancient Mariner* was already the longest poem in the collection and *Christabel* was to be longer still. From Wordsworth's point of view the whole collection was becoming unbalanced, and he began to feel that his own efforts to awaken the mind's attention from lethargy and direct it towards the hidden mystery in the here and now, to the landscape present before our eyes, unveiled by descriptions at once natural, simple and sublime, would be undermined by Coleridge's poetry, whose supernatural stories and archaic language would be a distraction rather than an awakening.

Coleridge visited Grasmere again in early October, a few weeks after Sara had given birth to their new baby, christened Derwent, after the river on whose banks Coleridge and his friends had walked with such joy. Wordsworth chose this visit to drop his bombshell: he would not be including *Christabel* in the *Lyrical Ballads* and indeed he even had doubts about retaining *The Ancient Mariner*. Dorothy noted the decision in her journal on 6 October. Coleridge says nothing in his notebooks on this day, but he set off for Greta Hall the next day alone, climbing over the mountains into the darkening weather as the first snow, of what would be a terrible winter, fell on Skiddaw.

Coleridge's response to this catastrophe was at once tragic and generous. He saw the point of his friend's reasoning, accepted Wordsworth's strictures, and submitted to his decision. Far from flouncing off or abandoning all his other parts in the project, as a lesser man might have been tempted to do, he continued to work hard on all the editing, correcting and proofing that the new edition required, even making the fair copy for the printer by hand of Wordsworth's long poem *Michael* which was to replace *Christabel*, and continuing to commend the new edition and the brilliance of Wordsworth's poetry to all and sundry. But inwardly he was deeply wounded. Wordsworth was growing in strength, deepening in vision and power, secure in his own place and the affections of all those he needed and counted on, including Coleridge himself. Coleridge had left behind all his other networks of support, and was still struggling in his marriage. Now he deeply internalised all of Wordsworth's criticisms and began, with terrible consequences, to doubt his own deepest vocation – his calling as a poet. Not long after this he was writing, on behalf of Wordsworth – who was too busy with his poetry – to a mutual friend, apologising for Wordsworth's delay in replying and saying of him: 'He is a great, a true Poet – I am only a kind of Metaphysician. – He has even now sent off the last sheet of a second volume of his Lyrical Ballads –.'[14]

At least *The Ancient Mariner*, with modernised spelling and other improvements, had been reprieved and it now came at the end of those proof sheets of his (Wordsworth's!) lyrical ballads.

Coleridge's name appeared nowhere. *Christabel* would not appear in print until 1816 and then only at Lord Byron's insistence. By that time it had been widely circulated in copied manuscripts and had, as Coleridge ruefully commented, furnished feathers for other men's quills, notably Walter Scott's. Coleridge would not publish *The Ancient Mariner* itself as his own poem set out as he wanted it until *Sibylline Leaves* was published in 1817.

Coleridge returned home and, as winter deepened, his first response to the turmoil of his largely suppressed emotions of resentment and betrayal at the rejection of *Christabel* was to throw himself into sudden bursts of almost self-punishing fell walking in all weathers. It was as though he thought he could exorcise the spiritual and emotional poisons by sheer exercise and relentless driving of the body. The inevitable result was that he collapsed and was ill. The rheumatic fevers that had plagued him since childhood and which had first led to his being dosed with opium even at Christ's Hospital, returned with a vengeance, giving him agonisingly painful swollen joints, especially his knee. He was once more prescribed and dosed with opium. But this time it was not such modest tinctures as might be administered by a school or college nurse; this time it was the now notorious Kendal Black Drop. Molly Lefebure gives a very full account of this particular 'medicine' in an appendix to her book *Samuel Taylor Coleridge: A Bondage of Opium*. It was between two and four times as strong as the 'common laudanum' which Coleridge had occasionally taken before and was administered in a mixture of vegetable oil and brandy to help the patient get and keep it down. It was advertised by its manufacturer 'Dr. Brathwaite' as an admirable specific against 'nervous and spasmodic affections, as pains of the head and stomach, depression of mind, anxiety, and irritability, in the gout, in wounds, inflammation and mortification; in chronic rheumatism, . . .' Not a word was breathed, for very little was known, about its desperately addictive nature or its many unpleasant side-effects. Coleridge later dated the beginning of his real and debilitating dependence on opium and his first encounters with its nightmarish effect on his dreams, and its sapping and corruption of his will, to this first winter in the Lakes of 1800–1. So it is worth reviewing the evidence from his own letters of his first encounters with and gradually increasing dependence on opium, a journey, like that of every addict, that leads from honeymoon to nightmare.

So innocent was the use of opium thought to be, that in 1798 Coleridge had written to his respectable brother George, the clergyman: 'Laudanum gave me repose, but not sleep: but YOU, I believe, know how divine that repose is – what a spot of inchantment, a green spot of fountains & flowers & trees, in the very heart of a waste of Sands.'[15] We catch here perhaps an echo of the opium enchantment that may have entered into some of the imagery of *Kubla Khan*. But after this winter the tone of his reference to the drug begins to change. He does not commit the full horror of what opium was doing to him to paper (at least not in letters – there are many harrowing notebook entries) until much later when he was going through the real death-throes of his futile attempts to throw off the drug, during his crisis of 1813–14. We will look at that crisis in more detail when we come to that part of this mariner's tale – the sinking of the ship and the pulling of his nearly drowned body from the water – but his later confessional letters, written in crisis, look back to this time so we will anticipate and quote some of them here.

Writing to Cottle in 1814 but remembering this winter of 1800–1 Coleridge wrote:

I had been almost bed-ridden for many months with swellings in my knees – in a medical Journal I unhappily met with an account of a cure performed in a similar case (or what appeared so) by rubbing in of Laudanum, at the same time taking a given dose internally – it acted like a charm, like a miracle! I recovered the use of my Limbs, of my appetite, of my Spirits – & this continued for near a fortnight – At length, the unusual Stimulus subsided – the complaint returned – the supposed remedy was recurred to – but I can not go thro' the dreary history – suffice it to say, that effects were produced, which acted on me by *Terror* & *Cowardice* of PAIN & sudden Death, not (so help me God!) by any temptation of Pleasure, or expectation of desire or exciting pleasurable Sensations. On the contrary, Mrs Morgan & her Sister will bear witness so far, as to say that the longer I abstained, the higher my spirits were, the keener my enjoyments – till the moment, the direful moment, arrived when my pulse began to fluctuate, my Heart to palpitate, & such a dreadful *falling-abroad*, as it were, of my whole frame, such tolerable Restlessness & incipient Bewilderment.[16]

Coleridge at last found the courage to speak plainly of what the full and terrifying effects of the drug had been on him in a letter to his friend John Morgan, written when he had passed through the final crisis which in a sense delivered him:

By the long Habit of the accursed Poison my Volition (by which I mean the faculty *instrumental* to the Will, and by which alone the Will can realize itself – it's Hands, Legs, & Feet, as it were) was completely deranged, at times frenzied, dissevered itself from the Will, & became an independent faculty: so that I was perpetually in the state, in which you may have seen paralytic Persons who attempting to push a step forward in one direction are violently forced round to the opposite. I was sure that no ease, much less pleasure, would ensue: nay, was certain of an accumulation of pain. But tho' there was no prospect, no gleam of Light before, an indefinite indescribable Terror as with a scourge of ever restless, ever coiling and uncoiling Serpents, drove me on from behind.[17]

By that time the echoes in his letters of the imagery of fearful pursuit he had first used in *The Rime of the Ancient Mariner* had become explicit and Coleridge had consciously identified himself with the mariner in both his nightmare and redemption. But even in the notebooks of this first serious descent into opium use in the Lakes, he seems, almost unconsciously, to draw on the poem. A brief, heart-breaking note from this time reads: 'Mind, ship-wrecked by storms of doubt, now mastless, rudderless, shattered, – pulling in the dead swell of a dark and windless Sea.'[18]

The 'Night-mare Life-in-Death' had indeed taken hold and in another notebook entry he records that he has seen her face to face in a dream:

Friday Night, Nov. 28, 1800, or rather Saturday Morning – a most frightful Dream of a Woman whose features were blended with darkness catching holding of my right eye & attempting to pull it out – I caught hold of her arm fast – a horrid feel – Wordsworth cried out aloud to me hearing my scream – hearing his cry & thought it cruel he did not come / but did not wake till his cry was repeated a third time – the Woman's name Ebon Ebon Thalud – When ~~my~~ I awoke, my right eye swelled –[19]

It is against this largely hidden background of his struggle and despair that we must set Coleridge's extraordinary achievements. Not only the achievement of sheer mental and spiritual survival, but all that he did in fact write and do in these years in the Lakes: the brilliant journalism and journal keeping, the editing for Wordsworth, the serious philosophical reading and thinking, the letters of comfort and support he poured out to the many friends in need who wrote to him at different times for solace and advice.

Remarkably, in the midst of the 'storms of doubt' he refers to in that earlier note, we can see from the letters and notebooks the dogged tenacity of his faith, often rising and clarifying in him, just at the point when he was weakest and others needed his insights most. A striking example comes in his long correspondence with Tom Poole. Poole's mother was ill and every letter from Coleridge ends with real concern and comment on her health and on Tom's own state of mind and soul. When, at last, Tom wrote to Coleridge saying his mother had died, Coleridge somehow drew out of his own depths a far from ordinary letter of condolence which shows how, even in the midst of these struggles, he still saw Christ as somehow the centre and depth of all our *Being*, as opposed to our mere existence. As this letter makes clear, this is not in some shallow personal pietism, but in a deep sense of Christ the sustaining and redeeming *Logos* in whom all things cohere. Coleridge wrote:

I have learnt, Poole! That your Mother is with the Blessed. – I have given her the tears & the pang, which belong to her Departure . . . what shall I say to *you*? I can only offer a prayer of Thanksgiving for you . . . The Frail and the too painful will gradually pass away from you; & there will abide in your Spirit a great & sacred accession to those solemn Remembrances and faithful Hopes, in which and by which the Almighty lays deep the foundations of our continuous Life, and distinguishes us from the Brutes that perish. As all things pass away, & those Habits are broken up which constituted our own & particular Self, our nature by a moral instinct cherishes the desire of an unchangeable Something, & thereby awakens or stirs up anew the passion to promote *permanent* Good . . . till *Existence* itself is swallowed up in *Being*, & we are in Christ even as he is in the father.

Then, in a postscript, he continues:

Come to me, Poole! – No-No-no. – You have none that love you as well as I – I write with tears that prevent my seeing what I am writing.[20]

One thing that appears to have kept Coleridge going through that dark winter and into the following year – though tragically it was also something that would ultimately crucify him with guilt and paralyse him emotionally – was the arrival in Grasmere, to stay with the Wordsworths, of Sara Hutchinson.

It was in these two years of 1801–2 that Coleridge's relationship with Sara Hutchinson would blossom, deepen, raise its sharp challenge, and ultimately be painfully renounced, with real nobility, self-sacrifice and devastating consequences on both sides. And yet in one way, certainly from a contemporary perspective, the relationship was entirely innocent and 'Platonic' (though for Coleridge, as we know, Platonic was a huge and important word). There has been occasional speculation, but there is no evidence, that Coleridge ever committed adultery; he may well have been tempted but it was absolutely against his deepest religious convictions, nor was it in Sarah Hutchinson's character either – she would have understood any temptation to adultery in the same terms: as desecrating and abasing all that was best and most to be cherished in their intimate friendship. An intimate and innocent friendship was what they both wanted it to be and hoped it would remain, deepening and blessing heart and soul, but casting no shadow or blame over their other relationships – but as their tenderness and feelings for one another grew they both came to realise that this was impossible – that neither of them could bear it. Coleridge was torn in his heart to find himself so deeply loving someone with whom he could never completely and exclusively share his life – for he was already committed, and however difficult his marriage became, he never forswore that commitment either to his wife or to his

children and Sara Hutchinson could not be asked to give herself
to a man who could not entirely give himself back. Even after
their grand renunciation, though, in April of 1802, which was
the occasion of *Dejection: An Ode*, one of Coleridge's last really
major poems, she continued to find ways to support and help
him, even acting as his amanuensis when he came to write his
wonderful journal series *The Friend*. But eventually he realised
he would have to leave her and distance himself from her, for her
sake as well as his.

In what then did the relationship really consist and how did it
develop?

Outwardly and visibly it was a series of visits, with Coleridge
going to Grasmere, and Sara, usually accompanied by the
Wordsworths, paying return visits to Keswick over that winter,
spring and summer. So they were most often in company, rather
than alone together, though sometimes they might walk together
a little apart when others were walking in a group. The relationship blossomed through conversation, through a common love
of the landscape, and most of all through 'Asra' and Coleridge's
shared love of poetry and story and her rich intuitive capacities
as a listener, an assistant, and ultimately a muse. Early in the
friendship Coleridge gave her a copy of Anna Seward's *Original
Sonnets*, which he inscribed 'to Asahara the Moorish maid'.
Asahara was soon shortened to Asra, an anagram for her own
name and the name he always used for her. Asra's is the only
hand, other than Coleridge's, to write in his precious and essentially private notebooks, and there is one entry only in which she
does so. But it is not an avowal of love or some heavily coded
outburst of passion. It is simply an alphabetical list of the names
of wildflowers, copied from William Withering's *British Plants*, a
book which Wordsworth had acquired as an aid to his and
Coleridge's work on the *Lyrical Ballads*. But as Asra copied these
names she added one or two of her own, local names unknown

to Withering perhaps, or ones that had a special meaning, and one of those additions was Forget Me Not. Now 'Forget Me Not' is the flower particularly mentioned in Coleridge's poem 'The Keepsake'. That poem was published first, like many of Coleridge's poems from this time, in the *Morning Post*, but he later included it in *Sibylline Leaves* of 1817. Interestingly, the OED gives Coleridge as the first person to introduce the country name *Forget Me Not* into print. We cannot tell whether the poem or this notebook entry came first, whether Asra was shyly reminding him of the poem with this interpolation or whether he took inspiration from her having written the name in the notebook to weave Forget Me Not into the poem. Either way, as Kathleen Coburn reflects in her notes to this notebook entry: 'It is not unpleasant to reflect that Coleridge and Sarah between them may have been responsible for re-introducing it into English Letters.'

On another occasion when Asra came to visit the Coleridges at Greta Hall, she and Coleridge spent a happy afternoon reading through his copy of *Bartram's Travels*, one of the beloved books of voyages that had supplied so much material for *The Ancient Mariner*.

Had their close friendship simply continued at this level it should not, ultimately, have presented a problem to either of them. It was not a secret. Sara Coleridge was certainly aware of it and may, at first, have been relieved that her husband had found such an amiable friend and companion, who could take him off her hands for a while as she had so much else to cope with, with her two young children and a third on the way. Had their marriage itself been in a better place and stronger at this time, then Sara might well have coped. In a letter from the autumn of 1802 Coleridge, one might say not unreasonably, pleads for space and openness in their relationship that might allow other friendships to flourish too. It begins 'My dear love' and speaks of 'pain and many struggles of mind, resolves and counter-resolves' which they had clearly both been going through. But in the end it makes this plea for a breadth and inclusiveness of affections:

> I can & do love many people, dearly – so dearly, that I really scarcely know, which I love the best. Is it not so with every good mother who has a large number of Children – & with many, many Brothers and Sisters in large & affectionate Families? Why should it be otherwise with Friends? Would any good & wise man, any warm & wide hearted man marry at all, if it were part of the Contract – Henceforth this Woman is your only friend, your sole beloved! All the rest of mankind, however amiable & akin to you must be only your *acquaintance*![21]

This allowance of space, this security that can accept other affections, was too much to ask of Sara Coleridge at this point, though it is interesting to note that later, when Coleridge was in Malta, Sara Coleridge went with the children to visit Asra and they became good friends, with Asra making visits back to Greta Hall. As Molly Lefebure remarks in her biography of Sara Coleridge, this rapprochement and long-lasting friendship between the two women would never have happened if either of them thought that Coleridge's relationship with Asra was the real source of the trouble in Coleridge's marriage. Both of them knew that the real culprit was opium.

> The stock romantic concept of Coleridge and Sarah Hutchinson as unrequited lovers has the ground cut from under it by Greta Hall's acceptance of Miss Hutchinson. The Southeys would never have received a woman whom they in any way believed to have been implicated in an intrigue with Coleridge, nor would Sara have cultivated friendship with such a woman, even to

please Samuel. But the better they knew her, the more the Greta Hall inmates liked the commonsensical, pithy, cheerful, in every respect decent Miss Hutchinson.[22]

But that rapprochement was still to come. This first deepening of Coleridge's relationship with Asra, about which up to that point he had made no secret, did lead to real resentment and jealousy on Sara's part. The consequence was that Coleridge, without forsaking the friendship, which he regarded as innocent, simply kept quiet about it, and this secrecy had the fatal consequence of intensifying the relationship it glossed over. When Asra returned to her brother's farm at Gallowhill, Coleridge, who had travelled up to Durham to consult books in the cathedral library, went over to stay with the Hutchinsons, without telling Sara. He was still suffering from the chronic rheumatic pains as before, particularly in his knee, and Tom Hutchinson's doctor recommended sea bathing, which was perhaps his excuse to himself for the visit. They enjoyed the sea at Scarborough over an idyllic ten days. But in the evenings, in the big fire-lit farmhouse kitchen, Coleridge, laid up on the sofa with his leg in bandages, was nursed by the two Hutchinson sisters, but perhaps with particularly tender care by Asra. Certainly there was playful flirtation, but it was the soothing tenderness of a kind of maternal nursing that entered most deeply into Coleridge's soul and turned intimate friendship into a deep and obsessive infatuation with which neither of them could cope.

Since many of their letters have been destroyed, it is difficult to reconstruct with certainty what happened next. But it would seem, from the subsequent poetry, that after his return, Coleridge began to send impassioned love letters to Asra, with which, quite understandably, she could not cope. It is clear from Coleridge's reference to 'my complaining scroll' in the long letter, subsequently published as the poem *Dejection*, that what made these letters so hard for Asra was not so much his affection as his insistent need for constant reassurance.

In February 1802, Coleridge heard from the Wordsworths that Asra had fallen ill at Gallowhill. Coleridge himself was not at Greta Hall, but in London trying to earn some more money for his family through journalism. As soon as he heard the news he rushed north and spent ten days at Gallowhill with Mary and Tom, helping to nurse Asra back to health while realising more and more deeply, and to his own great distress, that it was really his importunate and inordinate love that was the cause of her distress and illness. We have only the subsequent poetry and Coleridge's notebooks from which to reconstruct what happened, but it would seem that Coleridge and Asra agreed to some form of renunciation: Coleridge would go home and work on his marriage and try to reorder his feelings for Asra so that they might eventually resume an untrammelled friendship. Ironically, even as Coleridge and Asra, still desperately fond of one another, were trying to undo whatever unspoken troth plighting there might have been between them, Wordsworth and Asra's sister, Mary, were announcing their engagement and preparing to marry. It must have been unbearable for Coleridge. But the result was not, this time, a further spiral into the pit of self-pity and despair, but the composition of a truly great poem. The timing of its publication was exact: it was published in the *Morning Post* on 4 October 1802, the very day of Wordsworth's marriage: a strange and powerful wedding present.

The poem started life as a letter to Asra dated 4 April 1802, from which Coleridge later drew and shaped the famous *Dejection: An Ode*. Before turning to the poem that he eventually published, it is worth looking at the more personal passages that were later excised from the earlier draft.

In the letter he remembers looking up at the moon from the same places that Asra has seen it, and in a beautiful passage evokes the memory of listening late at night to a murmuring beehive.

> I would, that thou'dst been sitting all this while
> Upon the sod-built Seat of Camomile –
> And tho' thy Robin may have ceas'd to sing,
> Yet needs for my sake must though love to hear
> The Bee-hive murmuring near,
> That ever-busy & most quiet Thing
> Which I have heard at Midnight murmuring.[23]

Then he remembers in vivid detail the 'blameless' intimacies of the Gallow Hill kitchen.

> It was as calm as this, that happy night
> When Mary, thou, & I together were,
> The low decaying Fire our only Light,
> And listen'd to the Stillness of the Air!
> O that affectionate & blameless Maid,
> Dear Mary! On her Lap my head she lay'd –
>   Her Hand was on my Brow,
>   Even as my own is now;
> And on my cheek I felt the eye-lash play.
> Such Joy I had, that I may truly say,
> My spirit was awe-stricken with the Excess
> And trance-like depth of its brief happiness.[24]

Then, in great pain, he remembers

> . . . the fretting Hour
> Then when I wrote thee that complaining Scroll!
> Which even to bodily Sickness bruis'd thy Soul![25]

From thence he turns to their agreed renunciation:

> Be happy, & I need thee not in sight.
> Peace in thy Heart, & Quiet in thy Dwelling,
> Health in thy Limbs, & in thine eyes the Light
> Of Love, & Hope, & honorable Feeling –
> Where e'er I am, I shall be well content!
> To all things I prefer the Permanent.
> And better seems it for a heart, like mine,
> Always to know than sometimes to behold,
>   Their *Happiness* & thine –
> For Change doth trouble me with pangs untold!
> To see thee, hear thee, feel thee – then to part
>   Oh! It weighs down the Heart![26]

He cannot forbear, even so, from reflecting on the contrast between the happiness he hopes she will enjoy and his 'own peculiar lot'.

> My own peculiar Lot, my house-hold Life
> It is, & will remain, Indifference or Strife.
> While *ye* are *well & happy*, 'twould but wrong you
> If I should fondly yearn to be among you –
> Wherefore, O wherefore! should I wish to be
> A wither'd branch upon a blossoming Tree?[27]

These personal passages were all removed when the *Ode* was published, but what remained was still, in its own way, deeply personal and absolutely central to Coleridge's understanding, not only of poetry, but of the very ways in which we perceive the world.

At the heart of *Dejection: An Ode* is the struggle to know whether the transfiguring glimpses in nature which he had so powerfully celebrated in *This Lime-Tree Bower My Prison* and *Frost at Midnight* were really there, or whether they were just projections of his feelings. If there is a range or spectrum between an utterly confident transcendental vision in which all things speak of God and are drenched in his meaning, on the one hand, and on the other a bleak matter of fact-ness in which everything is opaque, dully and merely itself, speaking of nothing beyond its own materiality, then *Frost at Midnight* is at one end, the northern pole of that spectrum, but in *Dejection: an Ode* Coleridge has been plunged far south to the other pole, and the contrast and challenge between the two ways of seeing nature are an agony to him.

In the second stanza of the published poem he speaks of

A grief without a pang, void, dark, and drear,
A stifled, drowsy, unimpassioned grief,
Which finds no natural outlet, no relief,
In word, or sigh or tear—[28]

In such a state gazing at the western sky Coleridge becomes aware of a complete disjunction between sight and feeling: even though he can describe what he sees precisely and beautifully, there is no connection with anything within.

And still I gaze – and with how blank an eye!
And those thin clouds above, in flakes and bars,
That give away their motion to the stars;
Those stars, that glide behind them or between,
Now sparkling, now bedimm'd, but always seen:
Yon crescent Moon as fix'd as if it grew
In its own cloudless, starless lake of blue
I see them all so excellently fair,
I see, not feel how beautiful they are!
. . .

It were a vain endeavor,
Though I should gaze for ever
On that green light that lingers in the west:
I may not hope from outward forms to win
The passion and the life, whose fountains are within.[29]

Then, in the fourth section, Coleridge suddenly sees that the
glories that he had previously seen in nature had really issued out
from himself.

O Lady! we receive but what we give,
And in our life alone does nature live:
Ours is her wedding garment, ours her shroud!
And would we aught behold, of higher worth,
Than that inanimate cold world allowed
To the poor loveless ever-anxious crowd,
Ah! from the soul itself must issue forth
A light, a glory, a fair luminous cloud
Enveloping the Earth—
And from the soul itself must there be sent
A sweet and potent voice, of its own birth,
Of all sweet sounds the life and element![30]

In the fifth stanza, Coleridge identifies 'this fair luminous cloud'
with Joy: joy, which has been given by nature and is then returned
to nature as we see her.

Joy, Lady! is the spirit and the power,
Which wedding Nature to us gives in dower
    A new Earth and new Heaven,
Undreamt of by the sensual and the proud—
Joy is the sweet voice, Joy the luminous cloud—
    We in ourselves rejoice!

And thence flows all that charms or ear or sight,
    All melodies the echoes of that voice,
All colours a suffusion from that light.[31]

In the sixth stanza, Coleridge finally diagnoses the depth of his crisis: in losing joy he has also wounded in himself the spirit of imagination from which all his visionary poetry had actually flowed.

But oh! each visitation
Suspends what nature gave me at my birth,
    My shaping spirit of Imagination.
For not to think of what I needs must feel,
    But to be still and patient, all I can;
And haply by abstruse research to steal
    From my own nature all the natural man—
    This was my sole resource, my only plan:
Till that which suits a part infects the whole,
And now is almost grown the habit of my soul.[32]

Like his mariner, Coleridge is somehow only seeing things through the 'dungeon-grate' of his own afflictions.

 The paradox is that this lament for the loss of his 'shaping spirit of imagination' is itself expressed in beautifully shaped poetry of great imaginative force. Even as he mourns at seeing without feeling he is enabling us both to see and to feel. On one reading this poem appears to concede that everything we thought was actually glorious and beautiful *in* nature is merely a subjective feeling projected onto nature, and yet those very 'subjective' ideas are expressed in a beautifully made object, the poem itself, which is not fleeting but reliable and generative, always available to the reader. From henceforth, this apparent dichotomy and tension between the two poles of the subjective and the objective was to be the central preoccupation of Coleridge's thinking. What he needed was to find some mediating power between these apparent opposites that would not only reconcile them but would release the immense potential energies that each could bring out in the other. Like his mariner, he would find that resolution in a miraculous moonrise.

'In his loneliness and fixedness he yearneth towards the journeying moon …'
A turning point, a grace, a transfiguration, came first to the mariner and then
to his poet.

CHAPTER NINE

The Moving Moon

Part III of *The Ancient Mariner* ended with this ominous final gloss: 'But Life-in-Death begins her work on the ancient Mariner.'[1] In Part IV we begin to see the nightmare's dreadful work on the mariner; but we also see in the midst of it an unexpected trans-figuration, an unlooked-for and undeserved grace that changes everything.

We left the mariner alone on the deck, reminded of his deed by the death of each of the other crew members. The narrative picks up again with one of Coleridge's dramatic shifts of perspective. Suddenly we are back with the post-voyage mariner as he tells his tale to the wedding guest, and once more we are given the reactions of the listener:

The Wedding-Guest feareth that a Spirit is talking to him;

"I fear thee, ancient Mariner!
I fear thy skinny hand!
And thou art long, and lank, and brown,
As is the ribbed sea-sand.

"I fear thee and thy glittering eye,
And thy skinny hand, so brown."—
Fear not, fear not, thou Wedding-Guest!
This body dropt not down.

(Lines 224–31 with gloss)

The guest is afraid that the mariner is one of the dead! It is not so, but this alarm serves to underline what follows when the mariner tries in vain to die, rather than to be alone with the dead, and helps us to realise that from his perspective it was worse to have been 'won' by life-in-death than to have been given over to death himself.

Then comes one of the most famous and harrowing verses in the poem:

But the ancient Mariner assureth him of his bodily life, and proceedeth to relate his horrible penance.

Alone, alone, all, all alone,
Alone on a wide wide sea!
And never a saint took pity on
My soul in agony.

(Lines 232–5 with gloss)

The poem was written at the end of the eighteenth century, but in some respects the loneliness evoked in this verse may strike us even more deeply in the twenty-first century than it did its first readers. Loneliness of this profound kind, utter isolation, a sense of being cut off not only from other people but from the cosmos itself, has come to be one of the most common experiences, even perhaps the defining experience, of our own age. And this is not simply the loneliness of the increasing numbers in our society who are living alone, from the bereaved or abandoned elderly to the middle-aged divorced, to singles in their minimalist studio flats, but a deeper more endemic kind of loneliness: a sense of disconnection, anomie, alienation; that even when we are with people we are somehow all the more isolated in our own tiny absurd islanded consciousness, separated and marooned in the concavity of our own little skulls with a wide, wide sea of nothingness between us and any other. Ironically, this feeling of isolation is actually deepened rather than relieved by the plethora of online social networks and the almost manic fury with which we acquire virtual friends only to find that no one actually knows us, not even we ourselves.

The root cause of this loneliness is philosophical. It reflects the shift at the birth of modernism, from the living, sacral view of the cosmos as an interconnected web of human and angelic consciousnesses all participating, to a greater or lesser degree, in an all-pervasive divine presence, expressed in and through the physical, to the modern mechanistic, instrumental view of nature in which matter is dead, inert and essentially meaningless, its motion caused by blind mechanism and its apparent flashes of beauty and meaning no more than a mirage. Coleridge was living in the midst of this shift and he felt it from within, understood its consequences and turned to resist it with every effort of his being. *The Rime of the Ancient Mariner* is a poem of resistance: it prophesies the consequences of this loss of sacral vision, but it also prophesies a recovery of vision. That recovery is, I think, beginning in our midst, in these opening decades of the twenty-first century. The reductive Enlightenment modernist project is disintegrating all around us, and although it is not yet clear what will replace it, Coleridge, especially in this part of the poem which speaks so tellingly of our present condition, points to some exciting possibilities.

In the following verse Coleridge moves from expressing what many feel as a kind of existential loneliness, to giving voice to another phenomenon for which the twentieth century found it needed a special term: survivor guilt.

He despiseth the creatures of the calm,	The many men, so beautiful! And they all dead did lie: And a thousand thousand slimy things Liv'd on; and so did I.

(Lines 236–9 with gloss)

Psychologists first used the term survivor guilt when working with Holocaust survivors, but soon found that similar symptoms arose with people who had survived other traumas, including shipwrecks. At its core is a deep sense of guilt and loneliness for having survived at all; an intense perception of the worth and beauty of those who didn't, contrasted with an equally intense and perhaps distorted sense of self-loathing. Certainly the mariner experiences all of this, and his double sense of horror at the death of the crew coupled with a sense of their beauty speaks deeply from this poem into the lives of many who, long after it was written, experience trauma. It is small wonder that when David Jones came to write *In Parenthesis*, his masterpiece of survivor guilt about the experience of fighting as a private in the First World War, he called the opening section 'The Many Men so Beautiful'. Jones, an artist as well as a poet, went on after the war to make a series of striking copperplate engravings to illustrate *The Rime of the Ancient Mariner* (see picture section).

> And a thousand thousand slimy things
> Liv'd on; and so did I.
>
> *(Lines 238–9)*

This moment, the nadir of the poem, presents us with a strange inversion of that other archetypal voyage which haunts this poem: the voyage of Noah's Ark. The mariner afloat alone, 'despising' the only other living things around him, with the bird he has killed hung round his neck and the deck strewn with the dead bodies of the fellow crew, contrasts at almost every point with the biblical image of the Ark: full of living things of every species, with Noah, its own 'ancient mariner' preparing to let a living bird fly free to return with a sign of hope that will lead to a new covenant between God and all living things – not just humanity. Before he shot the albatross, the mariner and his crew might well have become a new ark, hospitable to the guiding bird and moving from the lifeless ice back into a new world of possibility as they round the cape. Indeed, Gustave Doré, who famously illustrated the poem with such power and resonance, makes just that connection when he portrays the vessel early in the poem guided by the albatross and orbed with a rainbow.(See Illustration on page 416) But the mariner chose otherwise, and in this despairing stanza he identifies himself with the 'slimy things', which become an outward expression of his inward self-loathing. We are back in a deliberate echo of the imagery we encountered in Part II of the poem:

> The very deep did rot: O Christ!
> That ever this should be!
> Yea, slimy things did crawl with legs
> Upon the slimy sea.
>
> *(Lines 123–6)*

This uneasy sense of reversion – of apparent progress suddenly lost, the ship in the doldrums, rudderless, rolling uneasily, drifting back and forth over the same spot – is a powerful outward expression of the inward state of mind and soul which the poem is trying to evoke.

This opens out the question of how the inward and outward are related, which was to preoccupy Coleridge so desperately and to which he was to find such a powerful and in every sense *imaginative* solution. For here the gloss gives us a different perspective and subtly subverts the mariner's assumption of loathing in the main text. Against this verse Coleridge sets the gloss: 'He despiseth the creatures of the great calm.' They are not, in this gloss, 'slimy things' but creatures of the calm,

creatures in the deeper theological sense: parts of the *creation*
made and shaped by the hand of God, with their own particular
beauty and meaning, even if the mariner, at this moment, cannot
perceive the beauty and misconstrues the meaning. Indeed, the
next time the gloss refers to them, eight verses later, they are
referred to as 'God's creatures of the great calm'. The very phrase
'the great calm' carries spiritual connotations that are prophetic
of what is to come.

But here the mariner is still in a state of desperation, an agony
of loneliness and self-loathing:

And envieth   I look'd upon the rotting sea,
that they should
live, and so   And drew my eyes away;
many lie dead.   I looked upon the rotting deck,
                 And there the dead men lay.

                 I look'd to Heaven, and tried to pray;
                 But or ever a prayer had gusht,
                 A wicked whisper came, and made
                 My heart as dry as dust.

                 I closed my lids, and kept them close,
                 And the balls like pulses beat;
                 For the sky and the sea, and the sea and the sky
                 Lay like a load on my weary eye,
                 And the dead were at my feet.

                             (Lines 240–53 with gloss)

The core of all this agony and isolation is, for the mariner, as it
would be for Coleridge, the inability to pray. Having broken the
threads of mutuality and communication at the horizontal
level, as it were, between himself and his fellow creatures, the

mariner now finds the vertical axis, the thread of connection with the divine in prayer, also broken, and his isolation is complete.

It is also characteristic of Coleridge that he should express this failure of prayer as dryness and dust; dryness just at the very place where the hidden spring or fountain should have been, where a prayer should have 'gusht'. The very imperfection of the rhyme of 'gusht' and 'dust' is itself an expression of the faltering and failure in the mariner's heart which is at the heart of this verse. For Coleridge, as we have seen and will see in his other poetry, the fountain, the inner welling source, the river itself as the stream of grace and inspiration, are all central images and so this reduction of the heart, the fountainhead, to dust is especially horrific.

The wicked whisper that makes the heart dry as dust, the voice of the accuser, is a kind of infernal opposite to the work of the Holy Spirit, whose emblems in wind, water and fire we are shortly to encounter.

In the Genesis narrative God originally creates humankind, forms his 'creature' out of the dust of the ground, and then stoops down and, in a kind of divine whisper, puts his breath within and breathes the human being into life. By contrast there is a kind of hideous 'decreation' taking place here in which the 'wicked whisper' comes and reduces the heart to dust again. As we shall see, Coleridge would soon enough find himself in this very place.

These stanzas also make it clear that this withering and desiccation of the heart affects not only prayer but vision itself: the cosmos turns from being a luminous series of symbols that speak of a beauty and meaning beyond themselves to being simply a dead oppression, a 'weary load' from which we seek in vain to escape, a 'huge heap of little things' as Coleridge had called it in an earlier letter. This failure of vision is the very thing he analysed, four years after writing *The Mariner*, in *Dejection: An Ode*. So here, in *The Mariner*, he wrote:

> For the sky and the sea, and the sea and the sky
> Lay like a load on my weary eye,
> And the dead were at my feet.

(Lines 250–2)

And in *Dejection: An Ode*:

> I may not hope from outward forms to win
> The passion and the life, whose fountains are within.[2]

Now, as he turns back from the sea and the sky to the 'rotting deck', even the beauty he had once perceived in the 'many men' has disappeared:

But the curse liveth for him in the eye of the dead men.

> The cold sweat melted from their limbs,
> Nor rot nor reek did they:
> The look with which they looked on me
> Had never passed away.
>
> An orphan's curse would drag to hell
> A spirit from on high;
> But oh! more horrible than that
> Is the curse in a dead man's eye!
> Seven days, seven nights, I saw that curse,
> And yet I could not die.

(Lines 253–62)

The Moving Moon

It is just at this point, after he has reached his worst agony, seven days and seven nights of longing but being unable to die, that we get the first intimations of change: initially in the imagery of the poem itself, and then in the course of what actually happens to the mariner. The motif – almost as it were, musically, the 'signature' – that accompanies these changes, is the image of the 'moving moon':

> *In his loneli-*
> *ness and fixed-*
> *ness he year-*
> *neth towards*
> *the journeying*
> *Moon, and the*
> *stars that still*
> *sojourn yet*
> *still move*
> *onward; and*
> *every where the*
> *blue sky*
> *belongs to*
> *them, and is*
> *their appointed*
> *rest, and their*
> *native country*
> *and their own*
> *natural homes,*
> *which they*
> *enter unan-*
> *nounced, as*
> *lords that are*
> *certainly*
> *expected and*
> *yet there is a*
> *silent joy at*
> *their arrival.*

The moving Moon went up the sky,
And no where did abide:
Softly she was going up,
And a star or two beside—

(Lines 263–6 with gloss)

Coleridge makes a beautiful and ambiguous play on the word 'moving'. This is a 'moving moon' in every sense. It is in the moon's very nature both that she moves through space and is the cause of movement in others, and also that she moves us emotionally, in the inner space of our hearts.

Accompanying this verse is the later gloss which forms a kind of counterpoint to and commentary on the verse. 'In his loneliness and fixedness, he yearneth towards the journeying Moon, and the stars that still sojourn, yet still move onward . . .' These glosses, as we have seen, were added years later, after Coleridge had himself lived through much of what the poem describes. They form almost a separate poem and yet one that is in profound conversation with the text it glosses. So, for example, this long and beautiful gloss on the 'journeying Moon, and the stars that still sojourn, yet still move onward', although set there apparently only to explain a single verse, acts as a kind of premonition of the redemption which is to come. At the lowest point in the mariner's journey, just when he has cried in agony that he wishes to die and yet he cannot, just at the point where his own journey seems endless and hopeless, and home is an unimaginable possibility – just at that point comes a gloss whose imagery moves us from journeying to homecoming. The narrative of the poem will not arrive at a homecoming for many stanzas yet, but the hope of its possibility is mediated to the reader through key words in the gloss; words such as 'belongs' and 'rest', 'native country', 'natural home', which gloss the text of the mariner's exile like the whispers of a good dream. The last phrase of that gloss, 'there is a silent joy at their arrival', antici-pates, with its echo of Christ's words about the joy in heaven over the sinner who repents, the final homecoming of the mariner – even at that point in the story at which such a homecoming seems least likely.

The way in which Coleridge's later gloss on the text of his poem allows us to return to a page we thought we knew and read it in a new way is rather like the Christian experience of repentance, confession and grace. One lives through a page of one's life, and looking back it can seem to have the finality of a printed text, a completed work. How can any of it ever be undone or unsaid, however much one wishes it could? But in prayer and confession, we offer that page to God for the commentary of His grace; we invite Him to surround the text of our life with a gloss that may reveal to us, many years later, glimpses of redeeming love that were hidden at the time.

The mariner's redemption can only come from a recognition of the truth he had denied when he shot the albatross: the truth that all creatures are God's and not his. In the following stanzas he looks out again at the water-snakes, which he had previously described as 'a thousand thousand slimy things', and sees them utterly transfigured in the moonlight:

The mariner ... "moon" first change in the water-snakes

258

<table>
<tr><td>By the light of the Moon he beholdeth God's creatures of the great calm.</td><td>Beyond the shadow of the ship,
I watch'd the water-snakes:
They moved in tracks of shining white,
And when they reared, the elfish light
Fell off in hoary flakes.</td></tr>
</table>

(Lines 272–6 with gloss)

[*verse omitted*]

<table>
<tr><td>Their beauty and their happiness. He blesseth them in his heart.</td><td>O happy living things! no tongue
Their beauty might declare:
A spring of love gushed from my heart,
And I blessed them unaware:
Sure my kind saint took pity on me,
And I blessed them unaware.</td></tr>
</table>

<table>
<tr><td>The spell begins to break.</td><td>The self-same moment I could pray;
And from my neck so free
The Albatross fell off, and sank
Like lead into the sea.</td></tr>
</table>

(Lines 282–91 with gloss)

It is as though by seeing these creatures in moonlight he is given, however briefly, some notion of how God sees them. Certainly Coleridge's own experiences of moonlight, especially moonlight on water, had something of that quality, as for example this brief passage from one of the notebooks shows: 'Quiet stream, with all its eddys [sic]& the moon light playing in them; quiet, as if they were Ideas in the divine Mind anterior to the Creation.'[3]

For Coleridge, the meaning of the moon and moonlight is not a purely human invention. It is a symbol, but it is not a randomly chosen or arbitrarily constructed human one; it is a symbol which is given, which is moulded by and participates in the reality it represents. Coleridge distinguished true symbols from artificial analogies; he summed up his distinction in a late work, *The*

Statesman's Manual: 'The Symbol is characterized by . . . the translucence of the Eternal through and in the Temporal. It always partakes of the Reality which it renders intelligible; and while it enunciates the whole, abides itself as a living part in that Unity, of which it is representative.' By contrast, analogies are 'but empty echoes which the fancy arbitrarily associates with apparitions of matter, less beautiful but not less shadowy than the sloping orchard or hill-side pasture-field seen in the transparent lake below'.[4]

Coleridge spent most of the second part of his life reflecting in a rigorous and philosophically disciplined way on the very question of what a symbol is, and on the relation between language considered as a set of symbols given and articulated by humanity, and nature considered as a set of symbols given and articulated by God. As we tell the story of the rest of Coleridge's life we will turn to some of his later prose works and travel with Coleridge on a journey that traces the full flow of his poetry back to its source in an Imagination which is more than the human.

But this is to anticipate. Remaining for a moment with these verses in the poem, we can see that what restores and re-orients the 'reversal of creation' we saw in 'a wicked whisper came, and made / My heart as dry as dust' is a blessing uttered by the mariner himself: 'I blessed them unaware'. And the blessing itself is a reversal both of the 'despising' of the 'creatures of the great calm' highlighted in the gloss and also a reversal of the language of 'curse'. The word 'curse' is repeated three times in one stanza (lines 257–62), and now we have the word 'bless', also repeated ritually in one stanza.

In these concluding stanzas of Part IV we can see the anticipatory echoes not only of what was to come later in the poem, but also of texts that Coleridge had already read but the full meaning of which he had not yet grasped, yet had somehow still intuited in the imaginative medium of his poem. One of these texts, as we

And "unjusted" too'.

have already seen in considering the relevance of the Ark, is of course the Bible.

In *The Rime of the Ancient Mariner* we can see the rich, intuitive, allusive way in which biblical images and motifs were feeding and informing Coleridge's imagination. The earlier images of the mariner's agonising thirst were already echoing the imagery of the Psalms, particularly Psalm 22, the psalm of crucifixion: 'My strength is dried up like a potsherd; and my tongue cleaves to my jaws; and thou has brought me unto the dust of death.'[5] And now, in this turning point of the poem, when the mariner receives unexpected and undeserved grace, perceived as the sudden arising of a spring or fountain, within, voiced in the line 'a spring of love gushed from my heart', there is a deliberate echo of the story of Christ and the woman at the well. In John (Coleridge's favourite Gospel) Jesus meets the woman in the heat of the day when they are both exhausted and thirsty. The conversation turns on the possibility or impossibility of drawing water from Jacob's well. The woman sees only the problems and difficulties in the 'outer well':

> The woman saith unto him, Sir, thou hast nothing to draw with, and the well is deep: from whence then hast thou that living water? Art thou greater than our father Jacob, which gave us the well, and drank thereof himself, and his children, and his cattle? Jesus answered and said unto her, Whosoever drinketh of this water shall thirst again: But whosoever drinketh of the water that I shall give him shall never thirst; but the water that I shall give him shall be in him a well of water springing up into everlasting life.[6]

In both the Gospel moment, and the turning point of *The Ancient Mariner*, what is offered is sheer grace at the zero point. Neither the woman nor the mariner have done anything to deserve it, but for both of them grace changes everything. As the story unfolds, the woman at the well turns from being an outcast from her community (which is why she is drawing water at noon) to being someone with a discovery made and a story to tell which will change the lives of those around her – and so it proves with the mariner.

With the exception of the seventh and final part, each of the parts of *The Mariner* ends with a return to the image or memory of the albatross; but here, at the end of the fourth part, it is at last an image of release, and what achieves the release, and is in its own way achieved by release, is prayer:

> *The spell begins to break.*   The self-same moment I could pray;
> And from my neck so free
> The Albatross fell off, and sank
> Like lead into the sea.
>
>   *(Lines 288–91 with gloss)*

Returning to Coleridge's own story, we find that, as with his mariner, reaching a turning point is one thing, but recovering and reaching home is quite another.

Composing *Dejection: An Ode* seems to have provided Coleridge with some real relief. In writing it he had had a brief return of that very shaping spirit of imagination, whose loss he was lamenting. He cared about the ode enough to work hard on its revision and it in turn spurred Wordsworth on to his great *Ode on Intimations of Immortality*; indeed, one can read the poems as a kind of dialogue, so it seemed, however briefly, that an old writing partnership had been resumed. But in *Dejection: An Ode* Coleridge was stating his problem, not solving it. As that spring turned to summer and another winter drew on, he found that the tensions and impossibilities that confronted him were deepening, not dissipating. Publishing *Dejection* on the day

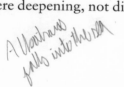

A albatross falls into the sea

of Wordsworth's marriage to Mary, Asra's sister, had been meant to help Coleridge draw a line under the whole Asra/Mary Hutchinson cluster of memories and longings. He and Sara had both agreed to make a serious new effort at their marriage and had set out some of the terms on which they would do so. Sara would try to be more warm-feeling and engaged and less disparaging of Coleridge's friends; Coleridge, in his turn, would be more attentive to and concentrated on his domestic life, and less irregular in his habits.

He also promised to attend to his 'mismanaged sensibility'. 'Mismanaged sensibility' was code for overuse of opium, and therein lay the problem. Deep down Coleridge must have known, as Sara already consciously knew, that it was not his flirtation with Asra as a muse that was destroying their marriage, but his utter bondage to opium. Sara rebuked him for it and he came, as all addicts do, to resent her deeply for pointing to the very things he knew were true but couldn't face. In normal circumstances, Coleridge, whose whole temper was genial and generous, would be the last person to have a habit of 'bitter censure', but opium was already impairing that gift of generosity. Indeed, his emotional outbursts against Sara, for which he apologises in some of his letters, were really displaced rages against opium, for opium was already not only possessing and distressing his waking hours and his bodily health, but invading his dreams.[7]

Coleridge needed to find a way of coping with these impossible tensions that didn't involve a heavier recourse to opium. He found two outlets, both of which seemed to provide, at the time, only temporary relief, but that ultimately did him great good and shaped and informed his mature writing. The first was fell walking, which Coleridge could be said to have invented.[8] Whereas most people in Coleridge's day, traversing the Lake District on foot, as often as not in foul weather, sensibly kept to the lowest

and most well-kept paths, Coleridge insistently and enthusiastically headed for the hills, striding out and upwards, pushing
himself through his bodily pains and into the elements with a
kind of manic and almost preternatural strength. The sheer intensity banished, for a while, the two other intense longings he was
really fleeing: the opium craving and the hopeless desire for Asra.
Though he was in one sense *driven* into these great expeditions
over many days and nights in all weathers, in another sense he was
lifted and occasionally experienced the utter openness to the
divine in nature, which had once come so easily to him. In the
letter to Thomas Wedgwood which we have already cited, written
as dark December had turned to the January of 1803, Coleridge
gives some account of what was really going on within him, and
this passage gives the wider context of that earlier citation:

> I never find myself alone within the embracement of rocks &
> hills, a traveller up an alpine road, but my spirit courses, drives,
> and eddies, like a Leaf in Autumn: a wild activity, of thoughts,
> imaginations, feelings, and impulses of motion, rises up from
> within me . . . The farther I ascend from animated Nature, from
> men, and cattle, & the common birds of the woods, & fields,
> the greater becomes in me the Intensity of the feeling of Life;
> Life seems to me then a universal spirit, that neither has, nor can
> have, an opposite. God is every where, I have exclaimed, &
> works every where; & where is there *room* for Death? In these
> moments it has been my creed, that Death exists only because
> Ideas exist / that Life is limitless Sensation; that Death is a child
> of the organic senses, chiefly of the Sight; that Feelings die by
> flowing into the mould of the Intellect, & becoming Ideas; &
> that Ideas passing forth into action re-instate themselves again
> in the world of Life. And I do believe, that Truth lies inveloped
> in these loose generalizations. – I do not think it possible, that
> any bodily pains could eat out the love & joy, that is so

substantially part of me, towards hills, & rocks, & steep waters!
And I have had some Trial.[9]

The disadvantage of these expeditions, however, was that
Coleridge would return home exhausted and soaked to the skin,
with the rheumatic pains more intolerable than ever, and retreat
to the very opium he had been trying to avoid.

His second stratagem, alluded to in *Dejection: An Ode*, was
what he called in that poem 'abstruse research'.

> But to be still and patient, all I can;
> And haply by abstruse research to steal
> From my own nature all the natural man—
> This was my sole resource, my only plan:
> Till that which suits a part infects the whole,
> And now is almost grown the habit of my soul.[10]

These annotations ×D

The abstruse research referred to here was Coleridge's deep reading
in philosophy and metaphysics. Not other people's summaries, but
a fiercely concentrated absorption of the primary texts themselves:
first the British empiricists, Locke, Hume, Hartley, and behind
them, Descartes and Newton, and then the counter-movement and
critique of that materialist empiricism in the various forms of transcendental idealism to be found in Spinoza and Kant. Many literary critics, especially those with scant knowledge of philosophy,
have taken Coleridge at his word in this passage of *Dejection: An
Ode* and assumed that it was the philosophy that killed the poetry,
that Coleridge was reading for distraction alone and that this
particular distraction and the thought that attended it confused
and diffused his real vocation, turning him from an accessible poet
into an inaccessible and obscure metaphysician. But this is emphat-
ically not the case. He may have needed distraction, but Coleridge
was reading and thinking for his life – and for ours.

Coleridge recognised that the material and instrumental view of nature which derived from Locke and Hume was utterly deadening and would eventually not only threaten faith but ultimately crush any notion of 'soul' or even 'person'. He also saw that it was not enough to reject these ideas emotionally and subjectively and write a little compensatory poetry as a retreat from grim reality; he saw that these philosophies, which he felt to be false, had also to be met head-on in their own terms and by the exercise of reason, if the counter-intuitions of poetry were to have any good grounding. Somehow he needed to find or to build the bridge between the dead but objective world of meaningless fact, on the one hand, and the world of rich subjective fancy with no claims to truth, on the other, which seemed to be the only two alternatives his contemporaries presented. He would still have much work to do in the future, but even in these desperate first three years of the nineteenth century, he was making great strides. His letters, especially to his beloved Tom Poole, are full of the discoveries which would be the building blocks of his great future synthesis. In a letter to Poole of March 1801, after alluding to another letter sent to Wedgwood, in which he carefully analysed the faults and inconsistences in Locke's philosophy, he goes on to say:

> Be not afraid, that I shall join the party of the *Little-ists* – I believe, that I shall delight you by the detection of their artifices – Now Mr Locke was the founder of this sect, himself a perfect Little-ist. My opinion is this – that deep Thinking is attainable only by a man of deep Feeling, and that all Truth is a species of Revelation. The more I understand of Sir Isaac Newton's works, the more boldly I dare utter to my own mind & therefore to *you*, that I believe the souls of 500 Sir Isaac Newtons would go to the making up of a Shakspere or a Milton. But if it please the Almighty to grant me health, hope, and a steady mind, (always

the 3 clauses of my hourly prayers) before my 30th year I will thoroughly understand the whole of Newton's works – At present, I must content myself with endeavouring to make myself master of his easier work, that on Optics. I am exceedingly delighted with the beauty & neatness of his experiment, & with the accuracy of his *immediate* Deductions from them – but the opinions found on these Deductions, and indeed his whole Theory is, I am persuaded, so exceedingly superficial as without impropriety to be deemed false. Newton was a mere materialist – Mind in his system is always passive – a lazy Looker-on on an external World. If the mind be not *passive*, if it be indeed made in God's Image, & that too in the sublimest sense – the Image of the *Creator* – there is ground for suspicion, that any system built on the passiveness of the mind must be false, as a system.[11]

There is much to be learned from this rich and beautiful letter. First, one should note Coleridge is not glibly or superficially dismissing the scientists and philosophers with whom he contends, but is making himself master of their works. Second, there is his unique and important emphasis on the *mode* of our knowing: he challenges the unquestioned assumption on the part of all materialists that the mind is a merely passive receptor, acted upon and only recording external impulses and stimuli. Given that assumption, their *immediate deductions* may be accurate as far as they go, but once we make the daring leap to frame things differently and understand the mind and imagination as prior and active agents then we can transcend this superficial frame without necessarily denying the immediate conclusions in that smaller reference. Coleridge's unease about the false neatness and pretended inevitability of the Newtonian system has proved prophetic and this letter, read in the light of Einstein and all that has developed since, seems less outrageous than it might have done to the astonished Tom Poole.

Third, we can see Coleridge reaching for a helpful and essentially rational integration between faith, philosophy and science. It is given in his brilliant association of truth with revelation and deepened in his crucial insight that mind itself, if it is made in the image of the creator, is essentially creative rather than reductively passive. This insight into the mind as exercising an active, shaping, creative power as it looks out into the world was to become a crucial element in his eventual definition of the Imagination as a 'living power and prime agent of all perception'. Finally, in his intuition that deep thinking is 'attainable only by a man of deep feeling' we can see him feeling his way towards a resolution of the apparent antipathy between reason and imagination, between objective and subjective. One might also note the passing reference to prayer, unnoticed by almost all the other writers on Coleridge who quote this letter: 'But if it please the Almighty to grant me health, hope, and a steady mind, (always the 3 clauses of my hourly prayers)'. 'My hourly prayers'! Coleridge may have bracketed that comment, but we should not ignore it. Prayer is not only the turning point, but almost the very subject of *The Ancient Mariner*, and any reader of Coleridge's letters and notebooks will be struck by the frequency, range and depth of the prayers that weave through his writing. They will also feel, with Coleridge, the agony he experiences when unable to pray; and yet in the vast literature on Coleridge there is almost nothing that really examines his writing about prayer, let alone his prayer life itself. One purpose of this book is to redress that balance.

Most writers about Coleridge have opted to tell only one of two apparently very different stories: the first and best known is the sublime yet tragic story of the poet of inspiration and of agony, of the lover who speaks with and from a broken heart, the poet of freedom who finds himself evermore deeply meshed in the bondage of opium, and ends his life, from that perspective, in apparent failure. The second is the story of Coleridge the thinker, the philosopher, the man of faith, the founder of literary criticism and the originator of almost every school of literary criticism we now possess. This story is often told without any reference to his life at all, as though the great literary criticism, the profound theories of poetry, the subtle and just appreciation of Shakespeare, were all achieved in some ideal ivory tower, free from pain or distraction. But the real story is much more moving. Owen Barfield's excellent book *What Coleridge Thought* presents us with a reconstruction of Coleridge's whole system of thought – 'The Dynamic or Communicative Philosophy' as Coleridge called it, as though that whole system had come to him in one piece with all its subtle connections and strong ramifications. When we see how Coleridge reached out towards, shaped and attained that dynamic philosophy, that integration of faith and reason, in the midst of the heartbreak of forsaken love and the corruption and damage of opium; how he achieved what he did not only in spite of the pain and despair through which he lived, but *with* that pain and despair, expressed in prayer and poetry, as his very materials; then we begin to see the greatness of his achievement.

So Coleridge struggled on with his impossible tensions, sometimes fending them off with the heights of fell walking, sometimes descending instead to the depths of the Kendal Black Drop, but it couldn't last. The tensions were too great even for Coleridge's agility and endurance to hold together.

In fact, for all his efforts to control and overcome his infatuation with Asra, Coleridge could not get her out of his heart. On 19 October 1803, his thirty-first birthday, and his last autumn in the Lakes before his self-imposed exile the following spring, he looked out again at the beautiful views from his study and confided to his notebook:

the vale, like a place in Faery, with the autumnal Colours, the orange, the re-brown, all & Birches, as they were blossoming

Fire & Gold! – & the Sun in slanting pillars, or illuminated small parcels of mist, or single spots of softest greyish Light, now racing, now slowly gliding, now stationary/ – the mountains cloudy – the Lake has been a mirror so very clear, that the water became almost invisible – & now it rolls in white Breakers, like a Sea; & the wind snatches up the water, & drifts it like Snow/ – and now the Rain Storm pelts against my Study window! – [Sara] why am I not happy! Why have I not unencumbered Heart! These beloved Books still before me, this noble Room, the very centre to which a whole world of beauty converges, the deep reservoir into which all these streams & currents of lovely Forms flow – my own mind so populous, so active, so full of noble schemes, so capable of realizing them / this heart so loving, so filled with noble affections – O [Sara]! Wherefore am I not happy! Why for years have I not enjoyed one pure and sincere pleasure! – one full Joy! – one genuine Delight, that rings sharp to the Beat of the Finger! – all cracked, & dull with base Alloy![12]

The paradoxes at the heart of this glorious piece of prose are almost unbearable. Coleridge gives an almost perfect picture of the alert, perceiving mind, alive to beauty, in and through which all the outer images of nature converge and find their inner meaning, and yet the encumbered and broken heart can make nothing of them, can no longer find in them the joy which should be their truest meaning.

Given these preoccupations and the deepening use of opium with which he tried to quell them, it is not surprising that things were difficult and cold again at home. Eventually Coleridge gave way to the fatal temptation to indulge in 'might have beens', to go back and unpick his earlier decisions and wish them away, to wish he had not married Sara. And, of course, as soon as he did so it was easy to look back and see how he had in many senses been hurried and pressurised into that marriage by Southey. In a heart-breaking letter to Southey himself he wrote:

> Assuredly, I have no right to do any thing that will in the least degree diminish Mrs Coleridge's Comforts & Tranquillity. In an evil Day for me did I first pay attentions to Mrs Coleridge; in an evil Day for me did I marry her; but it shall be my care & my passion, that it shall not be an evil day for her; & that whatever I may be, or may be represented, as a Husband, I may yet be unexceptionable, as her Protector and Friend.–
>
> O dear Southey! I am no Elm! – I am a crumbling wall, under-mined at the foundation! Why should the Vine and all it's clusters be buried in my rubbish?[13]

In another equally frank letter to William Godwin he put his finger on the terrible dilemma experienced by any couple who are contemplating separation, but who deeply love their children. He was, he says:

> struggling with sore calamities, with bodily pain and languor – with pecuniary Difficulties – & worse than all, with domestic Discord & the heart-withering Conviction – that I could not be happy without my children, & could not but be miserable with the mother of them.[14]

Coleridge began to find more and more reasons to be away from home, and Sara may have been relieved that he did so, for in some senses opium and depression had already taken away the man she married. His reasons to be away were still in their own way good ones.

There was his promise to look after the ailing Tom Wedgwood, who was, after all, one of his benefactors. He toured the West

Contemplating separation

Country and Wales with Tom searching for spas and dreaming with him of how they might go to some sunnier clime – Sicily perhaps. Tom's illness, diagnosed as thickening of the gut, was most probably cancer of the stomach, and like Coleridge he had been driven by pain to dependence on opium. In the end the only extended trips the two men took together were inner ones, Coleridge even going so far as to obtain quantities of Indian 'Bhang' (concentrated cannabis resin in powdered form) in case that might improve their health. The two men took prodigious quantities and speculated as to whether this substance was the 'nepenthe' mentioned in Homer, an elixir of the gods – but of course they had to come down, with the usual hideous drop from their narcotic Olympus, and that descent left both men more depressed and dependent than ever.

There was also Coleridge's promise to Daniel Stuart of more political journalism for the *Morning Post*, and he gladly made trips to London for that – it at least brought him income for the family, but it also dissipated his concentration. One good thing that came of it, though, was that when Coleridge did finally take ship for the Mediterranean he went with strong letters of recommendation as an acute political observer, which ended up being of great service to him in Malta.

Then there was the whole complex, ambivalent matter of his relationship with Wordsworth and the work they were still doing together. If the letter to Southey confessed that Coleridge felt his marriage had been mistaken and was now broken, there was still his friendship and collaboration with Wordsworth, strained though it had been by the omission of *Christabel* from the *Lyrical Ballads*. For Coleridge had swallowed his pride and still loved and sought to elevate and encourage Wordsworth in his work. The Wordsworths perceived their friend's restlessness and, in an attempt to tame or channel it, Wordsworth proposed that Coleridge should undertake a tour of Scotland with himself and

Dorothy. It would be just like the old days in the Quantocks, the three of them 'three persons but one God', but this time in the even grander and more sublime scenery of Scotland. Coleridge gladly accepted, but secretly both men knew that they were unlikely to recapture the fleeting magic of that Quantock summer that had given birth to the *Lyrical Ballads*. As Coleridge confided in a letter to Southey: 'I never yet commenced a journey with such inauspicious heaviness of heart before.'[15]

Coleridge's forebodings proved only too true. He had hoped to use the remoteness and exertion of this trip as a personal discipline, a way of forcing himself to break the opium habit – 'I have abandoned all opiates except Ether be one; & that only in *fits*', he wrote in a later letter to Southey – but of course he was racked by the bodily pains of withdrawal and tormented at night by the nightmares with which withdrawal also afflicted him. All this, of course, meant that Coleridge, who had been the very breath of inspiration on the walk that gave birth to *The Ancient Mariner*, now proved to be a terrible travelling companion: restive, desperate and screaming every night, as the Night-mare Life-in-Death continued her work.

Finally, on 29 August, just a fortnight into the tour, they parted company. At his parting, the Wordsworths, and perhaps Coleridge himself, assumed that he would now make his way on foot back home. But in fact he did the opposite. He headed north and in a manic, almost superhuman feat of walking, he went right up to Glencoe, circled down and came back to Edinburgh, covering 263 miles through mountainous country on foot in eight days, driven indeed, as he described the ship in *The Ancient Mariner*:

Like one, that on a lonesome road
Doth walk in fear and dread,
And having once turn'd round walks on,
And turns no more his head;

Because he knows, a frightful fiend
Doth close behind him tread.

(Lines 446–51)

There was little need to ask what that fiend was, for somehow
even in the midst of this feat of endurance he composed the
confessional poem 'The Pains of Sleep', which he enclosed in a
letter to Southey written from Perth. Once again, like so much of
The Mariner, the poem is focused on prayer. Coleridge starts with
an account of how he used to pray in less troubled times:

Ere on my bed my limbs I lay,
It hath not been my use to pray
With moving lips or bended knees;
But silently, by slow degrees,
My spirit I to Love compose,
In humble trust mine eye-lids close,
With reverential resignation.[16]

This gentle opening suggests the mature openness of someone
who feels they may have grown beyond the childish lisping of
their earlier forms of bedtime prayer, when they had prayed 'with
moving lips and bended knees'. But then the poem suddenly turns
and we realise that Coleridge's purpose is not to promote this
vague and hazy spirituality but rather to reveal its utter inade-
quacy. In the agonising confession that follows he makes it clear
that in confronting his demons and coming to the root of his
wretchedness, he needs to pray 'aloud, in anguish and in agony'.
Indeed, he goes on later in the poem to reconnect with the inner
child who had stopped praying in the old way and says:

But yester-night I prayed aloud
In anguish and in agony,

Up-starting from the fiendish crowd
Of shapes and thoughts that tortured me:
. . .
The third night, when my own loud scream
Had waked me from the fiendish dream,
O'ercome with sufferings strange and wild,
I wept as I had been a child;[17]

Here the strong rhythm and close rhyme of these four-stress lines seems to be a deliberate echo of the strongly rhymed traditional child's prayer, which was already well known by the late eighteenth century:

Now I lay me down to sleep,
I pray the Lord My soul to keep,
If I should die before I wake,
I pray the Lord My soul to take.

But if Coleridge needs to summon again the almost incantatory power of a child's remembered prayer, he does so because he must confront an adult's agony. One of the reasons Coleridge can speak very directly to our own age is that he lived in and confronted addiction, and its attendant self-loathing, which seems to be one of the deepest, if most hidden, curses of our own age. In an age which should theoretically offer us greater possibilities of freedom than in any previous generation, we have in fact used that freedom to devise our own trammels and cages, and our entire culture of consumption seems designed at once to promote and conceal addictive and obsessive patterns of behaviour. The specifics of the addictions may have changed since Coleridge's time, but he fearlessly enumerates their real psychological and spiritual consequences.

Even in the midst of this experience of chaos and depression Coleridge can see what is needful, though he cannot attain it. He concludes this confessional cry in the night with a gesture towards love:

> To be loved is all I need,
> And whom I love, I love indeed.[18]

In the end, like his mariner, Coleridge did recover something of that capacity to give and receive love, and returned, after many trials, to a fuller and profoundly held faith in Christ as one who could come down into the midst of his pain and set him free. But that was still to come.

The actual occasion of the letter to Southey which included this poem was some terrible news: Southey's only child, a little girl, had died. Coleridge, even in the midst of the agonies described in this poem, opened himself in complete empathy to his brother-in-law, his old friend and sparring partner, in these terms:

> O dear friend! it is idle to talk of what I feel – I am stunned at present – & this beginning to write makes a beginning of living feeling within me. Whatever Comfort I can be to you, I will. – I have no Aversions, no dislikes, that interfere with you – whatever is necessary or proper for you, becomes ipso facto agreeable to me. I will not stay a day in Edinburgh . . .
>
> Bless you, my dear Southey! I will knit myself far closer to you than I have hitherto done – & my children shall be your's [sic] till it please God to send you another.[19]

Coleridge returned to Keswick and immediately invited Robert and Edith to join him and his family there, for as long as they needed to stay. What followed was a strange exchange and reversal of roles. Even as Coleridge was trying to comfort Southey, taking him out for long walks and sitting up with him, it became clear that their presence was comforting Sara and bringing a kind of stability to the household, now that she had her sister and brother-in law with her. The Southeys loved and got on well with Sara and the children. And now there was a third – a little girl (also christened Sara!) had been born to the Coleridges late in the previous year and was thriving. She would prove the most brilliant of the Coleridge children, a fine writer in her own right, devoted to her so-often absent father. In happier times, they would work together, and in due course, after his death, she would help to edit his works. But now, in his desperation, realising that he was as much a burden to his own family as he had been to the Wordsworths, Coleridge saw a chance to make the complete break and the new beginning he needed to overcome his obsession with Asra and combat his addiction to opium, without leaving his wife to cope on her own.

Weaving in and out through all the letters of these years is the consistent yearning to move to a warmer climate to get away for a total cure and a new beginning. This was presented to his wider circle of friends as a 'cure' for rheumatism, but Coleridge and his immediate family knew what was really at stake. With Southey installed at Greta Hall, Coleridge suddenly saw that he could go and at least try to achieve that recovery from obsession and addiction, that new beginning. He began to set his affairs in order, as though a man preparing for his own death. He made over the whole of the Wedgwood annuity to Sara, thus leaving himself with no income but what he could make with his pen, and he took out a life assurance policy in her favour, payments for which he never failed to make despite all the vicissitudes that followed.

In the dying days of 1803 he made the journey to Grasmere to see the Wordsworths again, urging Wordsworth to continue his great poem *The Recluse*, to which, of course, the 'Poem to Coleridge' was intended as a prelude. Wordsworth arranged for a loan to speed Coleridge on his journey and gave him a precious manuscript book of what he'd written of the poem, thus far, for his commentary and advice. It was copied out by Dorothy and Asra, which made it all the more precious to Coleridge. He kept it close by him and in all the struggles, wrecks, flotsam and jetsam that trailed in his wake thereafter, this precious manuscript survived, returned later to Dove Cottage – its place of origin – where it can still be seen today.

After much correspondence with Daniel Stuart and other friends, Coleridge was offered, through their good offices and connections, an opening, working as an assistant to Sir Alexander Ball, the governor of the island of Malta, and possible further employment assisting the British envoy in Sicily. They were all agreed that the warmer climate, the change and the rest would do him good. In the new year, with good wishes and blessings from all, including his own family, Coleridge set off for London, to wait for a ship that might take him to Sicily via Malta. From London he wrote valedictory letters to all his friends. Rumours had begun to spread of Coleridge's ill health and many no doubt suspected that opium lay at the heart of it. Both writer and correspondents perhaps wondered if they would ever see each other again.

Then he was off, a mariner once more, in a Navy flotilla on its way to garrison Malta. His vessel was called the *Speedwell*, one of the flower names that Asra had written in his book. From afar, Wordsworth wrote in *The Prelude*:

> For thou art wandered now in search of health
> And milder breezes, - melancholy lot!
> But thou art with us, with us in the past,
> The present, with us in the times to come . . .
> Speed thee well![20]

The *Speedwell* set sail on 19 April 1804 and Coleridge, full of high hopes of renewal and reformation, began to fill his notebooks with a wonderful combination of close observation of ship-board life and powerful reflection on his reading and his inner life. He had taken with him a copy of Dante's *Commedia* and the necessary grammar books and dictionary to teach himself Italian. In later years, he would lecture brilliantly on Dante and be instrumental in making F.H. Carey's translation so popular. Already, Dante's story of mid-life crisis, of a journey down through darkness in order to ascend, and of a renewed faith that illuminates every speck of the cosmos, was beginning to grip his imagination. Perhaps when he came to the beginning of the *Purgatorio* he was particularly gripped by the image of a ship steered by an angel, whose great white wings outstretched are themselves the ship's sails taking mariners to the island where they will be purged of their sins, but through that purgation will come home at last.

Certainly, *The Rime of the Ancient Mariner* seems to have come back into focus for him on this voyage. An early notebook entry reads: 'Saw, a nice black-faced bright black-eyed white-toothed Boy running up to the Main Top with a large Leg of Mutton swung, Albatross-fashion about his neck.'[21] For a while 'the fair breeze blew, the white foam flew' and Coleridge also seemed to be faring well. He had brought a small quantity of laudanum with him, but for the first two weeks of the voyage managed to refrain from it. Things changed, however, after they passed Gibraltar and entered the waters of the Mediterranean: it grew hot and, like the mariner's ship before, they were becalmed. After five days of trying to sail on, they ended up back at the same spot. Coleridge, as ever, was alert to the ways the outer expresses the inner. He noted on 1 May:

Tuesday Afternoon, one o'clock, May Day – We are very nearly on the spot, where on Friday last about this same Hour we caught

A new Dante?

the Turtles – And what are 5 days' toiling to Windward just not
to lose ground, to almost 5 *years*! Alas! Alas! What have I been
doing on the Great Voyage of Life since my Return from Germany
but fretting upon the front of the Wind – well for me if I have
indeed kept my ground even![22]

In spite of this note of admonition, or perhaps because of it,
Coleridge became ill and depressed again, and broached his little
supply of laudanum which, of course, ultimately made things
worse: 'Wednesday, May 2nd / 1804. To this hour six o'clock,
afternoon, desperately sick, ill abed, one deep dose after another.'[23]

From here on, there begins to be an uncanny resemblance
between what Coleridge observes and chooses to remember in his
notebooks and the details of *The Rime of the Ancient Mariner*,
including this remarkable episode:

15.56 Hawk with ruffled Feathers resting on the Bowsprit – Now
shot at & yet did not move – how fatigued – a third time it made
a gyre, a short circuit, & returned again / 5 times it was thus shot
at / left the Vessel / flew to another / & I heard firing, now here,
now there / & nobody shot it / but probably it perished from
fatigue, & the attempt to rest upon the wave! – Poor Hawk! O
Strange Lust of Murder in Man! – It is not cruelty / it is mere un
non-feeling from non-thinking.[24]

One can only imagine how the author of *The Ancient Mariner*
felt when he witnessed outwardly and visibly this random cruelty
and contempt for the life of another, whose inner and spiritual
consequences he had mapped so unflinchingly; but the end of this
note does take us to Coleridge's own sense of the sheer mystery of
human evil, 'the Strange Lust of Murder in Man', and the crucial
insight that it is not cruelty, per se, but a failure of engaged
thought and feeling. In many ways, Coleridge's great work in the

Coleridge as the young Romantic in 1795 by Peter Vandyke:
'His eye . . . speaks every emotion of his animated soul . . .'

The fireside in Nether Stowey: 'You would smile to see my eye rolling up to the ceiling in a Lyric fury, and on my knee a *Diaper* pinned, to warm'

The cottage at Nether Stowey: a meeting place for 'A Mischievous gang of disaffected Englishmen' and a 'Sett of violent Democrats'

Coleridge in 1804 by James Northcote:
'he achieved what he did, not only in spite of the pain and despair through
which he lived, but *with* that pain and despair as his very materials'

'Deep Calleth unto Deep':
David Jones' intense take on
the creatures of the great calm

David Jones' central
engraving of the moment
the albatross is shot
places the bird, pierced,
and almost crucified, on
the cross tree of the mast

Survivor guilt: Mervyn Peake gives his figures 'that disquieting blend of the venerable, the pitiable and the frightful'

In Peake's beautiful illustration of the mariner kneeling to pray, the albatross, still round his neck, seems almost to have become part of him, as though he himself had wings

Greta Hall: the beautiful white house just outside Keswick and nestling near the shores of Derwentwater, in which Coleridge made an inner voyage to such heights and depths

Derwentwater: 'awakening the mind's attention . . . and directing it to the loveliness and the wonders of the world before us; an inexhaustible treasure'

Coleridge in 1811, at the time of the London lectures: 'his face when he repeats his verses hath its ancient glory, an arch angel a little damaged' – C Lamb

Beneath this stone lies the body of
SAMUEL TAYLOR
COLERIDGE
Born 21 October 1772. Died 25 July 1834.
Stop Christian passer-by! Stop Child of God
And read with gentle breast. Beneath this sod
A poet lies: or that which once seem'd he.
O, lift one thought in prayer for S.T.C.;
That he who many a year with toil of breath
Found death in life, may here find life in death
Mercy for praise - to be forgiven for fame
He ask'd, and hoped, through Christ.
Do thou the same!

'Stop Christian Passer-by!' Even in death this Ancient Mariner calls out and stops us in our tracks

As surely as the fallen albatross was an emblem of the mariner's wounded soul, Chris Jordan's image shows us who we are: bloated with emptiness, dying of excess second half of his life would be to try to move his readers from a state of 'mere non-feeling from non-thinking' to a more awakened response to nature, a new way of knowing the world.

Soon after the shooting of the hawk the ship was becalmed again: Coleridge descended deeply into what he called the 'gloom and anxious horror' of his 'nightmare life-in-death'. A harrowing note, written at midnight on 13 May, takes us from self-torture into desperate prayer

> for Sleep a pandemonium of all the shames & miseries of the past Life from early childhood all huddled together, & bronzed with one stormy Light of Terror & Self-torture / O this is hard, hard, hard! – O dear God! give me strength of Soul to make one thorough Trial – if I land at Malta / spite all horrors to go through one month of unstimulated Nature – yielding to nothing but manifest Danger of Life! – O great God! Grant me grace truly to look into myself, & to begin the serious work of Self-amendment – accounting to Conscience for the Hours of every Day. Let me live in *Truth* – manifesting that alone which *is*, even as it *is*, & striving to be that which only Reason shews to be love – that which my Imagination would delight to manifest! – I am loving & kind-hearted & cannot do wrong with impunity, but o! I am very, very weak – from my infancy have been so – & I exist for the moment! – Have mercy on me, have mercy on me, Father & God! omnipresent incomprehensible, who with undeviating Laws eternal yet carest for the falling of the feather from the Sparrow's Wing.[25]

For the mariner the possibility of prayer itself had been blocked, but at least Coleridge managed to utter this prayer, crucially a prayer for strength, and a recognition of his own weakness, which all former addicts and members of the recovery community will recognise as essential first steps. It is also wonderful how, woven into this prayer, is a glimpse, even through the veil of present horror, into how the two great faculties of reason and imagination might properly work and work together: a striving that imagination should delight to manifest what reason shows to be lovely. Like the 'gloss' on the mariner's agony which Coleridge would write later, somehow these great words, *reason*, *imagination*, *lovely*, *grace*, offer some kind of grace towards the other words: *pandemonium*, *shame*, *misery*, *horror*. It is also a truly Coleridgean touch that, remembering Jesus' words in Matthew, he finishes his prayer with the images of falling, of feathers and of flight – 'the falling of the feather from the sparrow's wing'.

Five days later they arrived in Malta and Coleridge presented himself to Sir Alexander Ball, the Governor of the island. Here something extraordinary happened. In spite of all his inner trials, Coleridge blossomed in the stimulating company of Ball, one of that heroic generation of Nelson officers and a friend of Nelson himself. Soon Ball found Coleridge indispensable and made him his public secretary. Suddenly Coleridge was part of the British naval effort in an heroic struggle for control of the Mediterranean, drafting political position papers, assessing intelligence reports of unfolding events in the Mediterranean theatre of war, helping the Governor to administer justice and make provision for the lives of the garrison and the islanders. For a while Coleridge managed a life of 'un-stimulated nature', his term for living opium-free, buoyed up and interested by his work, but at night the nightmares returned, the self-reproach, the desperate longing for Asra and the ever-deepening inner loneliness. For all his ebullience in company, when the door closed on his upper chamber in the Governor's house, Coleridge was indeed 'Alone, alone, all, all alone / Alone on a wide, wide sea'.

Eventually, in the pains of withdrawal, his reserves failed him, and he began to take opium again. He confided it to his notebook in a terse note written in a code he had developed for the most secret things; decoded it reads, 'no night without its guilt of opium and spirit!' Soon he was writing pitiable confessions without code; in one of these he suddenly becomes aware of the possibilities of posterity and imagines us for a moment, reading his notebooks. He writes:

> If I should perish without having the power of destroying these and my other pocket books, the history of my own mind for my own improvement. O friend! Truth! Truth! But yet Charity! Charity! I have never loved Evil for its own sake; & (no! nor) π ever sought pleasure for its own sake, but only as a means of escaping from pains that coiled round my mental powers, as a serpent around the body & wings of an Eagle![26]

That final image of the serpent and the eagle speaks both of Coleridge's sense of his own powers, as the winged eagle that should soar in the heavens, and also of his strong sense of his own failure and weakness, wrapped in the serpentine coils of addiction and despair. It also takes us back to the hidden wisdom embedded in *The Rime of the Ancient Mariner*, wisdom which Coleridge had yet to open out fully. In that poem he exercised the 'sacred power of intuition' and held open a shape into which reason and imagination could eventually grow. The mariner, too, is compassed with great wings above and coiling serpents below, but his liberation in that magical moonrise comes from learning to let these diverse powers live in harmony; not from self-loathing but from self-acceptance; not from destroying, but from blessing the water-snakes. Not dividing and rejecting but restoring and integrating the disparate powers of the soul.

Remarkably, on Coleridge too in the lonely watchtower of that upper room in Malta, the moon also rose and began a work of redemption. From the early months of 1805 the notebooks begin to be filled with glimpses of the moon. In one note, as Coleridge looks out at 2 o'clock in the morning, he sees the moon behind 'thin, pearl Cloudlets, hands, & fingers, the largest not larger than a floating Veil / unconsciously I stretched forth my arms as to embrace the sky . . .'[27] _Unconsciously_ is a wonderful word here, resonating with the mariner blessing _unaware_. The note finishes: 'have Mercy on me, O something out of me! For there is no power . . . in aught within me! Mercy! Mercy!'[28]

Then in April came the moonrise that, I believe, was the turning point for Coleridge as much as the moonrise had been for his mariner. For here Coleridge discerned something in the moon's transfiguring light that promised him, at last, the real link he so desperately needed between outer and inner, object and subject, nature and spirit, philosophy and faith. Coleridge recorded the core of his experience, and intuition, in a brief note:

> In looking at objects of Nature, while I am thinking, as at yonder moon dim-glimmering thro' the dewy window-pane, I seem rather to be seeking, as it were _asking_, a symbolic language for something within me that already and for ever exists, than observing any thing new. Even when the latter is the case, yet still I have always an obscure feeling as if that new phænomenon were the dim awaking of a forgotten or hidden Truth of my inner Nature! It is still interesting as a Word, a Symbol! It is _Logos_, the Creator! [and the Evolver!][29]

In some ways this notebook entry speaks directly into that space, that apparent gap and contradiction, between _Frost at Midnight_ and _Dejection: An Ode_ – the gap that had so much paralysed Coleridge. Both poems address our experience of apparent meaning in nature, and puzzle over where that 'meaning' comes from. _Frost at Midnight_ had suggested that the shapes and sounds of nature might themselves be a kind of language. In that poem, the phrase 'eternal language' tells us something about God, but doesn't help us to understand his language. In this note, Coleridge is trying to grasp what it might mean to say that the language of God is a 'symbolic' language.

Perhaps the most important of Coleridge's many insights is just this parallel he discerned between our experience of language and our experience of the world. We could describe language in purely exterior and physical terms. As soon as a word is used it has a quantifiable, 'objective' physical presence; black ink and paper weighing so many grams, an audible sound at so many decibels. Yet, however accurate the measurements and description of language as a purely physical phenomenon were to be, such a description would still say nothing of a speaker's, listener's or reader's actual experience of language. When we use language, we pass through the physicality of the words so swiftly we hardly realise they are there. For the words we use are, of course, not simply dead physical objects, opaque and referring to nothing but themselves. The words we use are living symbols taking us the instant they are uttered through and beyond themselves, connecting us with an intricate network of reference; reference to other words and reference to the realities in nature and in ourselves of which the words are symbols. For most of us this process of meeting the word only to be ushered through it to that meaning beyond itself to which it points is so familiar and unconscious we scarcely notice it is happening. We cease to be conscious of the words, only of the images they summon up. But poets are concerned not only with the meanings of words, but with savouring and celebrating the words themselves, the very sounds. And so it is that in reading great poetry, our vision is doubled: we become aware simultaneously both of the word as a thing in itself, a chosen sound, a kind of music in the air, and also of that other reality, that mystery of truth of which the word is the gatekeeper. In the language of poetry we meet something that is both itself and a mediator of that which is beyond itself. We can sometimes have the same experience, not just with words but with the world. Before the Enlightenment most people were free to read the world as being itself symbolic and constantly drawing us to truths beyond itself. For Coleridge this experience was so constant that it drove him first to doubt and then to demolish the new 'Enlightened' view that the world was a set of dead objects meaning nothing.

In his rich, dense, closely written note, trying to unravel what this particular moonrise meant, as a *word*, a *logos*, Coleridge begins, apparently, in a world clearly divided between subject and object, which he inherited in the eighteenth century. That phrase, 'in looking at *objects* of nature', could have been written by any materialist or mechanistic philosopher of Coleridge's day. But the sentence continues, 'while I am thinking' – and this touches on what he had noted in his letter to Tom Poole, that the mind in its act of perception is not passive. We are not merely *tabula rasa*, upon which the outside objects of nature impinge or impress themselves, on the contrary we are constantly active looking, thinking, shaping minds, and surely this constant awareness of our own conscious activity, of the movement of what Coleridge called 'the self-circling energies of the reason',[30] must itself have an influence both on the way in which we see nature, and perhaps on the very nature itself that we see. So Coleridge continues: 'In looking at objects of nature while I am thinking, as at yonder moon dim-glimmering through the dewy window-pane, I seem rather to be seeking, as it were asking . . .'[31] We move here from the ideas and language about mind as being passive, to the notion that the mind is actively *asking*, actively *seeking*. And what the mind seeks is not simply the exterior recording of the opaque outsides of dead objects, but *language*, intelligibility, meaning: 'I seem rather to be seeking, as it were asking for a symbolic language'. Coleridge has the experience as he sees the moon dim-glimmering through the window-pane, that, as it were, there is a meaning behind it, that it is like a *word*, that he could pass through it and see something beyond it; but he simultaneously has the experience that whatever is *beyond* it is also resonant with some-thing which is *within* him, something which 'already and for ever exists'. It is as though the experience of perception were a kind of medium or middle-state between a meaning which is beyond and a meaning which is within. Perception itself becomes a language of communication between the inner and the outer, between the immanent and the transcendent.

So Coleridge continues in this startling little note, and this time he introduces the word, *Word*, significantly with a capital W: 'It is still interesting as a Word, a Symbol!' Now, whose Word, whose Symbol is it? Coleridge in this note is certainly not suggesting that it is simply his own construct. Yes, this moonlight does seem somehow to correspond to something within Coleridge's inner nature, which only that moonlight could express; but Coleridge is not saying that it is he, privately, Coleridge himself, who is, as it were, casting upon the moonlight the spell of its meaning, which is what *Dejection: An Ode*, read on its own, might seem to suggest.

'It is still interesting', he says, 'as a Word, a symbol', but he goes on to say, in a sudden leap of understanding, 'It is *Logos*, the Creator! and the Evolver!' And here he anticipates by some years the formulation that he gives this idea in the famous thirteenth chapter of the *Biographia Literaria*, where he asks at last, 'What is the deepest and purest source of creativity, of imagination?' Is there a common source both for the outward and visible forms of nature, and for those inward and invisible imaginative apprehen-sions of that nature which we find in the human mind? Is there a common source for that beautifully expressed and ordered organic whole, that composition of one in many parts which we call the cosmos, and the beautifully expressed and ordered organic wholes in poetry and art which we call human creation? Might there be a single source for that ordering and imaginative power which is responsible for both? Coleridge anticipates and says, 'It is *Logos*, the Creator! and the Evolver!'

The question naturally arises: does this Word, this Logos, have anything to do with Christ, the Christ whom we encounter in the preface to John's Gospel, where it says: 'In the Beginning was the Word'? In John it is the Word through whom all things are made, but who is also the 'light that lightens every man that comes into the world'.

Coleridge, in beginning to answer that question, was feeling his way towards something important here, important for him and perhaps also for us. The word 'Logos' could mean many things. Primarily it meant 'Word', but by extension it meant order, coherence, intelligibility, and that is how it was used by Greek philosophers long before it was taken up by the writer of John's Gospel and identified with Christ, the 'eternal Word', the only begotten of the Father. In the word *Logos* Coleridge had found a focal point that brought together his deep sense, explored in his earlier poetry, that all the images of nature *meant*, or were *saying* something, and his equally deep need to make some new sense of the religion of his childhood, the faith of his own father, his inheritance as a Christian. Perhaps there was a link: perhaps we find in the world around us so many apt representations and symbols of our own inner states and experiences because the outer and the inner have the same source and are sustained and given their meaning by the same divine Word. Perhaps he could find, in a new understanding of Christ as *Logos*, a way of reconciling his insights as a poet with the faith into which he had been born.

This is the breakthrough, implicit in this note!

How that correspondence works between Christ the eternal Word and Christ the light within us, how it might renew our understanding of who we are, as persons made in his image, and how all of that might inform and encourage the life of the imagi-nation – all this was to be the great work of the second half of Coleridge's life when, like his mariner, he turned his sails for home. But in one sense it was all given and disclosed here as the April moonrise shone on a desperate and lonely man.

'Nine fathom deep beneath the keel' the Polar Spirit moves beneath the mariner's ship and a spirit stirs deeper still in the unfathomable reaches of Coleridge's mind

CHAPTER TEN

Nine Fathom Deep

As we take up the mariner's tale again we find that the fifth part
of the poem, the mariner's release into prayer and his freedom
from the physical burden of the albatross, ushers in a completely
new atmosphere and a change and variation in the imagery of
the poem. From here on the ship will be under angelic rather
than dæmonic guidance, and whereas previously Coleridge was
drawing on the folklore of the sea, and the deathly charnel
images of the gothic genre, now we suddenly have access to
images of the holy, the angelic, and to renewed images of nature
herself. It is not that the images of death and horror are
removed; far from it. The mariner still has a long journey ahead
of him and 'penance more to do'; he is still alone and still
surrounded by the bodies of the fallen, the cold sweat still on
their limbs and the curse still in their eyes; but now he is on the
path to redemption, and now the horror can be confronted and
redeemed.

This first stage of recovery begins, as so often with people
recovering from trauma, with the return of sleep:

> Oh sleep! it is a gentle thing,
> Beloved from pole to pole!
> To Mary Queen the praise be given!
> She sent the gentle sleep from Heaven,
> That slid into my soul.

(Lines 292–6)

At the time that Coleridge composed this verse his own patterns of sleep and waking were generally good and healthful, but as we have seen, he was soon to know the mariner's agony of nightmare sleeplessness and therefore also to know the blessed relief, the sense of sheer gift, when sleep comes at last to the sleepless. It is interesting to note how gently in the second line of this stanza he reminds us of the 'polar' frame in which his story is set. The journey moves from the northern to the southern polar hemispheres and back, and each occasion they reach or cross 'the line' is carefully emphasised in the poem. At a symbolic and thematic level the poem also operates in the tension between different polarities: freedom and constraint, community and isolation, blessing and curse, redemption and guilt, and indeed, sleep and waking; and all the transitions between these states, the crossings of invisible lines, are also significant. So Coleridge immediately goes on to note the importance of this sleep as spiritual gift, and specifically as a gift from the feminine:

> To Mary Queen the praise be given!
> She sent the gentle sleep from Heaven,

(Lines 294–5)

Mary has already been invoked earlier in the poem, in the brief prayer 'Heaven's Mother send us grace' (line 178), uttered when the spectre-ship first appeared, and now that prayer is answered in the grace of sleep and a prescient dream of further grace. This repeated invocation of Mary as the beneficent feminine ushers us into another of the poem's tensions and polarities; for in one sense Mary here counter-balances the demonic feminine, the 'Night-mare Life-in-Death' and helps to free the mariner from her curse. Coleridge emphasises this contrast even further in the gloss that accompanies this verse by introducing the word *grace*:

Nine Fathom Deep

By grace of the holy Mother, the ancient Mariner is refreshed with rain.

> The silly buckets on the deck,
> That had so long remained,
> I dreamt that they were filled with dew;
> And when I awoke, it rained.

(Lines 297–300 with gloss)

In this stanza Coleridge briefly reminds us of the long drought through which the mariner and the rest of the crew had struggled, with the image of the buckets set out on the deck to catch any rain or dew, but every morning always empty and dry till they become 'silly' in the sense that they are absurd and useless reminders of thirst, reminders of the water they fail to provide. But now he dreams that they are filled, and it almost seems as if the dream itself precipitates the rain that fills them.

> My lips were wet, my throat was cold,
> My garments all were dank;
> Sure I had drunken in my dreams,
> And still my body drank.

(Lines 301–4)

Here the verse again takes us back to the memory of drought, deliberately echoing but reversing the line:

> With throats unslaked, with black lips baked

(Line 162)

Then, blessedly, we move from the dream-life to the actual, from the soul to the body:

> Sure I had drunken in my dreams,
> And still my body drank.

(Lines 303–4)

There is great wisdom here. Psychologists and spiritual directors will be aware of the way a person's dream-life can anticipate, symbolise and ultimately guide them towards fulfilments and resolutions that are lacking in their waking lives. Indeed, all the key or guiding images in the poem are in some way prefaced or associated with the idea of a dream, or swoon – an altered state in which the soul is more alert to the emblems of its deepest life. As we have noted, the mariner hears the ice 'like noises in a swound' just before he sees the albatross, and it is when he falls into another swound or trance at the end of this section of the poem that he is able to hear and 'in my soul discern' the two voices which set out his true condition. Dreams and discernment always go together and in some ways this whole dream-like poem, with its richly laden emblems and symbols, is an instrument for spiritual discernment.

The other parallel, and in its own way polarity, is between sleep and death, something on which both the scriptures and the whole poetic tradition have richly dwelt, so that sleeping and waking become a constant reflection and anticipation of death and resurrection and therefore of all the little deaths and resurrections which constitute the rhythms of our spiritual life. Coleridge avails himself fully of all this in his account of the mariner's waking after his 'gentle sleep':

> I moved, and could not feel my limbs:
> I was so light—almost
> I thought that I had died in sleep,
> And was a blessed ghost.

(Lines 305–8)

Of course the deeper spiritual death and resurrection would come to the mariner later, as it would eventually come to Coleridge, when in profound baptismal imagery (for baptism is

also a death and resurrection) the whole ship goes down and the
mariner is pulled from the waters 'like one that hath been seven
days drowned' *(line 552)* and then, with a significant reference to
dreams,

The ancient   But swift as dreams, myself I found
Mariner is   Within the Pilot's boat.
saved in the
Pilot's boat.   *(Lines 554–5)*

Interestingly, when Coleridge finally disembarked from the
Speedwell at Malta, he described himself as stepping ashore 'light
as a blessed ghost'.[1] 'Blessed' is an important word here, and is a
deliberate reversal of the idea of curse, which has so dominated
the poem. He still has the curse to deal with and work through,
and later, in a piece of psychological realism, the mariner has a
relapse and flashback to the cursedness and loses for a while the
gift of prayer:

The pang, the curse, with which they died,
Had never passed away:
I could not draw my eyes from theirs,
Nor turn them up to pray.

                                    (Lines 438–41)

In the next four stanzas we look out with the mariner from himself
to the world around him and once more we find Coleridge realising his ideal for poetry that the outer and the inner should express
one another. We have just heard of the inner release of all that
was dry, tense and locked up in the mariner; now we see the same
thing in the outer elements. After so many stanzas about insistent
oppressive heat and there not being a breath of wind, we know
that all that heat and oppression must eventually be released in a
storm, and so it is. The light rain that refreshed the mariner and

filled the buckets is the presage of this bigger storm. The mariner himself is in its quiet eye and hears but does not feel the wind, but he witnesses the release of power as lightning falls, which also expresses the release of energy and movement at this point in the poem after so much stifling stillness in the preceding sections:

He heareth sounds and seeth strange sights and commotions in the sky and the element.

And soon I heard a roaring wind:
It did not come anear;
But with its sound it shook the sails,
That were so thin and sere.

The upper air burst into life!
And a hundred fire-flags sheen,
To and fro they were hurried about!
And to and fro, and in and out,
The wan stars danced between.

And the coming wind did roar more loud,
And the sails did sigh like sedge;
And the rain pour'd down from one black cloud;
The Moon was at its edge.

The thick black cloud was cleft, and still
The Moon was at its side:
Like waters shot from some high crag,
The lightning fell with never a jag,
A river steep and wide.

(Lines 309–26)

After the roaring of the distant wind a key line here is 'The upper air *burst into life*'. There is a sense that something is so charged and powerful in the new atmosphere that follows on from the mariner's prayer and the release of the albatross that everything that has hitherto been dulled and deadened is bursting into life. The verse itself, with its account of 'fire-flags sheen', waving in the heavens, with the stars appearing to dance between them, appears to be an account of an *aurora*, and Coleridge had certainly read descriptions of these, and would himself later witness the *aurora borealis* on his walking tour to Scotland. Among the descriptions he read in travel stories, as Martin Gardner notes: 'One writer says the lights "make a rustling and crackling noise, like the waving of a large flag in a fresh gale of wind" another writes of "fires of a thousand colours" that "light up the sky." The hyphenated word fire-flags is Coleridge's own happy invention.'[2]

The detail of the wan stars dancing in between these fire-flags, which is so magical at this point in the poem, is, in its own way, realistic. Just as if you fix your attention on the clouds, the moon and stars behind them seem to be moving even though it is actually the clouds, so if you fix your attention on the beautiful folds or curtains of an *aurora* the wan stars do indeed appear to dance between them. Indeed, this phenomenon of one thing 'giving away its motion to another' is something that Coleridge highlighted in a beautiful passage of *Dejection: An Ode*:

O Lady! in this wan and heartless mood,
To other thoughts by yonder throstle woo'd,
All this long eve, so balmy and serene,

Have I been gazing on the western sky,
And its peculiar tint of yellow green:
And still I gaze—and with how blank an eye!
And those thin clouds above, in flakes and bars,
That give away their motion to the stars;
Those stars, that glide behind them or between,
Now sparkling, now bedimmed, but always seen:

Yon crescent Moon, as fixed as if it grew
In its own cloudless, starless lake of blue;
I see them all so excellently fair,
I see, not feel, how beautiful they are![3]

In this part of *Dejection* Coleridge seems almost deliberately to recall the elements of this passage of *The Mariner*, with the recurrence of 'wan' and 'between' and the movement of the stars, the emphasis on the moon and the colouring of the sky. If the echoes of *The Mariner* are deliberate and intended to be heard by Asra, who of course knew *The Mariner* well, then there must have been for them both a sense of irony, for in *The Mariner* this glimpse of the dancing stars is a sign of recovered vision and feeling, whereas *Dejection: An Ode* is a lament for their loss.

But perhaps the allusion goes deeper. *Dejection* is a paradoxical poem, for in every line Coleridge exhibits just those powers of vision and imagination which he laments he is losing. To invoke a memory of *The Mariner* at his point of recovery, in a poem about Coleridge's own sense of loss, was itself a hidden sign of hope.

We now know the *aurora* to be caused by charged particles that stream from the sun, their energy transformed into these beautiful luminous veils. How Coleridge would have rejoiced to know that, and seen immediately how it deepened the solar symbolism of his poem. Later in this same section of the poem the mariner, in a trance, experiences the angels' song as a series of beautiful flying particles of sound and meaning rising to, and returning from, the sun, his symbol of the divine. Although he didn't know its solar origin, the fire-flags here are certainly a manifestation of the divine, which, as we shall see, he subtly associates with the gift and work of the Holy Spirit.

The middle lines of this stanza are also doing their own act of recollection:

To and fro they were hurried about!
And to and fro, and in and out,

These lines deliberately recall the earlier stanza, and the dreadful
night that falls on the becalmed ship after the mariner has shot
the albatross:

About, about, in reel and rout
The death-fires danced at night;

Now, nearly two hundred lines later, this incantation, with its echo
of the witches in *Macbeth*, is ritually reversed, another aspect of
reversing curse into blessing, so that the 'death-fires' in Part II of
the poem become the 'fire-flags bursting into life' in Part V.

So the description of the new life, motion and energy in the
atmosphere continues:

And the coming wind did roar more loud,
And the sails did sigh like sedge;
And the rain pour'd down from one black cloud;
The Moon was at its edge.

The thick black cloud was cleft, and still
The Moon was at its side:
Like waters shot from some high crag,
The lightning fell with never a jag,
A river steep and wide.

(Lines 318–26)

Now we have a further image of release: the rain falling first, and
then the lightning, 'Like waters shot from some high crag' falling
as 'A river steep and wide'. As we have seen, rivers and moving
waters are always beneficent signs of grace and renewal in
Coleridge's symbolic vocabulary, and here we see the release of a

river of light and power in the outer world which corresponds in some way with the 'spring of love' that has gushed from the mariner's heart at his own moment of release.

If we pause now and look at the total effect of these four stanzas, two remarkable things emerge. The first is that Coleridge here evokes in succession three of the four traditional 'elements' of the cosmos: air, fire and water. That he is playing with the idea of the elements is made clear by the suggestive use of the word 'element' in the gloss that accompanies the first of these four stanzas. The missing fourth element is *earth*, and it is missing from what the mariner sees because it is of course the mariner himself! By this time in the poem he is in some sense the archetypal human being, the one who stands for us all, the fallen 'Adam'. The name 'Adam' means 'man of earth', formed from the dust of the ground, but enlivened and lifted into spiritual being by the other three elements: the breath or spirit of God, the divine spark or fire, and the waters of baptism. The mariner's own baptism, a full immersion, is still to come, but here is its first foreshadowing. Which brings us to the second remarkable thing about the symbolism of these four stanzas: wind, fire and water are the three great biblical symbols of the Holy Spirit. Coleridge seems almost to be paraphrasing the famous description in the book of Acts of the coming of the Holy Spirit at Pentecost: 'And suddenly there came a sound from heaven as of a rushing mighty wind, and it filled all the house where they were sitting. And there appeared unto them cloven tongues like as of fire, and it sat upon each of them.'[4] Particularly notable is the way he emphasises first the sound of the wind and then the vision of fire:

He heareth sounds and seeth strange sights and commotions in the sky and the element.

And soon I heard a roaring wind:

. . .

The upper air burst into life!
And a hundred fire-flags sheen,

(Lines 309–14)

The gloss that follows these verses speaks, in its first draft (the first edition of *Sibylline Leaves*) of how 'The bodies of the ship's crew are *inspirited*, and the ship moves on'; and in subsequent editions this gloss is strengthened to 'the bodies of the ship's crew are *inspired*':

The bodies of   The loud wind never reached the ship,
the ship's crew
are inspired,   Yet now the ship moved on!
and the ship   Beneath the lightning and the Moon
moves on;   The dead men gave a groan.

(Lines 327–30 with gloss)

Coleridge sets up the narrative so that we can read this 'ghastly' scene in two quite different ways; indeed, we are obliged to do so. We can see it as just another horrific supernatural incident, a gothic thrill in a gothic ballad, keying in to the folk memory of innumerable mariners' tales of ghost ships manned by a crew of the living dead, from the *Flying Dutchman* onwards – the stuff of nightmare, and indeed the substance of Cruickshank's own nightmare, which partly inspired the poem. But then, when it is revealed to us that what 'inspirits' the bodies are not ghosts or evil spirits but blessed angels, we are obliged to read it again with a different insight, looking to the inner and not the outer. This double reading of the same event is actually dramatised for us by the wedding guest's own first reaction, which is to assume that the mariner who is talking to him may also be one of the dead, and by the mariner's response 'be calm', which discloses a new interpretation.

> The loud wind never reached the ship,
> Yet now the ship moved on!
> Beneath the lightning and the Moon
> The dead men gave a groan.

They groaned, they stirred, they all uprose,
Nor spake, nor moved their eyes;
It had been strange, even in a dream,
To have seen those dead men rise.

(Lines 327–34)

Taken by themselves the lines 'Beneath the lightning and the Moon / The dead men gave a groan' portray a scene of pure gothic horror, and yet there is something in the poetry, some suggestion that 'the lightning and the Moon' have already been forces for good in this poem (for the lightning preceded the rain and the moon transfigured the mariner's vision) and for this reason we are able to re-read this verse as somehow suggesting hope as well as horror.

The helmsman steered, the ship moved on;
Yet never a breeze up blew;
The mariners all 'gan work the ropes,
Where they were wont to do:
They raised their limbs like lifeless tools—
We were a ghastly crew.

(Lines 335–40)

This stanza, particularly the detail of the ship moving with 'never a breeze', brings us to the sudden realisation that, at least outwardly and visibly, the mariner's own ship is becoming the 'spectre-bark' that had visited them at the beginning of the curse:

And horror follows. For can it be a ship that comes onward without wind or tide?

See! see! (I cried) she tacks no more!
Hither to work us weal;
Without a breeze, without a tide,
She steadies with upright keel!

(Lines 167–70)

This parallel is further emphasised by the details of the sails being 'thin and sere' like the sails of the ghost ship, which were 'Like restless gossameres'. Indeed, when the mariner and his ship do eventually return home the hermit comments on its appearance in just the terms the mariners had used for the spectre-bark:

> The planks look warped! and see those sails,
> How thin they are and sere!
> I never saw aught like to them,
>
> *(Lines 529–31)*

But for all the outward and visible similarities, there is of course a huge difference between the two vessels and their crew. In the spectre-bark the Night-mare Life-in-Death briefly gives the outer appearance of attractive life and vitality:

Like vessel, like crew!

> Her lips were red, her looks were free,
> Her locks were yellow as gold:
>
> *(Lines 190–1)*

But inwardly she is deadly and 'thicks man's blood with cold'. By contrast the outer appearance of the re-animated crew on the mariner's vessel is 'ghastly', but inwardly they are full of life and light, 'a blessed troop of angelic spirits', who will not only steer the ship and guard the mariner but also make a profound and celestial music, which will be part of his inner healing. By means of this contrast in the symbolic architecture of the poem, Coleridge is conveying a spiritual truth about judgement and discernment. Although the essential inner change has already happened for the mariner, outwardly and visibly things look a lot worse than they did even before he prayed. Both he and the rest of the ship's company are apparently a 'ghastly crew', a portent of

303

evil, but by the end of the poem, the outer veils are removed and all are seen in their true colours. This passage was indeed, as we shall see, prophetic of Coleridge's own fate. It was in the second half of his life – when he had 'turned the corner' and begun an extraordinary recovery and was producing new work of unprecedented spiritual depth – that he was most reviled and condemned as a morally bankrupt addict, and it was even amid the poverty and chaos of the last phases of opium degradation on his return from Malta that the great renewal occurred and the lasting spiritual work was shaped.

So the narrative continues:

The body of my brother's son
Stood by me, knee to knee:
The body and I pulled at one rope,
But he said nought to me.

(*Lines* 341–4)

Humphrey House in his book on Coleridge makes a very pertinent comment on this stanza:

This brings home, as nothing else does, the horror of the deaths, the violation of family ties which the action has involved; it dramatizes to the Mariner's consciousness the utter ruin of the merry, unified community which had set out on the voyage. The curse in the stony eyes (lines 436–41) is made far more appalling by this specially intimate experience of the fact that intimacy has gone forever.[5]

This is certainly true, but I think there is something further going on here. The description of the re-animated crew as mere bodies, almost automata, who 'raised their limbs like lifeless tools' takes us to a distinction which was absolutely central to Coleridge's moral thinking: what he called the sacred distinction between a person and a thing. This distinction was at the heart of Coleridge's rational opposition to slavery, put very clearly in an essay of 1811:

> The Contra-distinction of PERSON and THING being the Ground and Condition of all Morality, a system like this of Hobbes's, which begins by confounding them, needs no confutation to a moral Being. A slave is a *person* perverted into a *thing*: *Slavery*, therefore, is not so properly a deviation from Justice, as an absolute subversion of all Morality.[6]

Although, as the mariner is shortly to tell the wedding guest, these bodies are not strictly 'things' since they are animated by the personhood of angels, Coleridge allows us for a moment to experience the horror of regarding a person as a thing – aware of the dreadful way that on the slave-ships people were reduced to bodies, to things. Indeed, his phrase 'they raised their limbs like lifeless tools' may be a wry allusion to Aristotle's chilling definition of a slave as 'a thinking tool'.

An interesting little book, *The Ancient Mariner and the Authentic Narrative*, links *The Ancient Mariner* with John Newton's account of his own conversion at sea, known as *The Authentic Narrative*.[7] The author, Bernard Martin, points to many parallels between the *Authentic Narrative* and the *Ancient Mariner*, and shows through Wordsworth, Clarkson and others that Coleridge had certainly read the text. The most interesting comparison is between the mariner and John Newton himself. Newton, now best remembered for the great hymn 'Amazing Grace', a hymn which could well serve as a gloss on *The Ancient Mariner*, felt compelled to make a series of reiterated confessions, telling again and again the story of his crimes as a slave-ship's captain in a kind of expiation and warning to others, just as the mariner does at the end of the poem. Indeed, Newton was compulsively and powerfully telling and retelling his story to transfixed listeners from the pulpits of London, even as Coleridge was composing this poem in the Quantocks.

After this glimpse of apparent horror we break out of the story and back into the narrative frame of conversation between the mariner and the wedding guest, as the mariner offers us a new reading of what we have just witnessed:

> *But not by the souls of the men, nor by dæmons of earth or middle air, but by a blessed troop of angelic spirits, sent down by the invocation of the guardian saint.*
>
> "I fear thee, ancient Mariner!"
> Be calm, thou Wedding-Guest!
> 'Twas not those souls that fled in pain,
> Which to their corses came again,
> But a troop of spirits blest:
>
> *(Lines 345–9 with gloss)*

These two stanzas are accompanied by a gloss which, as always, both elucidates and adds to the narrative. It continues and picks up from the previous gloss. In this gloss Coleridge reminds us of the whole supernatural frame of the poem for which he prepared us in the epigraph from T. Burnet. The gloss runs through the different categories of persons or rational beings with which we have to do in the poem: the souls of men, the dæmons of earth or middle air, the angels and the saints. One might add that beneath the lowest of these four categories is the genuinely hellish or demonic, represented by the 'Night-mare Life-in-Death', and above, the highest of these, is God himself, represented emblematically in the sun and the moon, and in the elemental emblems of the Holy Spirit: water, air and fire, and perhaps also in the albatross, always rhymed and associated with 'cross', as a sign of salvation.

As the poem progresses we see control of the ship being transferred across these categories of being. At first the ship is under the
control of human beings, the mariner and crew, then it is guided
through the ice by the albatross. At this point we see the natural and
the supernatural in harmony, brought together in the numinous
emblem of the albatross. Then comes the break in that harmony.
After the mariner's 'fall', after he has 'done a hellish thing', control
of the ship is first seized by the *dæmon* Polar Spirit and then the ship
encounters the genuinely *demonic* figures of Death and the Night-
mare Life-in-Death. That represents the low-point in this transition.
But now, at this new stage in the poem, following the intervention of
grace, the blessing and prayer under the moving moon, the ship and
the mariner are transferred to the guardianship of the angels 'sent
down by the invocation of the guardian saint'.

We are left suspended through one more ghastly night in which
the mariner stands working the sails among the dead, almost one
of the dead himself. Then comes the dawn and, as always in *The
Ancient Mariner*, the movements of the sun and moon are
moments of transition:

> For when it dawned—they dropped their arms,
> And clustered round the mast;
> Sweet sounds rose slowly through their mouths,
> And from their bodies passed.
>
> Around, around, flew each sweet sound,
> Then darted to the Sun;
> Slowly the sounds came back again,
> Now mixed, now one by one.

(Lines 350–7)

The mast, with its crossbar for the sail, is the central 'cross' on the
ship, and once more it becomes the focus of worship. The

albatross had perched there in the moonlight for 'vespers nine', and now as the sun rises the mariner is enabled for a moment to hear the worship of the angels, gathered round that same mast. The magical description is almost a kind of synaesthesia, with the sounds both heard and visually perceived as living shapes: circling, flying, darting, receding, returning, mixing and yet emerging singly. It is a beautiful account of how, in deep communion with the Spirit, one does hear music, but it is more than that: the 'sweet sounds' of the angels are part of an exchange, a communion, a perichoresis: they rise *to* the sun, the symbol of God in his true glory, at which the mariner cannot look directly, and they return *from* the sun, kindled and renewed.

At the time he wrote these verses Coleridge may well have been remembering a passage he had read in *Aurora*, one of the writings of the mystic Jacob Boehme, about the way angels worship and relate to God: 'An angel sendeth forth Nothing but the *Divine* power, which he takes in his Mouth, wherewith he kindles his Heart, and the Heart kindles all the members, and *that* he sends forth from himself again at the Mouth, when he speaks and praises God.'[8] If he was recalling this passage then it is significant that it speaks so much of *kindling* the heart, for this vision follows on the renewal of life in the mariner's heart. Interestingly, Coleridge later paid tribute to the mystics, specifically naming Jacob Boehme, George Fox and William Law, whom he continued to read even in times of dryness and doubt, and specifically thanked them for 'keeping the heart alive':

For the writings of these Mystics acted in no slight degree to prevent my mind from being imprisoned within the outline of any single dogmatic system. They contributed to keep alive the heart in the head; gave me an indistinct, yet stirring and working presentiment, that all the products of the mere reflective faculty partook of death, and were as the rattling twigs and sprays in winter, into which a sap was yet to be propelled from some root to which I had not penetrated, if they were to afford my soul either food or shelter. If they were too often a moving cloud of smoke to me by day, yet they were always a pillar of fire throughout the night, during my wanderings through the wilderness of doubt, and enabled me to skirt, without crossing, the sandy deserts of utter unbelief.[9]

It would be many years before Coleridge realised the full implications of what he had written, but already in this narrative he releases into the poem beautiful images from nature, drawn from his experience in Nether Stowey and the Quantocks, which in this context become indeed 'the lovely shapes and sounds intelligible' of God's 'eternal language'.

> Sometimes a-dropping from the sky
> I heard the sky-lark sing;
> Sometimes all little birds that are,
> How they seem'd to fill the sea and air
> With their sweet jargoning!
>
> And now 'twas like all instruments,
> Now like a lonely flute;
> And now it is an angel's song,
> That makes the Heavens be mute.

(Lines 358–66)

For Coleridge, birdsong was always a blessing, and music was the very condition to which poetry aspired. Here, even in a dawn far out at sea, he somehow summons for us the memory of a dawn chorus in his leafy garden in the Quantocks.

After these angelic matins, Coleridge shows us the ship sailing on and even there he manages to summon the image of a hidden

brook, whose real source we know is in the 'spring of love' that
gushed from the mariner's heart. It is the brook, also 'singing',
which completes this refreshing musical interlude:

> It ceased; yet still the sails made on
> A pleasant noise till noon,
> A noise like of a hidden brook
> In the leafy month of June,
> That to the sleeping woods all night
> Singeth a quiet tune.

(Lines 367–72)

Then we are brought back to the last of those significant, liminal,
transitional moments, always marked in the poem by the sun
directly above the mast, when the ship once more meets the equatorial line:

*The lonesome
spirit from the
south-pole
carries on the
ship as far as
the line, in
obedience to the
angelic troop,
but still
requireth
vengeance.*

> Under the keel nine fathom deep,
> From the land of mist and snow,
> The spirit slid: and it was he
> That made the ship to go.
> The sails at noon left off their tune,
> And the ship stood still also.
>
> The Sun, right up above the mast,
> Had fixed her to the ocean;
> But in a minute she 'gan stir,
> With a short uneasy motion—
> Backwards and forwards half her length,
> With a short uneasy motion.
>
> Then like a pawing horse let go,
> She made a sudden bound:

It flung the blood into my head,
And I fell down in a swound.

(Lines 377–92 with gloss)

Uplifted by the blessing of the angelic music, we have almost
forgotten the presence of the Polar Spirit under the keel nine
fathom deep, who is moving the ship, though it is the angels that
guide it. As always Coleridge is as much concerned in this poem
with the depths as with the heights, with the unappeased, unknown
beneath the keel of our consciousness as with the heavenly heights
above it. The tension between the two is perfectly expressed in the
beautifully balanced gloss, which sees the Spirit as acting 'in obedience' to the angelic troop and yet also 'requiring vengeance'. Grace
may deliver us utterly from our sins, but our actions still have
consequences. This sense of poise or balance, this need to release
a tension between polarities, is itself, of course, perfectly expressed
by the ship stopping still at 'the Line', which is the mid-point
between two polarities. The transition from movement to stillness
and then to an uneasy tipping between balances is perfectly
expressed in the very sound of the poem. We have the easy flow of
'The spirit slid and it was he / That made the ship to go', then the
stillness of 'the ship stood still also', and then the unbalancing of
the form of the next stanza itself with the repetition of the short
uneasy line which expresses the short uneasy motion:

But in a minute she 'gan stir,
With a short uneasy motion—
Backwards and forwards half her length,
With a short uneasy motion.

(Lines 385–8)

Once more we are stuck, and once more the resolution of that
impasse requires spiritual discernment. As so often, the

MARINER

discernment happens in a dream or trance-like altered state, in this case a 'swound', a word that deliberately recalls 'the noises in a swound' that had preceded the first appearance of the albatross.

In the following stanza Coleridge uses a word that is, in a sense, the key word of the poem: *discerned*. As we have seen, the whole poem is an instrument of discernment, and even Coleridge had to wait many years before he perceived some of the truths embedded in his own poem. At this point in the poem, the mariner's altered state allows him to discern the two voices representing the two sides of the tension and dilemma which has halted the ship, and to learn a key truth, without which he cannot cross the line and return home.

The Polar Spirit's fellow-dæmons, the invisible inhabitants of the element, take part in his wrong; and two of them relate, one to the other, that penance long and heavy for the ancient Mariner hath been accorded to the Polar Spirit, who returneth southward.

How long in that same fit I lay,
I have not to declare;
But ere my living life returned,
I heard and in my soul discerned
Two VOICES in the air.

"Is it he?" quoth one, "Is this the man?
By him who died on cross,
With his cruel bow he laid full low
The harmless Albatross.

"The spirit who bideth by himself
In the land of mist and snow,
He loved the bird that loved the man
Who shot him with his bow."

The other was a softer voice,
As soft as honey-dew:
Quoth he, "The man hath penance done,
And penance more will do."

(Lines 393–409 with gloss)

r_

The gloss here tells us two very important things. First, that the Polar Spirit is satisfied, its part has been played, and it 'returneth southward'. The mariner is now in the hands of the angels, and the ship will be able to cross the line, which it does while the mariner is still in his 'swound'. We also learn that the two voices are the Polar Spirit's 'fellow-dæmons' and that they 'take part in his wrong', that is to say they each take a different part: one is the voice of the accuser, making it utterly clear to the mariner what he has done; the other is the voice of the redeemer, offering him a way back out of guilt into freedom. If the mariner is to move forward from this point he must hear both voices.

> "Is it he?" quoth one, "Is this the man?
> By him who died on cross,
> With his cruel bow he laid full low
> The harmless Albatross."

(Lines 398–401)

The cruelty of the deed and the innocence of the albatross are made utterly clear, but that clarity is revealed to the mariner in the only context which can make it bearable: the passion of Christ. 'By him who died on cross' is the last and most important of the many occasions when Coleridge rhymes 'cross' and 'albatross'. The mariner has killed the innocent, as humanity crucified Christ, and the following stanza makes it clear that what is really being wounded and must be redeemed is Love:

> "The spirit who bideth by himself
> In the land of mist and snow,
> He *loved* the bird that *loved* the man
> Who shot him with his bow."

(Lines 402–5)

313

This is the first time that we, and the mariner, learn that the alba-tross loved the man who killed him, just as surely as Christ loved those who crucified him. But the circle of love extends further. In hearing the phrase 'he loved the bird that loved the man / Who shot him', we must hear some echo of the Christian affirmation that God the Father loved the Son, who loved the men who killed him on a cross. The mariner needs to understand the covenant of love that he has broken, in order that the one who restores that covenant can heal him. And so, having heard this declaration of that communion of love which the mariner has violated, we are ready to hear the other voice.

> The other was a softer voice,
> As soft as honey-dew:
> Quoth he, "The man hath penance done,
> And penance more will do."

> (Lines 406–9)

Now the mariner is able to understand that his sufferings thus far are not, in fact, random or meaningless, as the throw of dice by Death and the Night-mare Life-in-Death might have suggested, but that there is a deeper purpose working through them. Here it is important to draw the contrast between penance and vengeance. The offended Polar Spirit asks for vengeance, but in the economy of grace, under the influence of the angels, retributive vengeance is transformed into redemptive penance. Here, in the play between outer narrative and inner meaning, Coleridge is redeeming the word *penance* itself. He would have been well aware that the Greek word *metanoia*, meaning, as its etymology suggests, 'meta mind' or new mind, a whole new vision or way of seeing things, was mistranslated in the vulgate Latin text of the Bible as 'do penance'. For centuries Jesus' proclamation 'repent and believe the good news' was

314

misunderstood to mean 'do penance and believe the Gospel'. The triumph of the Reformation and the new translations of the New Testament was to restore the original meaning. *Metanoia* was not a series of ritual 'penitential' actions but an inner transformation, a new way of seeing yourself and the world. Since the setting of Coleridge's ballad is pre-Reformation, he needs, in the outer narrative, to preserve the whole frame of 'doing penance' and he does so brilliantly with the mariner's current sufferings, the rest of his journey, and his lifelong 'penance' of telling and re-telling his tale to the people who need to hear it. But at the same time, in the lucid inner meaning of his narrative, he gives us an almost perfect picture of true *metanoia*. The real repentance happens in that moment at moonrise when the mariner, freely and from his heart, blesses the very creatures he had previously despised. That is the 'new mind', the transfigured vision which changes everything for the mariner, and in the end for the wedding guest. Coleridge was himself to recover this transfigured vision and to spend the second half of his life helping others to see it too.

And so we return to Coleridge where we left him, gazing at 'yonder moon dim-glimmering through the dewy window-pane' and scribbling down the little note that would eventually become the key to the new vision, the *metanoia*, the new mind, that he was given to unfold. But at this moment, like the mariner on whom that other moon rose, Coleridge was still essentially lost at sea, still a long way from home, with more than half his strange voyage ahead of him: he had not yet even crossed the line.

Coleridge's outer life during his sojourn in the Mediterranean was, as we shall see, both active and at times daring, but it was the steady development, though not yet integration, of his inner life which would hold the key to his future. Outwardly he became, much to everyone's surprise – including his own – a successful civil servant and diplomat, even something of a man of action.

Metanoia = New mind
≠ repentance
(Protestants)

Sir Alexander Ball sent him as his emissary to Sicily, then neutral in the war, and he stayed with the honorary consul there, G.F. Leckie. Leckie showed Coleridge around his estates, where, ironically, the main crop was opium poppies. Leckie showed him how the poppy heads were incised to extract the drug, and remarked on what a lucrative trade it was. Coleridge's response is not recorded, but already he knew too well the real cost of opium.

While he was in Sicily a crisis called Coleridge to action. Quite apart from the hostile encounters of the warring English and French Navies, the Mediterranean was also full of privately fitted 'privateer' vessels, little more than pirates, indeed many of them 'ex-pirates' seeking to profit from the war. While Coleridge was in Syracuse, a French privateer sailed into the harbour with two captured British merchantmen, hotly pursued by the British naval cutter *L'Hirondelle*. The French claimed a lawful right to unload their prize in a neutral port, the British captain disputed it, and both vessels, in the same harbour, trained full guns on one another with their armed crews standing by ready to do battle. Coleridge, as Alexander Ball's emissary, was called down to the harbour to deal with the crisis. Coleridge and Leckie between them managed to defuse a very tense situation, saving the British captain from an angry crowd: they negotiated a truce until the privateer's papers could be examined the next day for the legality of their claim to unload. In the end the Governor of Syracuse decided in the privateer's favour, but Coleridge almost certainly saved the British captain's life, ensured the safe passage of his vessel out of the harbour, and sent a very favourable report of him to Sir Alexander Ball. News of this soon spread throughout the Navy in the Mediterranean theatre of war, and won Coleridge lasting friends for his swift action and support of a young naval officer. The whole episode was also observed by the famously gallant young American, Captain Stephen Decatur, who became perhaps America's greatest naval commander, coined the phrase 'my country right or wrong', and was eventually killed in a duel. He too befriended Coleridge and did a great deal to spread and enhance his reputation in America.

Coleridge returned to Malta, to congratulations all round and a salary rise, but also to letters from home and from Wordsworth, desperate to know when he would return to England. Wordsworth had now completed *The Prelude* (what we now know as the 1805 version – then still simply called 'The Poem to Coleridge') and he was anxious to read it to the man to whom it was addressed and who was its ideal audience. He was also hoping, as always, to improve his poem with Coleridge's comments and criticisms of the manuscript.

But Coleridge was not free to leave at once. The Mediterranean was a war zone and ships could only move safely in convoys, so he would have to wait for a convoy if he were to sail back the way he came, directly from Malta; but in any case he had been made temporary public secretary on the death of the previous holder of that post and Sir Alexander Ball couldn't really let him go, given the war situation, until his permanent replacement arrived. So Coleridge had to stay for another five months, a civil servant by day, and by night resuming his moonlit vigils and inner journeys in that high room whose baroque ceiling depicted angels circling round the quarters of a mariner's compass. It is to that all-important inner life we now return.

When the moon rose on the mariner, his vision was transfigured in an instant and he was able to bless the water-snakes from his heart. For Coleridge himself this process of transfiguration and renewal was not so simple, and was as much a matter of intellectual wrestling as it was of renewing the springs of love in his heart. During his time in Malta, Coleridge was thinking long and hard about the content and claims of Christian faith, and especially about the doctrine of the Trinity. He came to see two important and related truths at this time. First, that his previous speculations about the Trinity had been no more than a mind-game, a playful encounter with a philosophical conundrum, and what was needed now was something more thoroughgoing and all-embracing. Second, the recognition that any idea of Trinity rested on the claims of Jesus to be God, to be both human and divine, and thus that it was not sufficient simply to admire or follow his ethical teachings – there was a bigger claim at stake. So he confided to his notebook:

> it burst upon me at once as an awful Truth what 7 or 8 years ago I thought of proving with a hollow *Faith* and for an ambiguous *purpose*, my mind then wavering in its necessary passage from Unitarianism (which I have often said is the religion of a man whose ~~Understanding~~ Reason could make him an Atheist but whose Heart and Common sense will not permit him to be so) thro' Spinosism into Plato and St. John / No Christ, No God! – This I now feel with all its needful evidence of the Understanding, would to God my spirit were made to conform thereto – that No Trinity, No God . . . O that this Conviction may work upon me and in me / and that my mind may be made up as to the character of Jesus and of historical Christianity as clearly as it is of ~~Christ~~ the Logos and intellectual or spiritual Christianity, that I may be made to know either their special and peculiar Union, or their absolute disunion in any peculiar sense.[10]

There is a great deal in this fascinating passage. It is interesting that he dates the start of his intellectual journey away *from* Unitarianism '7 or 8 years ago', which would take us back to the period in which he was candidating for Unitarian ministry, and the year he wrote *The Ancient Mariner*. But it is also noteworthy that he recognises that there was something hollow and ambiguous in all his precocious religious reasoning at that time. Now this conviction, which he might have glibly 'proved' then, is beginning to 'burst upon him' as 'necessary', but he is also praying that it will 'work upon him'. What is the conviction? This ever-loquacious man puts it in four one-syllable words: 'No Christ, No God'.

What does this mean? It means first and foremost that Coleridge has come to see that Christ reveals the nature of God more fully than any rational system of philosophy ever could – though he also wants to acknowledge that Reason and Philosophy helped him on his journey to Christ. And Coleridge even tells us the path along which philosophy has guided him towards a fuller revelation in Christ: from the pantheism of Spinosa in which everything already is god and no one thing reveals any more of him than any other, through Platonism in which all the shadows of this world glimmer with and point towards a union of the true, the good and the beautiful which the intellect is drawn towards and delights to contemplate, and then to the Gospel of John in which the *Logos*, the Word behind all things, about whom the Greeks already knew, is absolutely identified with Christ, the eternally begotten Son of the Father.

Now, in John's Gospel Coleridge confronts the Christian claim that this same Eternal Word was 'made flesh' and dwelt among us, became the historical Jesus, and that therefore all that Jesus does and says, especially his proclamation of love, his death on the cross and his resurrection, also proclaim who God is and how we come to him. Knowing God through his Word is not only a matter of *intellectual* or *spiritual* ideas, but is also about *historical* fact, about encountering Jesus in the flesh, his flesh and ours. Christianity is not only about contemplation, it is about crucifixion, death and resurrection. This represented a big challenge for Coleridge who tended to retreat from life, retreat from 'the flesh', into philosophical speculation; but here he is confronted with the claim that something he would like to regard as only 'intellectual'

319

Coleridge is contemplating a reasoning about faith

and 'spiritual' actually became real and historical. In this note Coleridge confesses his need to bridge that gap, between an idealised Christianity of the mind and an historical Christianity in which he should participate: 'O that this conviction may work upon me and in me / and that my mind may be made up as to the character of Jesus and of *historical* Christianity as clearly as it is of Christ the Logos and *intellectual* or *spiritual* Christianity . . .'[11] But he has not made that step yet, indeed he is still open to two possibilities: 'that I may be made to know either their special and peculiar Union, or their absolute disunion in any peculiar sense'.[12]

How might this dilemma be resolved? How might the eternal Word of all this intellectual contemplation be made flesh in Coleridge's life? Years later, looking back on how he was poised in this very dilemma, Coleridge gave this account of his situation and of what was still needed, in his great *Biographia Literaria*:

> The admission of the Logos . . . in no respect removed my doubts concerning the Incarnation and the Redemption by the cross; which I could neither reconcile in reason with the impassiveness of the Divine Being, nor in my moral feelings with the sacred distinction between things and persons, the vicarious payment of a debt and the vicarious expiation of guilt. A more thorough revolution in my philosophic principles, and a deeper insight into my own heart, were yet wanting. Nevertheless, I cannot doubt, that the difference of my metaphysical notions from those of Unitarians in general contributed to my final re-conversion to the whole truth in Christ;[13]

Crucial here is the need for a 'deeper insight into my own heart'. That would indeed come, and with it a 'reconversion to the whole truth in Christ', but it would come to Coleridge in a profound experience of crucifixion, death and resurrection that still awaited him.

For Coleridge in Malta, the heart was still 'dry as dust', still waiting for the fountain of joy, the joy whose loss he had lamented in *Dejection: An Ode*. In another of these telling entries in the Malta notebooks he makes the distinction between pleasure and joy, and turns again to his favourite image of the fountain, the deep welling spring. The note is addressed in his mind and heart to Asra, though her name was later nearly, but not quite, erased from the text:

> Soother of Absence. Days & weeks & months pass on/& now a year / and the Sun, the Sea, the Breeze has its influences on me, and good and sensible men – and I feel a pleasure upon me, & I am to the outward view of all cheerful, & have myself no distinct consciousness of the contrary / for I use my faculties, not indeed as once, but yet freely – but oh [Sara]! I am never happy, never deeply gladdened – I know not I have forgotten what the *Joy* is of that which the Heart is full as of a deep & quiet fountain overflowing insensibly, or the gladness of Joy, when the fountain overflows ebullient. S. T. C.[14]

It is heart-breaking to see Coleridge who, by his very nature, had a heart that was capable of 'the gladness of Joy when the fountain overflows ebullient', remembering that joy from a place of exile and a dry, empty heart. But even the memory, even the capacity for it, was perhaps a promise of release. In some ways, Coleridge, like his mariner, was back at 'the line', waiting for the release which would allow him to return to his true hemisphere, caught for a while in the polar tension between heart and head, between exile and return, between nightmare and renewed vision – sawing back and forth in 'a short uneasy motion'.

Eventually, on 9 September (ten months after Coleridge had agreed to stay on for another five months!) his replacement arrived and Coleridge became an outward voyager again. He decided not

Reconversion

to wait for a safe convoy, but to take the more daring alternative of travelling first to Italy and then taking whatever vessel he might find from there. On 23 September 1805 he took ship back to Sicily, hoping to travel swiftly thence to Naples. It was not to prove so easy. The overland route through Italy was now being made dangerous, if not impossible, by Napoleon's new victories, and Coleridge was trapped for a while on the island, which was at that time given over to the production of opium – one vast pharmacopeia.

Coleridge was still there on 21 October, his thirty-third birthday and the day of Nelson's victory at Trafalgar. He eventually crossed over to Naples on 20 November. Characteristically, the first thing he did on his arrival was to visit Virgil's tomb outside the city. He had known and loved Virgil's poetry since he was a schoolboy, but now, an exile himself, travelling with his precious copy of Dante, he felt a new resonance with the poet whom Beatrice had sent to help a lovelorn middle-aged man who had lost his way.

It is almost impossible to track Coleridge's movements in Italy at this time, but by Christmas he was in Rome and there he met and befriended the American artist Washington Allston, who painted his portrait. Together they walked among the ruins, and Allston left us a vivid account of his time with Coleridge, from which we can tell that, at least conversationally, the magical fountain of Coleridge's mind was flowing again:

> To no other man whom I have known, do I owe so much intellectually, as to Mr. Coleridge, with whom I became acquainted in Rome . . . He used to call Rome the silent city; but I never could think of it as such, while with him; for, meet him when, or where I would, the fountain of his mind was never dry, but like the far-reaching acqueducts [sic] that once supplied this mistress of the world, its living stream seemed specially to flow for every

classic ruin over which we wandered. And when I recall some of our walks under the pines of the Villa Borghese, I am almost tempted to dream that I once listened to Plato, in the groves of the Academy.[15]

Given the turning tides of the Napoleonic wars, common sense dictated that Coleridge should have passed through Rome as swiftly as possible, but characteristically he did nothing of the sort. With his great capacity for friendship he joined the artistic and philosophical circles still flourishing in Rome, discussing Schlegel and transcendental philosophy with the Germans and art with the Americans, and then inevitably, in March, the French arrived and occupied the city. Eventually they gave orders for the expulsion of all British citizens; indeed, Coleridge later used to claim that Napoleon had given personal orders for his arrest, because of a then-famous character portrait of Napoleon he had published in the *Morning Post* before leaving England. Just – but only just – in time, Coleridge made his escape. He travelled north with an English art student, Thomas Russell, could not forbear to stop at Florence to see the Uffizi, and then, finally, they set off for 'Leghorn' as the English called Livorno, almost too late, as Coleridge wrote to Washington Allston: 'This day at noon we set off for Leghorn, . . . and heaven knows whether Leghorn may not be blockaded / However we go thither & shall go to England in an American ship.'[16] The letter discloses that he had been seriously ill in Florence, perhaps another opium crisis, and the whole feel of the letter is of darkness creeping over him again. He ends it:

My dear Allston! Somewhat from increasing age, but much more from calamity & intense pre-affections my heart is not open to more than kind good wishes in general; to you & to you alone since I have left England, I have felt more / and had I not known the Wordsworths, should have loved and esteemed you *first* and

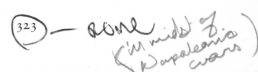

most / and as [it] is, next to them I love and honor you / Heaven knows, a part of such a Wreck as my Head & Heart is scarcely worth your acceptance –

S.T. Coleridge [17]

At Leghorn, where they waited for their ship, he gave in to complete despair, confiding to his notebook:

O my Children! – Whether, and which of you are dead, whether any, & which among you are alive, I know not / and were a Letter to arrive this moment from Keswick (Saturday Night, June 7th, 1806, Leghorn/ Gasparini's, or Arms of England Hotel) I fear, that I should be unable to open it, so deep and black is my Despair – O my Children, my Children! I gave you life once, unconscious of the Life I was giving / and you as unconsciously have given Life to me. / Yes! It has been lost – many many months ɫ past I should have essayed whether Death is what I groan for, absorption and transfiguration of Consciousness – for of annihilation I cannot by the nature of my Imagination have any idea / Yet it may be true – O mercy, mercy! Even this moment I could commit Suicide but for you, my Darlings (of Wordsworths – of Sara Hutchinson / that is *passed* – or of remembered thoughts to make a Hell of /) O me! now racked with pain, now fallen abroad & suffocated with a sense of intolerable Despair /& no other Refuge than Poisons that degrade the Being, while they suspend the torment, and which suspend only to make the Blow fall heavier/[18]

Eventually, his ship, the *Gosport*, arrived, and on 23 June they set sail for England. It was a terrible journey, lasting fifty-five days, of which we have little record, for Coleridge's suffering on that voyage was so great that he seems to have been unable to confide it even to the notebooks: they endured terrible storms and were boarded by Spanish privateers at one point and only released after many political papers and despatches – including, tragically, some of Coleridge's manuscripts – were thrown overboard. But for Coleridge the deepest suffering was once more from opium. Among its many terrible side-effects was a complete and life-threatening blockage of all his bowel movements and he had to endure the painful humiliation of violent enemas administered by the Captain, as Coleridge recalled in graphic detail in a later letter to Southey: 'tho' the Captain was the strongest man on board – it used to take all the force of his arm, & bring the blood up in his face before he could finish. Once I brought off more than a pint of blood – & three times he clearly saved my Life.'[19]

Eventually Coleridge alighted again on English soil, feeling 'more dead than alive', on 15 August. And just as the mariner, on his return, had rushed to the hermit and cried 'Shrieve me, Shrieve me, holy man', so Coleridge rushed to 'a curious little chapel at Lower Halstead', and 'offered I trust as deep a prayer as ever was sent up without words or thoughts by any human being'.[20]

[handwritten annotation: Coleridge returns to England]

'I heard and in my soul discerned
  Two voices in the air.'
The mariner and the poet discern at last the range and meaning of their pain

CHAPTER ELEVEN

The Two Voices

Part V of *The Ancient Mariner* ends with the mariner cast into a trance and in that altered state 'discerning' two voices that speak of his present state and of his future. One of them says that his purgation is not yet complete, that he has 'penance more to do', and that, paradoxically, is the voice that speaks softly, 'as soft as honey-dew'. That phrase was surely an allusion to his own poem *Kubla Khan*:

> For he on honeydew hath fed
> And drunk the milk of paradise.[1]

If it is a conscious allusion then it adds to the sense we have that these voices are 'paradisal' and not demonic.

Part VI resumes with the mariner still in his 'swound' or trance, still hearing the voices in the air. This time the mariner learns, not directly about his own fate, as before, but about the fate of his vessel. Here Coleridge uses the rapid dialogue of the two voices to change the tone of the poem's narrative and to move it swiftly forward, just as the vessel itself is suddenly accelerated with unnatural swiftness, and that sudden speed is indeed the very subject of their dialogue:

FIRST VOICE.

But tell me, tell me! speak again,
Thy soft response renewing—

What makes that ship drive on so fast?
What is the ocean doing?

(Lines 410–13)

This question about the ocean allows Coleridge to delay the answer about the speed of the vessel for a moment and insert a beautiful little pair of stanzas that draws out and emphasises once more the beneficent role of the moon and moonlight throughout the poem, as well as glancing graciously at an Elizabethan poet whom he particularly admired:

SECOND VOICE.

Still as a slave before his lord,
The ocean hath no blast;
His great bright eye most silently
Up to the Moon is cast—

If he may know which way to go;
For she guides him smooth or grim.
See, brother, see! how graciously
She looketh down on him.

(Lines 414–21)

Here we see the reciprocal relation of the moon and the ocean as she governs the movement of his tides, and although Coleridge knows Newton's mathematical and mechanistic account of this gravitational pull perfectly well, he complements it here with a sense of personal interdependency in nature which is of course one of the great themes of the poem, and in particular he highlights the role of the moon as a vessel of grace: 'how *graciously* / she looketh down on him'. Indeed, there is an ambiguity in the placing of this phrase. In its primary sense it refers to the way the moon looks down on the ocean, but in another sense it is a comment on how graciously the moon looks down on the mariner, how she allowed him to see, to re-envisage the water-snakes, in her gracious light and so released the blessing which itself released love and prayer in his heart.

Coleridge's source for this exchange of grace and obedience between the moon and the ocean is a poem called 'Orchestra, or A Poem of Dancing' by the Elizabethan poet Sir John Davies. The poem ostensibly tells the story of how Antinous, one of the suitors of Penelope in Ulysses' absence, woos her, and asks her to dance. When she refuses he launches into a great paean in praise of dancing which forms the main body of the poem. This 'narrative' is no more than the framework that enables Davies to set out a picture of the universe we inhabit animated by the double powers of love and dancing. It is a picture in which the traditional hierarchies and interconnections of 'the great chain of being', which can sometimes seem fixed, frozen and patriarchal in prose accounts, are all set in a swinging motion of delight, a dance which fallen man, if he could only purge himself sufficiently to hear the music, is invited to join. This is how Davies describes the parts played by the moon and the sea in this love-led cosmic dance:

> For lo the Sea that fleets about the Land,
> And like a girdle clips her solid waist,
> Music and measure both doth understand:
> For his great crystal eye is always cast
> Up to the Moon, and on her fixèd fast:
> And as she danceth in her pallid sphere,
> So danceth he about his center here.[2]

We can see how Coleridge's lines, 'His great bright eye most silently / Up to the Moon is cast', directly allude to this poem, and how the whole image of the movements of the cosmos as *dance* has been prepared for in Coleridge's earlier line 'the wan stars dance between'. But, as always, it is not sufficient just to notice a source; we must ask what Coleridge is doing with it. Why is he evoking Davies' poem, just at this point in his own poem? The answer lies in a return to another of the great themes of *The Mariner*, which we have touched on before: the difference between a mechanistic/instrumental and a personal/sacral vision of nature. We saw earlier that the mariner's 'fall' after shooting the albatross was a fall out of community and into alienation. The way he and the other crew members saw the bird as just an isolated 'thing', instrumental to their own purposes and ultimately expendable, is their downfall, because their instrumental/mechanistic view was false. The albatross was part of a whole delicate web of physical and spiritual community whose balance they offend with terrible consequences for themselves. And once he has lost that personal/sacral vision the mariner can only see what is loathsome and meaningless in nature and in himself, and he despises both. It is only as the moon looks down graciously on him that his earlier vision is restored both outwardly and inwardly and he can be released with a new life and a new vision, which he must share when he gets home. Davies' poem is perhaps the most perfect expression of that earlier personal/sacral view, and by the time Coleridge republished *The Mariner* with its gloss in 1817, he had come to see Davies as a prophet for his own time. He may be a prophet for our time too, giving us a glimpse of how to see the world that we will somehow have to recover and with which we will somehow have to integrate the insights of our new science.

If Coleridge felt this in his own day, then thoughtful people must feel it even more deeply now. Owen Barfield, the author of *What Coleridge Thought*, puts his finger unerringly on the central crisis of our own age when he writes:

Amid all the menacing signs that surround us in the middle of this twentieth century, perhaps the one which fills thoughtful people with the greatest sense of foreboding is the growing sense of meaninglessness. It is this which underlies most of the other threats. How is it that the more able man becomes to manipulate the world to his advantage, the less he can perceive any meaning in it?[3]

The 'whole scientific and common-sense concept of objectivity' is flawed, he argues; and these flaws are now surfacing. Barfield is, of course, not the only one to have observed this, and the trickle of unease about the intellectual validity of the Enlightenment project has since become a flood. Reviewing *Where the Wasteland Ends*[4] – Theodore Roszak's important critique of Western cultural and scientific method – and summarising its arguments, Barfield writes:

The vaunted progress of knowledge, which has been going on since the seventeenth century, has been progress in alienation. The alienation of nature from humanity, which the exclusive pursuit of 'objectivity' in science entails, was the first stage; and was followed, with the acceptance of Man himself as part of a nature so alienated, by the alienation of man from himself. This final and fatal step in reductionism occurred in two stages: first his body and then his mind. Newton's approach to nature was already, by contrast with older scientific traditions, a form of behaviourism; and what has since followed has been its extension from astronomy and physics into physiology and ultimately psychology.[5]

Such is the analysis of our present malaise that Barfield, Roszak and many others share. But Roszak does not leave us in this wasteland. As his title suggests, he is concerned with where the wasteland *ends*, and he goes on to argue that this modern reductionism, far from being, as has been generally assumed, a reflection of fact, is itself an arbitrary mental construct. It is a convenient and necessary assumption for the purpose of manipulation (technology) but in so far as it is assumed to reflect the whole truth, or the most important part of it, it is an illusion.

Roszak argues that the way out of this illusion will proceed in reverse order from the way in, first with psychology and then with the natural sciences. Completely reductive behaviourism in psychology is no longer seen as comprehensive and satisfying. We challenge it because we know that another person is more than the sum of their observed behaviour, and we know it of others because, by the mystery of our own consciousness, we know it of ourselves. But suppose, Roszak suggests, we extend this counter-mechanistic knowledge beyond the so-called subjective, or the realms of personal psychology:

> Suppose this ability we have to find something of ourselves in people should be expanded, so that the same personal transaction occurred with animal and plant . . .
>
> Suppose that ability began to reach out further still, discovering a reality of inventive pattern and communicative vitality even in what we once regarded as the dense dead stuff of the world . . .
>
> Suppose the whole of creation began to speak to us in the silent language of a deeply submerged kinship . . .
>
> Suppose . . . we even felt urged to reply courteously to this address of the environment and to join in open conversation . . .[6]

Barfield examines the consequences of these suppositions for science and society in his brilliant and prophetic essay 'The Coming Trauma of Materialism',[7] but in fact the vision, the integration, the imagined possibility of a courteous and open conversation with nature, had already been imagined and realised by the young Sir John Davies almost exactly 400 years before. Coleridge perceived all this long before Barfield and Roszak, and by including Davies here in his very first draft of *The Mariner* he was feeling his way towards a solution. When, like his mariner, Coleridge returned to his 'own countree', he would offer a way forward that integrated this sacral vision with our new developments in science, and Davies would make a second and crucial appearance in Coleridge's other great work of 1817, the *Biographia Literaria*.

Returning to the poem, the two voices conclude their dialogue with a comment on the ship's sudden acceleration, which includes a poetic expression of some of that new science:

FIRST VOICE.

But why drives on that ship so fast,
Without or wave or wind?

SECOND VOICE.

The air is cut away before,
And closes from behind.

Fly, brother, fly! more high, more high!
Or we shall be belated:
For slow and slow that ship will go,
When the Mariner's trance is abated.

(Lines 422–9)

As Gardner comments in his annotations to *The Mariner*:

The reference to the air being cut away in front and closing from behind, is apparently an attempt to introduce a quasi-scientific explanation of the event. A vacuum forms in front of the ship, then pressure of the air in back moves the ship forward.[8]

But, as we might expect from Coleridge, these verses contain both a scientific and a poetic allusion, for he was thinking of the passage in the *Odyssey*, another of the seminal texts that lie behind this poem, when Odysseus is also laid in a trance and is carried in his ship at supernatural speed towards his homeland. Here is the translation of the key passages as it is given in Lowes:

upon Odysseus' lids deep slumber fell, sound and most pleasant, very like to death . . . safely and steadily the swift ship ran; no circling hawk, swiftest of winged things, could keep beside her. Running vast rapidly she cut the ocean waves, bearing a man of godlike wisdom, a man who had before met many griefs of heart . . . yet here slept undisturbed, heedless of all he suffered.[9]

As ever, Coleridge tells us more of what we need to know in the gloss:

The Mariner hath been cast into a trance; for the angelic power causeth the vessel to drive north-ward faster than human life could endure.

FIRST VOICE.

But why drives on that ship so fast,
Without or wave or wind?

(Lines 422–3 with gloss)

Northward is the key word here; the mariner is back in his own hemisphere, his own polarity, having suffered and learned what he needs to suffer and know in the opposite polarity. It is neither the South Polar Spirit, nor his 'fellow-dæmons', but an 'angelic power' that is in charge of the ship. He may have 'penance more to do', but the mariner is on his way home.

With the departure of the 'fellow-dæmons' and their two voices, we make a transition from this swift pace, and as the mariner wakes from his merciful trance we return to a more gentle and natural pace in the movement of both the ship and the poem:

The supernatural motion is retarded; the Mariner awakes, and his penance begins anew.

I woke, and we were sailing on
As in a gentle weather:
'Twas night, calm night, the moon was high;
The dead men stood together.

(Lines 430–3)

Then comes a piece of subtle psychological realism. Even though the mariner is on the way home and his healing has begun, he experiences a flashback to trauma, something that many people with Post Traumatic Stress Disorder (PTSD) or survivor guilt are plagued with:

All stood together on the deck,
For a charnel-dungeon fitter:
All fixed on me their stony eyes,
That in the Moon did glitter.

The pang, the curse, with which they died,
Had never passed away:
I could not draw my eyes from theirs,
Nor turn them up to pray.

(Lines 434–41)

Once more the mariner endures a crisis of prayer: he is back for a moment in that place where

I look'd to Heaven, and tried to pray;
But or ever a prayer had gusht,

335

Mariner cannot pray (guilt?)

A wicked whisper came, and made
My heart as dry as dust.

(Lines 244–7)

He still feels the guilt, and even though, behind the apparently cursing eyes of the dead, there are angelic spirits who are there to bless him, he cannot for the moment perceive it. But this is a temporary flashback, and mercifully it vanishes as suddenly as it has come:

The curse is finally expiated.

And now this spell was snapt: once more
I viewed the ocean green,
And looked far forth, yet little saw
Of what had else been seen—

(Lines 442–5 with gloss)

Significantly, it is at this point that the gloss tells us that 'the curse is finally expiated'. This is important because it changes the character and meaning of the mariner's subsequent suffering. Later, when he is 'shriven' by the hermit, the gloss tells us that 'the penance of life' falls on him. But this is no longer a backward-looking penance of expiation for the past, but a forward-looking 'penance'; a penance which is about learning again to love, and to make his own story a means of releasing love and redemption in others. Once again, Coleridge was to experience just such a transition in his own 'penance of life'.

The snapping of the spell involves a restoration of the mariner's vision, again subtly suggested in the way phrases of the poem echo or reverse one another across the wide seascape of the text. In the great crisis after shooting the albatross the mariner says:

And envieth that they should live, and so many lie dead.

I look'd upon the rotting sea,
And drew my eyes away;

(Lines 240–1 with gloss from Part IV)

But now

> once more
> I viewed the ocean green,
> And looked far forth . . .

> *(Lines 442–4)*

Then, almost as an echo of the last flashback, comes the verse we have already noted about the sense of pursuit:

> Like one, that on a lonesome road
> Doth walk in fear and dread,
> And having once turned round walks on,
> And turns no more his head;
> Because he knows, a frightful fiend
> Doth close behind him tread.

> *(Lines 446–51)*

In the delicate, almost chiasmic architecture of the poem, this stanza, set late in the return journey northward, almost exactly parallels the similarly extended stanza early in the journey south, even down to the final rhyme sounds:

> With sloping masts and dipping prow,
> As who pursued with yell and blow
> Still treads the shadow of his foe,
> And forward bends his head,
> The ship drove fast, loud roard the blast,
> The southward aye we fled.

> *(Lines 45–50)*

But this is a false haunting; this time there is no pursuer.
  Then, in another of the subtle interconnections that thread

through this poem, we return to the wind as a symbol of the Holy
Spirit but this time modulated into a different key:

> But soon there breathed a wind on me,
> Nor sound nor motion made:
> Its path was not upon the sea,
> In ripple or in shade.
>
> It raised my hair, it fanned my cheek
> Like a meadow-gale of spring—
> It mingled strangely with my fears,
> Yet it felt like a welcoming.
>
> Swiftly, swiftly flew the ship,
> Yet she sailed softly too:
> Sweetly, sweetly blew the breeze—
> On me alone it blew.

(Lines 452–63)

In Part V, again just after the mariner has awoken from sleep, we
had the grand cosmic arrival of the Spirit with its deliberate echo
of Pentecost; the loud roaring wind, the upper air bursting into
life, 'a hundred fire-flags sheen'. But, significantly, we were told
'The loud wind never reached the ship' and it is 'moved on from
beneath', not by the wind. It is as though, at that point, the mariner can behold the energy of release and new life 'afar off in the
element' but it has not yet become his own personal, and more
gentle renewal of spirit. But now, just as he is being readied to
return home, the Spirit comes to him personally. Coleridge was
of course well aware that in the Authorised Version of the New
Testament the words 'wind', 'breath' and 'spirit' are all translations of the single Greek word 'pneuma'. When Jesus has that
remarkable conversation with Nicodemus about the possibility

of Nicodemus being born anew, he says (in the Authorised
Version):

> Verily, verily, I say unto thee, Except a man be born of water and
> *of* the Spirit, he cannot enter into the kingdom of God. That
> which is born of the flesh is flesh; and that which is born of the
> Spirit is spirit. Marvel not that I said unto thee, Ye must be born
> again. The wind bloweth where it listeth, and thou hearest the
> sound thereof, but canst not tell whence it cometh, and whither
> it goeth: so is every one that is born of the Spirit.[10]

But it is the translators who are choosing when to use 'wind' and
when to use 'Spirit'. It could equally well be translated: 'The spirit
bloweth where it listeth . . . so is everyone that is born of the
wind.' This cluster of water, spirit and wind is certainly part of
the resonance and meaning not only of these stanzas, but of the
whole poem. In one sense the wind/spirit that 'breathes' on the
mariner at this moment is the beginning of this new birth, but it
will not be completed until he is also 'born of water', and that is
precisely what happens in the final part of the poem when the
mariner is pulled, 'like one that hath been seven days drowned',
from the sea.

The phrase 'yet it felt like a welcoming' subtly prepares us for the
beautiful 'homecoming' verse that follows this spiritual interlude:

And the ancient	Oh! dream of joy! is this indeed
Mariner	The light-house top I see?
beholdeth his	
native country.	Is this the hill? is this the kirk?
	Is this mine own countree?

(Lines 464–7)

Here we are presented with a view of the land from far out at sea,
its familiar features gradually coming back into focus. There is a

sense of tantalising possibility: the mariner can see his own country, but isn't yet there, and there is to be one more dramatic incident in his life before he finally sets foot on dry land. But here the gradual approach to his 'native country' is beautifully done, with a reversal of the three features that had dropped out of sight in the opening stanzas, each returning to view; so in Part I we had the 'kirk . . . the hill . . . the light-house top', and now in this stanza we see first the light-house, then the hill, and finally, the kirk.

Apart from this delicate mirroring of the earlier stanza, the key word here is *Joy*. Just as there is a gradual approach to the harbour and the homeland, so there is a gradual approach to *Joy*, the positive counterpart to, and healing of, the mariner's lonely *agony*. Here, as we view the homeland from a distance, we have 'a dream of joy'; in the next verse we have a prayer that it may be more than a dream – 'oh let me be awake'; and then finally, with the arrival of the pilot's boat, it becomes a real joy which cannot, like a dream, be taken away, 'a joy the dead men could not blast'. As we have seen, when he wrote *Dejection: An Ode* four years after writing *The Mariner*, Coleridge came to identify Joy as an essential element of the shaping spirit of imagination, and as the gift we ourselves bring to nature:

> Joy, Lady! is the spirit and the power,
> Which wedding Nature to us gives in dower
> A new Earth and new Heaven,
> Undreamt of by the sensual and the proud—
> Joy is the sweet voice, Joy the luminous cloud—
> We in ourselves rejoice!
> And thence flows all that charms or ear or sight,
> All melodies the echoes of that voice,
> All colours a suffusion from that light.[11]

Interestingly, these apprehensions of Joy by the mariner at this point in the poem are swiftly followed by the perception of pure and luminous colour in the angels who have previously been invisible to him, concealed in the bodies of the dead. Indeed, this stanza with its 'dream of joy' acts as a prelude to some of the most lucid and beautiful stanzas of purely natural description in the whole poem:

> We drifted o'er the harbour-bar,
> And I with sobs did pray—
> O let me be awake, my God!
> Or let me sleep alway.

> The harbour-bay was clear as glass,
> So smoothly it was strewn!
> And on the bay the moonlight lay,
> And the shadow of the Moon.

> The rock shone bright, the kirk no less,
> That stands above the rock:
> The moonlight steeped in silentness
> The steady weathercock.

> *(Lines 468–79)*

Here indeed, this poem, which was the first in the *Lyrical Ballads*, fully achieves one of the joint aims of that book, as Coleridge later recalled it:

> to excite a feeling analogous to the supernatural, by awakening the mind's attention to the lethargy of custom, and directing it to the loveliness and the wonders of the world before us; an inexhaustible treasure, but for which, in consequence of the film of familiarity and selfish solicitude, we have eyes, yet

see not, ears that hear not, and hearts that neither feel nor understand.[12]

Once more we see that this scene of transfigured or heightened vision is preceded by prayer and presided over by the moon.

After this vision of nature so heightened as to be 'analogous to the supernatural' comes a vision of the supernatural itself; again, it comes gradually and by degrees:

The angelic And the bay was white with silent light,
spirits leave the
dead bodies, Till rising from the same,

Full many shapes, that shadows were,

In crimson colours came.

And appear in A little distance from the prow
their own forms
of light. Those crimson shadows were:

I turned my eyes upon the deck—

Oh, Christ! what saw I there!

(Lines 480–7)

It is important for us to remember the earlier sense of the word 'shadow' here. The word shadow was sometimes a synonym for a reflected image, and indeed this is the sense in which it is used a few lines earlier when he spoke of 'the shadow of the moon'.

So now when we see the 'crimson shadows' rising from the bay, which is white with the silent light of the moon, the mariner is seeing first the reflections and then the actual and true 'forms of light' of the angels who have accompanied him on this last stage of his journey. Once more, Coleridge is able to suggest deep mystery by means of gradual approach: first he hears the angelic music and almost mystically perceives the sounds as shapes flying to and from the sun; then he sees the reflections of the 'crimson shadows' in the water; finally he turns and sees the seraphim themselves:

> *And appear in their own forms of light.*
>
> A little distance from the prow
> Those crimson shadows were:
> I turned my eyes upon the deck—
> Oh, Christ! what saw I there!
>
> Each corse lay flat, lifeless and flat,
> And, by the holy rood!
> A man all light, a seraph-man,
> On every corse there stood.
>
> This seraph-band, each waved his hand:
> It was a heavenly sight!
> They stood as signals to the land,
> Each one a lovely light;
>
> This seraph-band, each waved his hand,
> No voice did they impart—
> No voice; but oh! the silence sank
> Like music on my heart.
>
> *(Lines 484–99 with gloss)*

The dramatic ending of the stanza 'Oh Christ! what saw I there!' teases us with the expectation of some new horror, some terrible further flashback, but instead we have not a catastrophe but what Tolkien calls a 'eucatastrophe' – a sudden turn to the good. The images of the living dead which had so haunted and tormented the mariner as he looked at the crew are replaced by the living light of the angels. And they are not just generic 'angels'; three times in these verses Coleridge emphasises that they are *Seraphim*, borrowing the shortening to 'seraph' that was first coined by

Milton. Of the nine orders of angels (first delineated by Pseudo-Dionysius and later consolidated by Thomas Aquinas) the Seraphim are the highest and nearest to God, and they burn with the fire of the Divine Love, as distinct from the Cherubim, who excel in knowledge. In medieval paintings, the Seraphim are traditionally shown as crimson and having six wings. It is with a vision of Christ amid the Seraphim, appearing himself almost like a Seraph, that St Francis receives the stigmata as the supreme seal of his suffering love, as for example in the famous painting by Giotto.[13] It is the Seraphim who are sent to the mariner because his crime is a failure of love and his redemption is supremely by and for love. It is the Divine Love, mediated through the Seraphim, which then flows down from them into the other orders of angels, who represent the purity and clarity of intellectual vision. In other words, it is Love that purifies Vision, and this is why, at last, the mariner can actually see the Seraphim who have been with him all this time.

In giving the mariner this moment of vision, just before he sets foot in his native country, Coleridge was also once more recalling the *Odyssey*, and this time not simply the poem itself, but the interpretation of Odysseus's own voyage out and back again which was given by the great Neo-Platonic sages such as Plotinus, in whose writings, as we know, Coleridge had delighted since his schooldays. In writing these stanzas Coleridge was probably remembering the allegorical interpretation of Odysseus's return in Plotinus's *Enneads*, as it was translated by Thomas Taylor, the Cambridge Platonist whose works Coleridge also admired and annotated:

In the third class is the race of divine men, who through a more excellent power, and with piercing eyes, acutely perceive the supernal light, to the vision of which they raise themselves above the clouds and darkness as it were of this lower world . . . being no otherwise delighted with the place which is truly and properly their own, than he who after many wanderings is at length restored to his lawful country.[14]

What Plotinus is saying here is that those who have purified themselves and attain visionary and transformative experience in this life are like Odysseus on his return to Ithaca, like long-lost mariners coming home. That the mariner should see the Seraphim 'in their own forms of light' is a testimony therefore that his redemption has begun, that he is becoming pure of heart. For Coleridge that long process of recovery and purification would take many years, even after he had returned to his own country, but certainly those who were with him in his last days felt very strongly that they were in the presence of a purified and visionary soul. A moving entry in his notebooks from 1833, the year before he died, touches strangely on this meeting of purity of heart, poetic vision and the Seraphim which he had intuited thirty years earlier in this poem: 'The pure of heart are not therefore poets; but no man can be a great poet, that apotheosis of the philosopher, the transfigured philosopher with seraph wings on his shoulders, who has not a pure heart.'[15]

The mariner is not the only one to see the light, though perhaps the only one to perceive that it is the light of the Seraphim, for we are told that 'they stood as signals to the land'. They are seen by the pilot and the hermit, though the text makes it clear that the pilot has only seen, as he takes it, distress flares or torches, whatever better thing the hermit has discerned. So the angels not only bring the mariner's ship back to his home port but also, even as they wave and depart, make the right human connections for him so that the work of redemption can continue on shore. This little sequence on the angels ends with a return to the theme of music, with which the angelic presence began, but this time music transposed into the key of silence:

No voice; but oh! the silence sank
Like music on my heart.

(Lines 498–9)

Once again there is a subtle reversal, and so healing, of an earlier
episode in the poem. When the mariner and the crew were still in
their fallen and alienated state after the killing of the albatross,
silence was oppressive to them, not musical or contemplative, and
the mariner tells us 'we did speak only to break / The silence of
the sea'. But now the silence itself becomes part of the inner music
of the heart.

The tone of spiritual vision and contemplation turns to action
again and we are back in the ordinary world with the sudden
sound of oars and voices:

But soon I heard the dash of oars,
I heard the Pilot's cheer;
My head was turn'd perforce away
And I saw a boat appear.

The Pilot and the Pilot's boy,
I heard them coming fast:
Dear Lord in Heaven! it was a joy
The dead men could not blast.

(Lines 500–7)

The sudden arrival of the pilot helps us make the transition from
the dream-like, sacral world we have been contemplating, to the
everyday human world to which we are returning, but the fact that
the pilot is accompanied by the hermit also provides a link
between the two worlds.

At first the mariner doesn't perceive the hermit, only the pilot
and the pilot's boy, and we get another 'flash of joy', but this time:

Dear Lord in Heaven! it was a joy
The dead men could not blast.

(Lines 506–7)

The phrase 'Dear Lord in Heaven' does not fall lightly here; indeed, as the mariner returns home the references to Christ, his cross and resurrection, increase in frequency and meaning. Here there is a reference once more to John, Coleridge's favourite Gospel, to the promise: 'And ye now therefore have sorrow: but I will see you again, and your heart shall rejoice, and your joy no man taketh from you.'[16] That particular verse in John could well stand as an epigraph to the whole of *The Ancient Mariner*.

When a large sailing vessel entered a harbour there was need for a local pilot to guide it to safe anchorage and to take its crew ashore; the pilot would be on the lookout for such vessels, and on this moonlit night has seen the 'signal lights'. So, at one level, his appearance at this point is a perfectly natural episode, but at another, as with so much else in the poem, it carries a spiritual truth. There has to be a transition between deep inner experience, the visions in the height and depth that may be given to an individual soul, and that person's return to the wider community. The mariner has to be helped back to land after his spiritual voyage; he has to be helped practically by the pilot and spiritually by the hermit. But most of all, he needs to find an outward and visible sign and expression of what has happened in the inner and spiritual world. This is one of the purposes and meanings of sacrament: that ritually and publicly we should make the great signs and enactments of what has already happened inwardly and spiritually:

I saw a third—I heard his voice:
It is the Hermit good!

347

He singeth loud his godly hymns
That he makes in the wood.
He'll shrieve my soul, he'll wash away
The Albatross's blood.

(Lines 508–13)

In one sense that blood has already been washed away, that sin has been forgiven: the burden of the albatross has been released and 'sunk like lead into the sea'. But at another level this inner event has to be acknowledged and ratified, brought into the scope and wider communion of the Church which the mariner will be re-joining and to which Coleridge was also to return. So we hear once more, for the sixth and last time, as at the ending of all the previous parts of the poem, of the mariner's crime. After this, however, it won't be mentioned again; the seventh and final part of the poem will end with the proclamation of love, and a new morning.

However new the morning may have been when Coleridge rose from his knees at the little chapel in Halsted, he was by no means a renovated man. He still had much further to travel than his mariner, even though for him, too, the lighthouse top of reason, the hill of nature, and most important of all, the kirk of his faith were coming back into view. If the mariner in his trance had heard two voices – the one revealing his guilt and the other his penance – then for Coleridge, too, in the desperate decade between his return in 1806, and his final shelter and sanctuary with Dr Gillman in 1816, there were likewise two voices 'taking part', taking sides, and sometimes tearing him to pieces.

There was the voice he had seemed to hear in that Malta moonrise: 'the logos, the creator, the evolver'. Intellectually, he was more than on the mend; he was beginning that great re-integration of faith and reason rooted in the Trinity and in our being made in the image of our maker, which would bear fruit in

Biographia Literaria and *Sibylline Leaves*, the two great publications of his new life post-1816. But for now, however true and beautiful, all that theology was still a matter of intellectual exploration and assent; it had not yet reached and renovated his heart. In his heart Coleridge was still haunted by 'wicked whispers', whispers that had yet to be exorcised. For the second of Coleridge's two voices was one of utter condemnation, guilt and despair.

Coleridge had set off to Malta with the blessings, good wishes, and it has to be said, financial investment, of his friends and his family. He and they had high hopes that he would return a new man, free of his addiction, financially solvent, restored to health and buoyant again, ready to be once more the ever-inspiring collaborator with his literary friends and the diligent provider for his family. He returned two years later a penniless wreck. He had sent much of the money he earned in Malta home, and what he kept he had squandered or spent on the expenses of travel and accommodation on his long journey back. He had left a lithe dark-haired epitome of Romantic Genius; he returned prematurely grey, overweight, listless, more deeply addicted than ever, and, secretly, more desperately and obsessively in love with Asra than he had been when he left. What was he to do? Of course he wanted to go straight home; he was desperate to see his children, anxious to see Wordsworth, but equally terrified, though in different ways, of confronting either his wife or Asra. What was he to do?

For a while he did nothing, falling back into his lifelong habit of evading or postponing difficult choices or confrontations. He stayed with his friend Daniel Stuart, from whom he borrowed clean clothes and money. Then he stayed with the Lambs and asked if Mary might write to Mrs Coleridge on his behalf, which she quite properly refused to do, insisting that Coleridge write himself. His family and friends, who had heard he was back at last, could not understand his delay and were both anxious and offended. Wordsworth wrote to their mutual friend and patron Sir George Beaumont:

> What shall I say of Coleridge? What can I say? My dear friend this is certain, that he is destined to be unhappy . . . in fact, he dare not go home, he recoils so much from the thought of domesticating with Mrs Coleridge . . . he is so miserable that he dare not encounter it. What a deplorable thing! I have written to him to say that if he does not come down immediately I must insist upon seeing him somewhere. If he appoints London, I shall go. I believe if any good thing is to be done to him, it must be done by me.[17]

Wordsworth's determination to 'do Coleridge good' was a bad sign, and the beginning of various futile attempts by Coleridge's friends to 'manage' him. But this would not be possible until he had really confronted his own darkness, and recognised his own helplessness; until he was ready and willing to be managed.

If we are to understand what happened, for good and for ill, over the next few years, then we must hear the second of Coleridge's two voices, the voice of accusation and despair, from his own lips, and to do so, we must look a little forward in time to the series of confessional letters that poured out of him during and after his final opium crisis in 1813/14.

First, there is the sheer sense of guilt he was enduring, for no one could accuse Coleridge of his faults more harshly than Coleridge himself. Eight years after his arrival back in England he was to write to Joseph Cottle, looking back over these years:

> for years the anguish of my spirit has been indescribable, the sense of my danger *staring*, but the conscience of my GUILT

worse, far far worse than all! – I have prayed with drops of agony on my Brow, trembling not only before the Justice of my Maker, but even before the Mercye of my Redeemer. 'I gave thee so many Talents. What hast thou done with them?'[18]

Alongside the guilt, and exacerbating it, was the sheer paralysis of the will, in which he could see the right course of action but somehow never take the action itself, and worse, the perverse lashing out at the very people he loved, precisely because they reminded him of his guilt. In chapter 8 we quoted briefly from a letter to his long-suffering friend John Morgan on the effects of opium (see chapter 8, pages 233–234); the passage from which we quoted continues in words which might be a summary of all the self-inflicted calamities that befell him during this 'lost decade':

> the worst was, that in *exact proportion* to the *importance and urgency* of any Duty was it, as of fatal necessity, sure to be neglected: because it added to the terror above described. In exact proportion, as I *loved* any person or persons more than others, & would have sacrificed my Life for them, were *they* sure to be the most barbarously mistreated by silence, absence, or breach of promise. – I used to think St. James's text he who offends in one point of the law, offended in all, very harsh; but my own sad experience has taught me it's [*sic*] awful, dreadful truth. – What crime is there scarcely which has not been included in or followed from the one guilt of taking opium? Not to speak of ingratitude to my maker for the wasted talents; of ingratitude to so many friends who have loved me I know not why; of the barbarous neglect of my family . . .[19]

After weeks of delay and prevarication in London, Coleridge finally pulled himself together and travelled north in October to face that neglected family and the unpalatable truths that encounter would bring home to him. But before he went he took the time to write to two other desperate men who had written to him about their faith.

The first was George Fricker, his wife's younger brother, who had passed through a spiritual crisis arising from a deep conviction of sin. Coleridge wrote to him with great patience and empathy, sharing something of his own story:

> I am far from surprised that, having seen what you have seen, and suffered what you have suffered, you should open your soul to a sense of our fallen nature; and the inability of man to heal himself. My opinions may not be in all points the same as yours; but I have experienced a similar alteration ... sorrow and ill health, and disappointment in the only deep wish I had ever cherished, forced me to look into myself. I read the New Testament again ...[20]

The letter concludes with a powerful peroration, addressed as much I think by Coleridge to himself as to the young George Fricker, saying that it's all very well to believe in the miracles and the outer evidences of the faith, but for the faith to be real and effective something must happen within – it must be 'a head-and-heart faith':

> Still must thou repent and be regenerated and be crucified to the flesh, and this not by thy own mere power; but by a mysterious action of the moral governor on thee ... of the Logos, or Word ... still will the vital head-and-heart FAITH in these truths be the living and only fountain of all true virtue.[21]

Curiously, Coleridge discloses here a number of important things which he did not disclose to people with whom he was much more intimate. First, that he was completely re-reading the New Testament, an act which would prove continuously fruitful for both his writing and his faith. Second, that he has recognised that it is not in his 'own mere power' to be regenerate but that he must be open to the 'mysterious action' of the Logos, that same Logos he had sensed in the Malta moonrise. Finally, there is the insight that what is needed is a link between head and heart: faith can only be vital – that is alive and life giving – when these two are joined.

The second letter was to Thomas Clarkson. Indeed, it was more than a letter. Clarkson was exhausted and depressed after so many setbacks in the campaign for the abolition of slavery and was beginning to have doubts even about his own Christian faith, and in his distress he appealed to Coleridge. Coleridge's response was immediate and helpful, for Coleridge took a side journey to visit the great campaigner on his way north, and stayed with him, writing this letter, which is really a three-thousand-word essay on the Trinity, while he was actually staying with the Clarksons. In this long philosophical letter he takes Clarkson back to the source of all things in the Mind of God, in the exchange of love between the Father and the Son, that love itself being the Holy Spirit. He reminds Clarkson that he and all things are continually spoken into being by the *Logos* as a reflection of the loving will of the Father: first, he shows Clarkson that his own individual soul is breathed into being by the loving Word and the Spirit, so that his own sense of being a little 'I Am' derives from and participates in the great 'I AM' who is God. He then goes on to show him that all of us as individuals are also called by the same love to grow together and to assist one another's growth, for

Man is truly altered by the co-existence of other men; his faculties cannot be developed in himself alone, & only by himself.

Therefore the human race not by a bold metaphor, but in a sublime reality, approach to, & might become, one body whose Head is Christ (the Logos).[22] ✓ ✓ ✓ ✓

And so, Coleridge draws Clarkson back to just those essential truths that lie behind the anti-slavery campaign: that every human being is made in the image of God and that the way we treat each other, the way we live in community, is an essential part of growing into what God has called us to be; not only unique individuals but also a single body with Christ as our head. Here, the better of Coleridge's two voices is speaking, and his intellectual insights, given generously and unstintingly, move others deeply in their hearts as well as their minds – even though Coleridge himself still awaits that integration.

So Coleridge returned to Keswick, but not before one last deviation to Penrith, to see Asra, only to find that Wordsworth had beaten him to it. The lease at Grasmere had expired and Wordsworth intended to set up household with Mary, Dorothy and Asra at Coleorton in Leicestershire in a farmhouse provided by Sir George Beaumont. They hadn't yet travelled south and were in fact staying a few miles away from Penrith in a house in Kendal. Notes were exchanged, and eventually, drawing a deep breath, Coleridge came over to Kendal to see them. They were all shocked at his appearance. Dorothy wrote later to her friend Catherine (Thomas Clarkson's wife): 'Never did I feel such a shock as the first sight of him. We all felt in the same way . . . and yet sometimes . . . I saw something of his former self.'[23]

Coleridge took rooms at an inn and the Wordsworth ménage delayed their journey south so that they could all talk things through. There was a lot to discuss. Could Coleridge go home and save his marriage or was it too late? Could he resume his friendship with Asra without it becoming obsessive again? Were there ways that he and Wordsworth could find to work together

Coleridge draws Clarkson back to faith

again? The upshot of these conversations was a generous offer that if things proved impossible for Coleridge at home then he could come and stay with them in Coleorton and they could find a new way of working together as before. This was indeed generous, in one sense, but in another it spoke to Wordsworth's continued need for Coleridge's inspiration and philosophical underpinning for his own work. While in London, Coleridge had had many offers of work, including invitations from Humphry Davy to give lucrative and prestigious lectures – offers which Coleridge eventually took up and could, perhaps should, have taken up sooner. Once again Wordsworth was effectively luring him away from his own independent literary life to share work that in the end would have only Wordsworth's name on it.

With this offer still warm in his mind, Coleridge finally arrived home on 30 October 1806, having been away nearly three years. Sara must have been as shocked at the change in his appearance as Dorothy had been, and deeply distressed to discover that none of the problems which Coleridge's Malta sojourn was meant to address had been solved. It must soon have become clear that his deepened opium use, with its attendant paranoia and delirium in the day and the nightmares at night, now made him extremely difficult to live with. There were certainly terrible 'scenes'. Sara could not forbear to make all the obvious and invidious comparisons between Coleridge and his sober, industrious brother-in-law Southey, whose literary career was forging ahead and who would soon be made Poet Laureate. Far from goading Coleridge into similar action, these harangues just increased his guilt-induced and opium-infused paralysis.

By the end of November they had agreed to a separation. Divorce was not an option in the early 1800s, except for adultery, and even this agreed separation was not a formal status, but a private arrangement. Indeed, there were a number of occasions when they came back together again, both at Greta Hall and, remarkably, at Tom Poole's back in Nether Stowey. At the heart of their 'negotiations' over this separation was, of course, access to the children. Here they seem to have made and kept a sacred agreement always to speak well of each other to the children and never to speak ill of the other parent in their presence. Coleridge was anxious to spend time with his children and to help personally in teaching and tutoring them when he could, which indeed he did, though sadly when the really crucial decisions had to be made and the funds found for Hartley's university education, Coleridge was in too deep a crisis, physically and mentally, to respond, and, to his everlasting shame, others had to do it for him.

By Christmas that year Coleridge had left home and returned to the Wordsworths and Asra, at Coleorton. Perhaps he should have gone to London and at last begun an independent literary life, but in a sense he had no choice. He must have known that, left alone in London with his weakness and addiction, the opium would probably kill him, as eventually it nearly did. He was not made to be 'alone on a wide wide sea', even the wide sea of the metropolis; he was made 'to love and to be loved'. He needed to be understood. His wife had long since ceased to read his poetry or take any interest in his other writings. It seemed to him, then, that the only four people in the world who really understood who he was or what he might yet become were in the Wordsworth household.

On 22 December he joined that household at Coleorton. It must have been a strange experience for all of them. At one level it was a great reunion. There were walks in the countryside, discussion of poetry, sharing of vision, much like the old days. But on another level everything had changed. Wordsworth was settled, mature, established, happy and highly productive and it gradually began to dawn on Coleridge that his own beloved Asra was now as much a part of the Wordsworth household as was her sister, or Dorothy. It was he, Coleridge, who was now, as he had predicted in the long first draft of *Dejection: An Ode*, 'A wither'd branch upon a blossoming Tree'.[24]

He was eaten away from within by agonising jealousy, the whispering of his dark voice, so much so that there came a crisis, two days after Christmas. There seems to have been a confrontation with Wordsworth and Asra in which Coleridge had the paranoid delusion that he had seen them in bed together. This seems highly unlikely and later Coleridge came to acknowledge to himself that it was a delusion, but he still made agonised references to it for years afterwards in his notebooks. And yet the household did not break. On the contrary, something near miraculous happened. Somehow composure was regained and only a week later, on 2 January, they all gathered in the big sitting room for the reading, over several nights, of 'The Poem to Coleridge', the text we now know as the 1805 version of *The Prelude*, and Coleridge was able to set aside every jealousy and open his heart and mind entirely to Wordsworth's great poem. More than that, he was stirred and moved to great verse himself. On the evening Wordsworth finished the reading, Coleridge stayed up all night and wrote the last of his great 'conversation poems' 'To William Wordsworth',[25] the first and perhaps best response to, and summary of, *The Prelude*, but also a poem in which Coleridge's own 'two voices' were somehow transmuted and brought into a kind of harmony.

He opens by praising *The Prelude* as 'more than historic', indeed as 'prophetic':

Friend of the Wise! and Teacher of the Good!
Into my heart have I received that Lay
More than historic, that prophetic Lay
Wherein (high theme by thee first sung aright)
Of the foundations and the building up
Of a Human Spirit thou hast dared to tell
What may be told, to the understanding mind

Revealable; and what within the mind
By vital breathings secret as the soul
Of vernal growth, oft quickens in the heart
Thoughts all too deep for words!——[26]

This whole opening section is about how poetry interconnects the head and the heart with its reciprocal movement: 'Into my heart . . . within the mind . . . secret as the soul . . . quickens in the heart'.

The poem goes on to recognise Wordsworth's extraordinary power as a poet, the very thing Coleridge's jealous heart might have wanted to deny:

Now in thy inner life, and now abroad,
When power streamed from thee, and thy soul received
The light reflected, as a light bestowed——[27]

He sees Wordsworth writing for all humankind, 'From the dread Watch-Tower of Man's absolute Self' (line 40) and sees him as having achieved immortality through this poem, as indeed he had:

O great Bard!
Ere yet that last strain dying awed the air,
With stedfast eye I viewed thee in the choir
Of ever-enduring men. The truly Great
Have all one age, and from one visible space
Shed influence! They, both in power and act,
Are permanent, and Time is not with *them*,
Save as it worketh *for* them, they *in* it.[28]

It is an extraordinary moment of self-forgetting humility to give this just praise to Wordsworth, for Coleridge had not the compensation of knowing that his own *Ancient Mariner* had also won for

him just such a place in 'the choir / Of ever-enduring men'. But he
goes on to say that the effect of hearing Wordsworth's poem seems
for a moment to rekindle the poet in him, significantly using a
metaphor drawn from the final part of *The Ancient Mariner*: the
resuscitation of one who seemed drowned:

> Ah! as I listened with a heart forlorn,
> The pulses of my Being beat anew:
> And even as Life returns upon the Drowned,
> Life's joy rekindling roused a throng of Pains—
> Keen Pangs of Love, awakening as a babe
> Turbulent, with an outcry in the heart;[29]

Then Coleridge gives utterance to his second, self-accusing voice,
but somehow by transmuting it into poetry he is able both to hear
it and to transcend it:

> And Fears self-willed, that shunned the eye of Hope;
> And Hope that scarce would know itself from Fear;
> Sense of past Youth, and Manhood come in vain,
> And Genius given, and Knowledge won in vain;
> And all which I had culled in wood-walks wild,
> And all which patient toil had reared, and all,
> Commune with thee had opened out—but flowers
> Strewed on my corse, and borne upon my bier,
> In the same coffin, for the self-same grave!
>
> That way no more! . . .[30]

He hears the voice, lets it speak, and dismisses it, 'The tumult rose
and ceased, for Peace is nigh' (line 87).

Then he gives a beautiful account of listening to Wordsworth's
poem, again using a maritime metaphor. This time the soul itself

is the sea and the poem becomes somehow both the breeze and the moonlight, in a glorious passage that recalls Coleridge's allusion to John Davies's lines about the moon and the sea in Part V of *The Ancient Mariner*:

> In silence listening, like a devout child,
> My soul lay passive, by thy various strain
> Driven as in surges now beneath the stars,
> With momentary Stars of my own birth,
> Fair constelled Foam, still darting off
> Into the darkness; now a tranquil sea,
> Outspread and bright, yet swelling to the Moon.[31]

Finally, Coleridge's poem modulates from intense literary appreciation, through personal friendship, into something far deeper still: spiritual perception and prayer:

> And when—O Friend! my comforter and guide!
> Strong in thyself, and powerful to give strength!—
> Thy long sustained Song finally closed,
> And thy deep voice had ceased—yet thou thyself
> Wert still before my eyes, and round us both
> That happy vision of beloved faces—
> Scarce conscious, and yet conscious of its close
> I sate, my being blended in one thought
> (Thought was it? or Aspiration? or Resolve?)
> Absorbed, yet hanging still upon the sound—
> And when I rose, I found myself in prayer.[32]

This ending was indeed prophetic of the whole direction Coleridge's thought and writing would take. In his lectures on Shakespeare, which were to be his next great achievement, and then in the *Biographia Literaria*, Coleridge would create a theology of the poetic imagination and make the link between the experience of the sublime, of heightened meaning in great literature, and the indwelling of the *Logos* in every soul.

Before either of those works emerged, there was the strange, and in its own way heartening interlude of *The Friend*. Stirred perhaps by Wordsworth's poem, Coleridge felt he must rouse himself, fight off the sense of failure and paralysis, and make something of his life. His first thought was to return, like his mariner, to his own native country, not just the West Country but to Ottery St Mary where he was born and where his respectable older brother George was now the vicar and schoolmaster, just as his father had been. Perhaps Coleridge could domicile and teach there. It seemed there might be an opening, but Coleridge thought he should let his brother know about the separation from Sara, and explain that the family would sometimes come down to see and stay with him, but for visits only, not permanently.

Unfortunately, at the least whiff of this 'scandal' of separation, the respectable George wrote withdrawing the offer. Coleridge never opened the letter (guessing it might contain bad news), but went ahead and travelled back to the west with the whole family, staying with Tom Poole at Stowey, only to discover that he wasn't welcome at Ottery. There was much mutual recrimination, but if Coleridge had faced up to the letter he'd received months earlier they would have been spared the trip and the embarrassment. Unfortunately, not opening crucial letters became something of a habit with Coleridge in the years that followed. This refusal even to look at potential bad news was, in its own way, the survival strategy of a man on the very edge, but of course it only made things worse in the end.

So Coleridge, Sara and the children retreated to Tom Poole's and Coleridge, while visiting Bristol to look up friends there, and almost certainly to obtain more opium, met with another young man who had long admired him from afar and was eager to meet his hero. This was the brilliant Thomas De Quincey, who would be first an overwhelmed fan and then a disillusioned foe of Coleridge's. Both the admiration and the opposition were complicated by the fact that De Quincey was a fellow addict, and in his *Confessions of an English Opium Eater* he accuses Coleridge of worse excesses than his, by way of excusing his own. It was also De Quincey who first accused Coleridge of plagiarism in some of his lectures and in the *Biographia*, mainly of citing translated passages of Schelling and Schiller without acknowledging the source. There was a time when these accusations were taken fairly seriously but recent scholarship has swung the other way, pointing out that Coleridge's use of these sources is not slavish but entirely original and that he had genuinely come through to similar conclusions and even phrasing since he and these German philosophers were themselves drawing on the same Platonic and Neo-Platonic sources.

For now, though, De Quincey proved a friend in need and gallantly accompanied Sara and the children back to the Lake District and loaned Coleridge money so that he could try his next stratagem, which was to take up the offer, initiated by Humphry Davy, of delivering public lectures at the Royal Institution in London. Coleridge's series was on 'Poetry and the Principles of Taste'. After a shaky start in which he made the mistake of reading a script instead of speaking more spontaneously, this first series of lectures in 1807–8 was a considerable success, and the second set, 1811–12, even more so. We will turn to those shortly, but in between these two lecture series Coleridge made one more attempt to find an outlet for his gifts and an independent income through journalism.

In spite of the complete financial failure of the fortnightly *Watchman* in his younger days, he decided to run and produce entirely by himself a weekly journal called *The Friend*. Whereas

The Watchman had been a campaigning journal, fiercely engaged with the politics of the day, Coleridge's idea with *The Friend* was to go back to first principles, and help people reframe their questions and think clearly from those first principles, rather as he had done in his letters to George Fricker and Thomas Clarkson. This encouragement of clear and principled thinking was to be interspersed with lighter travel stories and also with serious literature and literary criticism. Astonishingly, Coleridge managed to get subscribers and to keep *The Friend* going, producing his 6,000 words or so a week from June in 1809 to March in 1810. Even more astonishing is that he did it from the Wordsworths' new establishment, back up in the Lakes, at Allan Bank, and that Asra acted as his amanuensis. Their work together on *The Friend* was meant to re-establish their purely literary and platonic friendship, but Coleridge was still desperately in love and the tension, as many of his notebook entries show, was unbearable for him. It also proved unbearable for her, knowing herself to be the recipient of tumultuous unspoken love which she came to realise she could not ultimately return in kind. Eventually the strain became too much, and she left the household to go and live with her brother Tom.

Coleridge was heartbroken, as another of his fantasies, his delusory comforts, was pulled away from him. He collapsed and simply couldn't make the effort to bring out another issue of *The Friend*. It ended there, and it ended, as *The Watchman* had done, with debts and unsold copies. Coleridge might have been tempted to feel that all that heroic effort was in vain. Financially it was a disaster, but in other respects it had been important and helpful. *The Friend* was eventually reprinted in a three-volume edition in 1818 and many times after his death, and though it is not read so much now, it laid the essential groundwork for two classics which followed it: *Biographia Literaria* and *Aids to Reflection*, whose very title expresses the chief aim of *The Friend*.

Despondent and exhausted, thrown back again on the opium which the sheer work pressure of *The Friend* had helped him to resist, Coleridge returned to London, got permission to sleep in a tiny room above the newspaper offices of *The Courier*, to which he often contributed, and resumed his role as a lecturer.

When one considers the truly great lecture course on Shakespeare that ensued, the reprints and new editions of which are still a standard literary critical text, with many brilliant insights from them still being quoted in every new introduction to the plays, it is astonishing to contemplate the fact that the man who staggered into the lecture hall to deliver these masterpieces was deeply depressed, often suicidal, alternately battling the equally dreadful symptoms of opium indulgence on the one hand and withdrawal on the other. These lectures are often read in isolation from Coleridge's own life at the time, and also in isolation from his developing religious thought and convictions. This is a mistake. Coleridge was not a literary critic in one corner of his mind and a theologian in the other. On the contrary, the insights of his literary criticism into the power of the imagination and its ability to create and give life, organically, rather than mechanistically, to new works were precisely the insights that came deeply to inform his understanding of God as the divine creative artist, speaking us into being and freedom through his all-sustaining *Logos*.

In many ways, Coleridge could be credited with helping the English to rediscover the greatness of Shakespeare; to appreciate Shakespeare for the real virtues of his work, and not, as earlier critics, even Johnson, had done, to admit him grudgingly to the pantheon of great writers, as a kind of honorary rustic, a flawed, natural genius in whom many good things were to be found in spite of his woeful ignorance of the rules of composition. The pre-Coleridgean view of Shakespeare is best summed up in Milton's famously condescending praise, 'sweetest Shakespeare, fancy's child, warbles his native wood-notes wild . . .'[33]

This monumental critical failure to understand the power and subtlety of Shakespeare's art arose from the mistake of trying to apply a rigid and literalistic reading of Aristotle's *Poetics*, particularly the so-called 'unities', to Shakespeare's great tragedies. Shakespeare is shown as failing to apply the rules, and the power of his plays is conceded only as a success in spite of this failure. Following the lead of German Romantic philosophers and critics, Coleridge showed how beautifully and subtly wrought the plays are; that far from being 'native wood-notes wild' they are organic wholes, whose inner structure is perfectly accommodated to bear the weight of every line and animate the whole, whose smallest line or image carries and reiterates the meaning of the whole. However, in the course of rescuing Shakespeare from perverse criticism, he embraced rather than repudiated the notion that Shakespeare is 'natural', as distinct from 'artificial'. Indeed, he took this analogy more seriously than those who had used it as a slight, and it helped him not only to appreciate Shakespeare, but also to understand the distinction between the 'mechanic' and the 'organic' in many other spheres as well. This pair of contrasting terms was important to Coleridge in his understanding of 'cosmos' as well as his understanding of literature:

> The form is mechanic when on any given material we impress a predetermined form, not necessarily arising out of the properties of the material – as when to a mass of wet clay we give whatever shape we wish it to retain when hardened. The organic form, on the other hand, is innate; it shapes as it develops itself from within, and the fullness of its development is one and the same with the perfection of its outward form. Such is the life, such is the form. Nature the prime genial artist, inexhaustible in diverse powers, is equally inexhaustible in forms: each exterior is the

physiognomy of the being within, its true image reflected and thrown out from the concave mirror; and even such is the appropriate excellence of her chosen poet, our own Shakespeare – himself a nature humanized, a genial understanding directing self-consciously a power and a[n] implicit wisdom deeper than consciousness.[34]

Here, the parallel between human and divine making is explicit; it is not simply that images from nature provide Coleridge as a critic with metaphors like 'organic', but rather that there is a genuine continuity and reflection between the 'creativity' of nature, the prime genial artist, and the power of imagination in Shakespeare. The key to understanding the way imagination works in Shakespeare and what it teaches not only about his art, or about art in general, but about nature herself, is that Shakespeare's art is not simply the embroidering by fancy on the grave-clothes of the cold corpse of 'dead' nature, as though nature were meaningless in itself and only receives meaning from the 'artificial' work of the poet, but rather is the operation in and through Shakespeare as an artist of the very same power which itself gives nature life, and that power is the power of Imagination.

What Shakespeare is doing, as an artist, as distinct from what we all do in merely perceiving nature, is 'directing self-consciously a power and an implicit wisdom deeper than consciousness'. By the time he came to write the *Biographia Literaria*, Coleridge was prepared to name the source of that 'power and implicit wisdom' as 'the adorable I AM in that I am'.[35]

But in the midst of all this, another axe-blow fell. Even as Coleridge was still reeling from what he perceived as his 'desertion' by Asra, Wordsworth had chosen to confide to Basil Montague, a mutual friend with whom Coleridge hoped to stay, a few 'home truths' about Coleridge's desperate addiction, his night screams, his general unreliability. Wordsworth advised Montague not to take in Coleridge as a houseguest. Wordsworth thought he was sharing these comments in confidence; Montague stupidly, perhaps mischievously, passed them on to Coleridge and told him that Wordsworth had 'authorised him to do so'.

For Coleridge this was a shattering blow. He felt utterly humiliated and betrayed by his old friend. He reflected on how often he had swallowed his own pride, how often he had helped and encouraged Wordsworth; now he felt cast aside, and looking back began to see how often and how consistently Wordsworth had been the dominant partner, made decisions that suited him, and turned things to his own advantage. For a while Wordsworth didn't realise that Montague had committed these indiscretions, but when he did he in turn retreated into stiffness and pride. There was a bitter period of two years in which neither man would acknowledge or communicate with the other, and the whole rift was a great scandal, for Wordsworth and Coleridge were among the most famous literary figures of the day; everybody had a view and took a side.

Eventually their friends, Charles Lamb chief among them, arranged a meeting and there was a reconciliation, though never perhaps quite the same intimacy. The immediate effect on Coleridge of this rift was to destroy his last emotional reserves, his last banks of resistance against opium. He had found an alternative household in London with a kind and generous family – the Morgans. Curiously – as with Wordsworth, Mary and Asra – the Morgan household consisted of a husband, wife and wife's sister. As Coleridge sank into opium reverie he began to project his feelings for Asra, and perhaps his even earlier feelings for both Asra and Mary, onto Mary Morgan and her sister Charlotte, even going so far as to publish a piece of doggerel in *The Courier* called 'Two Sisters'. Once again it was all gentle teases and mild flirtations; it was manageable, but a little uncomfortable for Mary and Charlotte.

It was while he was with the Morgans that Coleridge descended into the deep and final crisis towards which he had been sliding ever since his return to England from Malta seven years before. It happened in the exhaustion following great efforts he had been making on their behalf. In 1813 there was a financial crash and John Morgan's investments crashed with it and left him ruined and in debt. He had to go to Ireland to avoid debtors' prison while he tried to reorder his finances. Coleridge was suddenly roused into action, especially as he could gallantly defend the two damsels in distress whom he was now looking after. They had to leave the London house and went to Bristol, where Coleridge undertook a gruelling course of further lectures to keep them all afloat, fuelling himself on brandy and laudanum, coming 'home' each evening exhausted and demanding. Bristol became too expensive and they moved to the tiny hamlet of Ashley near Box, with the thought that Coleridge would lodge wherever he could in Bristol and come home at weekends.

But early in this arrangement something seems to have gone badly wrong. Coleridge was meant to start a new course of lectures in Bristol on 7 December, but he left Ashley on foot on 5 December in atrocious weather, clearly intending to leave for good, or feeling flung out. It is not clear what happened, but later in notebooks and letters Coleridge was to accuse himself of 'cruelty' to Mary and Charlotte when they were both ill. With the paranoid 'opium voice' speaking, he was probably making impossible demands or false accusations that they were planning to abandon him. Whatever happened, Charlotte and Mary Morgan had had enough of Coleridge's emotional extremes and volatility, and told him so. Coleridge's response, as so often before, was to 'bolt', simply to leave, to retreat somewhere and lick his wounds. And so Coleridge staggered through the snow as far as the nearest inn, The Grey Hound on the outskirts of Bath, was shown upstairs into an attic room, and collapsed, probably taking there, or having taken earlier, the massive overdose of opium that ought to have killed him. His ship had gone down beneath him, and he plunged deeper into the murky water of opium delirium, 'like one that hath been seven days drowned', hoping never to surface.

[handwritten annotation: Coleridge's opium addiction gets much worse]

'It reached the ship, it split the bay;
  The ship went down like lead...'
The emotional depth charges go off at last; all is lost, all is recovered

CHAPTER TWELVE

He Prayeth Best Who Loveth Best

The last voice we hear in Part VI of *The Rime of the Ancient Mariner* is that of the hermit, who seems already to have been known to the mariner before he set off. There is almost a cry of recognition: 'I heard his voice / It is the Hermit good!' And what the mariner remembers in that moment is that the hermit is himself a poet and 'singeth loud his godly hymns / That *he makes* in the wood', much as Coleridge had done when he chanted his extemporary hymn to the echoes on Scafell. The opening two stanzas of Part VII give us a more vivid and detailed introduction to the hermit:

The Hermit of This Hermit good lives in that wood
the Wood, Which slopes down to the sea.
     How loudly his sweet voice he rears!
     He loves to talk with marineres
     That come from a far countree.

     He kneels at morn, and noon, and eve—
     He hath a cushion plump:
     It is the moss that wholly hides
     The rotted old oak-stump.

           (Lines 514–22 with gloss)

Here, with the woods sloping down to the sea, we are back in the landscape of the seaward side of the Quantocks where the tale began, and with the appearance of the hermit we are in the literary terrain not only of the medieval ballad, but of the Arthurian romance. But, once more, Coleridge casts a fresh light on his sources. For he re-imagines the hermit as a Romantic poet, a figure who is the priest both of nature and of God. So the key language and outer images of worship – the 'godly hymns', even the 'cushion' for a kneeler – are all transposed out of the confines of the church and into a natural setting, but without losing any of their sanctity or sacramental power, which is why the hermit is able to 'shrieve' the mariner. Indeed, Coleridge goes out of his way to emphasise the continuous prayer that forms the pattern of the hermit's life, since prayer is, as we have seen, the central theme of the poem and prominent at all its turning points. Coleridge adds a further detail:

> He loves to talk with marineres
> That come from a far countree.

(Lines 517–18)

This is perhaps why we are to surmise that the mariner and the hermit have met before, even though the hermit does not immediately recognise the mariner, so utterly changed is he. Coleridge has given the hermit something of his own heart and nature, for as we have seen he also loved to talk with mariners both *viva voce* and through the pages of every book of mariners' tales he could lay his hands on.

Then, as so often before in crucial moments of transition, such as the shooting of the albatross or the mariner's swoon when the ship re-crosses the equator, our perspective shifts and we see the mariner and his ship from the point of view of the approaching skiff:

Approacheth the ship with wonder.

> The skiff-boat near'd: I heard them talk,
> "Why, this is strange, I trow!
> Where are those lights so many and fair,
> That signal made but now?"

"Strange, by my faith!" the Hermit said—
"And they answered not our cheer!
The planks look warped! and see those sails,
How thin they are and sere!
I never saw aught like to them,

(Lines 523–31)

Here we are once more made aware of how the mariner's vessel has itself somehow become the spectre-bark which was the emblem of his punishment; indeed, the mariner's ship is now full of the dead and the hermit goes on to compare its thin sails to skeletal leaves.

This is why the mariner's first movement and speech so frightens those in the skiff for they have assumed that he too is one of the dead. The hermit's extended metaphor to describe the sails (he is indeed a poet!) also adds to the atmosphere of the uncanny:

". . . I never saw aught like to them,
Unless perchance it were

The skeletons of leaves that lag
My forest-brook along;
When the ivy-tod is heavy with snow,
And the owlet whoops to the wolf below,
That eats the she-wolf's young."

(Lines 531–7)

This verse draws on two pieces of English folklore: first, the association of owls with ivy bushes, which were believed to be a favourite habitat, hence the common phrase 'He looks like an owl in an ivy bush'; and second, the (unfounded) belief that in times of extreme hunger the male wolf would eat its cubs. However ill informed, this is certainly not a sentimentalised view of nature, and we feel that the hermit has looked on things unflinchingly as they are; that like the mariner he too may have experienced horrors but lived to see beyond them and renewed his vision. Certainly he shows much greater composure than the pilot, as they approach what they fear is a 'ghost ship'.

> "Dear Lord! it hath a fiendish look—
> (The Pilot made reply)
> I am a-feared"—"Push on, push on!"
> Said the Hermit cheerily.

> *(Lines 538–41)*

Then comes the last of the great turning points and moments of transition in the poem, and arguably the most important: the sinking of the ship, and the mariner's complete submersion and recovery from the water:

> The boat came closer to the ship,
> But I nor spake nor stirred;
> The boat came close beneath the ship,
> And straight a sound was heard.

The ship suddenly sinketh.

> Under the water it rumbled on,
> Still louder and more dread:
> It reach'd the ship, it split the bay;
> The ship went down like lead.

The ancient Mariner is saved in the Pilot's boat.

> Stunned by that loud and dreadful sound,
> Which sky and ocean smote,
> Like one that hath been seven days drown'd
> My body lay afloat;
> But swift as dreams, myself I found
> Within the Pilot's boat.

> *(Lines 542–5)*

What causes the ship to sink? The description is almost as of a delayed depth charge, shaking the ship to pieces. Because it comes from under the water, some commentators have seen it as a last act of vengeance by the aggrieved Polar Spirit, but this cannot be so because the gloss specifically tells us that he returned south again, and Coleridge's understanding of the *numen* or local *genii* of places, the dæmons of the elements, was that they each had to stay in their own hemisphere. It is nevertheless significant that the ship is sunk from beneath; something hidden in the depths, waiting to detonate, finally brings it down.

This is certainly true psychologically. People who are wrestling at depth with dreadful dilemmas or depression can retain apparent surface composure for a remarkably long time, and then suddenly, for no apparent reason, they sink. Certainly there were emotional depth charges in Coleridge going right back to his first passion for Asra and his first jealousy of Wordsworth, which were waiting to go off and which finally sank him in that bleak December at the Grey Hound Inn.

There is, though, another way of looking at the sudden sinking of the mariner's ship. The real question is not why did the ship sink here, but why has it not already sunk – how did it get so far? The sails are in rags, the planks are warped, there is no one at the helm. The ship should have sunk back in the tropics, and should certainly not have held together when it was being driven northward at supernatural speed. The answer seems to be that the ship is held together by the angelic power for the express purpose of bringing the mariner back to his beginning and enabling his redemption and new life. Once the angels leave the ship, it falls to pieces.

And for the angelic mission to succeed, the mariner's apparent drowning, his complete immersion, is also necessary. Earlier in the poem we saw him being 'born again of wind', born again of the spirit, as the breeze blew specifically and particularly on him.

Baptism

Now we see him born again of water. The baptism imagery is utterly clear and vital to the meaning of the poem. 'Know you not that as many of you as are baptised are baptised into the death of Christ', says Paul.[1] Baptism is a ritual enactment of dying and rising, of drowning and breaking the waters, coming to new birth.

The lines

'Like one that hath been seven days drown'd /
My body lay afloat' (lines 552–3)

are, for this reason, significant, for it was believed that after a week drowned bodies rise to the water's surface. Clearly the mariner has not been under that long, but he is '*like* one that hath been seven days drowned' in that his body has emerged from the depths. There is also an echo here in the words 'seven days' of an earlier part of the poem, which as so often is delicately 'answered' in the poem's resolution:

An orphan's curse would drag to Hell
A spirit from on high;
But oh! more horrible than that
Is the curse in a dead man's eye!
Seven days, seven nights, I saw that curse,
And yet I could not die.

(Lines 256–62 in Part IV)

Before his redemption the mariner tries for seven days to die physically and cannot, but now in this baptismal regeneration he is enabled to die spiritually, 'like one that hath been seven days drowned', so that he may rise to new life.

Strangely, Coleridge was himself seven days and nights in deadly agony looking into a kind of infinite darkness in his soul before he rose again. For, as we shall see later in this chapter, the time he spent at the Grey Hound Inn near Bath, where he had collapsed after leaving the Morgan sisters, was to be both traumatic and transformative. As Molly Lefebure puts it:

> The seven days and nights of . . . agony at the Grey Hound, Bath, formed the culminating point of horror of the long years, stretching from late adolescence to early middle age, during which STC had become sucked forever further and ever further into the current of the vortex of morphine reliance.[2]

But this is to anticipate.

The second half of this verse is just as significant as the first. Once more, at a point of transition we have a dream reference, and here we are to suppose that the mariner is so stunned by the shock of the sinking of his ship and his own immersion that he falls into a dream-like state and wakes simply to find himself in the pilot's boat. He has been rescued, and it is not by his own agency. This distinction became very important to Coleridge. In another two verses the mariner will indeed 'take the oars', but for now he must accept that another's arms, another's strength, another's benevolence have lifted him from the sea and that, left to himself, he would have drowned. As we shall see, this was the very thing Coleridge needed to learn, and did learn, with respect to his addiction and to his faith, during the seven days of agony at the Grey Hound.

> Upon the whirl, where sank the ship,
> The boat spun round and round;
> And all was still, save that the hill
> Was telling of the sound.

(Lines 556–9)

The image of the pilot's little boat whirling round in the whirlpool caused by the sinking ship is again very realistic both physically and spiritually, and is dramatically and beautifully illustrated by Gustave Doré, who really captures the sense of danger at this point (see illustration, p. 370). For a moment even the pilot and the hermit have lost control, pushed by the waves of the mariner's calamity. So it is also for those who act as pilots and rescuers to their friends, in the first transition, bringing the rescued on board, they occasionally risk capsizing themselves. But soon the boat steadies, the mariner tries to speak, and life returns enough for him to take some initiative of his own:

> I moved my lips—the Pilot shrieked
> And fell down in a fit;
> The holy Hermit raised his eyes,
> And prayed where he did sit.
>
> I took the oars: the Pilot's boy,
> Who now doth crazy go,
> Laughed loud and long, and all the while
> His eyes went to and fro.
> "Ha! ha!" quoth he, "full plain I see,
> The Devil knows how to row.'

(Lines 560–9)

Again we see this through the responses of the other three, and we are reminded of how appearances can be deceptive. We know, within the grand narrative of the poem, that the mariner is indeed redeemed, living a new life and has been guided by angels, but he gives every appearance of being one of the 'undead' or even demonically possessed, hence the pilot's shriek and the boy's hysteria. The hermit, by contrast, suspends his judgement and meets this new development steadily and with prayer.

Pilot's boat
twirls in
a whirlpool cause by ship

He Prayeth Best Who Loveth Best

So the mariner 'takes the oars'. Just as the first stage in spiritual and physical recovery for Coleridge was to be an admission of helplessness, an acceptance of rescue, so the second was to be action, careful modest action, not trusting too greatly in his own strength but acting nevertheless. And it is this combination of passion and action, of helplessness and willingness to help, that brings the mariner at last to land:

> And now, all in my own countree,
> I stood on the firm land!
> The Hermit stepped forth from the boat,
> And scarcely he could stand.
>
> *(Lines 570–3)*

The mariner may be safely ashore but he still has a life to live and a calling to fulfill, and it is here that the gloss tells us, in a curiously rich and ambiguous phrase that 'the penance of life falls on him':

The ancient Mariner earnestly entreateth the Hermit to shrieve him; and the penance of life falls on him.

> "O shrieve me, shrieve me, holy man!"
> The Hermit cross'd his brow.
> "Say quick," quoth he, "I bid thee say—
> What manner of man art thou?"
>
> Forthwith this frame of mine was wrench'd
> With a woeful agony,
> Which forced me to begin my tale;
> And then it left me free.
>
> *(Lines 574–81)*

To be 'shriven' is to confess one's sins and receive the cleansing and release of forgiveness. The word 'shrieve' derives from an Anglo-Saxon word 'shrift' meaning to hear someone's confession. (This is the origin also of 'Shrove Tuesday', a day of confession

379

before Lent.) It was the duty of priests, especially, to hear the confession and grant forgiveness and spiritual counsel to those who were facing execution, and when prison chaplains failed to do this properly – with time, care and attention – there was a complaint that prisoners were being 'given short shrift', which is where that phrase comes from. To be shriven, then, is to receive the sacrament of confession and absolution. Coleridge would have been familiar with the definition of a sacrament in the 39 Articles, in The Book of Common Prayer, as 'an outward and visible sign of an inward and spiritual grace'. In one sense, of course, the 'inward and spiritual grace' has already been given to the mariner, but he also needs the outward and visible sign. Such is the mariner's outward appearance that the hermit still crosses himself and asks 'What manner of man art thou?' to make sure he is dealing with a human being, who can therefore repent and be forgiven, rather than a re-animated or demon-possessed corpse.

It is in answer to the question 'What manner of man art thou?' that the mariner tells his tale. In one sense the story, the whole story with its balanced mysteries of random evil and undeserved grace, is an answer to that question. The mariner is a living man, so the hermit need have no fear, but he is also a man who has done evil, survived nightmare and just, only just, been touched and reached by grace. His penance, clearly ordained not by the hermit but by the angels, partly in response to the grieved Polar Spirit, is simply to tell the story over and over again and always to just the right person. Interestingly, the mariner is in physical pain until he begins his tale, but once he starts he is 'left free'. Those who deal with PTSD and survivor guilt will recognise this almost physical need to retell and re-live the events, though clearly, in this sacramental frame, there is also a higher moral purpose in the re-telling of the tale.

The phrase 'the penance of life' is interesting. If it had been 'the penance of his life' one would have felt the penance referred only to this constraint to keep retelling the tale, but somehow the phrase 'the penance of life' suggests more, as though in some circumstances life itself were a penance. For all the joys and graces of life there is also some sense in which we endure it: we are pilgrims and strangers, we have a sense of elegy and exile, of unappeased longing which lies just under everything we do, and we long to complete our penance, to fulfil the term of our exile, and come home.

A further sense of 'the penance of life' is brought out in the next couple of verses in their play on the myths of the Wandering Jew and the wanderings of Cain, which as we know were very much on Coleridge's mind when he began writing the poem:

And ever and anon throughout his future life an agony constraineth him to travel from land to land;

Since then, at an uncertain hour,
That agony returns:
And till my ghastly tale is told,
This heart within me burns.

I pass, like night, from land to land;
I have strange power of speech;
That moment that his face I see,
I know the man that must hear me:
To him my tale I teach.

(Lines 582–90 with gloss)

Coleridge was haunted by two 'biblical' legends of wanderers who could not die but were forced to be the continual witness of the nightmare of history. One was Cain, the primal and archetypal murderer, who slays his brother Abel. His story is told in Genesis chapter 4. A significant detail of this story comes in verse 15 where we are told: 'The Lord put a mark on Cain so that no one who came upon him would kill him.' From this verse grew the legend that Cain wandered the earth, a fugitive and exile, seeking to expiate the blood of his brother. The other was the legend of the 'wandering Jew', which arose from Jesus' saying, 'Verily, verily I say unto you there be some standing here, which shall not taste of death, till they see the son of man coming in his kingdom.'[3] Out of this and some other similar Gospel passages arose the idea that there must be someone who has not tasted and will not taste death until the Second Coming. Needless to say, such a figure presented rich possibilities for storytellers so the legend grew, taking on particular life in the thirteenth century when it was associated with an apocryphal story of a Jew who taunted Jesus on the way to the crucifixion. This story was also the subject of a ballad in Percy's *Reliques*, published in 1765, a collection of old ballads that Coleridge knew and drew from, and it may be that Coleridge is drawing on some elements of it here. Indeed, we know from a passage of Coleridge's conversation in the *Table Talk* that he had something like this in mind: 'It is an enormous blunder . . . to represent the ancient Mariner as an old man on board ship – he was in my mind the everlasting wandering Jew – Had told this story 10,000 times since the voyage which was in his early years and 50 years before.'[4] In that sense the 'penance of life' may be quite literally the penance of living a preternaturally long life.

Certainly the phrase in the gloss 'an agony constraineth him to travel from land to land' with its strange paradox of 'constraineth to travel' must have had particular frisson for Coleridge when he added it to the poem in 1817, having himself been 'constrained to travel' by the agonies of addiction and broken love.

The whole dream-like and magical quality of the tale and its teller is further emphasised in the phrase 'I pass like night from land to land' – as though the mariner could travel like the ever-moving shadow of night swiftly and silently round the earth, and like night, bring strange dreams. Finally, we are given a really crucial piece of information, which in a sense makes us revise our whole reading of the poem:

> That moment that his face I see,
> I know the man that must hear me:
> To him my tale I teach.

> *(Lines 588–90)*

Here at last is the answer to the question asked back in the opening stanza of the poem: 'Now wherefore stoppst thou me?' This particular wedding guest was meant to hear the mariner's story. There is something in it for him, something searching, telling, life changing. His two other friends can do without it for now, but he needs to hear the tale.

And this accounts for the powerful effect the story does in fact have on him. At the beginning of the tale the wedding guest is constrained, distracted, anxious to get away, but gradually he has become transfixed and indeed transformed by the tale. Now, when we have another burst of distracting sound reminding us that the wedding is still going on, the wedding guest is not distracted, but is listening to the pith and conclusion of the mariner's tale. And the wedding guest is of course our proxy in the poem, as the listener to the tale, so perhaps this verse poses the question to us too. Is there a particular reason why I need to hear this tale? This sense of the power and purpose of the telling and the importance of the listener's response is there in the word 'teach' rather than 'tell', as well as in the phrase 'strange power of speech'.

Once more we are brought out of the frame of the tale and reminded of the wedding we have been missing:

> What loud uproar bursts from that door!
> The wedding-guests are there;
> But in the garden-bower the bride

He missed the wedding when

383

And bride-maids singing are;
And hark the little vesper bell,
Which biddeth me to prayer!

(Lines 551–96)

This sudden re-emergence of ordinary life in a little interlude between the strangeness of the mariner's tale and the universal applicability of what he will teach from it is very effective. Although he draws the wedding guest aside from the wedding to teach him the tale, and although at the end the wedding guest turns from the bridegroom's door, the mariner is not dismissing the life the wedding represents, but rather pointing beyond it to something which for him, in his circumstances, is 'sweeter far': the life of prayer. And that life calls in the small bell at the close of this stanza:

And hark the little vesper bell,
Which biddeth me to prayer!

(Lines 595–6)

Again we hear an echo running across the poem, for the mariner was first called to vespers by the albatross:

In mist or cloud, on mast or shroud,
It perched for vespers nine;
Whiles all the night, through fog-smoke white,
Glimmered the white moon-shine.

(Lines 75–8 from Part I)

And so *Vespers* is the form and time of prayer that must primarily and especially be restored for the mariner. Vespers is, of course, evening prayer, and that the mariner should be especially called to that office is part of his whole association with night, with dreams, and with the rising and shining of the moon.

In his last farewell, the mariner sums up all that has gone before and draws out its meaning:

> O Wedding-Guest! this soul hath been
> Alone on a wide wide sea:
> So lonely 'twas, that God himself
> Scarce seemed there to be.
>
> O sweeter than the marriage-feast,
> 'Tis sweeter far to me,
> To walk together to the kirk
> With a goodly company!—
>
> To walk together to the kirk,
> And all together pray,
> While each to his great Father bends,
> Old men, and babes, and loving friends
> And youths and maidens gay!

(Lines 597–609)

We are reminded in the unforgettable phrase 'alone on a wide wide sea' of the earlier agony, and also that at the root of that loneliness was an existential or theological loneliness: 'So lonely 'twas that God himself / Scarce seemed there to be' – though the word 'seemed' is carefully chosen. As we have seen, God was there all the time: in the emblem of the sun, the reflected light of the moon, the presence of the angels, and perhaps in the albatross itself; but the mariner could not perceive it until he received the grace to clarify and restore his powers of perception, discovering that the real source of vision is not in the eyes but in the heart.

This loneliness contrasts directly with the following verse and its mention of walking 'together to the kirk / With a goodly company'. At the beginning of the whole poem we sense that the kirk mentioned by the mariner was little more than a landmark; now it is the heart of community. Just as we had 'alone' and 'lonely' repeated in one verse, so now over the next two verses we have its opposite, 'together', repeated three times. Having lost and then been given back the gift of prayer, the mariner now builds his life around prayer, both alone and in community. There is a sense of both here: 'All together pray' on the one hand, and yet something personal and individual in '*each* to his great father bends'.

These verses lead into the much-discussed two-verse 'moral' or conclusion of the poem:

And to teach, by his own example, love and reverence to all things that God made and loveth.	Farewell, farewell! but this I tell To thee, thou Wedding-Guest! He prayeth well, who loveth well Both man and bird and beast.

He prayeth best, who loveth best
All things both great and small;
For the dear God who loveth us,
He made and loveth all."

(Lines 610–17 with gloss)

In one way these clear, simple verses go right to the heart of the matter and both in sound and meaning ring out like a bell, precisely like the vesper bell that calls to prayer; for these verses are a call to prayer. So we have the continual tolling and chiming on the 'bell' sound in full and half rhyme: farewell, farewell . . . tell . . . well . . . well . . . small . . . all.

The whole poem has turned on the two hinges of prayer and love, now brought together and seen as mutually enfolded: the loving is the praying, the praying is the loving. This is so clear and

Kirk = Whole of community

simple as almost to seem simplistic, and therein lies our difficulty. Coleridge and the mariner are bringing us home to certain essential truths, or rather bringing them home to us. These truths were always there; always there in the gospel and in our deepest instincts, but they are almost too close and familiar for us to see. Just as the mariner has returned to the familiar kirk and hill and lighthouse top after his long circumnavigation, and now must recognise what he always knew and also in a sense see it and its true meaning for the first time, so we have to recognise the familiar in a new light. He and we are in that place described by T.S. Eliot in the *Four Quartets*:

> We shall not cease from exploration
> And the end of all our exploring
> Will be to arrive where we started
> And know the place for the first time.[5]

And there is genuinely new knowledge in our return to this link between love and prayer, which is rooted in the new commandment in John's Gospel 13:34–5: 'A new commandment I give unto you, That ye love one another; as I have loved you, that ye also love one another. By this shall all *men* know that ye are my disciples, if ye have love one to another.'

The mariner's new understanding arises directly from the experiences of guilt and alienation, from having wantonly destroyed life and precisely from having passed through a sense of all things being 'loathsome', of having 'despised God's creatures of the great calm'. It is because he has passed through that and discovered how to bless, as 'happy living things', the very creatures he had previously despised that he can say, 'he prayeth best that loveth best' with a conviction that lifts the phrase out of truism and back into discovery.

But there is something more, hidden in the 'truism' of the

poem's moral: a comprehensive and hidden radicalism, and it is hidden in the little word 'all' repeated twice in the text and also used in the gloss:

He prayeth best, who loveth best
All things both great and small;
For the dear God who loveth us,
He made and loveth *all*."

(*Lines 614–17*)

And again:

And to teach, by his own example, love and reverence to *all things* that God made and loveth.

(*Gloss to lines 610–13*)

If this is a gospel, then it is an utterly inclusive gospel. *Everything* is to be brought on board, *every* creature is to be salvaged. All living things, not just human beings, are loved by God and have a place in his world and in the web of life in which he has woven us as only one of many elements. This is both a return to the beautiful covenant with all creation in the Noah story to which we alluded earlier, and a powerful and prophetic word to our own culture. If Coleridge could, *per impossibile*, have seen Lynn White Junior's hugely influential paper 'The Historical Roots of our Ecological Crisis', published in *Science* in 1967,[6] he would have read it with great interest and shared its concern for how our faith and the roots of our thinking influence the way we treat the world, but he would I think have resisted its sweeping dismissal of the Christian and biblical material and would have offered this poem as part of that resistance. White asserts (I think correctly): 'What people do about their ecology depends on what they think about themselves in relation to things around them.

Human ecology is deeply conditioned by beliefs about our nature and destiny – that is, by religion.'⁷ But he goes on (I think erroneously) to suggest that for Christianity 'nature has no reason for existence save to serve [humans]'. For White, Christianity is 'the most anthropocentric religion the world has seen'. He suggests that this arrogant anthropocentricity means that the Judaeo-Christian tradition 'bears a huge burden of guilt for the contemporary environmental crisis'.

In fact, many of the attitudes to nature White most castigates are not scriptural but arose during the Enlightenment period when earlier more holistic understandings of nature embedded in the poetry of faith were being overthrown, although it is true that these 'Enlightenment' attitudes were 'Christianised' and the Church either adopted them alongside the rest of society or did very little to speak against them. White's own way of reading the Bible is entirely rooted in Enlightenment/modernist ways of thinking, reading attitudes back into the text that are simply not there. In fact, as Coleridge shows in this poem, both the Bible and the Christian tradition are full of a vital but neglected wisdom that would make for a far more integrated and sustainable relation with the wider ecology if we could recover and develop it. Precisely because the tradition is Theo-centric, not anthropocentric, and because the God on whom it centres is the lord of all creation, of angels as well as albatrosses, water-snakes as well as human beings, it offers a far richer basis for correcting anthropocentrism then secular humanism (which is of course human-centred by definition). Coleridge began that recovery and development of a lost 'inclusiveness' of all life in this poem and developed it much further in his later works. Indeed, he was working on a 'Theory of Life', which was a kind of meeting place of biology and theology, when he died.

Another factor which may subtly diminish for us the full impact of these two verses is something Coleridge could not have

389

anticipated, and that was the 'borrowing' from his text by the sentimental Victorian children's hymn writer Mrs C.F. Alexander:

All things bright and beautiful
All creatures great and small
All things wise and wonderful
The Lord God made them all.[8]

At first blush these words sound so close to Coleridge's text that we can't help reading them back into the text, or hearing some echo of the hymn as we read the poem. But to do so is a grave mistake. Mrs Alexander's cheerful, if facile, little ditty is a world away from *The Rime of the Ancient Mariner*. The problem with her hymn is precisely that it is all sweetness and light. It begs the question: what about the darkness? What about fearfulness and pain? Even as a small boy I can remember wanting to sing 'counter verses' that would start 'All things dark and dangerous / all creatures fierce and fell . . .' Of course Mrs Alexander was perfectly entitled to write a hymn in praise of creation, but sadly it peters out into mere picturesque sentiment – and even worse, becomes complicit with the various social hierarchies and injustices against which Coleridge was protesting, as in the verse which is usually not sung these days:

The rich man in his castle,
The poor man at his gate,
God made them high and lowly,
And ordered their estate.

By contrast (provided we can exorcise the echoes of Mrs Alexander), Coleridge's words have particular power at this point precisely because he has earlier included verses with words like 'a thousand thousand slimy things / Lived on; and so did I'. When it

comes at the end of this poem, the inclusivity of love and prayer
is not sentimental; on the contrary, it is such a radical challenge
that we have not yet risen to it.

> The Mariner, whose eye is bright,
> Whose beard with age is hoar
> Is gone: and now the Wedding-Guest
> Turned from the bridegroom's door.
>
> He went like one that hath been stunned,
> And is of sense forlorn:
> A sadder and a wiser man,
> He rose the morrow morn.

(Lines 618 to the end)

And so the poem ends. It has taken us out, away from the familiar
and out to the ends of the earth; it has made us conscious of the
spirit in our depths and of the beautiful numinous flight of wings
in the highest places of our being; it has reminded us of the deep
capacity for evil in each of us and how easy it is to unleash hell; it
has shown us moments of utterly undeserved and unlooked for
grace, moments when the sheer beauty of things can teach us
almost everything. And finally it has brought us home, home to
ourselves, sadder perhaps, but wiser, home to our situation in the
world, as the balance we have wantonly broken in nature unleashes
terrifying forces on us foretold in the breaking of polar ice and
death of the albatrosses on Midway Island, and home to the
chance to change, to begin again, with that rich intertwining of
love and prayer upon 'the morrow morn'.

Coleridge's poem has brought us home, but we left Coleridge
in deep crisis, 'like one that hath been seven days drowned' in the
Grey Hound Inn. We can only reconstruct what happened, physically and spiritually, in this crisis from the letters written

afterwards, though crucially we do have one written three days into the crisis from the inn itself. Coleridge had been due to start his Bristol lectures on the 8 December, and on that date he managed to get a scribbled note, some parts of which were later inked out, to his friend Josiah Wade, cancelling the lecture, but the note ends with a desperate appeal for prayer:

> Pray for my recovery—and request Mr Robart's prayers—but for my infirm wicked Heart, that Christ may mediate to the Father to lead me to Christ, & give me a living instead of a reasoning Faith!—And for my health . . . only as it may be the condition of improvement and final redemption . . .[9]

The next thing we have is a transcription of a letter sent on 19 December to Thomas Roberts, only part of which survived. This letter seems to bring us to the crux and turning point of the crisis, as well as giving us a glimpse of the physical symptoms and distress through which Coleridge was passing:

> You have no conception of what my sufferings have been, forced to struggle and struggle in order not to desire a death for which I am not prepared, – I have scarcely known what sleep is but like a leopard in its den have been drawn up and down the room by extreme pain, and restlessness, worse than pain itself.
>
> Oh how I have prayed even to loud agony only to be able to pray! Oh how I have felt the impossibility of any real *good will* not born anew from the Word and the Spirit! Oh I have seen far, far deeper and clearer than I ever saw before the ground of pernicious errors! Oh I have seen, I have felt that the worst offences are those against our own souls! That our souls are infinite in depth and therefore our sins are infinite and redeemable only by an infinitely higher infinity; that of the Love of God in Christ Jesus. I have called my soul infinite come but oh infinite in the depths of

darkness, an infinite craving an infinite capacity of pain and weakness, and excellent only as being passively capacious of the light from above. Should I recover I will – no – no may God grant me the power to struggle to become *not another* but a *better man* . . . O God save me – save me from myself . . .'[10]

We certainly glimpse the outer crisis brought on by the drug itself here: the sleeplessness, the driven restlessness, the sweating and extreme muscular pain which itself somehow expresses or embodies the spiritual pain of his deeper restlessness; but then in and through this we see something else altogether, something that need not necessarily have happened, but did. Coleridge could have spent seven days drowning in the kind of remorse that is no more than self-pity, but he didn't. Instead, like his mariner, Coleridge turned to prayer, and like his mariner, at first he could not pray: 'Oh how I have prayed even to loud agony only to be able to pray!' Then he seems to remember the very verse in John alluded to in *The Ancient Mariner* about new birth, about the necessity for real *good will* to be 'born anew from the Word and the Spirit'.

He gives us a glimpse for a moment of his soul, poised like the mariner's ship, between infinite depths and infinite heights, between the infinite depths of a brokenness and guilt and the 'infinitely higher infinity' of the Love of God in Christ Jesus'. Then, finally, he comes to actually praying, and the prayer, formed, broken off and reformed, becomes the great resolve of the rest of his life, the point from which he turned and grew: 'Should I recover I will – no – no may God grant me the power to struggle to become *not another* but a *better man*.'[11] Everything is in that break and turn from 'I will' to 'may God grant me the power to struggle to become'. Coleridge catches himself, even as he prays, in the very act of self-dependence which has been at the root of all his troubles, and he breaks it off and reframes it as a prayer not for private

strength, <u>but for grace *to become*, grace of transformation. This</u>
<u>is the turning point for every addict, as many in the recovery</u>
<u>community will avow: the turn from self-reliance to reliance on a</u>
<u>power greater than oneself.</u> But it is also a turning point, theologi-
cally, from the Law to the Gospel, from a sense of God as a distant
judge who has to be satisfied with a long list of perfectly executed
righteous deeds achieved in one's own strength, <u>to God as the</u>
<u>friend and redeemer whose blood we have unjustly shed, but</u>
<u>whose Love is so triumphant that the very blood we shed now</u>
<u>avails *for* us rather than witnessing *against* us.</u>

In that first letter from the crisis on 8 December, Coleridge had
asked to be given 'a *living* instead of a *reasoning* Faith'; here that
prayer is granted. Granted in the sense that head-knowledge, the
reasoning faith Coleridge had already attained, finally enters his
heart and becomes 'a living faith'. Of course Coleridge never
ceased to reason about and from his faith and to commend it to
the reason of anyone who would hear him, but now he had
another and deeper way of knowing and a surer foundation for
the great intellectual work which was to come.

As this crisis unfolded, no one else knew where Coleridge was.
Eventually, the landlady of the Grey Hound, distressed by the
pacing and screaming coming from her upper room, and the
evident illness of her guest who had not come down for food or
drink for days, summoned a doctor. It might have been anyone,
and it might have been a doctor who failed to recognise the symptoms or who even prescribed the very drug that was causing the
trauma, but the man who walked through the door turned out to
be Caleb Parry, the father of two young Englishmen whom
Coleridge had met on his German travels and who had returned
home with tales of the wonderful and loquacious poet Coleridge
who had befriended and helped them. Parry instantly recognised
Coleridge, and now he in his turn did the befriending and helping. He visited three times a day, he sat at Coleridge's bedside

wiping the sweat from his brow, he realised his suicidal tendencies and made sure that watch was kept upon him, he got in touch with Josiah Wade so that there would be somewhere for Coleridge to go when he was able to get up from his bed and leave the inn. As Coleridge said in a note to Mary Morgan on the 19th, the day he did leave the inn, it was to Dr Parry '& to him under God's Mercy I owe that I am at present still alive.'[12]

It was only as the months passed and Coleridge began a new regime of life and a slow recovery, that he himself began to grasp the full spiritual significance of what had happened. When John Morgan finally returned from Ireland in May, Coleridge wrote to him, summarising the spiritual heart of the crisis in these terms:

> If it could be said with as little *appearance* of profaneness as there is feeling or intention in my mind I might affirm; that I have been crucified, dead, and buried, descended into *Hell*, and am now, I humbly trust, rising again, tho' slowly and gradually.[13]

In a sense this says it all. It is the very meaning of baptism, the meaning of the immersion of the mariner in Part VII of the poem. In one sense Coleridge had always known, intellectually, what it meant to call Christ a redeemer, and could have given an eloquent verbal account of the meaning of atonement; but now, at last, that intellectual knowledge had become an embodied, irrevocable event in his life, had moved as he once prayed it would, from the head to the heart.

However, he still needed pulling out of the water and setting on dry land, and not surprisingly at first the pilot's boat was itself spinning a little on the whirl of so great a wreck. In the first instance, Coleridge was taken to his friend Josiah Wade in Bristol and stayed there for nine months, making a slow and painful return to health and the first of several attempts to get someone else, an external authority, to regulate and diminish his doses of

Coleridge finally leaves the inn

opium. He realised that this was essential, but it was easier said than done. Wade had a good doctor with some grasp of what was needed, and he also employed a serving man acting as Coleridge's 'valet' to supervise him when he went out. But none of this was really working well. Ultimately, Coleridge would need to stay permanently with a doctor who could both regulate and diminish the doses of opium he still needed and also deal with all the alarming symptoms of even gradual withdrawal.

One stratagem, and a sign of Coleridge's recovery, was intense writing, for creative effort was always far more stimulating to Coleridge than any drug could ever be, and he had long since come to see that the opium sapped rather than stimulated the true creative flow. Like the mariner, he began with a period of almost compulsive confession, making a 'serious moral inventory'. From Wade's house in Bristol he wrote a series of detailed confessional letters about his opium abuses and the other abuses to which these had led, addressed to a number of his closer friends in Bristol, including, unfortunately, Joseph Cottle, the publisher of *Lyrical Ballads*. Very shortly after Coleridge's death and against the express wishes of the family, Cottle published a version of these letters, which, taken out of context, and particularly the context of Coleridge's productive Highgate years, gave a very false impression and damaged his reputation.

Over the course of his nine-month sojourn and gradual recuperation with Wade, Coleridge, remarkably, achieved reconciliation with the Morgans, who were of course grateful for the way he had bailed them out of their debts, and very fond of him, though now also very wary. They had moved out of London to Calne in Wiltshire and Coleridge moved in with them and, as a sign of – indeed as part of – his recovery began to dictate the *Biographia Literaria*, another form of confession, though now as much a confession of faith as of failing. During that time at Calne, Coleridge was stable enough for the sixteen-year-old

Hartley to come and visit him. Hartley was brilliant and wayward like his father and was fascinated by the *Biographia*, which was in a sense partly addressed to him. It was also during this interlude at Calne in 1815 that Coleridge himself re-read *The Ancient Mariner* in light of all that had since happened and wrote for it the beautiful and revealing 'gloss'.

But once more this temporary pilot boat proved unstable. Coleridge needed something absolutely steady, committed and permanent to get him to the shore; he needed to be able to put himself entirely in the hands of a competent doctor and absolutely surrender his power of obtaining the drug himself. Eventually a Dr Adams, a friend of John Morgan's, saw that Coleridge needed some form of residential care and wrote to a friend of his, a Dr Gillman who had just set up practice in Highgate, in the following terms:

> Dear Sir,
>
> A very learned, but in one respect unfortunate gentleman, has applied to me on a singular occasion. He has for several years been in the habit of taking large quantities of opium. For some time past he has been, in vain, endeavouring to break himself off [*sic*] it. It is apprehended his friends are not firm enough, from a dread lest he should suffer by suddenly leaving it off, though he is conscious of the contrary, and has proposed to me to submit himself to any regimen, however severe. With this view he wishes to fix himself in the home of some medical gentleman, who will have courage to refuse him any laudanum, and under whose assistance, should he be the worse for it, he may be relieved . . .[14]

Gillman was intrigued and agreed to an interview with Coleridge. Coleridge came alone and laid his whole case with great frankness before Dr Gillman. He also talked, as Gillman later recalled, about life, love, poetry, friendship and faith. Gillman was deeply moved indeed, as he put it afterwards, in words that seem to echo the effect the mariner had on his listeners: 'I felt indeed almost spell-bound, without desire of release.'[15]

Gillman agreed to take on the case and took Coleridge to live with him in Highgate in 1816. In making this offer Gillman became in a sense the pilot who brought this wandering mariner, who had made such a shipwreck of his life, back to terra firma, back to a stable place in which he could be productive again. Gillman looked after Coleridge until his death at the age of sixty-one in 1834, the poet having lived far longer than anyone could reasonably have hoped.

The relationship was not always an easy one, but over the years it deepened into great confidence and trust. To begin with Coleridge did indeed have to submit, and had trouble submitting to a 'severe regime'. Gillman immediately reduced and strictly controlled his opium intake. He also restricted Coleridge's social life and vetted those who came to see him. Coleridge tried smuggling opium into the house wrapped up (ironically) in the proofs of 'The Pains of Sleep', which were being delivered from Murray the publisher, but Gillman found it and kept a closer watch thereafter. In June, a month or so into the regime, Coleridge wrote to Morgan to let him know how he was getting on and was very frank about the pains and difficulties. He writes of:

A sensation of indefinite *Fear* over my whole frame . . . I fought up against it . . . I had a wretched night - and the next morning the few drops, I now take, only increasing my irritability, about noon I called on G. for the performance of *his* part of our mutual Engagement, & took enough and *barely* enough (for more, I am certain, would have been better) to break the commencing Cycle before the actual Craving came on. – To day I am much better.[16]

Gradually the new regime began to have a beneficent effect: the cravings were incrementally reduced and, along with the doses, the fear receded. Coleridge began to return to the far deeper and more helpful stimulus of conversation and composition. He moved from formality to deep friendship with the Gillmans; Ann Gillman, the doctor's wife, was particularly helpful and sympathetic to Coleridge. In September of that year they deemed Coleridge well enough to take him with them on a little holiday in Mudeford near Christchurch, for change and rest. On their return, more of his friends were allowed to call and he proved he could be trusted to go out and socialise with them. He began to work on a regular pattern of reading and writing again. All this bore fruit in the last of the great literary works which we will consider now, some of which were started and partly written before he got to Gillman's, but all of which were published once he'd arrived there.

Chief of these is the *Biographia Literaria*, perhaps Coleridge's most widely read prose work. It is an eclectic mix of autobiography, philosophical history, literary criticism, rambling anecdote and radical new theology, all held together and threaded through with a constant witness to the power of the *Logos*, to the great analogy of language. At its heart is the idea that the cosmos is spoken into being by Mind, that nature is itself a kind of language, and that our own use of language is therefore a series of clues as to the meaning of both mind and cosmos. So the literary criticism and the theology are not separate and disparate parts of the book; they are the same thing.

The key to the whole book is the thirteenth chapter 'On the Imagination', and its core is this definition:

The imagination then, I consider either as primary or secondary. The primary IMAGINATION I hold to be the living Power and prime Agent of all human Perception, as a repetition in the finite mind of the eternal act of creation in the infinite I AM. The secondary Imagination I consider as an echo of the former, co-existing with the conscious will, yet still as identical with the primary in the *kind* of its agency, and differing only in *degree*, and in the *mode* of its operation.[17]

Here, the intimation which Coleridge had in the notebook of 1805, that the phenomena of nature might form a symbolic language, and that the words of this language might both articulate hidden truths about our inner nature and point to God the Creator as *Logos*, is made explicit and grounded in a philosophical system.

It is vital that we understand what it means for Coleridge to call the Imagination a 'living power' and an 'agent'. Throughout the first part of the *Biographia*, and indeed throughout the first part of his life, he battled with, and in the end defeated, a system of thought in which not only the imagination and all perception, but mind itself was understood as a 'passive faculty' rather than a living power, a patient, not an agent. It was a view of the world that saw the mind as at best passively recording material phenomena, and at worst as merely a mirage, the accidental by-product of the movement of atoms in a mechanical universe. Coleridge saw the falsehood at the bottom of this view, and this new definition of Imagination is a kind of cry of triumph in winning that victory. He understood that from Descartes onwards to Newton, we had simply been beginning from the wrong end of things; as he put it in the letter to Thomas Poole we cited earlier:

Newton was a mere materialist – *Mind* in his system is always passive – a lazy Looker-on on an external World. If the mind be not *passive*, if it be indeed made in God's Image, & that too in the sublimest sense – the Image of the *Creator* – there is ground for suspicion, that any system built on the passiveness of the mind must be false, as a system . . .[18]

The Cartesian-Newtonian system, for all its immediate lucidity, ultimately made for a universe devoid of mind and intrinsically unintelligible, and made mind itself almost an absurdity, and something which was to be experienced in isolation, individually, and only ever on the inside of one's small part of a cosmos which otherwise consisted of nothing but the meaningless concatenation of atoms. Coleridge was now in a position to see things from an entirely different perspective; he was no longer obliged to confine his sense of mind, intelligence, joy or wonder within the circle of the human skull, but could find it radiating through all the phenomena of the cosmos.

For Coleridge, the physical universe, which is the supposed 'object' of our perception, is not something that merely strikes us from the outside, but something that is, as it were, being formed continuously, both from our side of it by our perceiving Imaginations, and from an apprehended but as yet unknowable other side beyond it. The insight of this chapter is that there is a deep connection between that which is below the level of our consciousness and is continually giving us the gift of ourselves and our mind, and that which is behind or beyond the *phenomena* and is continuously giving them their being, allowing them to well up from its own *inexhaustible* depths. Even so seemingly simple a thing as perception itself, let alone composition or art, results from the active powers of our imagination, meeting and reflecting the active power of that Imagination which is always causing all things to be.

By means of our Primary Imagination, we are constantly participating in a cosmos whose every part is fraught with the meaning of the Mind of God. For Coleridge, our Secondary Imagination (what we would now call poetic imagination, or the imagination of the artist) is of the same kind and comes from the same source as this Primary Imagination, and when we cooperate with it, it too produces and articulates eternal symbols. By

Secondary is cooperation of primary

contrast, the Fancy simply manufactures artificial equivalences which are not, in Coleridge's terms, worthy of the name of 'symbol'. They have, as he would put it, 'mechanic form' rather than 'organic form', because they are not rooted in the Mind which is the source of the organic wholeness of the cosmos, for that cosmos is God's act of *poiesis*.

Coleridge had been speculating in this direction for many years, but had drawn a very strict dividing line between philosophy and religion in general, let alone full-blooded Trinitarian Christianity in particular. But by the time he came to write the *Biographia*, he had indeed experienced 'a more thorough revolution in my philo-sophic principles and a deeper revelation into my own heart', and, 'my final reconversion to the whole truth in Christ';[19] and so, here, he names the Mind and Imagination behind all things, in an allusion to God's self-disclosure to Moses at the Burning Bush, 'I AM that I AM'.

The second part of this sentence on the Primary Imagination is equally important; Coleridge calls it 'a *repetition* in the finite mind of the eternal act of creation in the infinite I AM'. In other words, the human mind, far from being an epiphenomenon, a 'ghost in the machine', or a kind of mist thrown up by the mere movement of matter, is, in all its imaginative perceiving, corre-spondent to something else beyond itself, and beyond the cosmos it inhabits. It is scarcely surprising that we find everywhere tanta-lising repetitions and echoes of ourselves in nature, that the mind is 'everywhere echo or mirror, seeking of itself', since our mind itself is a repetition, an echo, of the Mind of the Maker, in whose image we are created.

Because our Primary Imagination is a repetition in our finite mind of God's eternal act of creation, it enables us so to read God's works as to glimpse through them the Mind of their Maker. Unless, of course, we perversely choose to refuse that glimpse, refuse to hear 'that eternal language' which 'God utters', just as

402

we might choose to describe our own language entirely in terms of its physicality and not in terms of its meaning. What we see in *The Rime of the Ancient Mariner* is the story of someone who starts in this fully participatory mode of reading and perceiving the cosmos, falls out of it into an isolated, opaque refusal of that meaning, and is then restored back into that participative vision.

Coleridge has asserted that the power and prime agent of all human perception is not a material mechanism leaving its mark on the passive mind, but, on the contrary, is a living power of imagination, 'the repetition in our finite minds of the eternal act of creation in the infinite I AM'. It is as though the creative Word which speaks the cosmos into being raises its echo in us, and echoes back to God from our minds, made in His image. Where our echo meshes with His Word, we perceive His world.

Certainly, if we are to understand the vision and power behind those many moments in Coleridge's prose and poetry, not least in *The Mariner* itself, in which an account of natural beauty becomes a revelation of truth, then we will reach that understanding by tracing *both* world *and* word back to their single source in the holy *Logos*, the Imagination of God.

Coleridge came to comprehend a unity and continuity between his reason and his faith, both of them welling up from and animated by imagination. In the last words of the *Biographia*, he seems to revisit that evening walk as a little boy, holding his father's hands while the stars came out, but this time the grown man has found himself drawn into the life of another Father, with the Son, and Holy Spirit:

Christianity, as taught in the Liturgy and Homilies of our Church, though not discoverable by human Reason, is yet in accordance with it; that link follows link by necessary consequence; that Religion passes out of the ken of Reason only where the eye of Reason has reached its own Horizon; and that Faith is

Coleridge begins to understand faith & reason

then but its continuation: even as the Day softens away into the sweet Twilight, and Twilight, hushed and breathless, steals into the Darkness. It is Night, sacred Night! The upraised Eye views only the starry Heaven which manifests itself alone: and the outward Beholding is fixed on the sparks twinkling in the aweful depth, though Suns of other Worlds, only to preserve the Soul steady and collected in its pure *Act* of inward Adoration to the great I AM, and to the filial WORD that re-affirmeth it from Eternity to Eternity, whose choral Echo is the Universe.[20]

In a sense, everything else Coleridge was to write in this last stage of his life at Highgate arose out of these insights so lavishly, but sometimes randomly, scattered through the pages of *Biographia Literaria*. In 1817 he published his collected poems *Sibylline Leaves* and *Biographia Literaria* as a pair of companion volumes. He also published various lay sermons and, in 1825, his important *Aids to Reflection* on the principles of Christian thinking, and in this time he also produced a collected edition of *The Friend*, and two further magnificent editions of his own *Collected Poetry*.

But his new life at Highgate involved a great deal more than writing. The regime and restrictions to control his opium habit meant that he no longer travelled freely and called on friends far and wide, a change and a loss which many of his friends deplored and resented, but Coleridge and Gillman knew it was the only way he could survive. But what Coleridge discovered by staying still in Highgate was that many people from different walks of life were drawn to seek him out, drawn to his ideas, drawn to the new vision of a world kindled and quickened by imagination and calling us to a renewal of spiritual life which he was articulating in the *Biographia* and the poems of *Sibylline Leaves*. Like his mariner, Coleridge emerged at Highgate as a figure who could speak compellingly to the young, and offer them a renewal of vision, and so he came to be known as 'the sage of Highgate'. Gradually, a rising generation began to realise whom they had in their midst, and to gather in his rooms at Highgate, sit at his feet and listen, spellbound. As Carlyle has portrayed him in a famous (and ultimately hostile) account:

> Coleridge sat on the brow of Highgate Hill in those years looking down on London and its smoke-tumult, like a sage escaped from the inanity of life's battle; attracting towards him the thoughts of innumerable brave souls still engaged there. His express contributions to poetry Philosophy or any specific province of human literature or enlightenment having been small and sadly intermittent but he had, especially among young enquiring men, a higher than literary, a kind of prophetic or magician character.[21]

Carlyle was manifestly wrong in saying that Coleridge's contributions to human literature were small, however intermittent, but he was right in saying that he still had this magical power to draw new listeners, and to transform their vision. Coleridge was recognised, at least by some, as Carlyle went on to say, as 'A sublime man; who alone in those dark days, had saved his crown of spiritual manhood; Escaping from the black materialisms and revolutionary deluges, with "God, Freedom, Immortality" still his: a king of men'.[22]

So why the hostility, why the belittling of his achievement even in the midst of praise? The answer, in another phrase from this same description, is that Coleridge could 'still . . . profess himself an orthodox Christian and say and print to the Church of England, with its singular old rubrics, and surplices at Allhallowtide, *Esto perpetua!*'

For those who had been true radical French revolutionaries and who still wanted a revolution that would confine the Church along

Coleridge last years spent at Highgate

with the monarchy to oblivion, and equally now, to those who were espousing the new capitalism with its materialist worldview, its utilitarian economics and its 'captains of industry' (the phrase is also Carlyle's), it seemed scarcely credible that Coleridge, the radical campaigner, the sometime Jacobin celebrant of the French Revolution, and one of the great intellects of his age, should have become, of all things, an adherent not only of Christianity, but of the Church of England! Coleridge had never in fact formally left the Church of England, as he would have had to do to become a Unitarian minister, but now he was regularly attending his parish church in Highgate, and more significantly defending the Church in print and, in the *Biographia Literaria*, encouraging the young intelligentsia to become its ministers.

In one sense this reaction against Coleridge is understandable. The Church of England in Coleridge's day was not on the whole an edifying spectacle: its bishops had supported slavery; its system of the sale of parish patronage and livings (soon to be reformed) was clearly corrupt; and its clergy were often the youngest sons of landed families, given their posts for the sake of income and entirely unsuited to their vocation. There were shining exceptions among bishops and clergy; and though there was shortly to be revival and renewal, it was not visible in 1816. All these were reasons why Coleridge had rejected the Church in his youth. But now he had a different vision. Coleridge had seen, in that Malta moonrise, in that reaffirmation of the '*Logos*' within and without, not only a renewed way of seeing the world in the light of Christ, the Divine Imagination, but also a new way of seeing the Church. Like his mariner he saw that 'the kirk' could become the focus of renewed community, that it could stand in simple steady witness against the excesses and distortions of the new 'isms' both capitalist and materialist, ideas which he developed and articulated later in *Aids to Reflection* and *The Statesman's Manual*. Most of all, he saw that in the Bible and the Sacraments the church could continue to offer to the world a set of living symbols which opened out a sacral, vivifying view of nature, over against a meaningless mechanical one. For that reason he thought the Church itself should learn to rediscover the rich symbolism of biblical poetry and offer it as a fresh gift to the world. In *The Statesman's Manual*, the first of his 'Lay sermons' published the year after he arrived at Highgate, he wrote a brilliant critique of the poverty of literalism, whether it is peddled by scientists on the one hand or biblical literalists on the other:

> A hunger-bitten and idea-less philosophy naturally produces a starveling and comfortless religion. It is among the miseries of the present age that it recognises no medium, between Literal and Metaphorical. Faith is either to be buried in the dead letter, or its name and honours usurped by a counterfeit product . . .[23]

The aim of *The Statesman's Manual* was to present the Bible as 'the best guide to political skill and foresight', as the title suggests, to the hearts and minds of political leaders.

Carlyle, Hazlitt and others mistakenly thought that because Coleridge had returned to the Church of England he had 'sold out' on his earlier radical concerns. On the contrary, Coleridge took the practical and social implications of his renewed faith equally seriously. Where he had once campaigned against slavery he now became involved in campaigning against its new form, the atrocious conditions of child labour in the new factories. This activism brought him into direct contact at last with the other great seer and prophet of his age, William Blake, then living in old age, obscurity and poverty in London. Coleridge met Blake, and read his *Songs of Innocence and Experience*, through a mutual friend Charles Tulke, an unorthodox Swedenborgian who was helping with the campaign about factory conditions. So although Coleridge had returned to the Church of England he was still happy to move in radical circles. It would be fascinating to know what Blake and Coleridge talked about when they met. Both men had, by different pathways, realised that Christianity must be renewed from within by a deep engagement with the Imagination. Unfortunately, all Tulke tells us is that 'Blake and Coleridge, when in company seemed like congenial beings from another sphere, breathing for a while on our earth'.[24]

So Coleridge's return to the Church was not exhaustion, but a renewal of his radicalism which led him back to campaigning on social issues. He had a new vision, too, for the particular local life of the parish, which is the heart of the English Church. One of the most engaging chapters of the *Biographia Literaria* is the 'affectionate exhortation' to young men of literary gift and inclination. It starts by advising men of letters to get another profession as well as writing so that they are not chained to the desk and their genius blighted by mere necessity. But then Coleridge's prose suddenly opens up and lifts as he proposes a union of Christian and literary excellence and encourages young writers to deepen their faith and seek holy orders! What Coleridge sees is a rich new vision of the parish, and a central place for the Church in the education and cultural life of the nation:

> among the numerous blessings of Christianity, the introduction of an established church makes an especial claim on the gratitude of scholars and philosophers . . . that to every parish throughout the kingdom there is transplanted a germ of civilisation; that in the remotest places there is a nucleus round which the capabilities of the place may crystallise and brighten . . . the clergyman is with his parishioners and among them; he is neither in the cloistered cell nor in the wilderness, but a neighbour and a family man . . . Finally that man must be deficient in sensibility, who would not find an incentive to emulation in the great and burning lights which in a long series have illustrated the Church

of England; who would not hear from within an echo to the voice from their sacred shrines.[25]

Coleridge was certainly drawing ever more deeply on 'those great and burning lights', filling his notebooks and the margins of his own copies with rich and incisive notes on the writings of George Herbert and John Donne, and later Archbishop Leighton, around whose writings he would organise his own *Aids to Reflection*. He was also addressing the whole issue of how we read the Bible itself, having seen how it was ignored on the one hand and reduced to a false pseudo-scientific literalism on the other. He began a series of 'letters to a young friend' on intelligent and spiritually open ways of reading the Bible in the modern world, which was only published after his death as *Confessions of an Inquiring Spirit*. In the opening letter of the book he says that in the Bible:

> I have found words for my innermost thoughts, songs for my joy, utterances for my hidden griefs, and pleadings for my shame and my feebleness. In short whatever finds me bears witness for itself that has proceeded from a Holy Spirit even from the same Spirit *which remaining in itself yet regenerateth all other powers and in all ages entering into holy souls maketh them friends of God and prophets.*[26]

Word began to spread that, miraculously, Coleridge had risen again from the ashes. The new generation of younger poets all recognised his power, veiled as it might be. Shelley loved Coleridge's verse and had tried to visit him, and missed him when he was in the north. When Coleridge heard this, he regarded it as a missed opportunity, believing that he could have drawn Shelley away from his atheism. As it was, Shelley in exile in Italy wrote a verse letter to his friend Maria Gisborne telling her to search out Coleridge:

You will see Coleridge – he who sits obscure
In the exceeding lustre and the pure
Intense irradiation of a mind
Which, with its own internal lightning blind,
Flags wearily through darkness and despair
A cloud encircled meteor of the air
A hooded eagle among blinking owls.[27]

Byron also recognised Coleridge's genius and it was he who had encouraged Coleridge to publish *Christabel*, *Kubla Khan* and the *Pains of Sleep* in a pamphlet for Byron's publisher Murray, which Coleridge did in order to get money to pay off Morgan's debts. The other great Romantic poet of the new generation, John Keats, was already an ardent reader of Coleridge when they met by chance on Hampstead Heath in April 1819. Whereas most people who met Coleridge describe him as a great talker but don't give us an exact idea of what he actually said, Keats produces a fair menu:

I walked with him . . . for near two miles I suppose. And in these two miles he broached a thousand things – let me see if I can give you a list – Nightingales, Poetry – on Poetical sensation – Metaphysics – Different genera and species of Dreams – Nightmare – a dream accompanied by a sense of touch – single and double Touch – a Dream related – First and Second Consciousness – the difference between Will and Volition – so many metaphysicians from a want of smoking – the second consciousness – Monsters – the Kraken – Mermaids – Southey Believes in them – Southey's belief too much diluted – A Ghost Story – Good morning –[28]

Coleridge remembered, of this encounter: 'after he had left us a little way, he came back and said: "Let me carry away the memory, Coleridge, of having pressed your hand."'[29] Indeed, Keats may have carried away far more than that. He was on the cusp of his own great *annus mirabilis*, and later that April he would write *La Belle Dame Sans Merci*, drawing as it does in phrase and form on Coleridge's poem 'Love' which had been republished in *Sibylline Leaves*; then, in the coming two months, the *Ode to a Nightingale* and the other great odes, all of which draw on something of the rich music and tone of intimate conversation which Coleridge had pioneered in the conversation poems.

Coleridge's old London friends, as well as these rising poets, were glad to have him nearby. Lamb was at first sceptical at the new efforts to control opium – he had seen it so many times before – but he rejoiced to have Coleridge close again. In a famous account of his old friend he wrote to Wordsworth:

> Coleridge is absent but 4 miles & the neighborhood of such a man is as exciting as the presence of 50 ordinary persons. Tis enough to be within the whiff and wind of *his* genius, for us not to possess our souls in quiet ... I think his essentials not touched ... and his face when he repeats his verses hath its ancient glory, an arch angel a little damaged.[30]

From this new position of comparative stability Coleridge was even able to build bridges back to his family. His three surviving children, of whom he was immensely proud, came to visit him. Hartley had become a tutor at Oriel College in Oxford and Derwent had just won an exhibition as a student at St John's Cambridge, but it was Sara who was perhaps the most brilliant of them all. She would eventually marry her cousin Henry Nelson Coleridge and with him become the first editor of her father's works. When they did marry, they also settled in Hampstead and her mother, Sara Coleridge, came down to live with them there, so that in the end, the whole family were all together again for the christening of Coleridge's granddaughter,[31] and able:

To walk together to the kirk
And all together pray,

(Lines 605–6)

Hartley was the most volatile, and shared his father's restlessness, waywardness and propensity to addiction. He lost the fellowship on a charge of public drunkenness, which caused Coleridge terrible distress, and he did his best, in vain, to try and get his son reinstated. But Hartley had one more thing in common with his father: he had become a poet of some distinction, and in particular a master of the sonnet form. Notwithstanding all the times they had tried each other, fallen out and reconciled, Coleridge, in the year before he died, received one last lovely gift from his son: a copy of *Poems*, Hartley's first and only volume. Hartley had dedicated the whole volume to his father, and the dedicatory sonnet looked back to the very scene Coleridge described in *Frost at Midnight* and recalled all his hopes for Hartley:

Father, and Bard revered! to whom I owe,
Whate'er it be, my little art of numbers,
Thou, in thy night-watch o'er my cradled slumbers,
Didst meditate the verse that lives to show,
(And long shall live, when we alike are low)
Thy prayer how ardent, and thy hope how strong,
That I should learn of Nature's self the song,
The lore which none but Nature's pupils know . . .[32]

'Thy prayer how ardent, and thy hope how strong' seems a good summary of two deep and related themes of Coleridge's life. He must certainly have seen a great deal of himself in his son, both for good and ill.

But beneath all these outwards achievements, events and reconciliations – the publications, the growing recognition, the regular evenings when the ardent young came and sat at his feet – hidden away, as it must be, there was for Coleridge, as for every recovering addict, the heroic daily struggle, the daily resistance to temptation, the daily submission to a higher power. Towards the end of his life Coleridge composed his extraordinary *Nightly Prayer*, which sustained him with its reminder of the essentials of his faith, and above all as an act of essential communion with his maker and redeemer:

> Thy mercies have followed me through all the hours and moments of my life; and now I lift up my heart in awe and thankfulness for the preservation of my life through the past day, for the alleviation of my bodily sufferings and languors, for the manifold comforts which thou hast reserved for me, yea, in thy fatherly compassion hast rescued from the wreck of my own sins or sinful infirmities;—for the kind and affectionate friends thou hast raised up for me, especially for those of this household . . . but, above all, for the heavenly Friend, the crucified Saviour . . .[33]

It was a reminder and a thanksgiving, given one day at a time because, for all the outer ease of his conversation and his returning powers of mind, Coleridge understood, from that crisis in the Grey Hound onwards, that he could not depend on any of his many strengths and gifts but only on grace, and perhaps began to see that *The Ancient Mariner*, the great poem he had written in the full flower of all his gifts was, in the end, also a poem about grace. Certainly the mariner was on his mind when he came to compose his own epitaph:

> Stop, Christian Passer-by! stop, Child of God!
> And read with gentle breast. Beneath this Sod
> A Poet lies, or that which once seem'd He.
> O, lift one thought in prayer for S. T. C.

That he who many a year with toil of Breath
Found Death in Life, may here find Life in Death!
Mercy for Praise—to be forgiven for Fame
He ask'd, and hoped, thro' Christ. Do Thou the Same![34]

Here we seem to be back at the opening of *The Ancient Mariner* with Coleridge, mariner-like, compelling the passer-by to stop and hear a life-changing tale; but now Coleridge introduces a beautiful reversal and renewal of his phrase 'life in death'. He sees that the false life of his addictions and their nightmare consequences had been not so much 'life in death' as 'death in life'. Now Coleridge knows he is passing through the grave and gate of death to the true Life, turning at last upstream to the source of those very fountains of love he had so often celebrated in his verse. And this brief poem has the same turn at the end that the mariner does, a turn back from the speaker to the listener, 'He asked, and hoped, through Christ. Do thou the same!'

The rheumatic illness and the enlarged heart he had borne with him all these years were finally taking their toll. Coleridge's illnesses became more frequent and he became aware that he was dying. He was deeply conscious of how much he owed to the Gillmans and wrote a little note to Ann Gillman thanking her in case he had not the chance before the end. The note is not only deeply personal but also richly theological, concerning how we glimpse the light of God's goodness in and through one another. Indeed, its strong image of 'the light of life seen within the body of death' seems very like the mariner's seeing at last the light of the angels at the end of the *Rime*:

I not only hope but have a steadfast faith that God will be your reward: because your love to me from first to last has begun in, and been caused by what appeared to you a translucence of the love of the good, the true, and the beautiful from within me—as a relic of glory gleaming through the turbid shrine of my mortal imperfections and infirmities—as a light of life seen within 'the Body of this Death!' because in loving me you loved our Heavenly Father reflected in the gifts and influences of his Holy Spirit![35]

This is pure Coleridge; even the phrase 'the good, the true, and the beautiful' is a summary of all he loved in Plato, and the imagery of translucence, the shining of one truth in and through another, takes us back to the heart of his poetic vision.

Early in the morning of 25 July 1834, Coleridge finally slipped his moorings in this world. He had been talking lucidly until nearly the end and said his mind was quite clear, indeed his last words were 'I could even be witty . . .' We can never know his last thoughts, but perhaps he remembered the words he had once written, as he set off for Malta all those years ago: 'Death *itself* will be only a Voyage – a Voyage not *from* but to our native country.'[36]

The ship 'before the fall', orbed with a rainbow and led by the albatross . . .
'a lucid vision of how things could have been'

The Morrow Morn

The Mariner, whose eye is bright,
Whose beard with age is hoar
Is gone: and now the Wedding-Guest
Turned from the bridegroom's door

He went like one that hath been stunned,
And is of sense forlorn:
A sadder and a wiser man,
He rose the morrow morn.

(Lines 618–end)

For all of us who have read the poem, who have been stopped like the wedding guest, been held by that glittering eye and heard the mariner's transformative tale, it is now 'the morrow morn', the time after the poem, the time to reflect and find new directions. And here it is worth remarking on a curious reversal and re-reading of a parable that is embedded in the narrative structure of the whole poem. Coleridge's 'gloss' on the first verse of the poem contains a strangely reversed allusion to one of Jesus' parables. The gloss reads 'An Ancient Mariner meeteth three Gallants bidden to a wedding-feast, and detaineth one.' The phrasing of this gloss is bound to call to mind Jesus' parable of the Wedding Feast (Matt. 22:1–14) in which each of the invited guests makes an excuse to say they can't come, distracted by the cares of this world; as a result, the Master sends out his servants to the high-ways and byways, where they actually stop and compel the passers-by. But in Christ's story the passers-by are compelled *to* the wedding feast rather than withheld *from* it. Since in Christ's parable, the wedding feast represents the kingdom of God, the first priority of spiritual life, and the excuses which detain the guests who have been bidden to the feast represent distractions, a conventionally pious poem would make the mariner and his tale a distraction or digression from the important things in life for the bidden wedding guest, but in fact the reverse is the case. By the time the story is over, the wedding guest has realised that going into the church and attending the wedding feast, and all the pleasures and social duties tied up with it, was the distraction, and in the final verses, released from the spell of the mariner's eye, the wedding guest turns 'from the bridegroom's door' to begin his life again a sadder and a wiser man.

Why did Coleridge make this daring reversal of the expected norm? Perhaps because he had heard this parable abused from the pulpit, as it so often is, and preached on as though it were a parable about church attendance rather than the kingdom of God, as though the preachers thought that transformative kingdom events only happen inside their own precincts! Perhaps he had come to perceive that the Church's conventional pieties and its social role had dulled and tamed the spiritual challenge in Jesus' parable, and that the really shaking and profound experiences, the experiences of spiritual death and resurrection that could actually convert a person, and make sense of an inherited Christian faith, were more likely to happen outside the Church than in it. This certainly proved to be the case in Coleridge's own life. At the end of the poem the mariner does indeed return to the physical space of the church, responding to the 'little vesper bell', but his enlarged and transformed vision would never confine the God of the cosmos into that particular little box.

'The mariner . . . is gone', but even as Coleridge left this world, he must have known that the poetry he was leaving behind would live on; and so it does, most especially *The Rime of the Ancient Mariner*. Like the mariner himself, the poem passed 'like night from land to land' and had 'strange power of speech'; and as it has travelled the world and the centuries beyond Coleridge's own sphere, this poem, again like the mariner himself, has seemed to seek out and find its own particular readers, hold them spellbound, and leave them changed.

In particular the poem has reached out and found other artists, poets and writers, who then found themselves in the story in different ways. This epilogue will mention just a sample of those subsequent writers and artists who listened to Coleridge's poem, spellbound like the wedding guest, and whose work was decisively influenced by Coleridge's vision.

Gustave Doré was two years old when Coleridge died; when he came to illustrate *The Ancient Mariner*, in his full maturity in 1870, it became his master work and his engravings have become for many the defining imagery of the poem, particularly his sense of the vast uncharted spaces, the eerie sublime of the ice, the loneliness of the isolated human figure, the luminous beauty of the albatross itself. But, like all Coleridge's best illustrators, Doré felt able to add his own imaginative responses rather than slavishly illustrate, and nowhere more so than in the depiction of the ship 'before the fall', orbed with a rainbow and led by the albatross. In a sense it's that lucid vision of how things could have been, how things should be, that gives all the other illustrations their poignancy. This poem found Doré at the height of his art, his success and fame, and perhaps it whispered something in his ear about fallibility and the frailty of all human endeavour; it certainly seems to be more than hinted at in the mariner's haunted expression.

Twenty-one years after Doré illustrated *The Mariner* another writer, theologian and poet published a novel at whose heart was a close reading of *The Ancient Mariner*. This was George MacDonald and his novel *There and Back*, published in 1891.

Macdonald was a ten-year-old boy when Coleridge died but he discovered *The Mariner* early and it became a lasting influence, as did Coleridge's whole theory of Imagination. Coleridge's writing gave MacDonald the perspective and the intellectual purchase he needed to set himself free from the rigid Calvinism of the Congregationalist church in which he had been brought up and to develop his own gifts as a creative writer. He is now widely acknowledged as the father of the modern fantasy novel, for Macdonald was, in turn, to exercise a huge influence on the two greatest fantasy writers of the twentieth century: J.R.R. Tolkien and C.S. Lewis. Indeed, Lewis always called MacDonald 'My Master'. Macdonald himself published a series of essays on Faith and Imagination called *A Dish of Orts*, which very much develop the lines of thought laid out by Coleridge in the *Biographia Literaria* and *Aids to Reflection*, but it is in *There and Back* that he gives us a vivid account of how *The Mariner* might reach and transform its readers, or hearers. In a chapter of the novel called 'The Rime of the Ancient Mariner' there is a scene in which Barbara Wylder, a young child, running free and wild, finds a pigeon with a broken wing and brings it to a craftsman called Richard, who is a bookbinder by trade. He knows he cannot heal the bird and realises that this encounter with suffering and death may be of great importance to the young child. He hesitates as to what to say, for he is an atheist, and the seemingly random suffering of innocent creatures is part of the grounds of his atheism, but he is reluctant to convey his doubts to the child. As they tend to the wounded bird he begins to recite to her *The Rime of the Ancient Mariner*. Even at the beginning of the encounter the whole episode is framed in terms of the gates of life and death:

> Richard was piecing the broken cords of a great old folio—the more easily that they were double—in order to re-attach the loosened sheets and the hanging board, and so get the book

ready for a new cover. She carried in her hand something yet more sorely in need of mending—a pigeon with a broken wing, which she had seen lying in the park, and had dismounted to take. It kept opening and shutting its eyes, and she knew that nothing could be done for it; but the mute appeal of the dying thing had gone to her heart, and she wanted sympathy, whether for it or for herself she could hardly have distinguished. How she came to wake a little more just then, I cannot tell, but the fact is a joint in her history. The jar to the pigeon's life affected her as a catastrophe. She felt that there a crisis had come: a living conscious thing could do nothing for its own life, and lay helpless. Say rather—seemed so to lie. Oh, surely it is in reason that not a sparrow should fall to the ground without the Father! To whom but the father of the children that bemoan its fate, should the children carry his sparrow? But Barbara was carrying her pigeon where was no help for the heart of either.

'Ah, poor thing,' said Richard, 'I fear we can do nothing for it! But it will be at rest soon! It is fast going.'

'Ah! but where?' said Barbara, to whom that moment came the question for the first time.

'Nowhere,' answered Richard.

'How can that be? If I were going, I should be going somewhere! I couldn't go nowhere if I tried ever so. I don't like you to say it is going nowhere! Poor little thing! I won't let you go nowhere!'[1]

. . .

'Is it not strange,' he said, and would have taken from her hands the wounded bird, but she would not part with it, 'that men should take pleasure in killing—especially a creature like that, so full of innocent content? It seems to me the greatest pity to stop such a life!'[2]

. . .

'Did you ever notice,' he said, 'in *The Rime of the Ancient Mariner*, the point at which the dead bird falls from the neck of the man?'

It was a point, however, at which neither he nor Barbara was capable of seeing the depth of the poem. Richard thought it was the new-born love of beauty that freed the mariner; he did not see that it was the love of life, the new-born sympathy with life.

'I don't even know what you are talking of,' answered Barbara. 'Do tell me. It sounds like something wonderful! Is it a story?'
    'Yes—a wonderful story.'[3]

So he goes on to recite the poem to her and as he does so it begins to transform them both. At various key moments the child interprets the poem for the adult and renews his sense of faith and vision, makes him begin to question his own bleak outlook, while at the same time the child learns from the adult's responses something of the sorrows and burdens of life. There is a wonderful passage in which having reached the part of the poem in which the mariner sees the moving moon, Richard and Barbara walk together through moonlight still reciting and thinking about the poem:

Higher and higher rose the moon. Her light on the grass-blades wove them into a carpet with its weft of faint moonbeams. The small dull mirrors of the evergreen leaves glinted in the thickets, as the two went by, like the bits of ill-polished glass in an Indian tapestry. The moon was everywhere, filling all the hollow over-world, and for ever alighting on their heads. Far away they saw the house, a remote something, scarce existent in the dreaming night, the gracious-ghastly poem, and the mingling, harmonizing moon. It was much too far away to give them an anxious thought, and for long it seemed, like death, to be coming no nearer; but they were moving toward it all the time, and it was even growing a more insistent fact. Thus they walked at once in the two blended worlds of the moonlight and the tale, while Richard half-chanted the music-speech of the most musical of poets, telling of the roaring wind that the mariner did not feel, of the flags of electric light, of the dances of the wan stars, of the sighing of the sails, of the star-dogged moon, and the torrent-like falls of the lightning down the mountainous cloud.[4]

There is darkness and distress in store for both characters as the novel unfolds, but somehow the very images of Coleridge's poem have become for both of them an imaginative language with which to interpret their lives.

As the twentieth century dawned, the poem went on to find others in darker places, where perhaps the mariner in his distress was the only one who could be their companion. One such was David Jones, the Welsh artist and poet who had served as a private through all the horrors of the Great War. In 1929, just as he was beginning, in response to mental breakdown, to piece together the beginnings of *In Parenthesis*, his masterly poetic account of his war experience, he was asked to make a series of copperplate illustrations of *The Ancient Mariner*. Jones's response to the poem was immediate and visceral; he knew it was a fluent and beautiful poem but he found:

> It is something far deeper than that which characterises this poem. It is that behind the fluent artistry and the popular ballad form, sustained without a lapse through the many stanzas of its seven parts, it conceals or discloses deeps and strata of meaning, where, in the words of the Psalmist, *abyssus abyssum invocat* (Deep calleth unto Deep).[5]

Certainly this poem called out great depths in Jones. His own experience of undeserved grace in the midst of horror had been a glimpse of Mass celebrated in the ruins of a barn amid a wrecked village during the First World War, and he keenly recognised the sacral world in which the poem begins and to which it returns, as well as the terrible wasteland through which it passes. Just as in his *In Parenthesis* he would glimpse Christ in and through the bodies of soldiers hanging on the wires, so his central engraving of the moment the albatross is shot places the bird, pierced, and almost crucified, on the cross tree of the mast with the sailors below looking up with raised arms in a gesture of horror that might equally be, or at any moment become, recognition and worship.

Some years later, in the midst of another terrible war, the poem found its way to another gifted artist and writer, also recovering from a nervous breakdown: Mervyn Peake. He knew the poem by heart and in 1943 he published an astonishing series of illustrations for it. Dark, nightmarish, unsettling, yet with a haunting beauty, many of the images show the mariner so utterly as one of the dead himself that there seems no possibility of redemption, except in the strange beauty of the art itself. As C.S. Lewis, who saw and loved these illustrations, wrote in a letter to Peake: 'The Mariner himself has just the triple character I have sometimes met in nightmares – that disquieting blend of the venerable, the pitiable and the frightful.'[6] The venerable, the pitiable and something more – the graceful and holy – predominate in Peake's beautiful illustration of the mariner kneeling to pray; the albatross still round his neck seems almost to have become part of him, as though he himself had wings, his head cast down and just a faint glimmer of light on the sea suggesting the moonrise that is about to change everything.

C.S. Lewis was himself pre-eminent among the writers whom this poem was to find 'on the morrow morn'. Lewis engaged with

Coleridge in many ways throughout his life, not least in the way Coleridge's thought was mediated to him through the writing of George MacDonald, and in a verse letter to his fellow poet Roy Campbell he brilliantly summarised what it had been Coleridge's mission to achieve, and what, in spite of everything, he had achieved. In the poem, Lewis approaches Coleridge through Cardinal Newman's appreciation of him:

> . . . Newman in that ruinous master saw
> One who restored our faculty for awe,
> Who re-discovered the soul's depth and height
> Who pricked with needles of the eternal light
> An England at that time half numbed to death
> With Paley's, Bentham's, Malthus' wintry breath.[7]

Though Lewis is writing about the whole of Coleridge's achievement, there could not be a better summary of *The Mariner*'s spiritual reach in 'rediscovering the soul's depth and height', and in restoring 'the faculty of awe'. We might even see a foreshadowing in this poem, written before the Narnia series was begun, of Lewis's own imaginative Christ-figure who frees Narnia, 'half-numbed to death' from a White Witch's 'wintry breath'. In fact, it is in *The Voyage of the Dawn Treader*, a book that begins with 'a painted ship upon a painted ocean', that Lewis gives us his deepest reading of *The Rime of the Ancient Mariner*. The key 'Coleridgean' episode is when the children and Prince Caspian, sailing east towards the rising sun, encounter on their way a 'dark island'. They cannot see it, but it is as though they are sailing into night itself:

> Suddenly, from somewhere . . . there came a cry, either of some inhuman voice, or else a voice of one in such extremity of terror that he had almost lost his humanity . . . "Mercy" cried the voice,

"Mercy! Even if you are only one more dream have mercy! Take me on board."[8]

When they eventually pull this lost mariner on board, Lewis gives an unforgettable description:

> Edmund thought he had never seen a wilder looking man. Though he did not otherwise look very old his hair was an untidy mop of white, his face was thin and drawn, and for clothing, only a few wet rags hung about him. But what one mainly noticed were his eyes, which were so widely opened that he seemed to have no eyelids at all, and stared as if in an agony of pure fear . . .[9]

The stranger reveals that this is the island where dreams come true, 'not daydreams, dreams'.

Suddenly everyone on the ship becomes vividly aware of their worst nightmares and realises that this is what they are sailing towards. They try to row back the way they have come, but as in a dream or a nightmare, they make no progress. Horrors from their nightmares creep gradually and vividly over the minds of the crew, and they all begin to panic. Lucy, from the fighting top, makes a desperate prayer: 'Aslan, Aslan, if you ever loved us at all, send us help now.' After that, they see a light shining like a beam on the ship. Lucy looked along the beam and saw something in it. 'At first it looked like a cross.'[10] It turns out to be an albatross, which Lewis, following Coleridge carefully, associates with the cross. The albatross circles three times round the mast and then guides the ship out of the darkness. 'But none except Lucy knew that as it circled the mast it had whispered to her, "Courage, dear heart", and the voice, she felt sure, was Aslan's.'[11]

Within the parameters of a children's book Lewis is playing with, indeed celebrating, some of the great themes of the poem, particularly the fear and quality of nightmare, but he is also offering, as David Jones did, a very clear identification, at this moment, of the albatross with Christ himself. The poem clearly held great salvific depth for Lewis, as throughout the rest of his Narnia Chronicles his Christ-figure is either a Lion or a Lamb, both biblical images, but here he quietly allows one of his characters to encounter Aslan in the mariner's albatross.

A world away from Lewis's robust Christian apologetics, and a couple of generations later, Coleridge found another deep reader in the poet-priest R.S. Thomas. Thomas has perfected, perhaps more than any other contemporary poet, the art of the tentative suggestion, the feel for gaps and spaces, the poetry of bleak waiting sustained by only the slenderest thread of hope. Thomas was a bird-watcher, fascinated and drawn by all forms of bird life, and finding in the 'twitcher's' long, often fruitless vigils, waiting to see a bird one may or may not have identified correctly, a metaphor for the long patience of his priestly life, his sense of tending a dimly burning wick, his unwillingness to trust mirages or false consolations in the long wait for the true God. But there is a late poem about finding, not losing, about knowing, not doubting, called 'A Thicket in Lleyn', in which far from fleeing or avoiding the bird-watcher, the birds fly towards him in great numbers and surround him. This poem, a celebration of sudden presence and renewed vision, all the more credible for Thomas's usual reticence, is soaked in the work and thought of Coleridge. It directly alludes to the passage on Imagination and perception in the thirteenth chapter of the *Biographia*, and its final image of travel and replenishment is entirely Coleridgean:

'A Thicket in Lleyn', by R.S. Thomas
I was no tree walking.
I was still. They ignored me,
the birds, the migrants
on their way south. They re-leafed

the trees, budding them
with their notes. They filtered through
the boughs like sunlight,
looked at me from three feet
off, their eyes blackberry bright,
not seeing me, not detaching me
from the withies, where I was
caged and they free.
                    They would have perched
on me, had I nourishment
in my fissures. As it was
they netted me in their shadows,
brushed me with sound, feathering the arrows
of their own bows, and were gone,
leaving me to reflect on the answer
to a question I had not asked.
'A repetition in time of the eternal
I AM.' Say it. Don't be shy.
Escape from your mortal cage
in thought. Your migrations will never
be over. Between two truths
there is only the mind to fly with.
Navigate by such stars as are not
leaves falling from life's
deciduous tree, but spray from the fountain
of the imagination, endlessly
replenishing itself out of its own waters.[12]

This poem takes us to the heart of Coleridge's teaching, which is that each human consciousness, each unique imagination that perceives and shapes the world it apprehends, is itself 'a repetition in time of the eternal and infinite I Am'! We participate in the imagination of God who shapes and makes the world with us even as we perceive it. And we are called to be voyagers, like the mariner 'to navigate' not by the signs of death (the leaves falling from life's deciduous trees), but by such stars as are formed by the spray of that eternal fountain, in the divine I AM, from the 'spring of love' that rises so unexpectedly in the mariner's heart, which is also 'the fountain / of the imagination, endlessly / replenishing itself out of its own waters'.

And what of us, at the beginning of the twenty-first century, two hundred years after this poem was published in its final form? Where does the poem find us, where does it leave us, as a culture and a society? I have tried to show in this book how Coleridge himself lived through the whole tale after he wrote it, how he passed through early joy, out into shipwreck and loneliness, into alienation and anomie, and returned at last, through a renewal of vision, to prayer and compassion. Over the course of his life Coleridge, in a sense, completed the tale: he lived through every phase of the prophecy even to its redemptive conclusion. But that may not be true of us. In one sense we have not yet caught up with Coleridge. Looking out at our present situation, at our exploitation and pollution of the world, at our crisis of faith and meaning, but also at our spiritual yearning, at our renewed interest in imagination and symbol, it seems to me that as a culture we are still on the voyage, still only part way through, still trapped in the loneliness and loathing of a wide wide sea, but perhaps just beginning to see the first glimmer of a moonrise, of a new vision, of a repentance, a new way of seeing and feeling, a new more chastened and humble account of our relations with nature and with the numinous, that may yet redeem and bring us home. Perhaps this prescient poem has more truths yet to tell us, new prophecies to fulfil. Coleridge may help us to read the signs and interpret the new light when it comes.

The Rime of the Ancient Mariner has passed like night from land to land, has passed from one generation to another, finding its ideal readers, finding the listeners to hear the tale, from Coleridge to Doré and MacDonald, from Macdonald to Jones and Lewis, from Lewis to Peake, from Peake to R.S. Thomas, and out to our own generation, out to Chris Jordan photographing the slain albatrosses on Midway Island and weaving verses from *The Ancient Mariner* into his film. This tale found me also, and drew me into its orbit, transfixed me with its spell, sent me out again, 'a sadder and a wiser man'. Perhaps, as you close the pages of this book, it will find you too.

'Stop, Christian passer-by!—Stop, child of God!'
You made your epitaph imperative,
And stopped this wedding guest! But I am glad
To stop with you and start again, to live
From that pure source, the all-renewing stream,
Whose living power is imagination,
And know myself a child of the I AM,
Open and loving to his whole creation.
Your glittering eye taught mine to pierce the veil,
To let his light transfigure all my seeing,
To serve the shaping Spirit whom I feel,
And make with him the poem of my being.
I follow where you sail towards our haven,
Your wide wake lit with glimmerings of heaven.[13]

Notes

Introduction

1 *Biographia Literaria*, Vol. 1, pp. 241–2.
2 *The Road to Xanadu: A Study in the Ways of the Imagination*, by John Livingston Lowes.
3 *Samuel Taylor Coleridge: A Bondage of Opium*, by Molly Lefebure.
4 *Coleridge: Early Visions* and *Coleridge: Darker Reflections*, both by Richard Holmes.
5 *Minding the Modern: Human Agency, Intellectual Traditions, and Responsible Knowledge*, by Thomas Pfau.
6 From a translation from the original Latin included in Martin Gardner's *The Annotated Ancient Mariner*.

Chapter One

1 *Lectures 1808–1819 on Literature*, Part 1, ed. R.A. Foakes.
2 *Poetical Works*, Part 1, poem 171, *Frost at Midnight*, p. 455, lines 27–33.
3 *Coleridge's Letters*, Vol. 1, letter 179 to Thomas Poole dated March 1797, pp. 310–12.
4 *Coleridge's Letters*, Vol. 1, letter 208 to Thomas Poole dated 9 October 1797, p. 347.
5 *Coleridge's Letters*, Vol. 1, letter 210 to Thomas Poole dated 16 October 1797, pp. 354–5.
6 *Coleridge's Letters*, Vol. 1, letter 208 to Thomas Poole dated 9 October 1797, p. 348.
7 Ibid., p. 347.

8 *Coleridge's Letters*, Vol. 1, letter 210 to Thomas Poole dated 16 October 1797, pp. 352–3.

9 *Coleridge's Father: Absent Man, Guardian Spirit*, by J.C.C. Mays.

10 *Coleridge's Letters*, Vol. 1, letter 210 to Thomas Poole dated 16 October 1797, p. 354.

11 *The Prelude or, Growth of a Poet's Mind*, by William Wordsworth, Book VI, 'Cambridge and the Alps', lines 265–76.

12 *Poetical Works*, Part 1, poem 140, 'Sonnet to the River Otter', p. 300, lines 3–11.

13 *Coleridge's Letters*, Vol. 1, letter 234 to Thomas Poole dated 19 February 1798, p. 387.

14 For a brilliant account of Coleridge as a spontaneous talker, and of his growing reputation, see *Coleridge the Talker*, ed. Richard Willard Armour and Raymond Floyd.

15 *The Life of Samuel Taylor Coleridge*, by James Gillman, first published 1838, p. 20.

16 Ibid., p. 17.

17 Ibid., p. 20.

18 Charles Lamb, 'Christ's Hospital Five-and-Thirty Years Ago', *The Essays of Elia*, First Series [1820]. Cited in Campbell, p. 14.

19 *Coleridge: Early Visions*, by Richard Holmes, p. 33.

20 *Coleridge the Visionary*, by John Beer, p. 167.

21 From William Wordsworth's poem *The French Revolution as It Appeared to Enthusiasts at Its Commencement*.

22 *Poetical Works*, Part 1, poem 13, *An Ode on the Destruction of the Bastille*, verse 6, pp. 20–1.

23 *Coleridge's Letters*, letter to Thomas Allsop dated 1822, Vol. v, p. 218.

Chapter Two

1 *Coleridge's Letters*, Vol. 1, letter 9 to George Coleridge dated November 1791, pp. 16–17.

2 Ibid.

Notes

3   *The Gentleman's Magazine*, December 1834: Charles Valentine Le Grice (1773–1858) of Christ's Hospital and Trinity College, Cambridge.

4   *The Statesman's Manual*, p. 29.

5   *Coleridge's Letters*, Vol. 1, letter 39 to George Coleridge dated 4 March 1794, p. 71.

6   See also the introduction to *The Greek Ode* (*Sors misera servorum in insulis indiae occidentalis*) in *Poetical Works*, Part 1, p. 72.

7   It is interesting to see how Coleridge attempts to Hellenise Wilberforce's name, as there is no 'w' in Greek. It comes out as 'ilbrephofsen'. In a manuscript note, Coleridge refers to this as 'gotho-Greek for Wilberforce'. See also *Poetical Works*, Part 1, p. 82.

8   All passages from this translation are taken from *Poetical Works*, Part 1, pp. 76–7.

9   See also *Coleridge: Early Visions*, by Richard Holmes, p. 48.

10 From *Coleridge's Letters*, Vol. 1, letter 44, to George Coleridge dated 30 March 1794, p. 78.

11 From *Coleridge's Letters*, Vol. 1, letter 25 to Mary Evans dated 7 February 1793, p. 52.

12 Some of this dissipation seems to have involved visiting prostitutes, not uncommon among eighteenth-century undergraduates in Cambridge. Unlike many of his contemporaries, Coleridge's indulgence here was brief, not repeated, and a cause of deep shame. Some memories of this period in his life may have surfaced in the description, in *The Ancient Mariner*, of the figure of the '*Nightmare Life-in-Death*'.

13 From *Coleridge's Letters*, Vol. 1, letter 23 to George Coleridge dated 13 January 1793, p. 46.

14 From *Coleridge's Letters*, Vol. 1, letter 36 to George Coleridge dated 23 February 1794, p. 68.

15 Ibid.

16 From *Coleridge's Letters*, Vol. 1, letter 35 to James Coleridge dated 20 February 1794, p. 66.

17 *Samuel Taylor Coleridge: A Biographical Study*, by E.K. Chambers, p. 23.

18 *Coleridge's Letters*, Vol. 1, letter 33 to George Coleridge dated 8 February 1794, p. 63.

19 *Coleridge: Early Visions*, by Richard Holmes, p. 55.

20 *Coleridge's Letters*, Vol. 1, letter 33, to George Coleridge dated 8 February 1794, pp. 63–4.

21 Ibid., p. 64.

22 Ibid.

23 *Coleridge: Early Visions*, by Richard Holmes, p. 58.

24 *Coleridge's Letters*, Vol. 1, letter 36 to George Coleridge dated 23 February 1794, p. 67.

25 *The Rime of the Ancient Mariner*, lines 238–9.

26 *Coleridge's Letters*, Vol. 1, letter 36 to George Coleridge dated 23 February 1794, p. 67.

Chapter Three

1 See below, chapter 12, pages 408–9

2 *The Notebooks of Samuel Taylor Coleridge*, Vol. 2, note 2398.

3 Born Sarah Fricker, her name was spelled 'Sara' on Coleridge's insistence after her marriage, and has been called Sara throughout this book. She must be distinguished from her daughter Sara Coleridge (1802–52), who married her cousin Henry Coleridge, and also Sara Hutchinson (known to Coleridge as 'Asra'), Mary Wordsworth's sister.

4 *Coleridge's Letters*, Vol. 1, letter 73 to Robert Southey dated 9 December 1794, p. 132.

5 *The Friend*, Vol. 11, pp. 146–7.

6 *Coleridge's Letters*, Vol. 1, letter 69 to George Coleridge dated 6 November 1794, p. 126.

7 *Coleridge's Letters*, Vol. 1, letter 93 to Robert Southey dated 13 November 1795, p. 165.

8 *Coleridge's Letters*, Vol. 1, letter 77 to Robert Southey dated 29 December 1794, p. 145.

9 Ibid.

10 *Coleridge's Letters*, Vol. 1, letter 93 to Robert Southey dated 13 November 1795, p. 164.

11 See *Poetical Works*, Part 1, poem 115, pp. 231–5.

12 Ibid., p. 231, lines 1–12.

13 Ibid., lines 12–22.

14 Ibid., p. 234, lines 44–8.

15 Ibid., pp. 234–5, lines 52–3 and 58–64.

16 *Poetical Works*, Part 1, poem 129, p. 263, lines 43–8.

17 Ibid., lines 60–2.

18 See *Coleridge: Early Visions*, by Richard Holmes, p. 107.

19 Article from *The Watchman: On the Slave Trade*, from No. 4, Friday, 25 March 1796, and taken from a *Lecture on the Slave Trade* given by Coleridge at the Assembly coffeehouse in Bristol in June 1795, pp. 130–3.

20 *Coleridge's Letters*, Vol. 1, letter 105 to Joseph Cottle dated 22 February 1796, p. 185: referred to in *Coleridge Early Visions*, by Richard Holmes, pp. 109–10.

21 Pinney's townhouse is now an excellent museum in Bristol, 'The Georgian House', and tells the story of his merchant and slave-owning enterprises, partly through the eyes of Pero, an African slave he had brought over to Bristol.

22 *Coleridge: Early Visions*, by Richard Holmes, p. 28.

23 See note to letter 125 to Thomas Poole dated 13 May 1796 in *Coleridge's Letters*, Vol. 1, p. 210.

24 Ibid., p. 210–1.

Chapter Four

1 Coleridge began *The Mariner* in November 1797, working through the additions and revisions in February before the first full version was read to his friends in March 1798.

2 *William Wordsworth: A Biography*, by Mary Moormon, Vol. 1, p. 317. Quoted in *Coleridge: Early Visions*, by Richard Holmes, p. 149.

3 *The Letters of William and Dorothy Wordsworth: The Early Years*, p. 168. Quoted in *Coleridge: Early Visions*, by Richard Holmes, pp. 149–50.

4   William Shakespeare, *Complete Works: A Midsummer-Night's Dream*, Act 5, Scene 1.

5   For example, Harriet Martineau said of Coleridge, 'His eyes were as wonderful as they were represented to be — light gray, extremely prominent, and actually "glittering".' For a fuller account see *The Power of the Eye in Coleridge*, by Lane Cooper, published 1910. Reprinted from Studies in Language and Literature in honour of Professor James Morgan Hart.

6   *Biographica Literaria*, Vol. 1, p. 304.

7   *Coleridge's Letters*, Vol. 1, letter 195 to Joseph Cottle dated 3 July 1797, pp. 330–1.

8   *Coleridge's Letters*, Vol. 1, letter 190 to Joseph Cottle dated 8 June 1797, p. 325.

9   '. . . blessed trinity' of friends, 'we were three persons, it was but one God'. As quoted in chapter 1, footnote 3, letter to William Godwin.

10 *Coleridge's Notebooks*, Vol. 1, note 73.

11 *Coleridge's Letters*, Vol. 1, letter to John Thelwall dated 6 February 1797, p. 308.

12 Ibid.

13 *Coleridge's Letters*, Vol. 1, letter 184 to Joseph Cottle dated early April 1797, p. 319. The final three lines are quoted from Milton's *Samson Agonistes*, lines 594–6.

14 *Coleridge's Letters*, Vol. 1, letter 184 to Joseph Cottle dated early April 1797, pp. 319–20.

15 Don Locke, *A Fantasy of Reason: The Life and Thought of William Godwin* (Routledge, 1980), pp. 181–2. For an account of these conversations, see Richard Holmes' *Coleridge: Early Visions*, p. 258.

16 As an example of the way the Inklings and writers could collaborate in so many ways see Diana Glyer's *The Company They Keep* (Kent State University Press, 1 December 2006).

17 C.S. Lewis, *The Four Loves*, chapter 4, 'Friendship' (Fontana books, 1963), p. 64.

18 From *Coleridge's Letters*, Vol. 11, p. 709.

19 *Coleridge's Letters*, Vol. 1, letter 184 to Joseph Cottle dated early April 1797, pp. 320–1.

20 *Coleridge's Letters*, Vol. 11, letter 384 to Josiah Wedgwood dated February 1801, p. 709.

21 *Coleridge's Notebooks*, Part 1, notes 32 and 45.

22 *Poetical Works*, Vol. 1, poem 160, *The Wanderings of Cain*, from p. 358.

23 *Coleridge's Notebooks*, Vol. 1, note 45.

24 Ibid., note 161.

25 Ibid., Vol. 1, note 174.

26 *Biographia Literaria*, Vol. 1, pp. 195–6.

27 See Edmund Blunden and Earl Leslie Griggs, *Coleridge: Studies by Several Hands* (Constable, 1934), p. 82. There is also a fuller account of this episode in Holmes, *Early Visions*, pp. 159–62.

28 'My First Aquaintance with Poets', in Hazlitt's *Selected Essays*, ed. George Sampson (Cambridge University Press, 1940), p. 3.

29 *Hazlitt's Letters*, Vol. I, p. 374. Quoted in *Coleridge: Early Visions*, by Richard Holmes, pp. 179–80.

Chapter Five

1 For a full account of Coleridge as a pioneer fell walker see *Coleridge Walks the Fells: A Lakeland Journey Retraced*, by Alan Hankinson.

2 *William Hazlitt's Essays*, ed. Rosalind Vallance and John Hampden (Folio Society, 1964), p. 17.

3 *Poetical Works*, Part 1, poem 156, *This Lime-Tree Bower My Prison*, pp. 349–54, Introduction.

4 Ibid., lines 1–5.

5 Ibid., lines 5–20.

6 Ibid., lines 20–37.

7 *The Letters of Charles and Mary Lamb*, Vol. 1, letter 143 to Samuel Taylor Coleridge, p. 128.

8 Ibid., p. 224.

9 *Poetical Works*, Part 1, poem 156, *This Lime-Tree Bower My Prison*, pp. 349–54, lines 37–43.

10 Ibid., lines 43–60.

11 Ibid., lines 60–7.

12 Ibid., lines 68 to the end.

13 There is some scholarly dispute about the exact dating; for a fuller discussion see *Poetical Works*, Part 1, p. 509.

14 *Poetical Works*, Part 1, poem 178, *Kubla Khan: or, A Vision in a Dream*, p. 511.

15 *The Crewe Manuscript* was probably written in 1798 and had been sent by Coleridge to Mrs Southey, who later gave it or sold it to a private autograph collector. It was auctioned in 1859 and purchased by another autograph collector and subsequently passed to the Marquess of Crewe, who donated it, in 1962, to the British Museum, where it is now on display.

16 *Coleridge's Notebooks*, Vol. III, note 4006.

17 *Poetical Works*, Part 1, poem 178, *Kubla Khan: or, A Vision in a Dream*, pp. 512–14, complete poem.

18 Ibid., pp. 349–54, lines 51–4.

19 From *Anima Poetae*, reprinted in *The Portable Coleridge*, ed. I.A. Richards, p. 315.

20 Extract from *The Fenwick Notes of William Wordsworth*, ed. Jared Curtis (Bristol Classical Press, 1993), p. 2.

21 *The Complete Poetical Works of William Wordsworth in Ten Volumes*, Vol. II (1798–1800) (Cosimo Inc., 2008), p. 6.

22 *Coleridge's Letters*, Vol. II, letter 459 to William Sotheby dated 10 September 1802, p. 864.

23 *Poetical Works*, Part 1, poem 171, *Frost at Midnight*, pp. 452–6, lines 1–3.

24 Ibid., lines 4–10.

25 Ibid., lines 10–13.

26 Ibid., lines 13–23.

27 Ibid., lines 23–33.

28 Ibid., lines 36–41.

29 Ibid., lines 44–51.

30 Ibid., lines 51–3.

31 Ibid., lines 54–64.

32 Ibid., lines 65 to the end.

33 *Poetical Works*, Part 2, poem 293, *Dejection: An Ode*, pp. 695–703, line 38.

Notes

Chapter Six

1 *Poetical Works*, Part 1, poem 115, *The Eolian Harp*: *Composed at Clevedon, Somersetshire*, p. 233, lines 26–31.

2 *The Annotated Ancient Mariner*, with notes by Martin Gardner, pp. 46–8, note 25.

3 Herman Melville's *Moby-Dick* (chapter 42, 'The Whiteness of the Whale'), page 190, *Moby Dick, Or The Whale*, Vol. 6, Scholarly Edition, ed. Herman Melville, Harrison Hayford, Hershel Parker and G. Thomas Tanselle (Northwestern University Press, 9 September 1988).

4 *Shorter Works and Fragments*, Part II, pp. 1486–7.

5 See above, pages 107–8.

6 *Coleridge's Letters*, Vol. 1, letter 254 to Sara Coleridge dated 18 September 1798, p. 416.

7 Ibid.

8 *Coleridge's Letters*, Vol. 1, letter 256 to Sara Coleridge dated 3 October 1798, p. 425.

9 Ibid.

10 *The Friend*, ed. Barbara E. Rooke, Vol. 11, No. 19, p. 257 dated 28 December 1809.

11 *Coleridge's Letters*, Vol. 11, letter 484 to Thomas Wedgwood dated 14 January 1803, p. 916.

12 Letter of 1 November 1798, quoted on p. 105 in *The Bondage of Love: A Life of Mrs Samuel Taylor Coleridge*, by Molly Lefebure.

13 Letter from Thomas Poole to Coleridge dated 15 March 1799, quoted on pp. 114–15 of *The Bondage of Love: A Life of Mrs Samuel Taylor Coleridge*, by Molly Lefebure.

14 Letter from Sara Coleridge to Coleridge dated 24 March 1799, quoted on pp. 116–17 of *The Bondage of Love: A Life of Mrs Samuel Taylor Coleridge*, by Molly Lefebure.

15 *Coleridge's Letters*, Vol. 1, letter 275 to Sara Coleridge from Göttingen in der Wende Strasse dated 8 April 1799, pp. 481–4.

16 *Coleridge's Letters*, Vol. 1, letter 276 to Sara Coleridge from

Göttingen in der Wende Strasse dated 23 April 1799, pp. 484–9.

17   Ibid., p. 488.

18   Quote attributed to Southey on p. 117 of *The Bondage of Love: A Life of Mrs Samuel Taylor Coleridge*, by Molly Lefebure.

Chapter Seven

1   *The Annotated Ancient Mariner*, with an introduction and notes by Martin Gardner, illustrated by Gustave Doré, p. 52, note 38.

2   Descriptive Catalogue, 1810, *The Vision of Judgement*.

3   Lines 31–2.

4   *Poetical Works*, Part 1, poem 156, *This Lime-Tree Bower My Prison*, p. 352, lines 32–3 and 32–43.

5   *Poetical Works*, Part 1, poem 175, *Fears in Solitude: Written in April 1798, During the Alarm of an Invasion*, p. 470, lines 10–12.

6   Ibid., lines 79–86.

7   *Coleridge the Visionary*, by John Beer, p. 155.

8   I am quoting from the slightly expanded version printed by J. Shawcross in the appendix to his edition of the *Biographia Literaria*, Vol. II, p. 257. Coleridge's own notes for this lecture are printed in *Lectures 1808–19 on Literature*, Part 2, pp. 217–25.

9   Extract from *Voyage to the Pacific Ocean*, Vol. 11, 257, quoted in *The Road to Xanadu: A Study in the Ways of the Imagination*, by John Livingston Lowes, on p. 81.

10   Quoted in *The Road to Xanadu*, by John Livingston Lowes, on p. 84.

11   *Macbeth*, Act I, Scene 3, lines 32–4.

12   Ibid., lines 8–11.

13   Ibid., lines 19–26.

14   *The Tragedy of Macbeth: The Oxford Shakespeare* (Oxford World Classics), ed. Nicholas Brooke, p. 62.

15   *Coleridge's Letters*, Vol. 1, letter 156 to John Thelwell dated 19 November 1796, p. 260.

16 For further reading see Owen Barfield's *History in English Words*, published in 1967 by Steiner Books.

17 Cited in *The Road to Xanadu*, by John Livingston Lowes, p. 216.

18 Coleridge's *Lectures 1808–1819 on Literature*, Part I, p. 495.

19 Matthew 7:1–2 KJV.

20 *The Rime of the Ancient Mariner*, illustrated by Mervyn Peake, (Chatto & Windus, 1949).

21 *Flowers of Evil*, by George Dillon (Harper and Brothers, 1936).

22 *Coleridge's Letters*, Vol. 1, letter 276 to Sara Coleridge dated 23 April 1799, p. 484.

23 *Coleridge's Letters*, Vol. 11, letter 431 to William Godwin dated 21 January 1802, p. 781.

24 *Coleridge's Letters*, Vol. 1, letter 294 to Robert Southey dated 30 April 1799, pp. 533–4.

25 For a full analysis of Coleridge's medical history, see Molly Lefebure's *A Bondage of Opium*, Introduction, Part II: 'The Tyranny of the Body'.

26 *Coleridge's Letters*, Vol. 1, letter 290 to William Wordsworth dated circa 10 September 1799, p. 527.

27 *Coleridge's Notebooks*, Vol. 1 (1794–1804), note 495 f55 dated October 1799.

28 *Poetical Works*, Part 1, poem 253, *Love*, lines 1–4, p. 606.

29 *Coleridge's Notebooks*, Vol. 1 (1794–1804), note 578 dated November 1799.

30 Coleridge's *Notebooks*, Vol. 1, note 1575 dated October 1803 (with translation from Kathleen Coburn's notes).

Chapter Eight

1 *The Road to Xanadu: A Study in the Ways of the Imagination*, by John Livingston Lowes, p. 223.

2 Ibid., p. 277, the second part being a quote from *Northern Mythology*, Vol. III, by Thorpe.

3 *Poetical Works*, Part 1, poem 161, *The Ancyent Mariner* as published in 1798, p. 386, lines 189.1.1–194.1.

4 See the article by Dana K. Nelkin on 'Moral Luck' in the *Stanford Encyclopedia of Philosophy*, ed. Edward N. Zalta (winter 2013 edition), URL: <http://plato.stanford.edu/archives/win2013/entries/moral-luck/>.

5 See *Coleridge: Darker Reflections*, by Richard Holmes, p. 3.

6 There is a learned discussion in Livingston Lowes' book *The Road to Xanadu* as to whether this is intended as a natural or supernatural event. You could see a star almost touching the nether tip of a crescent moon but you could never see a star 'within the nether tip' for that darkness is not transparent space but the darkened surface of the moon itself – these details need not concern us here: the key point is that in this deathly state, he and the mariners can only perceive the moon as star-dogged; they are not yet open to her full redemptive beauty.

7 *Coleridge's Letters*, Vol. 1, letter 332 to Josiah Wedgwood dated 21 April 1800, p. 587.

8 *Coleridge's Letters*, Vol. 1, postscript to letter 341 to Josiah Wedgwood dated 24 July 1800, p. 611.

9 *Coleridge's Notebooks*, Vol. 1, note 718 (written in March/April 1800).

10 *Coleridge's Letters*, Vol. 1, letter 343 to James Webbe Tobin dated 25 July 1800, p. 612.

11 *Poetical Works*, Part 1, poem 171, *Frost at Midnight*, p. 456, lines 55–8.

12 *Coleridge's Letters*, Vol. 1, letter 342 to Humphry Davy dated 25 July 1800, p. 612.

13 *Biographia Literaria*, ed. James Engell and W. Jackson Bate, Vol. 2, pp. 6–7.

14 *Coleridge's Letters*, Vol. 1, letter 371 to Francis Wrangam dated 19 December 1800, p. 658.

15 *Coleridge's Letters*, Vol. 1, letter 238 to George Coleridge dated circa 10 March 1798, p. 394.

16 *Coleridge's Letters*, Vol. III, letter 919 to Joseph Cottle dated 26 April 1814, pp. 476–7.

17 *Coleridge's Letters*, Vol. III, letter 927 to John Morgan dated 14 May 1814, p. 489.

18 *Coleridge's Notebooks*, Vol. 1, note 932 dated April–November 1801.

19 · *Coleridge's Notebooks*, Vol. 1, note 848 dated November 1800.

20 *Coleridge's Letters*, Vol. 11, letter 412 to Thomas Poole dated 19 September 1801, p. 758.

21 *Coleridge's Letters*, Vol. 11, letter 470 to Mrs S.T. Coleridge dated 22/23 November 1802, pp. 887–8.

22 Extract from *The Bondage of Love: A Life of Mrs. Samuel Taylor Coleridge*, by Molly Lefebure, chapter 16.

23 *Coleridge's Letters*, Vol. 11, letter 438 to Sara Hutchinson dated 4 April 1802, p. 792.

24 Ibid., pp. 792–3.

25 Ibid., p. 793.

26 Ibid., p. 794.

27 Ibid.

28 *Poetical Works*, Part 11, poem 293, *Dejection: An Ode*, p. 698, lines 17–21.

29 Ibid., lines 30–8, pp. 698–9, lines 42–6.

30 *Poetical Works*, Part 11, poem 293, *Dejection: An Ode*, Part IV, p. 699, lines 47–58.

31 *Poetical Works*, Part 11, poem 293, *Dejection: An Ode*, Part V, pp. 699–700, lines 67–75.

32 *Poetical Works*, Part 11, poem 293, *Dejection: An Ode*, Part VI, p. 700, lines 84–93.

Chapter Nine

1 Gloss to lines 220–3.

2 *Poetical Works*, Part 11, poem 293, *Dejection: An Ode*, Part 3, p. 699, lines 45–6.

3 Cited in *Coleridge The Visionary*, by John Beer, p. 147.

4 From 'The Statesman's Manual' in *Lay Sermons*, ed. R.J. White, pp. 30–1.

5 Psalm 22:15.

6 John 4:11–14.

7   See also footnote 16 in chapter 8.

8   See *Coleridge Walks the Fells: A Lakeland Journey Retraced*, by Alan Hankinson.

9   *Coleridge's Letters*, Vol. 11, letter 484 to Thomas Wedgwood dated 14 January 1803, p. 916.

10 *Poetical Works*, Part 2, poem 293, *Dejection: An Ode*, Part VI, p. 700, lines 88–93.

11 *Coleridge's Letters*, Vol. 11, letter 388 to Thomas Poole dated 23 March 1801, pp. 708–9.

12 *Coleridge's Notebooks*, Vol. 1, note 1577 dated 19 October 1803. Sara's name in square brackets was written in Greek text, so this is addressed to Asra.

13 *Coleridge's Letters*, Vol. 11, letter 491 to Robert Southey dated 17 February 1803, p. 929.

14 *Coleridge's Letters*, Vol. 11, letter 432 to William Godwin dated 22 January 1802, pp. 783–4.

15 *Coleridge's Letters*, Vol. 11, letter 513 to Robert Southey dated 14 August 1803, p. 975.

16 *Poetical Works*, Part 11, poem 335, *The Pains of Sleep*, p. 753, lines 1–7.

17 Ibid., p. 754, lines 14–17 and 37–40.

18 Ibid., p. 755, lines 51–2.

19 *Coleridge's Letters*, Vol. 11, letter 516 to Robert Southey dated 10 (and 11) September 1803, p. 982.

20 *The Prelude; Or, Growth of a Poet's Mind*, by William Wordsworth. First published in 1805, Book VI, lines 240–6.

21 *Coleridge's Notebooks*, Vol. 11, note 1997 dated 11 April 1804.

22 Ibid., note 2063.

23 Ibid., note 2064.

24 Ibid., note 2090.

25 Ibid., note 2091.

26 Ibid., note 2368.

27 Ibid., note 2453.

28 Ibid.

29 Ibid., note 2546.

30   'The Statesman's Manual', *Lay Sermons*, p. 29.

31   Ibid., p. 29.

Chapter Ten

1   *Coleridge: Darker Reflections*, by Richard Holmes, p. 16.

2   *The Annotated Ancient Mariner* with an Introduction and Notes by Martin Gardner, note 105, pp. 76–7.

3   *Poetical Works*, Part 2, poem 293, *Dejection: An Ode*, Part II, pp. 698–9, lines 13–38.

4   Acts 2:2–3.

5   Extract from *Coleridge: The Clark Lectures, 1951–52* published in 1952 and quoted by Martin Gardner in *The Annotated Mariner*, p. 80, note 112.

6   The Catholic Petition Letter III in *Essays on his Times*, Vol. 3, p. 235, with the following footnote: 'The former must not be used, as a Means, without being likewise included in the End: the latter may. I may feed Sheep, or fell Timber, for my own advantage exclusively; but not so with the Shepherd or Wood-cutter whom I employ. I must make them amends, i.e. the advantage must be reciprocal. A Slave is a Person perverted into a Thing: Slavery, therefore, is not so properly a deviation from Justice, as an absolute subversion of all Morality.'

7   *The Ancient Mariner and the Authentic Narrative*, by Bernard Martin.

8   Quoted in *Coleridge the Visionary*, by John Beer, p. 164.

9   *Biographia Literaria*, Vol. 1, chapter 9, p. 152.

10   *Coleridge's Notebooks*, Vol. 11, p. 2448 dated 12 February 1805.

11   Ibid.

12   Ibid.

13   *Biographia Literaria*, Vol. 1, chapter 10, pp. 204–5.

14   *Coleridge's Notebooks*, Vol. 11, note 2279 dated November 1804–5.

15   *Washington Allston: A Study of the Romantic Artist in America*, by Edgar Preston Richardson, (Chicago, 1948), p. 75.

16 *Coleridge's Letters*, Vol. 11, letter 620 to Washington Allston sent from Florence on 17 June 1806.

17 Ibid.

18 *Coleridge's Notebooks*, Vol. 11, note 2860 dated June 1806.

19 *Coleridge's Letters*, Vol. 11, letter 622 to Robert Southey dated 19 (20) August 1806, p. 1176.

20 As referred to in *Coleridge: Darker Reflections*, by Richard Holmes, pp. 62–3.

Chapter Eleven

1 *Poetical Works*, Part. 1, poem 178, *Kubla Khan*, p. 514, lines 53–4.

2 *Orchestra, or A Poem of Dancing*, verse 49, from *The Poems of Sir John Davies*, ed. Robert Krueger (Oxford University Press, 1975), p. 103.

3 *The Rediscovery of Meaning and Other Essays*, by Owen Barfield (Barfield Press, 2nd edition, 2006), p. 11.

4 *Where the Wasteland Ends: Politics and Transcendence in Post-industrial Society*, by Theodore Roszak.

5 *The Rediscovery of Meaning*, Barfield, p. 216.

6 Ibid., pp. 216–17.

7 Ibid., pp. 215–30.

8 *The Annotated Mariner*, by Martin Gardner, p. 86, note 130.

9 Extracts from *Odyssey XIII*, quoted in *The Road to Xanadu*, by John Livingston Lowes, pp. 286–7.

10 John 3:5–8.

11 *Poetical Works*, *Dejection: An Ode*, Part V, pp. 699–700, lines 67–75.

12 *Biographia Literaria*, Vol. 2, pp. 6–7.

13 'Saint Francis Receiving the Stigmata' – a painting in tempura on a wooden panel, painted between 1294 and 1300, by Giotto. Formerly displayed in the transept chapel of the Church of San Francesco in Pisa, it is now in the Musée du Louvre, Paris.

14 Quoted in *Coleridge the Visionary*, by John Beer p. 167.

15 Ibid., p. 293.

16 John 16:22.

17 *The Letters of William and Dorothy Wordsworth, Vol. II, The Middle Years, Part 1: 1806–11*, rev. Mary Moorman (Oxford University Press, 1969), p. 78. Wordsworth to Sir George Beaumont, 8 September 1806.

18 *Coleridge's Letters*, Vol. iii, p. 476, letter 919 to Joseph Cottle dated 26 April 1814.

19 *Coleridge's Letters*, Vol. iii, p. 489, letter 927 to J.J. Morgan dated 14 May 1814.

20 *Coleridge's Letters*, Vol. ii, letter 631 to George Fricker dated 4 October 1806, p. 1189.

21 Ibid. pp. 1189–90.

22 *Coleridge's Letters*, Vol. ii, letter 634 to Thomas Clarkson dated 13 October 1806, p. 1197.

23 *The Letters of William and Dorothy Wordsworth, The Middle Years*, pp. 86–7 (quoted by Richard Holmes in *Coleridge: Darker Reflections*, p. 75).

24 *Coleridge's Poetical Works*, Part 2, 289, 'A Letter to . . .', p. 685.

25 *Coleridge's Poetical Works*, Part 2, 401, 'To William Wordsworth, Composed on the Night After his Recitation of a Poem on the Growth of an Individual Mind', p. 815.

26 Ibid., p. 816, lines 1–10.

27 Ibid., p. 816, lines 17–19.

28 Ibid., p. 817, lines 47–54.

29 Ibid., p. 818, lines 61–6.

30 Ibid., p. 818, lines 67–76.

31 Ibid., p. 819, lines 95–101.

32 Ibid., p. 819, lines 102–12.

33 'L'Allegro', lines 133–4 in Milton's *Complete Shorter Poems*, p. 138.

34 *Lectures 1808–1819 on Literature*, by Samuel Taylor Coleridge, ed. R.A. Foakes, Vol. 1, p. 495.

35 From *Anima Poetae: From the Unpublished Note-Books of Samuel*

Taylor Coleridge, reprinted in the Portable Coleridge, ed. I.A. Richards, p. 315.

Chapter Twelve

1   Romans 6:3.

2   *Samuel Taylor Coleridge: A Bondage of Opium*, by Molly Lefebure, p. 480.

3   Matthew 16:28.

4   From *Table Talk recorded by Henry Nelson Coleridge and John Taylor Coleridge*, ed. Carl Woodring, Vol. 1, p. 273. Quoted in *The Annotated Ancient Mariner, by Samuel Taylor Coleridge with an Introduction and Notes*, by Martin Gardner, on p. 103.

5   *The Four Quartets*, V, Beginning of verse 3. Page 197 of *The Complete Poems and Plays of T. S. Eliot* (Faber & Faber, 1969).

6   *The Historical Roots of our Ecological Crisis*, by Lynn White, Jr, published in *Science*, 10 March 1967, Vol. 155, Issue 3767, pp. 1203–7. Also located at website http://science.sciencemag.org/content/155/3767/1203.

7   Ibid.

8   'All Things Bright and Beautiful' is an Anglican hymn, with words by Cecil Frances Alexander, and was first published in her *Hymns for Little Children* in 1848.

9   *Coleridge's Letters*, Vol. 111, letter 908 sent to Josiah Wade on 8 December 1813, p. 462.

10 *Coleridge's Letters*, Vol. 111, letter 909 sent to Thomas Roberts on 19 December 1813, p. 463.

11 Ibid.

12 *Coleridge's Letters*, Vol. 111, letter 910 sent to Mrs J.J. Morgan on 19 December 1813, p. 464.

13 *Coleridge's Letters*, Vol. 111, letter 927 sent to J.J. Morgan on 14 May 1814, p. 489.

14 "Letter from Joseph Adams, Hatton Garden to James Gillman, Highgate" dated 9 April 1816. Quoted in *Samuel Taylor Coleridge: A Bondage of Opium*, Molly Lefebure, p. 19.

15 Quote from chapter IV of *The Life of Samuel Taylor Coleridge*, by James Gillman. Quoted in *Samuel Taylor Coleridge: A Bondage of Opium*, by Molly Lefebure, on p. 20.

16 *Coleridge's Letters*, Vol. VI, letter 1013 A to J.J. Morgan dated 24 June 1816, pp. 1041–2.

17 *Biographia Literaria*, Vol. 1, pp. 304–5.

18 *Coleridge's Letters*, Vol. 11, letter 388 to Thomas Poole dated 23 March 1801, p. 709.

19 *Biographia Literaria*, Vol. 1, p. 205.

20 *Biographia Literaria*, Vol. 2, pp. 247–8.

21 Carlyle's *The Life of John Sterling*, 1851 – this and the other quotations from Carlyle are all drawn from the extract from *The Life of John Sterling* given in *Coleridge the Talker*, ed. Richard Willard Armour and Raymond Floyd, pp. 113 onwards.

22 Ibid.

23 'The Statesman's Manual', in *Lay Sermons*, ed. R.J. White, p. 30.

24 See *Blake* by Peter Ackroyd (The Folio Society, 2008), p. 403. I am also grateful to Richard Lines for sharing his unpublished researches on the other possible Blake–Coleridge lines of connection, including their mutual friend Henry Crabbe Robinson.

25 *Biographia Literaria*, Vol. 1, pp. 226–8.

26 *Confessions of an Inquiring Spirit* (Adam and Charles Black, 1956), pp. 42–3. This edition was based on H.N. Coleridge's later editing of Coleridge's manuscript; the original manuscript itself was entitled 'Letters on the Inspiration of the Scriptures'. The original draft is printed in *Shorter Works*, Vol. 2, pp. 1111–71. The Bible quote is taken from the Book of Wisdom 7:27.

27 'Letter to Maria Gisborne', a poem written by Percy Bysshe Shelley in 1820, lines 202–8.

28 *The Letters of John Keats, 1814–1821*, Vol. 2, *1819–1821*, ed. Hyder Edward Rollins. Letter to George Keats dated 15 April 1819.

29 *Table Talk*, Part 2, pp. 186–7.

30 *The Letters of Charles and Mary Lamb*, Vol. III, ed. Edwin J. Marrs, Jr, p. 215. Quoted in *Coleridge: Darker Reflections*, by Richard Holmes, p. 430.

31 Edith Coleridge was christened in Hampstead on 9 August 1832, as Sara mentioned in a letter to Emily Tevenen dated 12 August 1832: 'Over abundantly were we rewarded for some little inconvenience which this arrangement occasioned . . . by seeing my dear Father in such health and spirits and animation as we have not known him enjoy for several years' – as quoted in *The Regions of Sara Coleridge's Thought: Selected Literary Criticism*, by P. Swaab.

32 *Poems*, by Hartley Coleridge, started with this sonnet dedicated to S.T. Coleridge, and was published a year before Coleridge's death in 1834.

33 *Shorter Works*, Vol. 2, p. 1487.

34 *Poetical Works*, Part 2, pp. 1145–6.

35 *Coleridge's Letters*, Vol. VI, pp. 832–3. I am grateful to Graham Davidson for drawing my attention to this little note.

36 *Coleridge's Letters*, Vol. II, letter 595 to Sir George Beaumont dated 6 April 1804, p. 1123.

Epilogue

1 *There and Back*, by George Macdonald. In three volumes: Vol. I (London, 1891), pp. 301–3. Available online at http://www.ccel.org/ccel/macdonald/there_back.xxiv.html.

2 Ibid., p. 304.

3 Ibid., p. 305.

4 Ibid., pp. 336–7.

5 *The Ancient Mariner*, by David Jones (1895–1974) with an afterword by Thomas Dilworth.

6 Quoted in *The Rime of the Ancient Mariner: The Poem and its Illustrators*, by Samuel Taylor Coleridge et al. p. 104.

7 *The Collected Poems of C.S. Lewis*, ed. Walter Hooper (Harper Collins, 1994), p. 80. Used with permission.

8 Extracts from *The Voyage of the Dawn Treader*, by C.S. Lewis, the fifth of the seven volumes of *The Chronicles of Narnia*. First published by Geoffrey Bles in 1952. These extracts are from Collins 1988 edition, chapter 12, pp. 135–45.

Notes

9   Ibid.
10 Ibid.
11 Ibid.
12 From R.S. Thomas, *Collected Poems 1945–1990* (Orion Publishing Group, London, 1993), p. 511.
13 'Samuel Taylor Coleridge' a sonnet from *The Singing Bowl*, by Malcolm Guite (Canterbury Press, 2013).

Bibliography

Works Cited

Works by Coleridge

The Collected Works of Samuel Taylor Coleridge (*Complete Coleridge*), ed. J.C.C. Mays, 'Bollingen Series', including:

Volume 2: *The Watchman*, ed. Lewis Patton, Princeton University Press, 1970.

Volume 3: *Essays on His Times in the Morning Post and the Courier*, ed. David V. Erdman, Princeton University Press / Routledge & Kegan Paul, 1978.

Volume 4: *The Friend*, ed. Barbara E. Rooke, Princeton University Press, 1969.

Volume 5: *Lectures 1808–1819 On Literature*, ed. R.A. Foakes, Princeton University Press, 1987.

Volume 6: *The Statesman's Manual; Or, The Bible, the Best Guide to Political Skill and Foresight: A Lay Sermon, Addressed to the Higher Classes of Society: with an Appendix, Containing Comments and Essays Connected with the Study of the Inspired Writings by S T Coleridge, Esquire*, first published in 1816, ed. Kathleen Coburn, Princeton University Press, 1972.

Volume 7: *Biographia Literaria*, ed. James Engell and W. Jackson Bate, Princeton University Press, 1983. (*Biographia Literaria* throughout footnotes).

Volume 11: *Shorter Works and Fragments*, ed. H.J. Jackson and J.R. de J. Jackson, Princeton University Press, 1995.

Volume 14: *Table Talk recorded by Henry Nelson Coleridge (and John Taylor Coleridge)*, ed. Carl Woodring, Princeton University Press / Routledge, 1990.

Volume 16: *Poetical Works* I (Parts 1 and 2) ed. J.C.C. Mays, Princeton University Press, 2001 (*Poetical Works* throughout footnotes).

The Notebooks of Samuel Taylor Coleridge, ed. Kathleen Coburn, Bollingen Series L, Bollingen Foundation, New York, 1957–90:

Volume I (1794–1804) (*Notebooks*, Vol. I throughout footnotes).

Volume II (1804–8) (*Notebooks*, Vol. II throughout footnotes).

Volume III (1808–19) (*Notebooks*, Vol. III throughout footnotes).

Biographia Literaria or Biographical Sketches of My Literary Life and Opinions, by Samuel Taylor Coleridge, edited with his Aesthetical Essays, by J. Shawcross, Oxford University Press, 1979.

The Collected Letters of Samuel Taylor Coleridge, ed. Earl Leslie Griggs, Clarendon Press, 1956.

Volume I (1785–1800) (*Coleridge's Letters*, Vol. I throughout footnotes).

Volume II (1801–6) (*Coleridge's Letters*, Vol. II throughout footnotes).

Volume III (1807–14) (*Coleridge's Letters*, Vol. III throughout footnotes).

Volume V (1820–1825) (*Coleridge's Letters*, Vol. V throughout footnotes).

Volume VI (1826–34) (*Coleridge's Letters*, Vol. VI throughout footnotes).

Secondary Sources

Coleridge the Talker, by Richard Willard Armour and Raymond Floyd Howes, Ithaca, NY, Cornell University Press, 1940.

The Life of Samuel Taylor Coleridge, by Rosemary Ashton, Blackwell, 1996.

What Coleridge Thought, by Owen Barfield, Wesleyan University Press, 1971.

The Rediscovery of Meaning, and Other Essays, by Owen Barfield, Wesleyan University Press, 1977.

Coleridge the Visionary, by John Beer, Chatto & Windus, 1959.

Samuel Taylor Coleridge: A Biographical Study, by E.K. Chambers, Oxford, Clarendon Press, 1938.

The Annotated Ancient Mariner, by Samuel Taylor Coleridge, with an Introduction and Notes by Martin Gardner and illustrated by Gustave Doré, Anthony Blond Ltd, 1965.

The Life of Samuel Taylor Coleridge, by James Gillman, first published 1838; http://www.fullbooks.com/The-Life-of-Samuel-Taylor-Coleridge1.html

Coleridge Walks the Fells: A Lakeland Journey Retraced, by Alan Hankinson, Ellenbank Press, 1991.

Coleridge: Early Visions, by Richard Holmes, Hodder & Stoughton, 1989.

Coleridge: Darker Reflections, by Richard Holmes, HarperCollins, 1998.

The Ancient Mariner, by David Jones with an afterword by Thomas Dilworth, Enitharmon, 2005.

Samuel Taylor Coleridge: A Bondage of Opium, by Molly Lefebure, Victor Gollancz Ltd, 1974.

The Bondage of Love: A Life of Mrs Samuel Taylor Coleridge, by Molly Lefebure, Victor Gollancz Ltd, 1988.

The Road to Xanadu: A Study in the Ways of the Imagination, by John Livingston Lowes, Houghton Mifflin Company, 1927.

The Letters of Charles and Mary Lamb, 3 vols, ed. Edwin J. Marrs Junior, Cornell University Press, 1975.

Coleridge's Father: Absent Man, Guardian Spirit, by J.C.C. Mays, Friends of Coleridge, 2014.

The Ancient Mariner and the Authentic Narrative, by Bernard Martin, William Heinemann, 1949.

William Wordsworth: A Biography, by Mary Moorman in two vols, Oxford University Press, 1957–65.

The Rime of the Ancient Mariner, by Samuel Taylor Coleridge, illustrated by Mervyn Peake, Chatto and Windus, 1978.

Minding the Modern: Human Agency, Intellectual Traditions, and Responsible Knowledge, by Thomas Pfau, University of Notre Dame Press, 2013.

Anima Poetae, reprinted in *The Portable Coleridge*, ed. I.A. Richards, Penguin, 1978.

Washington Allston: A Study of the Romantic Artist in America, by Edgar Preston Richardson, Chicago, 1948.

Where The Wasteland Ends: Politics and Transcendence in Post-industrial Society, by Theodore Roszak, Faber, 1973.

The Letters of William and Dorothy Wordsworth: ed. Ernest De Selincourt, Mary Moorman and Alan G. Hill, Oxford University Press, 1969 especially:

The Early Years, 1796–1805.

The Middle Years, Part 1, 1806–1811.

The Middle Years, Part 2, 1812–1820.

The Prelude or Growth of a Poet's Mind, by William Wordsworth (text of 1805), edited from the manuscripts with Introduction and Notes by Ernest de Selincourt, Oxford University Press, 1933).

The Grasmere and Alfoxden Journals, by Dorothy Wordsworth, edited with an Introduction and Notes by Pamela Woof, Oxford University Press, 2002.

The Rime of the Ancient Mariner: The Poem and its Illustrators, by Samuel Taylor Coleridge et al., published by The Wordsworth Trust, Dove Cottage, 2006.

The Holy Bible – throughout this book *The Authorised Version* has been referred to, as this is the version Coleridge would have known and used. Also known as the *King James Bible*, it was translated between 1604 and 1611 for use in the Church of England and is still in use today.

The Book of Common Prayer (*The Book of Common Prayer and Administration of the Sacraments and other Rites and Ceremonies of the Church according to the use of the Church of England together with the Psalter or Psalms of David pointed as they are to be sung or said in churches; and the form and manner of making, ordaining, and consecrating of bishops, priests, and deacons*) was originally put together early in the Reformation in the reign of Edward VI, but was revised several times before it was printed in 1662, two years after the Restoration of Charles II. It is this '1662' version that Coleridge would have known and used and it has, therefore, been used throughout this book.

Acknowledgements

This book could not have been written in isolation, and I am grateful for the network of friendships that has sustained, shaped and supported the whole endeavour. First to my editor Katherine Venn, who suggested I write this book and supported me throughout with patience, encouragement and detailed critical and editorial advice, which has proved invaluable. My own college, Girton in Cambridge, have been supportive and encouraging, especially in granting me the term's sabbatical in which this book was begun, and I owe a debt to our Fellow Librarian Frances Gandy whose foresight and whose own interests meant that our college Library had an extensive Coleridge collection with critical editions of almost all the primary sources I needed. The Divinity School at Duke University provided me with a great base for the first part of my sabbatical and the chance to meet scholars like Thomas Pfau, whose assessment of Coleridge and Modernity has been so helpful. St. John's College Durham made me welcome as a visiting fellow for the second part of my sabbatical and it gave me great pleasure to reflect that Coleridge too had come up to Durham to consult books in the great cathedral library. The poet, scholar and literary critic Grevel Lindop has encouraged me throughout, not least in taking the time to walk with me in the Lake District of whose literary history he is such a formidable expert, and to arrange for me to see precious books and manuscripts in the keeping of the Wordsworth Trust. Here in Cambridge I have benefited greatly from conversation with the Coleridge scholar Douglas Hedley who has done so much to re-establish Coleridge's importance as a theologian. Fellow scholars and members of the 'Friends of Coleridge' like Graham Davidson and Richard Lines have helped me in conversation and correspondence. Jeremy Begbie, who pioneered so much of the current thinking on the relation of Theology and the Arts has been encouraging throughout and Kevin Belmonte, an expert on Wilberforce and John Newton, and author of many biographies, has helped me with many details and suggestions, passages and citations, and again, with sheer encouragement and goodwill.

I have been blessed with the help of two great amanuenses, first Travis Helms, who was one of my Doctoral students at Cambridge, and then Judith Tonry, with whom I have shared a love of literature and an exploration of its links with faith over many years of common Christian pilgrimage. My old friend and former student Niki Lambros, who helped me with my earlier book, *Faith Hope and Poetry*, kindly stepped in again to help me with proof corrections and some final clarifications. Without their help I could not have done this.

My wife Maggie has been supportive and helpful throughout. It was she who booked us to stay at Tom Poole's book room in the Old House in Nether Stowey one beautiful spring and walked with me from Porlock up to Culbone and beyond along the paths that lead deep into *Kubla Khan* and *The Mariner*. And it was she who helped make sure that not too many 'Persons from Porlock' called on business or detained me whilst I was trying to write these pages.

Finally, reaching deep, as Coleridge would, into the memories of my own childhood, I would like to thank my mother, Shiona, for first introducing me to *The Ancient Mariner* as she chanted verses from it on the deck of a ship when we were far out at sea. It is to her that I dedicate this book.

List of Illustrations

Index

Page numbers in *italics* refer to figures.

MARINER

Index

Index

Index

Index

Do you wish this wasn't the end?

Join us at www.hodder.co.uk, or follow us on
Twitter @hodderbooks to be a part of our community
of people who love the very best in books and reading.

Whether you want to discover more about a book
or an author, watch trailers and interviews, have the
chance to win early limited editions, or simply browse
our expert readers' selection of the very best books,
we think you'll find what you're looking for.

And if you don't,
that's the place to tell us what's missing.

We love what we do, and we'd love you to be part of it.

www.hodder.co.uk

@hodderbooks

HodderBooks

HodderBooks